MANET

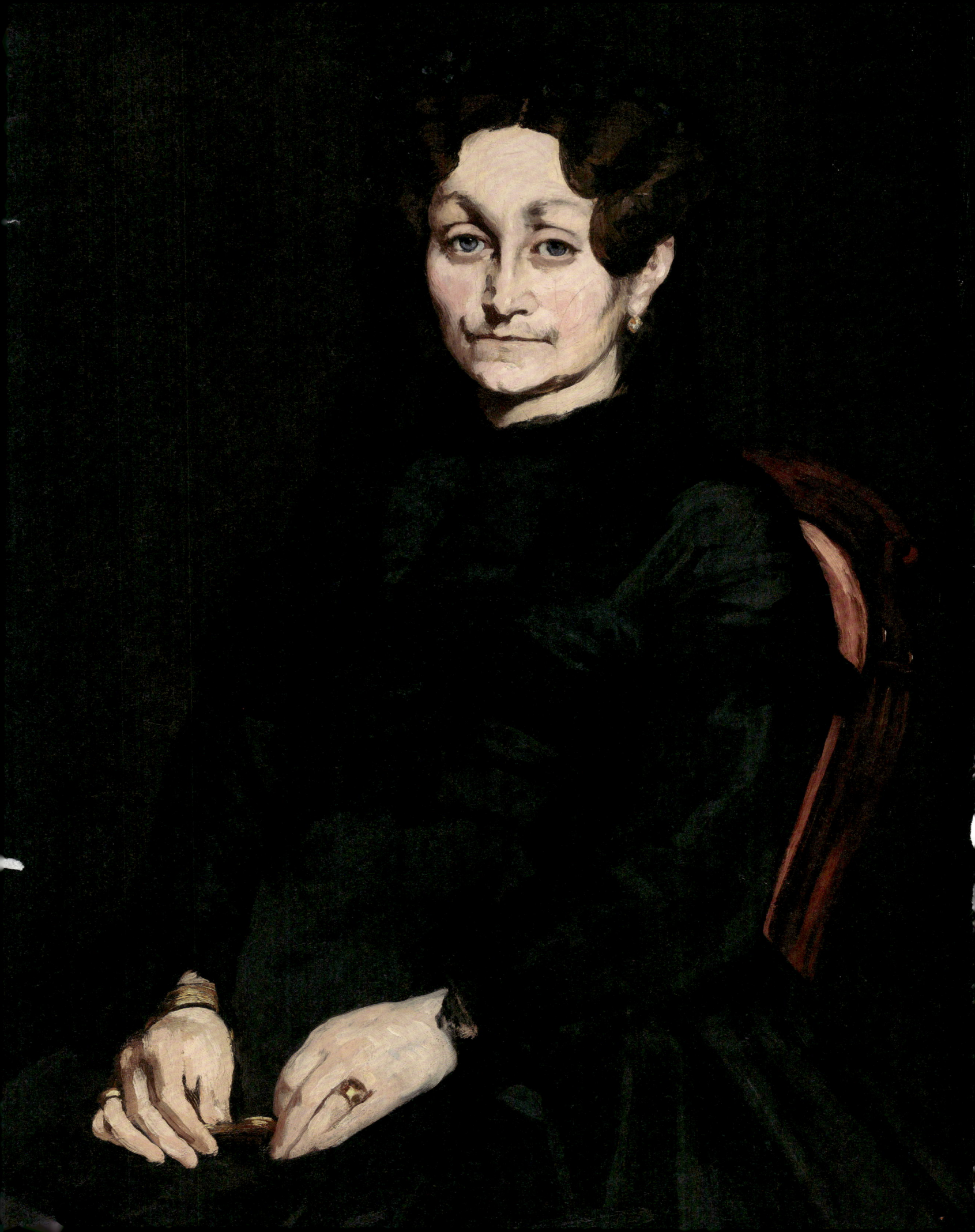

MANET

A Model Family

EDITED BY

Diana Seave Greenwald

WITH CONTRIBUTIONS BY
Hilton Als
Emily A. Beeny
Adrienne Chaparro
Aimee Marcereau DeGalan
Kathryn Kremnitzer
Nancy Locke
Gianfranco Pocobene
Isolde Pludermacher
Samuel Rodary
Bill Scott
Juliet Wilson-Bareau
Alex Zivkovic

Isabella Stewart Gardner
Museum, Boston

IN ASSOCIATION WITH
Princeton University Press,
Princeton and Oxford

Contents

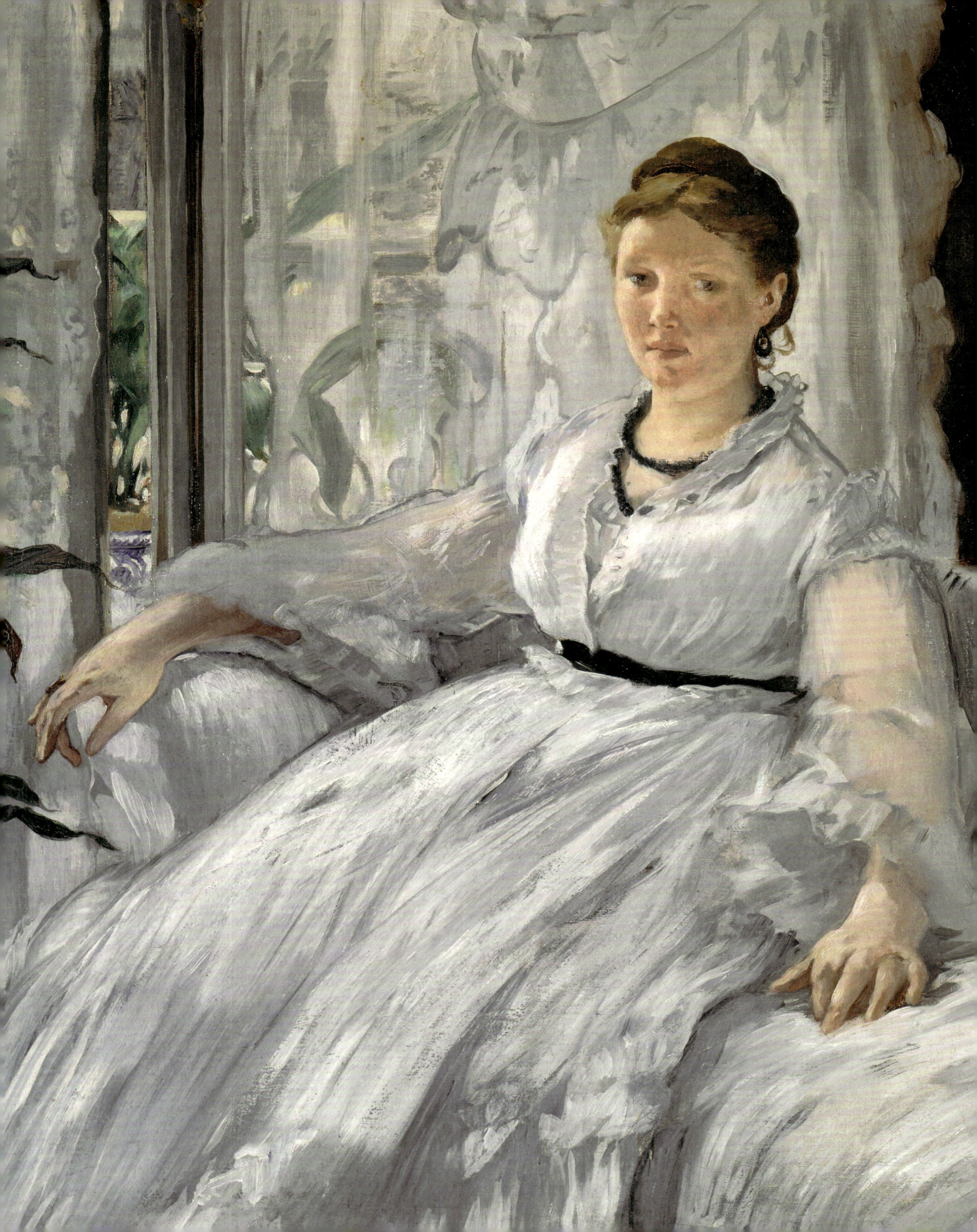

Director's Foreword

Leo Tolstoy famously wrote that "all happy families are alike, but every unhappy family is unhappy in its own way." The family of groundbreaking painter Édouard Manet defies this dictum: they were happy in their own unique, complicated way. Anchored by the exceptional portrait, *Madame Auguste Manet* (about 1866) in the Isabella Stewart Gardner Museum's collection, *Manet: A Model Family* examines his innovative artwork in the context of complex family relationships.

The artist married Suzanne Leenhoff, a Dutch piano teacher who worked for his wealthy Parisian family. She gave birth to a child—Léon Koëlla, better known as Léon Leenhoff—out of wedlock and conceived while in the Manets' employ. It is unclear who fathered Léon. After their marriage, Suzanne and Édouard did not legitimize him, and he was presented publicly as Suzanne's younger brother. Manet's father, Auguste, was possibly Léon's father, which would ultimately make the boy both the artist's stepson and half-brother. As wealthy nineteenth-century elites, the Manets could neither divulge nor acknowledge this ambiguity. Like many families, past and present, they left things unsaid and carefully navigated the permeable boundaries between public and private.

Perhaps against the odds, the family lived happily together. Léon and Suzanne served as the artist's two most frequent models. The artist's mother—the subject of the Gardner portrait—lived with her son and daughter-in-law and presided over the family's Thursday evening gatherings starting in the 1860s, which leading modern artists attended regularly. The famous Impressionist Berthe Morisot posed for Manet more than ten times and later joined the family when she married the artist's younger brother. The Manet family was, in short, a nexus of artistic creativity and innovation, as well as a source of emotional and financial support for a revolutionary painter.

In particular, the tension between revelation and obfuscation in Manet's family life provides a fruitful perspective for analyzing his specific brand of modernism. Sometimes Manet's family members are clearly identified, but often they serve as semi-anonymous models cast in scenes that blend images of nineteenth-century Parisian life with inspiration from the Old Masters. This blending resulted in a series of compelling and confounding works—works that Isabella Stewart Gardner specifically sought to add to her collection.

After years of searching, Gardner acquired a Manet for her museum in 1910 with the purchase of *Madame Auguste Manet*. Located by her art advisor Bernard Berenson, he excitedly wrote: "You must . . . trust me when I tell you that I have found at last what I have been looking for for years, what you yourself, when you were here last, urged me to find for you, a great Manet, if possible a portrait, and one worthy of hanging beside your Degas." She immediately placed the painting on an easel in the Long Gallery and later moved it to the Blue Room, where it currently resides. Beautifully cleaned and conserved for this exhibition, with support from the Richard C. von Hess Foundation, one can now clearly see what Berenson described as "a colossal thing" with "the touch most vigorous."

The decision to dedicate a show to this topic is a credit to Isabella's interest in Manet and her specific choice to acquire a family portrait. The Gardner—led by William and Lia Poorvu Curator of the Collection Diana Seave Greenwald—has assembled an exceptional checklist and scholarly catalogue to create the first exhibition specifically dedicated to the topic of Manet's family. Like Isabella, the Museum she founded does not avoid complicated or even slightly scandalous topics, such as complex family relations, that shed light on artistic creativity and human experience. In fact, our founder—who occasionally enjoyed courting drama and scandal in the press—may have enjoyed this particular take on Manet's work.

For their generous support of our exhibition and publication, I thank the Ford Foundation, Amy and David Abrams, and the Arthur F. and Alice E. Adams Charitable Foundation. Additional support is provided by the Mellon Foundation and the National Endowment for the Humanities.

Peggy Fogelman
Norman Jean Calderwood Director

Acknowledgments

Creating an exhibition and its catalogue is never a solitary effort. In this case, I needed to rely on my amazing team at the Isabella Stewart Gardner Museum and on a close-knit community of nineteenth-century French art scholars—Manet scholars, in particular—to turn this dream project into a reality. I arrived at the Gardner in 2019 with a project about Manet's family in mind. Nathaniel Silver, then Curator of the Collection and now Associate Director, encouraged me to pursue the idea. It has been an incredible five-year journey.

I am grateful to the many colleagues at lending institutions who answered my cold calls and emails asking to meet about their Manet paintings, drawings, and prints. Thank you to Susan Stein and Stephan Wolohojian at the Metropolitan Museum of Art. In addition to supporting several loan requests, Isolde Pludermacher at the Musée d'Orsay has been a generous contributor and friend to this project; she wrote a fabulous essay for this catalogue. Thank you to Esther Bell at the Clark, Joachim Homann and Miriam Stewart at the Harvard Art Museums, Vibeke Waallann Hansen at the Nasjonalmuseet in Oslo, Magnus Olausson at the Nationalmuseum in Stockholm, Madeleine Viljoen at the New York Public Library, Patrick Murphy and Edward Saywell at the Museum of Fine Arts in Boston, Luísa Sampaio at the Calouste Gulbenkian Museum in Lisbon, Maureen O'Brien at the RISD Museum, Andrew Renton formerly at Amgueddfa Cymru–Museum Wales, and the staff at the Phillips Collection in Washington, DC. Sal Robinson at the Morgan Library & Museum supported essential loans of archival material and gave a fantastic presentation about the Tabarant archive at a roundtable held in preparation for the exhibition. Jennifer Heuer and Cynthia Peng also gave illuminating presentations at that event. I also want to acknowledge the private collectors who have generously agreed to part with their works, including Cathy Lasry, Denys Wilcox, and others who wish to remain anonymous.

Gathering the checklist was one feat; gathering enough knowledge to do a thoughtful and innovative Manet show was another. While I have long studied nineteenth-century French art, Édouard Manet and the vast literature dedicated to his work represent another kind of challenge. In this journey, I was helped enormously by Katie Hanson from the Museum of Fine Arts in Boston, who generously introduced me to several colleagues at other museums. Kathryn Kremnitzer, whom I have known for decades, became my guide to all things Manet. I am grateful for her expertise and friendship. Nancy Locke, the definitive expert on the Manet family, welcomed me with open arms and gamely fielded my many emails asking about specific elements of family history. Both she and Kathryn have written excellent essays, biographies, and catalogue entries for this publication. For this volume, Emily Beeny wrote one of the most beautiful scholarly essays I have ever read. In addition to this generous contribution, she has always been available to talk about this project and its development.

Relatively early in planning this exhibition, I enjoyed visiting the painter Bill Scott in Philadelphia. Since that visit, he has lent his insights and deep knowledge of the Manet and Morisot families to this project both at our roundtable and in written form in this catalogue. He has been an invaluable partner, from reading drafts to sharing works by Edma Morisot and Eugène Manet. Samuel Rodary also shared his deep knowledge of Manet and his correspondence by providing a fantastic selection of letters and writing two excellent catalogue entries. Finally, I would like to thank Juliet Wilson-Bareau for her incredible knowledge about Manet and her deep commitment to his legacy. Her helping me navigate sources and ideas about the artist improved this exhibition and catalogue. She helped me shift its framing, form the checklist, and contributed her wisdom to the publication. I was also able to redate the Gardner's

Manet with her support and guidance. I am eternally grateful for her time, effort, and patience.

I have the privilege of working with an exceptional team at the Isabella Stewart Gardner Museum. Thank you to Gianfranco Pocobene for his transformative conservation treatment of *Madame Auguste Manet* and excellent research on the painting. It was a pleasure to co-author a catalogue entry with him. I am also grateful to Holly Salmon for helping to coordinate the treatment and study of the painting. Adrienne Chaparro provided invaluable research assistance, good cheer, and two excellent contributions to the catalogue. Elizabeth Reluga, as always, kept everything organized, on schedule, and moving forward. She is a dream partner in bringing museum publications to life. Thank you to Rebecca Ehrhardt and her team for raising the funds to support this ambitious show and publication. Caitlin Lowrie is the organizational force behind the exhibition. I am grateful to our director, Peggy Fogelman, for her continued support of bold exhibition projects like this one.

Beyond the Gardner, many other people helped make this book a reality. Thank you to Dominique Clément at the French Library in Boston, who translated our French contributors' submissions. Thank you to Alex Zivkovic, our incredible research assistant and the author of two wonderful catalogue entries, who expertly checked all the notes and compiled the bibliography. Diana Jaskierny helped source an otherwise difficult-to-find image of *Madame Manet in the Conservatory*. I am eternally grateful to Michelle Komie at Princeton University Press for her continued partnership, trust, and guidance. Finally, thank you to Miko McGinty and Julia Ma for designing such a beautiful book and to Helen Riegle and Kurt Weidman for their wonderful exhibition design.

Diana Seave Greenwald
William and Lia Poorvu Curator of the Collection

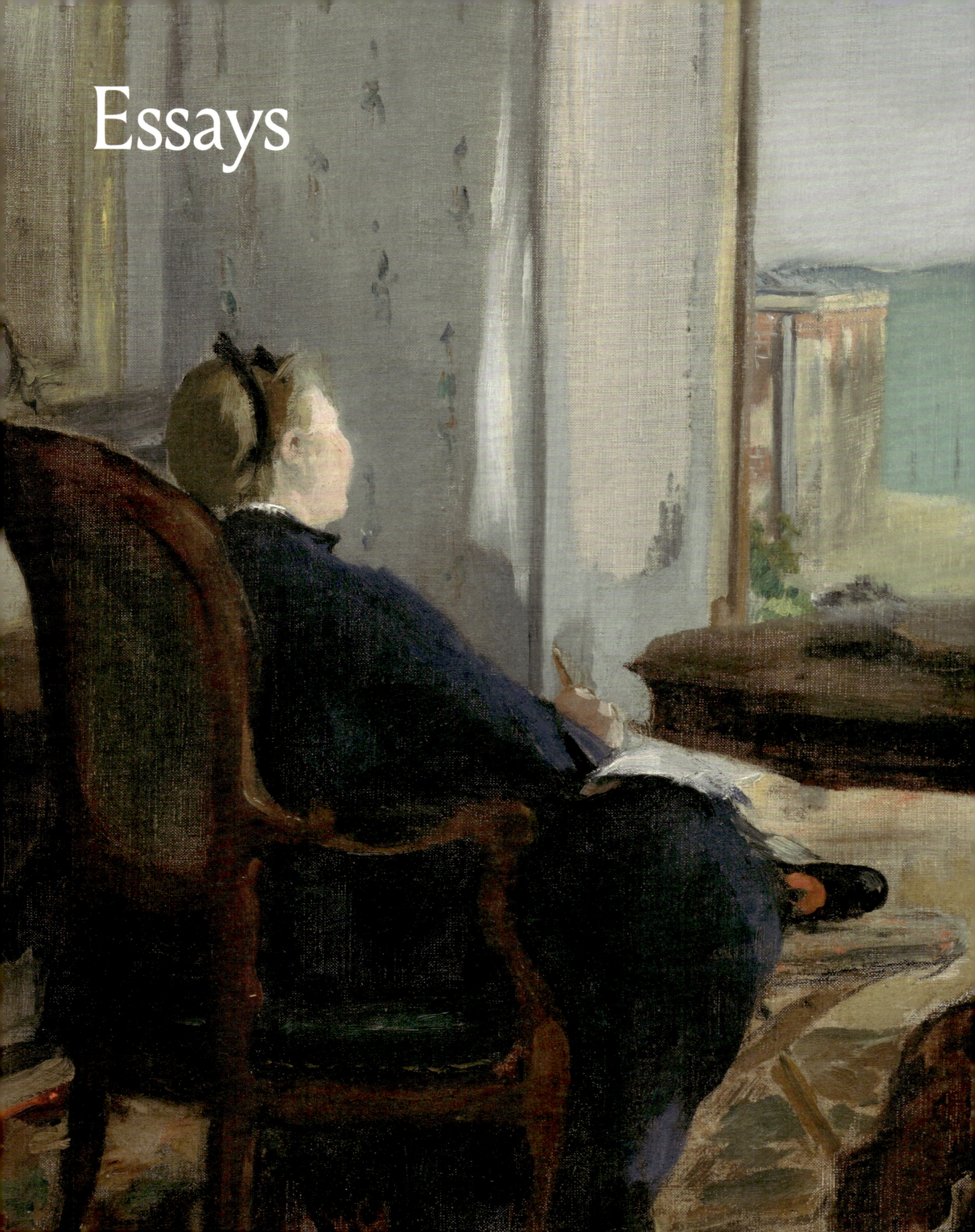

Essays

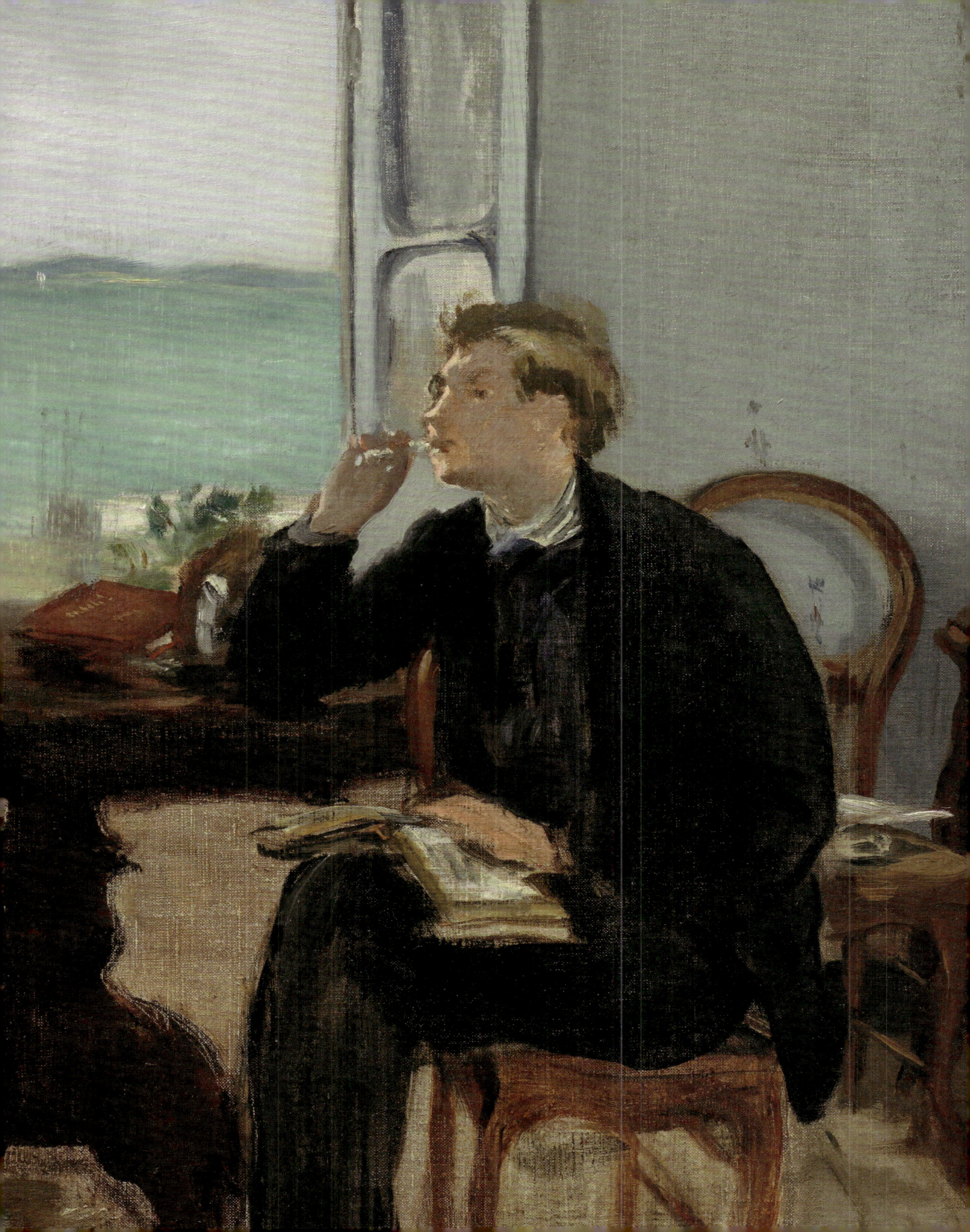

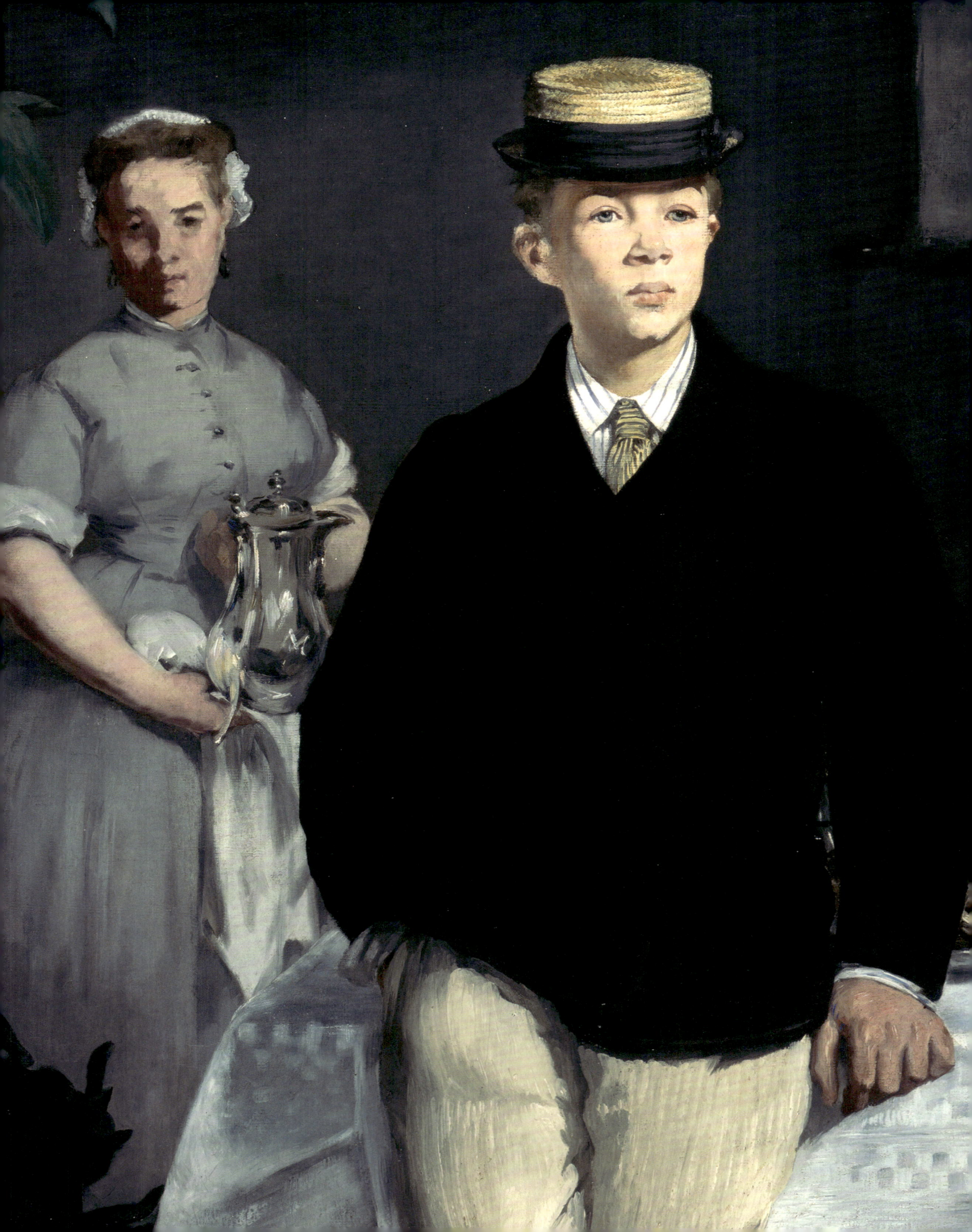

Édouard Manet: A Family Story

DIANA SEAVE GREENWALD

Families are complicated. The family of Édouard Manet (1832–1883) was no different. It was, in fact, more complicated than most. Despite these complexities, family members—from his mother, to a son of indeterminate legitimacy, to an extraordinarily talented sister-in-law—inspired and supported this groundbreaking artist. The principal source of this complication relates to the birth of Léon-Édouard Koëlla (1852–1927), known as Léon Leenhoff for much of his life. Léon, the son of Manet's future wife, Suzanne Leenhoff (1829–1906), was born out of wedlock. He was presented as Suzanne's younger brother in public, and in private he called Suzanne and Édouard his godmother and his godfather. His paternity remains speculative. Édouard was long assumed to be his biological father, but more recent scholarship suggests it could be either a traveling musician or Édouard's own father, Auguste. This latter situation would make Léon both Édouard's stepson and half-brother.

Suzanne's initial position within the Manet family added another layer of complexity: a Dutchwoman who immigrated to France, she met the family when they employed her as a piano teacher. Therefore, not only was she a single mother of an illegitimate child when she married Édouard in 1863, but she was also a foreigner and of a lower social class than the bourgeois Manets. Add to this mix that Manet's father, a government official, died of syphilis (as would Édouard). His mother, Eugénie, was a strong matriarch who oversaw the financial and social life of the family long into widowhood. Manet's brother Eugène married the Impressionist painter Berthe Morisot (1841–1895)—Édouard's close friend, colleague, and frequent model. In surviving correspondence, the bourgeois Parisian Morisots were not always kind to Suzanne. From the outside, this web of relationships looks like it could be a recipe for drama and familial instability. Yet the opposite was true.

Crucially, the family seems to have been both happy and central to a seismic change in art over which Édouard presided. They served as his frequent models and provided him with a stable home life and—essentially—independent financial resources that allowed him to pursue an avant-garde art career in which sales were few and far between. After his death, they took responsibility for inventorying his work and shepherding his legacy. Suzanne, Léon, Eugénie, and many other members of the family—including Berthe and Eugène—deserve long-overdue credit for their role in Édouard's career.[1]

There are many reasons that the Manet family has never been the subject of a dedicated exhibition and catalogue. Some of this neglect is perhaps related to the fact that biographical approaches to art history have, for the past few decades, been out of scholarly fashion. With one notable exception—Nancy Locke's *Manet and the Family Romance* (2001)—the art historical research about the Manets has been spread across disparate sources, mentioned primarily when a painting showing a family member is presented in a broader thematic or theoretical context.[2] This catalogue presents new research about the family, returns to a biographical approach that can deliver scholarly insights, and brings information about the family together in one cohesive work.

Importantly, the marginalization of Manet's family in studies about the artist can also be traced to events in his own life. In October 1863 his friend Charles Baudelaire reported, "Manet has just announced . . . the most unexpected news. He is leaving this evening for Holland, when he will bring back *his wife*. He does, however, have some excuses for it would seem that she is very beautiful, very kind, and a very fine musician, so many treasures in a single female individual, isn't that monstrous?"[3] It is surprising that Baudelaire would not have known the woman Édouard was about to marry. His family's own commentary sometimes reinforces the image that Manet kept his creative and family lives separate. In a letter to the painter Henri Fantin-Latour, Manet's mother complained that her son spent so much time in a *villain* (horrible) café alongside fellow artists.[4] Yet, Eugénie's correspondence with Fantin indicates that Manet's artistic life outside of the home and his family life could sometimes overlap. The artist's mother was writing to invite Fantin to a gathering of creatives at the family's apartment. The line between private family and public friends, between the drawing room and the cafes, was not as impenetrable as one might think.

Turning to the visual evidence, we find Manet's family members—most often Léon and Suzanne—at the very center of his artwork. Léon appears in eighteen canvases and frequently features in prints and drawings; Suzanne may have posed for as many as twenty oils, one beautiful pastel, a range of drawings, and at least one print; Berthe Morisot is in eleven canvases, as well as additional works on paper.[5] Thus each of these family members appears in more canvases than Victorine Meurent, perhaps Manet's best-known model, who appeared in his landmark paintings *Olympia* (1863, see fig. 54) and *Le Déjeuner sur l'herbe* (1863, see fig. 84). Quantity of depiction is, of course, not the only metric of the importance of a model or a subject to an artist's practice. Nonetheless, the volume of visual evidence gathered in this exhibition is compelling: Manet's family helped fuel his creativity. This essay introduces the Manet family story and his family-related oeuvre. It is, however, just an overview of the topic that the contributors to the rest of this volume delve into in greater, moving, and revelatory detail.

Bourgeois Beginnings

For more than a century, the Manet family were prosperous landowners in Gennevilliers, a then-rural and now-suburban town six miles north of Paris. Édouard's grandfather, a former judge, was a major property holder in the town and its mayor.[6] Auguste (1797–1862), the artist's father, had followed a predictable path: he studied the law and later worked for the Ministry of Justice. He was awarded the Légion d'Honneur and became a judge on a lower-level civil court.[7]

Édouard's mother, Eugénie-Désirée Fournier (1811–1885), came from a French family that made its fortune in Sweden and played a role installing a Frenchman on the Swedish throne (cat. no. 1).[8] She married Auguste Manet on January 18, 1831; she was nineteen and he was thirty-three. With Fournier family money, income derived from landholdings in Gennevilliers, and Auguste's salary from the Ministry of Justice, the couple started a comfortable life together. On January 23, 1832, almost exactly a year after his parents' marriage, Édouard Manet was born in the couple's large Paris home at 5, rue des Petits-Augustins (now rue Bonaparte). He would be the eldest of three brothers, with Eugène born in November 1833 and Gustave in the spring of 1835.[9]

Being the firstborn son came with expectations; Édouard fell short of these early in life. He struggled with the academic subjects necessary for him to become a lawyer, as his father expected. However, he quickly discovered his passion for art. As a boy, his maternal uncle Edmond Fournier took him to the Louvre and other Parisian museums.[10] Manet developed an enthusiasm for sketching and told his family he wanted to be an artist. This was distressing and unacceptable to Auguste.[11]

After months of wrangling over his future, Édouard agreed to pursue a naval career to appease his father. In the summer of 1847 he failed his first attempt at the naval officers' corps entrance exam; a candidate only had two attempts.[12] His family decided to take advantage of a newly created loophole to ease his admission to the navy: there was a lower bar for admission for candidates who had sailed on a vessel across the equator. Alongside other bourgeois young men, teenage Édouard sailed for Rio de Janeiro from the port of Le Havre in December 1848 on the merchant ship *Havre et Guadeloupe*.[13]

Letters sent to his mother, father, brothers, and cousin during this journey are early evidence of his love for family.[14] Just before his departure, he wrote to his mother: "If I hadn't been afraid of another separation and the goodbyes which are always so upsetting, I would regret your not having come with me to Le Havre."[15] Despite disputes about his future, Édouard clearly loved and respected Auguste. "Papa will . . . say goodbye to me tomorrow; I'm happy he has been here until my departure, he's been so good to me throughout our stay."[16] Nevertheless, Édouard understood which of his parents most appreciated his artistic talents. Evocative, descriptive letters to Eugénie recount how he created drawings of his shipmates, while those addressed to Auguste focus on geographic detail and an extensive description of the "baptism" held for the boys on board when the ship crossed the equator.[17] Manet would not, however, excel at sea. He wrote to his mother, "A sailor's life is so boring!"[18]

With political upheaval in France during Manet's trip—the Republic established after the 1848 revolutions was chaotic and unstable, ultimately yielding to the Second Empire— there was a change in the naval admission rules. Édouard did not make a second attempt at the entrance exam, and upon returning home in June 1849 he announced he was going to be a painter. This time, his father apparently grudgingly accepted the decision, and Manet became a student of the painter Thomas Couture.[19] From this point forward, the most compelling records of his love for his family were visual. It was also at this moment that he met Suzanne Leenhoff, his future wife, who would become a critical inspiration.

Old Masters, New Family

Suzanne was born in Delft, in the Netherlands, in 1829. Her family soon moved to Zaltbommel in the country's south, where her father was appointed the city's music master.[20] The eldest of seven siblings (six of whom survived to adulthood), she was a gifted pianist.[21] She likely performed for Franz Liszt when he visited the Netherlands in 1842, and the famed composer may have suggested she move to Paris to continue her musical training. In 1847 Suzanne, her mother, and five younger siblings moved to the French capital.[22] Presumably,

Suzanne continued to study the piano in Paris, though where she studied is unclear—she was not admitted to the famed Paris Conservatory.[23] What is certain is that in 1849 she was hired by the Manet family to teach the piano to all or some of the boys—probably Eugène and Gustave, considering Édouard was at sea for much of the year.[24] Some have suggested that Liszt himself recommended her for the job, though definitive proof is lacking.[25] Her employment presumably lasted until 1852, when she gave birth to her son, Léon, or at least until she was visibly pregnant and could therefore no longer work.

Suzanne's introduction to the Manet family coincided with the beginning of Édouard's formal artistic education in Couture's studio, where he remained from 1850 until 1856. During this time, he also began to study paintings by the Old Masters, including Titian, Veronese, and Velázquez, both through publications and on frequent outings to sketch and copy at the Louvre. These studies of historical painters continued during his first trips to the Netherlands and Italy, in 1852–53.[26] He also had access to the many reproductive prints circulating in nineteenth-century Paris, including those in the collection of the Bibliothèque Nationale (then the Bibliothèque Imperiale).[27]

Suzanne's relationship with the Manet family in general—and with Édouard in particular—in the years following Léon's birth is unclear. Suzanne and Léon did not have a permanent address but lived in different places around Paris with her siblings, their significant others, and her paternal grandmother. The only formal evidence of the continued relationship between her and the artist is that in 1855 Suzanne named Édouard as Léon's godfather even though Léon was baptized in the protestant Dutch Reformed church and Manet was Catholic.[28] In his written recollections from the first decade of the twentieth century, Léon implies that he and Suzanne lived with Édouard for a period before the couple's marriage and that Eugène visited them frequently.[29] Given that this sole account relies on the memories of a very young child, the relationship between Suzanne, Léon, and the Manets during this time will likely remain a mystery.

In 1856 Manet left Couture's studio frustrated with what he viewed as the artificiality of history painting.[30] His own preoccupations were veering toward the depiction of living, breathing, and present-day subjects, and he sought to fuse his interest in the present with a deep engagement with the art of the past. Suzanne was a catalyst for this fusion. In both drawings and paintings from the period, Suzanne was a frequent model often cast in poses that echo those found in works by Titian, Veronese, and other Italian Renaissance painters. These drawings, oil sketches, and fragments of oil paintings (see cat. nos. 4, 5) featuring Suzanne document Édouard's struggle to create a significant composition for submission to the Paris Salon, a juried public art exhibition at the center of the nineteenth-century art world.[31]

During this period of artistic flourishing in the wake of the artist's departure from Couture's studio, Édouard created two works of art featuring family members that were intended for the Salon. The first, and the only one accepted by the jury, was *Monsieur and Madame Auguste Manet* (cat. no. 3). Executed between 1859 and 1860, it was shown at the Salon of 1861, where it received some negative critical reactions.[32] Simply titled *M. and Mme M . . .* , it was painted when his father was suffering from tertiary syphilis. Already seriously ill and partly paralyzed, Auguste is presented with a grizzled dignity. Eugénie appears behind him in a position of support and care.[33]

If Édouard depicted his parents as an aging bourgeois couple, his effort to show Suzanne in a work intended for the Salon—but that was never exhibited there—is radically different.[34] A nude Suzanne sits by a river in *Surprised Nymph* (fig. 1).[35] This is the only time Édouard painted a large oil of Suzanne in the nude—in later works she is portrayed as a

Fig. 1. Édouard Manet, *Surprised Nymph*, 1861. Oil on canvas, 144.5 × 112.5 cm. Museo Nacional de Bellas Artes, Buenos Aires

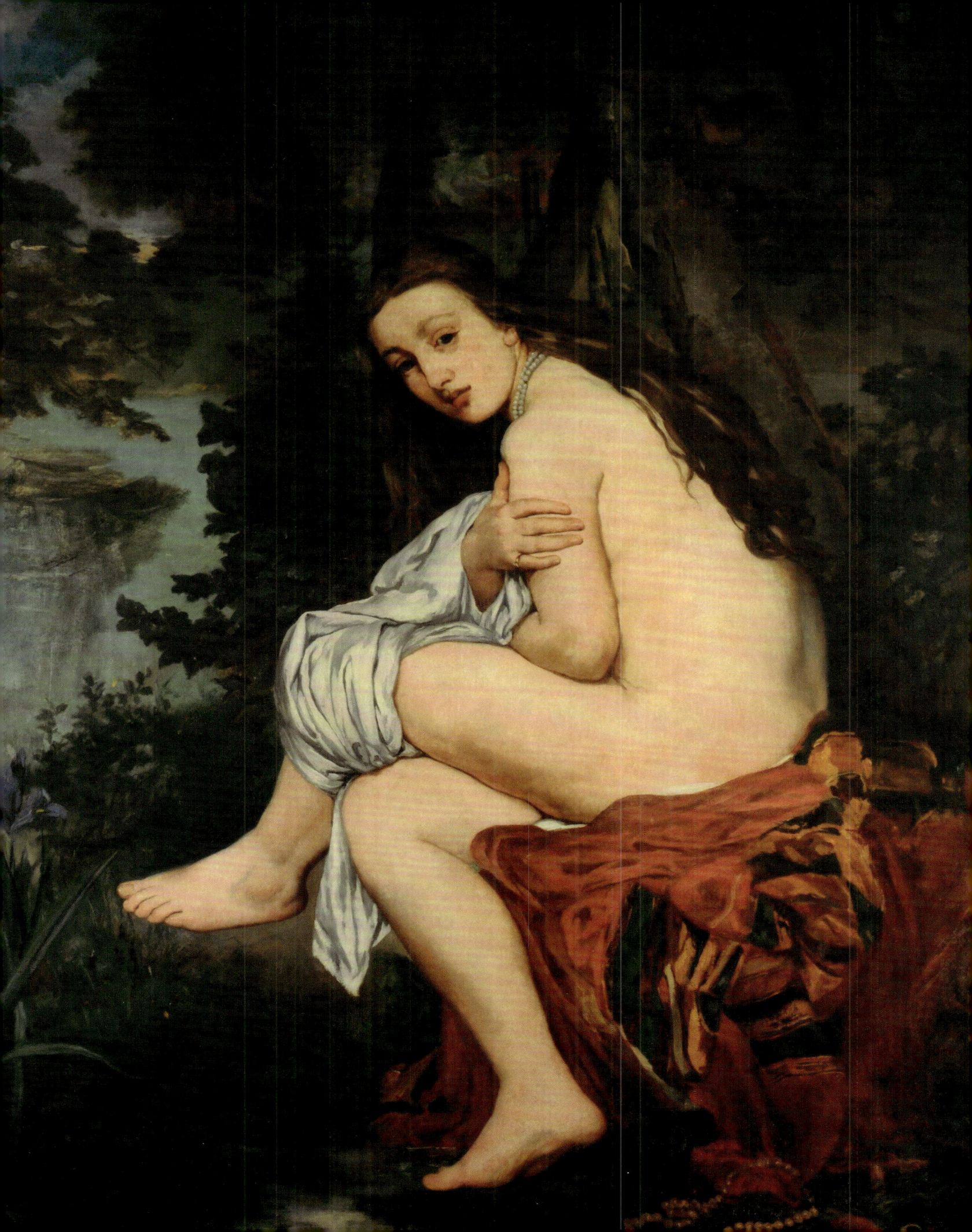

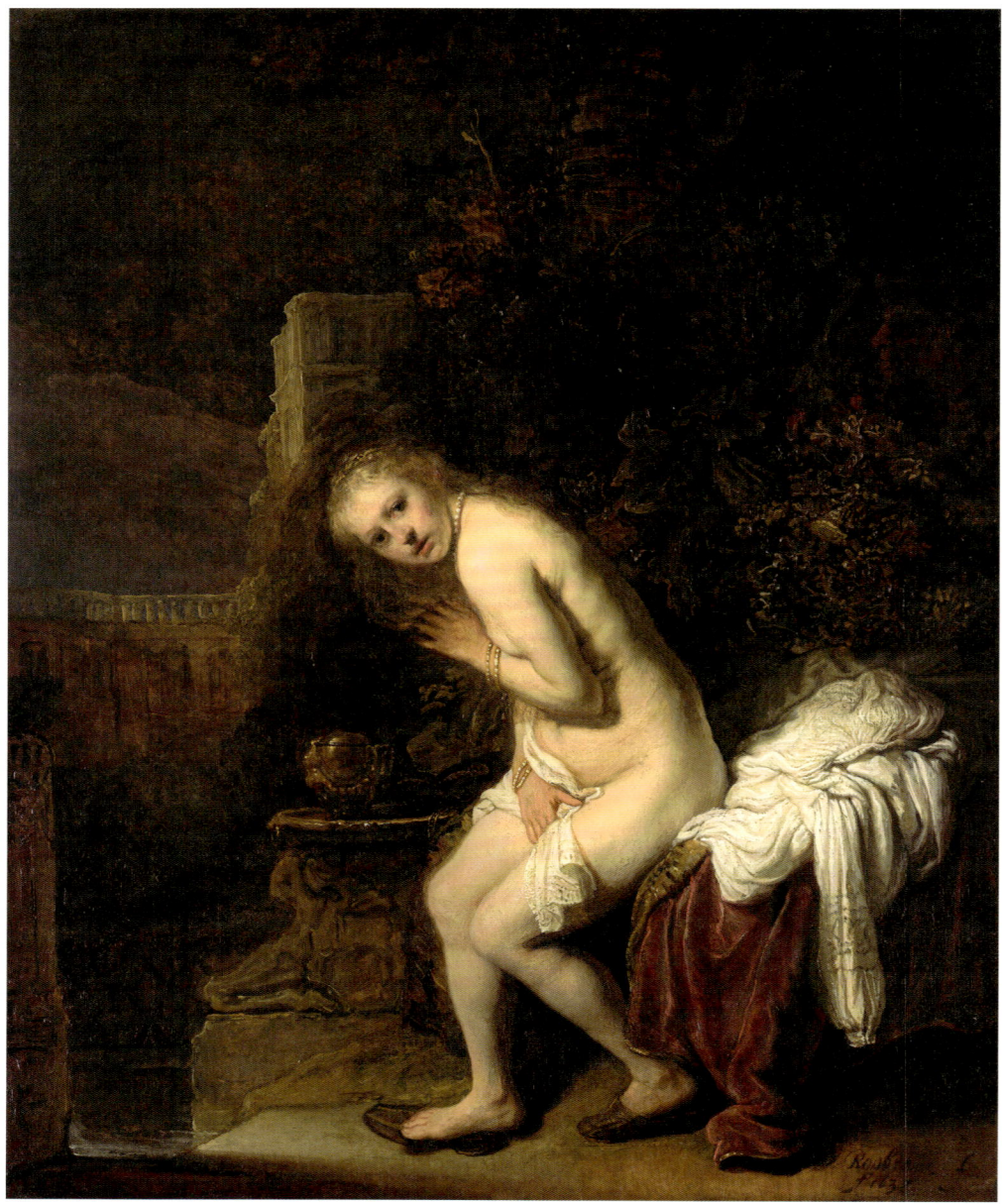

Fig. 2. Rembrandt van Rijn, *Susanna*, 1636. Oil on panel, 47.4 × 38.6 cm. Mauritshaus, The Hague

fully clothed bourgeois wife.[36] Scholars have linked this painting to sources ranging from prints after Giulio Romano's sixteenth-century fresco in Mantua's Palazzo del Te showing the *toilette* of Bathsheba to eighteenth-century French nudes like François Boucher's *Diana Leaving Her Bath* (1742, Louvre.) X-radiographs reveal extensive revision and complexity beneath the painting's surface.[37] Considering that scholars can locate so many art historical influences in one painting—as well as the fact that the surface masks another composition—it is one of Manet's most intriguing canvases.

Some of the obvious art historical references in *Surprised Nymph* are the works of two Dutch masters: Rembrandt's and Rubens's interpretations of the story of Susanna and the Elders (figs. 2, 3). Both were reproduced in prints (the Rubens is now lost), and

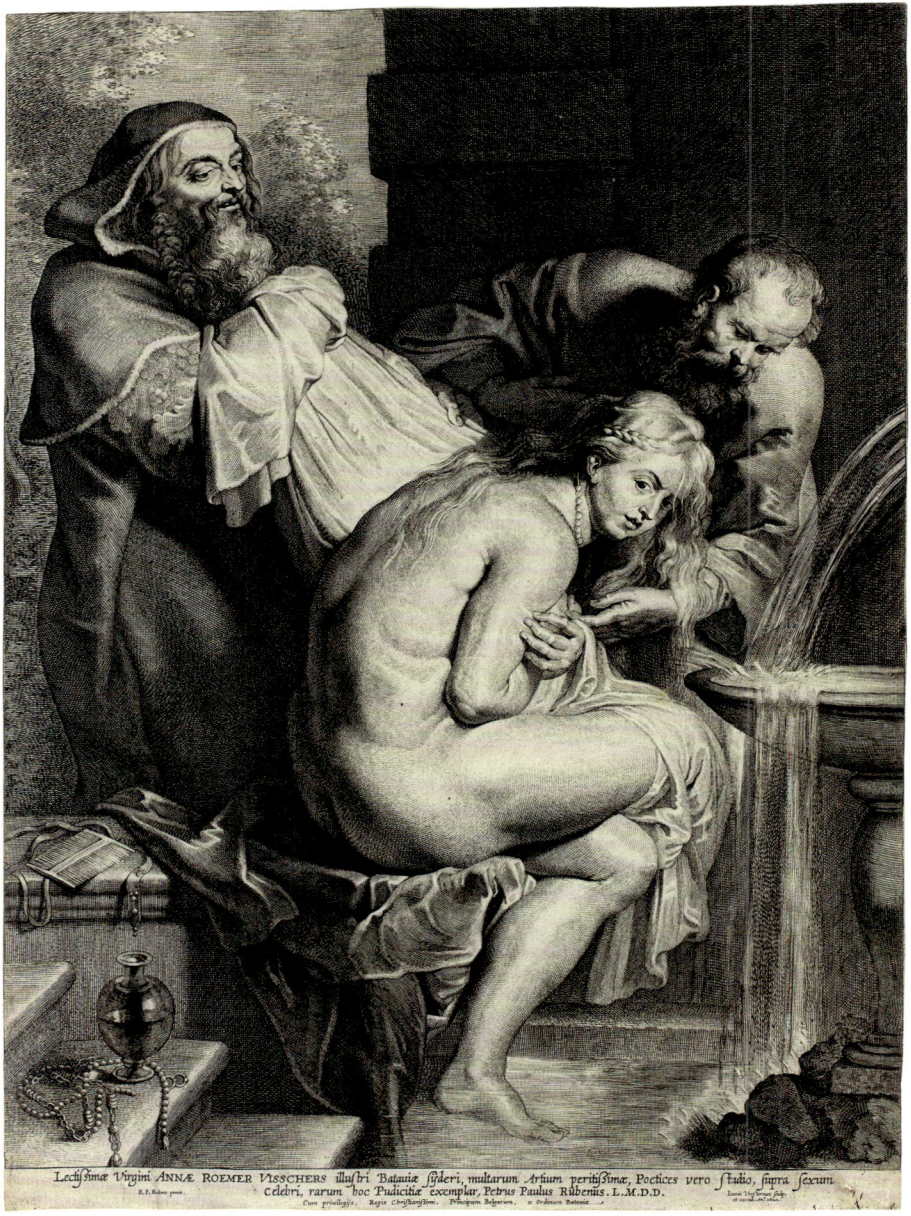

Fig. 3. Lucas Vorsterman after Peter Paul Rubens, *Susanna and the Elders*, 1620. Engraving, 38.2 × 27.7 cm. The Art Institute of Chicago

Édouard may have seen the Rembrandt in person during his first trip to Holland, in 1852. With allusions to paintings from his model's home country that feature a biblical character with her same name, Édouard could be making a personal reference to her true identity. Beyond these subtle associations with Suzanne's name and nationality, casting her in the story of the Susanna and the Elders feels weighted with meaning. The biblical story revolves around two old men spying on Susanna, a young married woman bathing in her garden. Lusting after her, the men try to force her to have sex with them. When she refuses, they falsely accuse her of adultery, a crime punishable by death. The intervention of the young hero Daniel and the exposure of the old men's lies save Susanna from condemnation; instead, the spying old men are sentenced to death.[38]

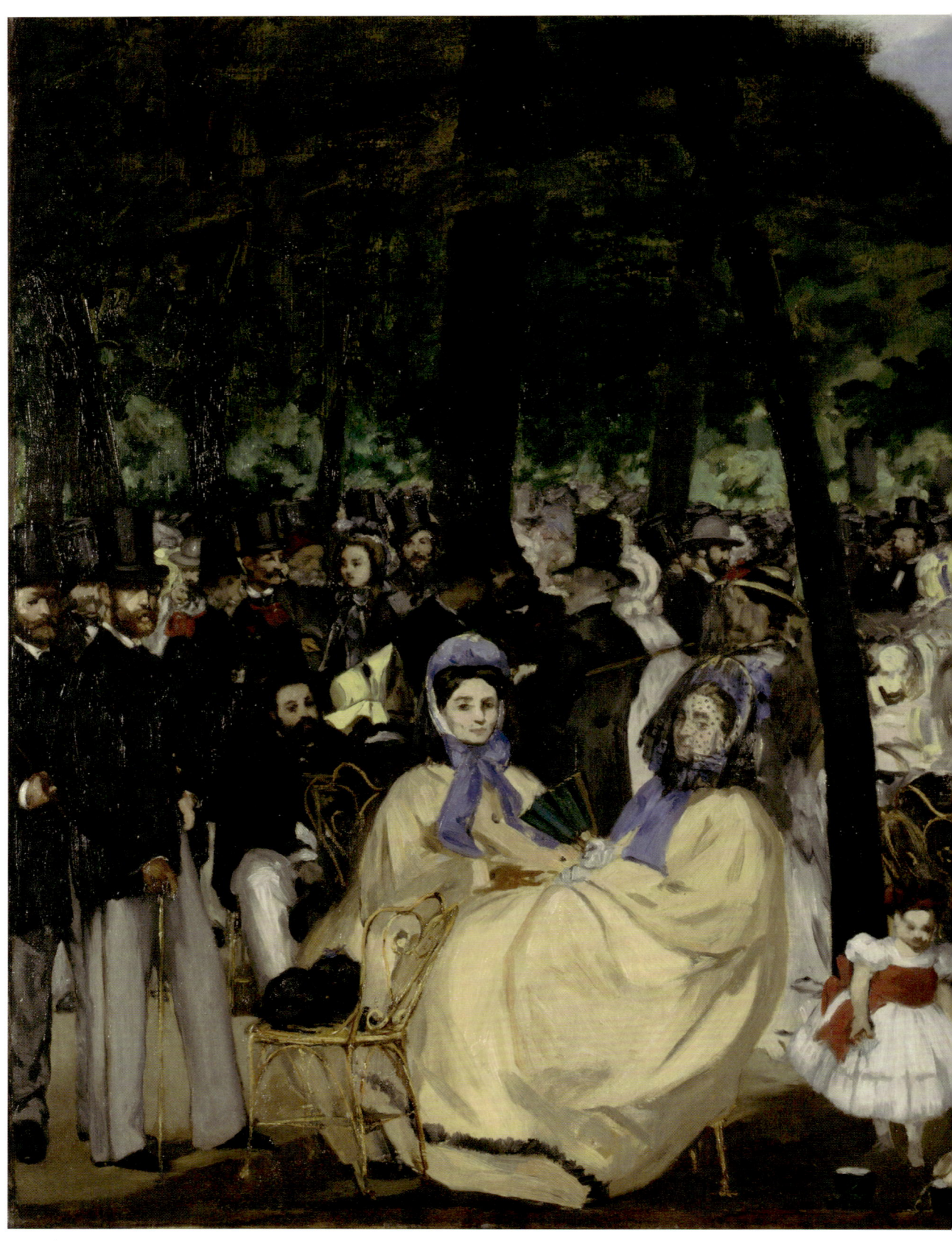

Fig. 4. Édouard Manet, *Music in the Tuileries*, 1862. Oil on canvas, 76.2 × 118.1 cm. National Gallery, London. Sir Hugh Lane Bequest, 1917, The National Gallery, London. In partnership with Hugh Lane Gallery, Dublin

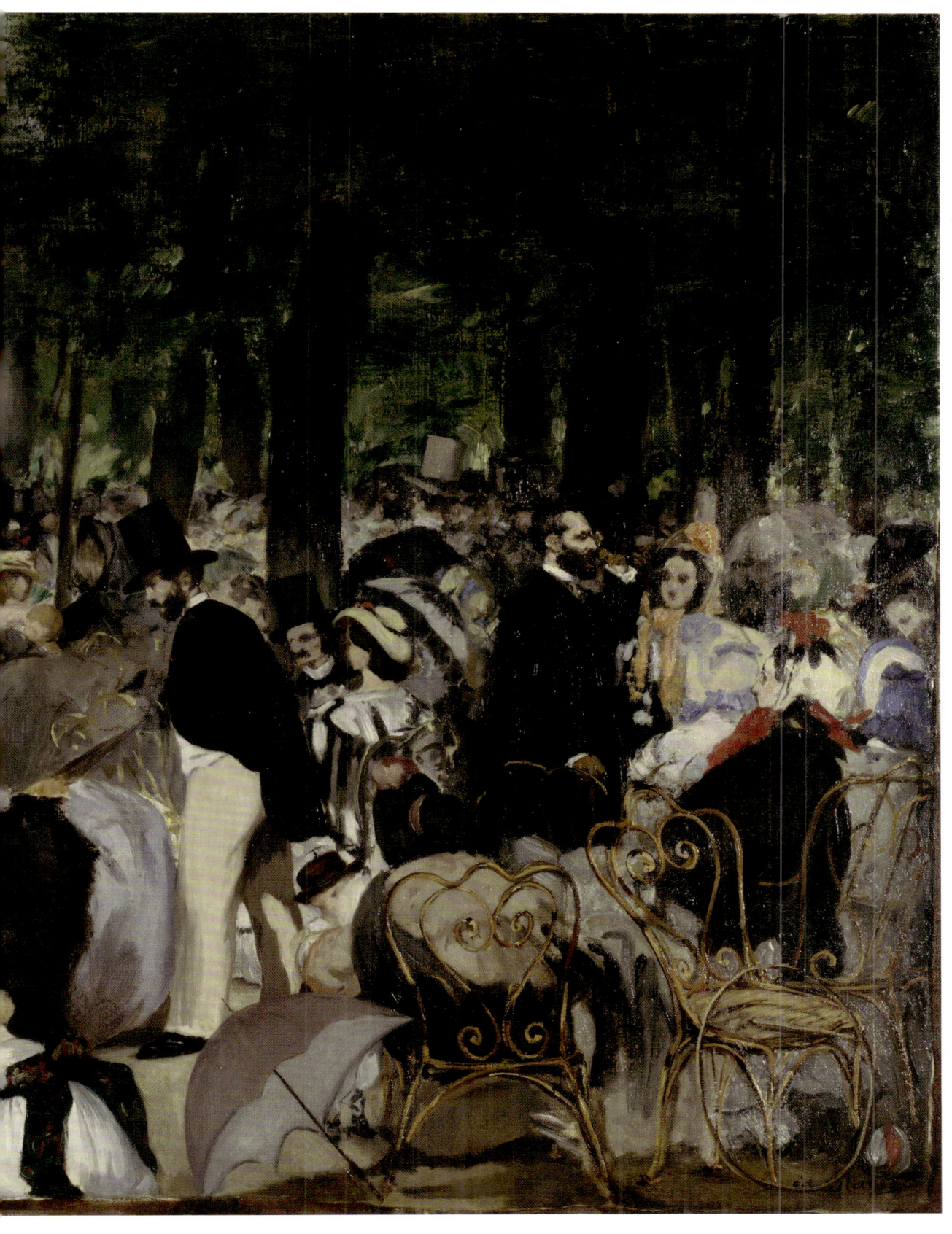

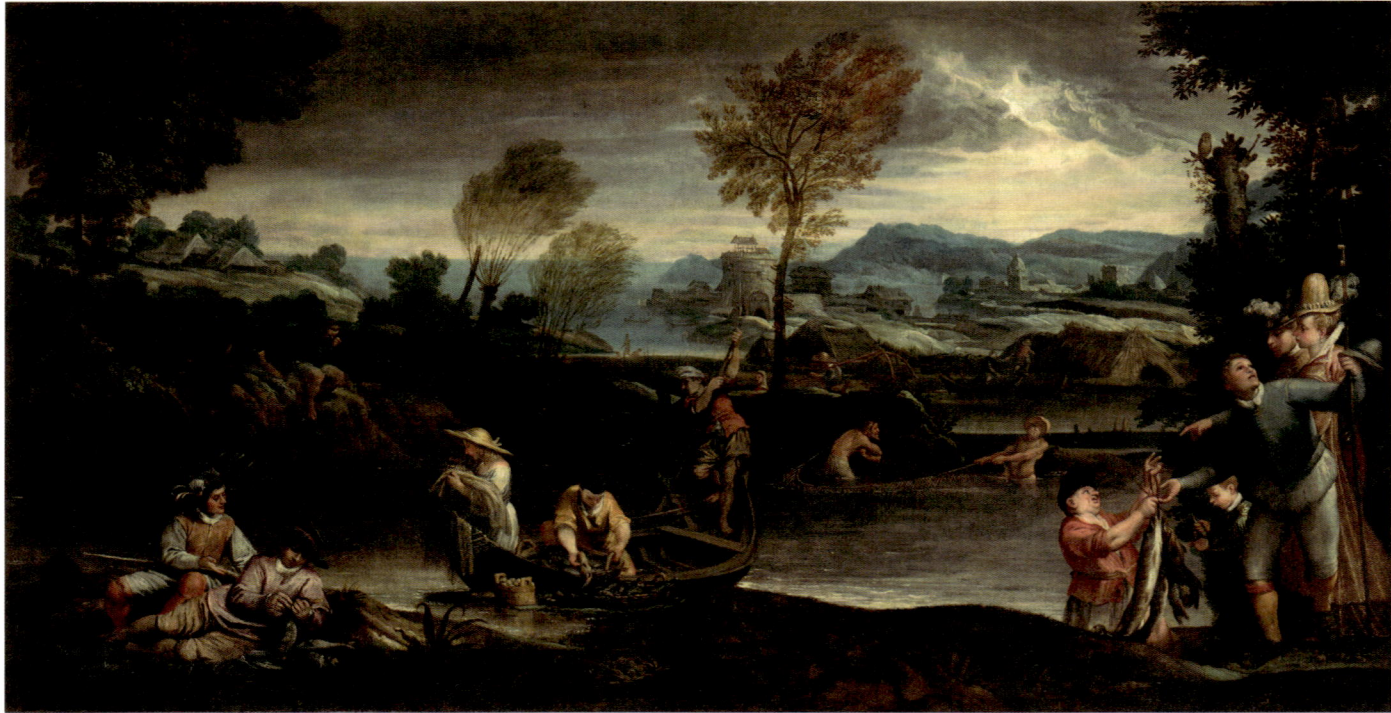

Fig. 5. Annibale Carracci, *Fishing*, 1575–1600. Oil on canvas, 136 × 155 cm. Musée du Louvre, Paris

Considering Auguste may have fathered Léon, Édouard's choice to feature a story where older men make unwanted sexual advances toward a young woman is poignant. The intervention of a young hero also carries weight considering the artist's impending marriage to Suzanne and the formalized family role he would take on to ensure her future and that of her son. Édouard could be considered Suzanne's Daniel, ensuring her social respectability and, of course, financial security. The couple married on October 28, 1863, in Zaltbommel in the Netherlands, just one year after Édouard's father died. Auguste's death seemingly cleared the way for the marriage. It also allowed the artist to become financially independent, as he and his brothers sold several properties they had inherited.[39]

Two paintings created during this period and often considered pendants exemplify Édouard's ability to fuse his artistic and family lives: *Music in the Tuileries* (fig. 4) and *Fishing* (cat. no. 6). The first, *Music in the Tuileries,* is an early manifesto of his interest in painting modern Parisian life. Although its composition and brushwork speak to his fascination with Velázquez, the cast of characters is a who's who of creative colleagues—a roster of the intellectual energy gathering in Parisian cafés at the time, including a self-portrait in the left side of the canvas.[40] Amid this bohemian mélange, Édouard positioned his own family. Eugène is a central standing figure.[41] To the left of the composer Jacques Offenbach is a veiled woman in black. A faceless blonde child leans against her lap. This duo could be Eugénie and Léon. After Auguste's death, Eugénie wore black for the rest of her life, making her easily recognizable.[42] Suzanne, who often wore gray, seems to be nearby.[43]

The pendant to *Music*, the canvas best known as *Fishing* (1862), is an unequivocal if enigmatic tribute to Suzanne and the inauguration of married life. Filled with references to the Old Masters, the landscape depicted has been identified as the area near the Manet family landholdings in Gennevilliers.[44] In the bottom right corner, in period dress, Édouard casts himself as Peter Paul Rubens. Suzanne appears by his side dressed as Rubens's wife and muse, Helena Fourment.[45] Manet's aspiration is clear: he is the future Rubens, supported by his Helena. The rest of the composition, however, muddies the waters. Referencing Annibale Carracci's *Fishing* (fig. 5), the center of his composition shows two fishermen maneuvering nets on a boat. On the far bank, separated from the happy couple, is a faceless blonde figure holding a fishing rod: Léon.[46] Édouard's painting places Suzanne clearly by the painter's side as he discovers an artistic landscape. Yet, Manet seemingly equivocates about the boy's position in that same landscape. Even though Léon is Suzanne's biological son, Édouard has separated him from the betrothed couple. Not totally edited out of the picture, he is almost a prop—a faceless formal element less clearly resolved than even the anonymous fishermen. This composition is a poignant summary of Léon's position within Édouard's oeuvre and within the family in general: frequently present but never clearly identified.

We Need to Talk About Léon

Léon was one of Édouard's most frequent models.[47] From childhood in the 1850s until young adulthood in the early 1870s, he was a consistent presence in the artist's works. In many instances—*Music in the Tuileries, Fishing, Spanish Cavaliers* (cat. no. 2) and *The Balcony* (fig. 6)—he is faceless or marginal. In other works, he migrated to the center, as in *Boy with a Sword* (see fig. 34), *Luncheon in the Studio* (fig. 7), *Boy Blowing Bubbles* (cat. no. 7), and *Young Boy Peeling a Pear* (cat. no. 8). Whatever his position, Léon is consistently presented in a scene reminiscent of an Old Master painting or as the quintessential Parisian dandy. In contrast to other family members, he was never the subject of an unambiguous solo portrait. This creates a tension between his status as an identified member of the family and the artist's use of him as a studio model in ways one would associate with someone intended to be anonymous or at least unrelated to the painter. Léon's mutability under Édouard's brush and across media heightens this tension. He ages radically from one painting to another, and his features oscillate between anonymity and specificity. His figure is often cropped and isolated in drawings and prints.[48]

Juxtaposing two paintings that feature teenage Léon—*Boy Blowing Bubbles* and *Young Boy Peeling a Pear*—exemplifies this mutability. The two paintings are dated roughly a year apart, about 1867 and about 1868, respectively.[49] In *Boy Blowing Bubbles,* Léon looks younger than his fifteen years. In *Young Boy Peeling a Pear,* he appears older than sixteen, with a small mustache, broad shoulders, and a square jawline. Adolescent boys can, of course, change rapidly from one year to the next. Both paintings, of similar size, include details—a delicate soap bubble and a perishable pear—associated with themes of *vanitas,* the fleeting nature of worldly pleasures.[50] If considered as pendants, they could be Manet's attempt—one that feels parental and sentimental—to record and pay homage to Léon's fleeting youth. This dramatic shift in appearance can, however, be seen in another way. The lack of resolve in his features and chameleon-like presence seems to make Léon's physical attributes respond at will to Manet's own artistic needs. The Old Master source related to *Boy Blowing Bubbles,* a work by Jean Baptiste Chardin, features children, and Manet presents Léon in a way that mirrors the youthful eighteenth-century subjects that inspired him.[51] In contrast, the inspiration for *Young Boy Peeling a Pear* is likely a Jusepe de Ribera image featuring an old man.[52] The age of Ribera's subject seems to rub off on Léon's suddenly much more mature appearance. He is a strikingly flexible—almost unrealistically flexible—model.

The lack of resolution around Léon's features across Manet's oeuvre presages scholars' evolving and fluid understanding of the boy's status within the Manet family. Just as scholarship about the Manet family has, in the past, often been scattered across disparate sources—the same is true of scholarship about Léon's paternity and familial position. This research often appears in connection with a single painting in which he features or has been the subject of scholarly articles that propose to have discovered the "secret" of his birth. Most importantly, new scholarship has appeared since Locke wrote her account of the family story twenty years ago. In many ways, the complexity of the Manet family swirls around Léon, so it is useful to survey the current arguments in one place. Rather than clearly privilege one theory over another, this survey aims to present the arguments for and against each scenario.

There have been three proposed candidates for Léon's father: one of four Swiss musicians with the last name Koëlla; Édouard Manet himself; and Auguste Manet. Koëlla, the single name listed as Léon's father on his birth certificate, was long thought to be a fabrication or bastardization of a generic Dutch name. Scholars have, however, since identified the musical Koëlla brothers, who performed around Europe and could have crossed paths with Suzanne. One of them—Giovanni—is the most likely candidate based on age and resemblance to a figure in *The Old Musicians* (1862; National Gallery of Art, Washington). The declaration of Koëlla's occupation as an "artiste-musicien" on Léon's birth certificate supports this identification.[53] This theory, however, does not address one critical question: why would Édouard and his family continue to engage with and support Suzanne, their hired piano teacher, after she had given birth out of wedlock to a son fathered by a traveling musician?[54] Was the artist's connection to her already strong enough to overcome this scandal? Possibly. However, Giovanni Koëlla (or another brother) could also have sold or volunteered his surname to provide Léon with at least some legitimacy. A vague name listed as father was more respectable than no name at all.[55]

There are two other hypotheses. The first is that Édouard was Léon's biological father. Evidence supporting this theory includes Léon's second name being Édouard and the artist being named his godfather.[56] Finally, Manet's marriage to Suzanne after his father's death suggests the artist had an enduring attachment to her and possibly Léon as well. Some scholars simply ask a sexist rhetorical question to support this scenario: Why else would Manet marry this quiet, average-looking Dutch musician below his social standing if she were *not* the mother of his child?[57]

There is, however, also evidence against Édouard being Léon's biological father. The first is that he and Suzanne never officially recognized him as their legitimate son after their marriage. This process was relatively straightforward under the laws of the Second Empire, which emphasized the protection and preservation of traditional nuclear families.[58] Furthermore, many of Manet's fellow artist friends, including Paul Cézanne and Claude Monet, *did* recognize their natural children after marrying the children's mothers.[59] In contrast, it would have been difficult—and possibly illegal—for Manet to recognize Léon as his son if he were not his biological father.[60]

Further evidence that Léon was not Édouard's son comes from a letter that the artist wrote to Zacharie Astruc in 1865. Manet congratulates his friend on the news of his wife's pregnancy: "Give Mme Astruc all our good wishes for the arrival of your heir. We would love the same thing to happen to us."[61] The implication is, of course, that he and Suzanne want but cannot have children. While he could be referring to additional children, this comment implies they have no children together—Léon was Suzanne's son, not Édouard's, and therefore not his heir. In a letter sent after the artist's death, his brother Gustave recounts Eugénie's anger at Suzanne's refusal to reimburse 10,000 francs she gave to the couple upon their marriage. The marriage contract had a condition that the money should be returned if Édouard predeceased his mother and left behind no natural heirs. Gustave quotes Eugénie as saying: "There are some things about which I will not change my mind,

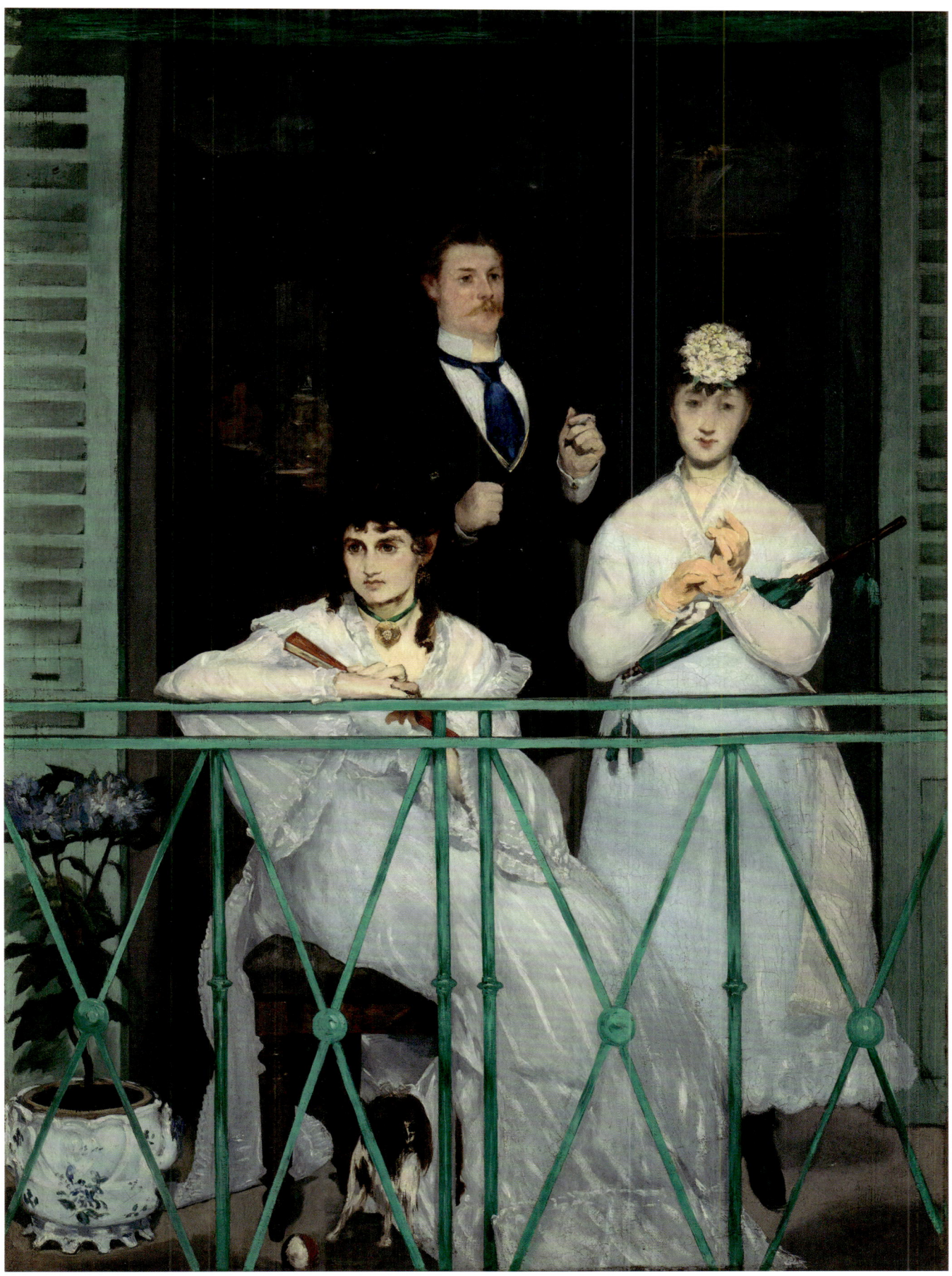

Fig. 6. Édouard Manet, *The Balcony*, 1868–69. Oil on canvas, 170 × 125 cm. Musée d'Orsay, Paris

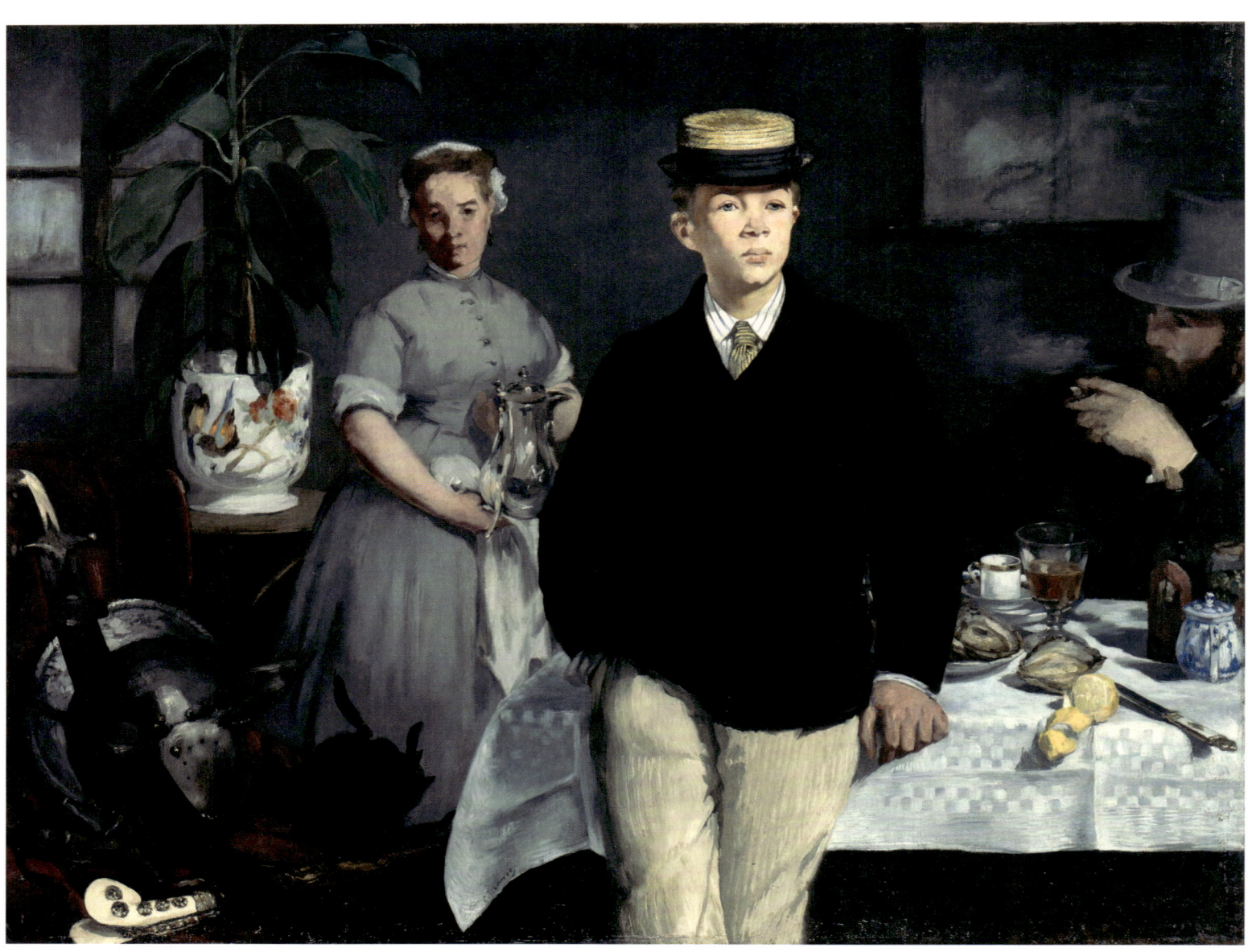

Fig. 7. Édouard Manet, *Luncheon in the Studio*, 1868. Oil on canvas, 118.3 × 154 cm. Neue Pinakothek, Munich

namely the crime she committed out of affection for that dear boy who is merely a victim of his unhappy birth. . . . That is the punishment for her crime, let her suffer it."[62] Her words make clear she did not think "that dear boy" was her legitimate grandson.

The final theory about Léon's paternity is that he is Auguste Manet's biological son. This would make him both Édouard Manet's half-brother and stepson. Auguste's paternity explains the paradox of the Manet family's continued engagement with Suzanne after she gave birth—concluding in her marriage to Édouard—but failure to officially recognize Léon as a legitimate son and official family member.[63] If Auguste fathered Léon while Suzanne was employed in his household, it would be a serious crime made even more disgraceful by his position as a judge.[64] To openly admit Léon's true paternity would admit the patriarch's breach of both family expectation and the law. Édouard's will suggests a family understanding that Léon, despite not having official recognition, deserved his portion of the Manet family wealth. It states: "I appoint Suzanne Leenhoff . . . my universal legatee. In her last will, she will leave everything I have left to her to Léon Koëlla, called Leenhoff . . . I believe my brothers will find these arrangements perfectly natural." In an addendum, he reiterates that Suzanne's inheritance should pass to Léon upon her death.[65]

Ultimately, we will never know who fathered Léon. Léon himself did not seem to know—he may have only discovered Suzanne was his mother and not his sister when his uncle Ferdinand Leenhoff helped him obtain a replacement birth certificate in 1871.[66] Despite the shock of learning Suzanne was his mother, he had positive memories about his upbringing. He wrote: "In the Manet and Leenhoff families, I always said 'godmother' and 'godfather' . . . in society, they were my brother-in-law and sister. A family secret of which I never learned the last word, having been pampered and spoiled by both of them, who indulged all my whims. We lived happily, the three of us; above all I lived happily with no concerns. Therefore, I had no need to question my birth."[67] This happiness is apparent in a small group of works and a wonderful cache of letters from the early 1870s.

"We Lived Happily"

The Franco-Prussian War (July 1870–January 1871) and the Paris Commune (March–May 1871) exploded the Manets' Parisian world. With the capital under siege, Édouard and his brothers stayed to defend Paris while he sent his mother, Suzanne, and Léon to the southwest of France for safety.[68] This separation was the longest from his mother since his trip to Brazil, and he had never been far from Suzanne and Léon for so long. This physical distance prompted an extensive and moving stream of letters that provide real-time evidence of how Léon, Édouard, and Suzanne lived happily.

Filled with lines that worry about everything from Léon having forgotten a woolen shirt to reassuring his mother that he is looking after his brothers, they reveal the artist's genuine and touchingly quotidian concern for his family.[69] After several months apart, Manet wrote to Suzanne: "I woke up last night thinking I heard you calling me."[70] This is just one of many similarly emotional letters sent to his wife, which also hint at his desire for a compelling visual record. He wrote in November 1870, "I think of you all the time and have filled the bedroom with your portraits."[71]

Manet would soon produce a handful of new images of Suzanne and Léon together that serve as tender double portraits. The complicated *Reading* (cat. no. 11) is an adaptation of a painting that previously featured only Suzanne; the artist almost certainly added Léon at a later date, likely in the early 1870s.[72] Two others—the watercolor and painting, both titled *Interior at Arcachon*—are a visual complement to the stream of Siege letters (cat. no. 10). They were completed when Manet rejoined his family in the southwest of France. While Suzanne is the star of *Reading*, in the two *Interior at Arcachon* works, Léon takes center stage and—particularly in the watercolor—has an air of maturity distinct from earlier depictions (see fig. 93). During the war, Léon had become a man and would soon begin his professional life in Paris in earnest.[73] These were among the last depictions of Léon; with manhood came a lack of visual interest from Manet.

Another Madame Manet

While Léon stopped modeling in the 1870s, Suzanne did not, and another soon-to-be Madame Manet also captured Édouard's attention. He first met Berthe Morisot (1841–1895) in 1868. She had already been painting for a decade and had exhibited at the Paris Salon.[74] Soon after they met, Berthe started modeling for Manet—first in *The Balcony* (1868–69). Manet and Morisot developed a friendship, mentorship, and artist-model relationship. The surviving correspondence between Berthe; her mother, Marie-Joséphine; and her sisters, Edma and Yves, demonstrates a clear admiration for Manet. As Marie-Joséphine wrote to Edma in 1869, "He naively said that Berthe [as his model] was bringing him luck. He seems to me very nice because he is interested in Berthe."[75] The Morisot family—also part of the Parisian bourgeoisie—started socializing regularly with the Manets. Berthe ultimately appeared in eleven oils and numerous prints and drawings. This visual engagement was intense but relatively short compared to that of Suzanne and Léon. Morisot started modeling for the artist in 1868 and stopped in 1874, when she married Eugène Manet, becoming Édouard's sister-in-law.[76]

In her correspondence, it is clear Berthe saw Manet both as a friend and mentor. In one account from 1870, she describes how the Morisot family "spent Thursday evening at Manet's. He was bubbling over with good spirits, spinning a hundred nonsensical yarns, one funnier than another."[77] Manet's alternating praise and critiques of her paintings seem to have been both encouraging and frustrating. In one typical account, she wrote to Edma: "Manet exhorted me so strongly to do a little retouching on my painting of you that when you come here, I shall ask you to let me draw the head again and add some touches at the bottom of the dress, and that is all. He says the success of exhibition [at the Salon] is assured and that I do not need to worry; the next instant he adds that I shall be rejected. I wish I were not concerned with all this."[78] Some have theorized that there was a romantic element—or at least a yearning—in Manet and Morisot's connection to one another.[79]

For his part, Manet seriously engaged with Berthe's art, though he clearly saw that her career could be limited by the fact that she was a woman. In an exchange not long after their initial meeting, Manet wrote in a letter to Fantin-Latour: "I agree with you: *les demoiselles* Morisot [Berthe and her sister Edma] are charming. What a pity they are not men. However, they could, as women serve the cause of painting by each marrying an Academician and bringing discord into the camp of those old fogies."[80] Of course, Berthe would not marry an establishment academic painter and influence his painting. Instead, in marrying Eugène, she found a partner who was dedicated to supporting her artistic career—perhaps in ways that mirrored how he had long been his brother's travel partner, frequent companion, and sometime model. Eugène was already accustomed to supporting a great artist, and he brought this skill to his relationship with Berthe.[81] Unlike her sister Edma, Berthe continued her career as a painter after her marriage. As a married woman and Manet's sister-in-law, she showed her paintings in the Impressionist exhibitions alongside those of many of Édouard's closest friends and colleagues.[82]

Fig. 8. Édouard Manet, *Repose*, about 1871. Oil on canvas, 150.2 × 114 cm. RISD Museum, Providence. Bequest of Mrs. Edith Stuyvesant Vanderbilt Gerry

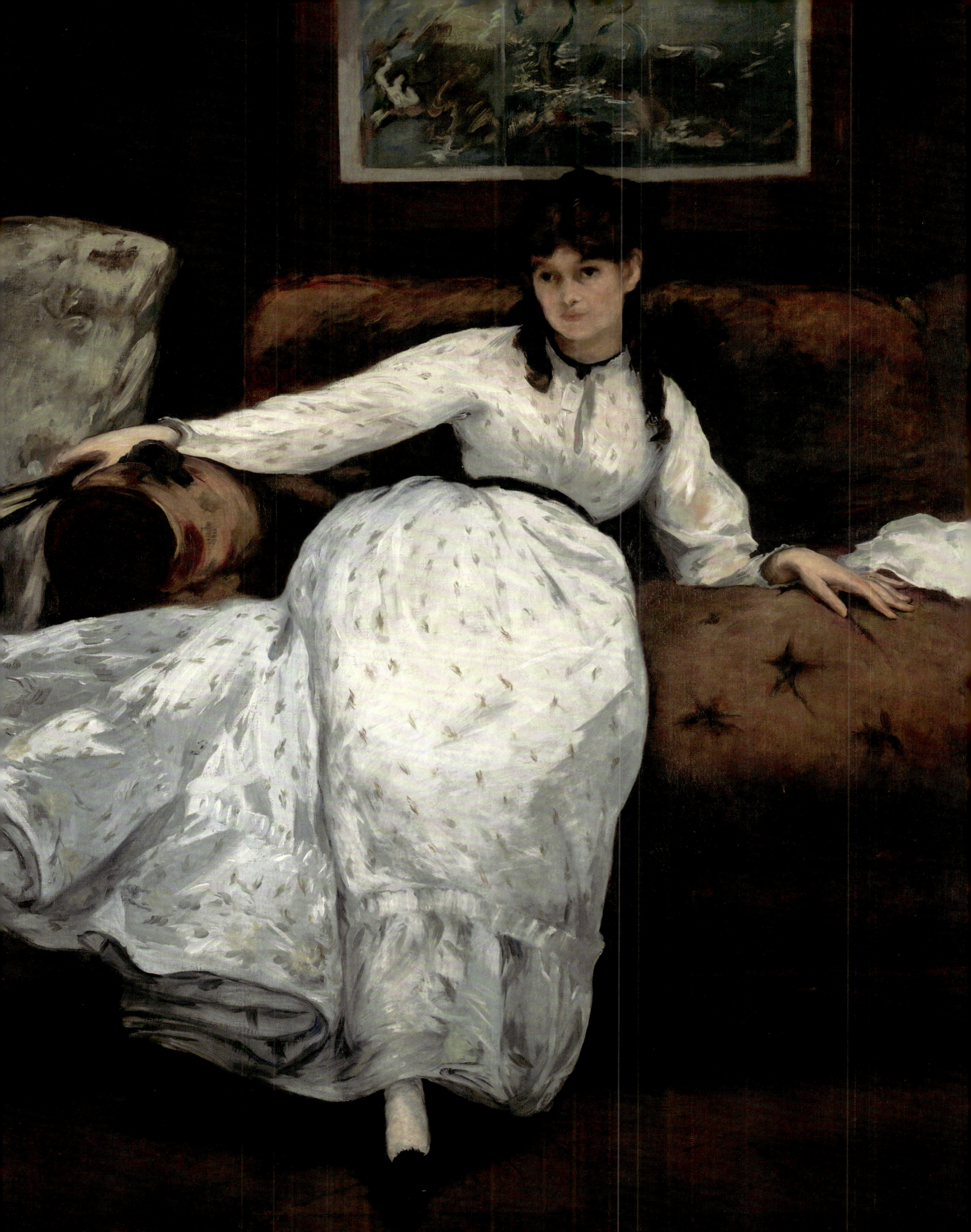

In many ways, Berthe seems like a foil to Suzanne. French, upper class, and an innovative visual artist, she successfully straddled a bourgeois family life and the bohemian artistic world—just like Édouard. The Manet family and their friends do not seem to have viewed Suzanne as an artistic and social peer in the same way that they viewed Berthe. Although a talented piano player, the foreign and lower-class Suzanne has often been relegated to a secondary role within the Manet story. She was not Édouard's primary hostess—Eugénie, who lived with the couple starting in 1867, retained that responsibility after their marriage. She contributed to the family's social life mostly by providing musical entertainment at their gatherings. This apparent contrast between Suzanne and Berthe has been heightened by the surviving correspondence between the Morisot women. Before her marriage to Eugène, Berthe, her sisters, and their mother often describe Suzanne in less than flattering terms—perhaps tinged with a touch of jealousy and indignation.[83]

These surface-level contrasts, however, mask the striking similarities in Manet's depictions of the women—whether it is painting them reclining (see figs. 8 and 28) or casting them in works inspired by the Old Masters. *Berthe Morisot* (cat. no. 13) and *Madame Édouard Manet (Suzanne Leenhoff)* (cat. no. 14) demonstrate the similarities of some of these pictorial schemes. Both appearing in profile with elaborate hats, these images of Suzanne and Berthe are sketchy, particularly around the hands. Suzanne—like in many other images of her—is in gray, a trait that makes her recognizable across Manet's canvases. In this painting, Morisot does not have the gaunt appearance that she has in many other pictures; instead, her figure is filled out with a fur coat and muff. So dressed, her silhouette resembles Suzanne's. While Suzanne sold the painting of herself to a dealer in the 1890s, she kept the portrait of Berthe until her death; it then went to Léon, who sold it in 1910.[84] This provenance points to an understudied yet essential role that the family played: shepherding Manet's works and legacy after he died. The two women, in fact, sometimes worked together in this shared project. The wealthier Berthe helped to support her financially struggling sister-in-law after Édouard's death, likely to help her to survive without selling off works of art.[85] Rather than being foils, they had become family.

Keepers of the Manet Legacy

By the late 1870s Édouard was suffering from progressively debilitating symptoms of advanced syphilis—the same disease that had killed his father. He continued to paint and produce important works like the portrait of his cousin Jules Dejouy (cat. no. 15) and the Salon-medal-winning *Monsieur Pertuiset: the Lion Hunter* (1881; Museu de Arte de São Paulo). However, as Manet's condition deteriorated, he needed more care, which was provided by Léon, Suzanne, and his brothers. In his will, dated September 1882, the artist specifically says Léon "has given me the most devoted care." Édouard Manet died of an infection related to syphilis on April 30, 1883. His family was by his side.[86]

Manet's will dictated that "the pictures, sketches, and drawings remaining in my studio after my death are to be sold at auction," specifically charging his friend Théodore Duret to manage the sale and decide what was saleable and what should be destroyed. The proceeds would support Léon and Suzanne. The family helped Duret arrange both a posthumous exhibition and the sale (fig. 9).[87] Léon created a comprehensive inventory of works in the studio and hired a photographer to document every piece (see fig. 44).[88] The family also retained certain works. Suzanne held back some things from sale, and Eugène and Berthe bought eight works; in the following years Berthe continued to purchase additional pieces.[89]

Despite a shared love for and loyalty to Édouard and his art, growing tension was evident between Suzanne, Léon, and the other members of the Manet family. As Léon wrote to Eugène shortly after the artist's death, "Your brother raised me like his own son; I have always lived in your family, and it would be a great wrench to leave you."[90] Eugénie's letter to Gustave, in which she complains about Suzanne and Léon's claims to Édouard's family money, followed a few months later. Tensions increased between "Leenhoff world"—as Eugénie referred to them—and the legitimate Manets. Suzanne and Léon fell into financial hardship.[91] The mother-son pair started to sell the paintings they had retained, which Suzanne recorded in a notebook (fig. 10).[92] As time went on, these sales were not necessarily kosher—they sold parts of sketchbooks, unfinished works that were "completed" by another hand, and Léon likely sold a handful of copies originally made as keepsakes for Suzanne when she had to part with her favorite paintings (see figs. 11 and 33).[93] Julie Manet (1878–1966), Berthe and Eugène's daughter, was deeply concerned about this practice.[94]

While Léon's handling of the sale of Manet's works is questionable, what is beyond contention is the critical role he played in preserving Manet's legacy through his collaborations with scholars, notably Adolphe Tabarant and Étienne Moreau-Nélaton. By the time

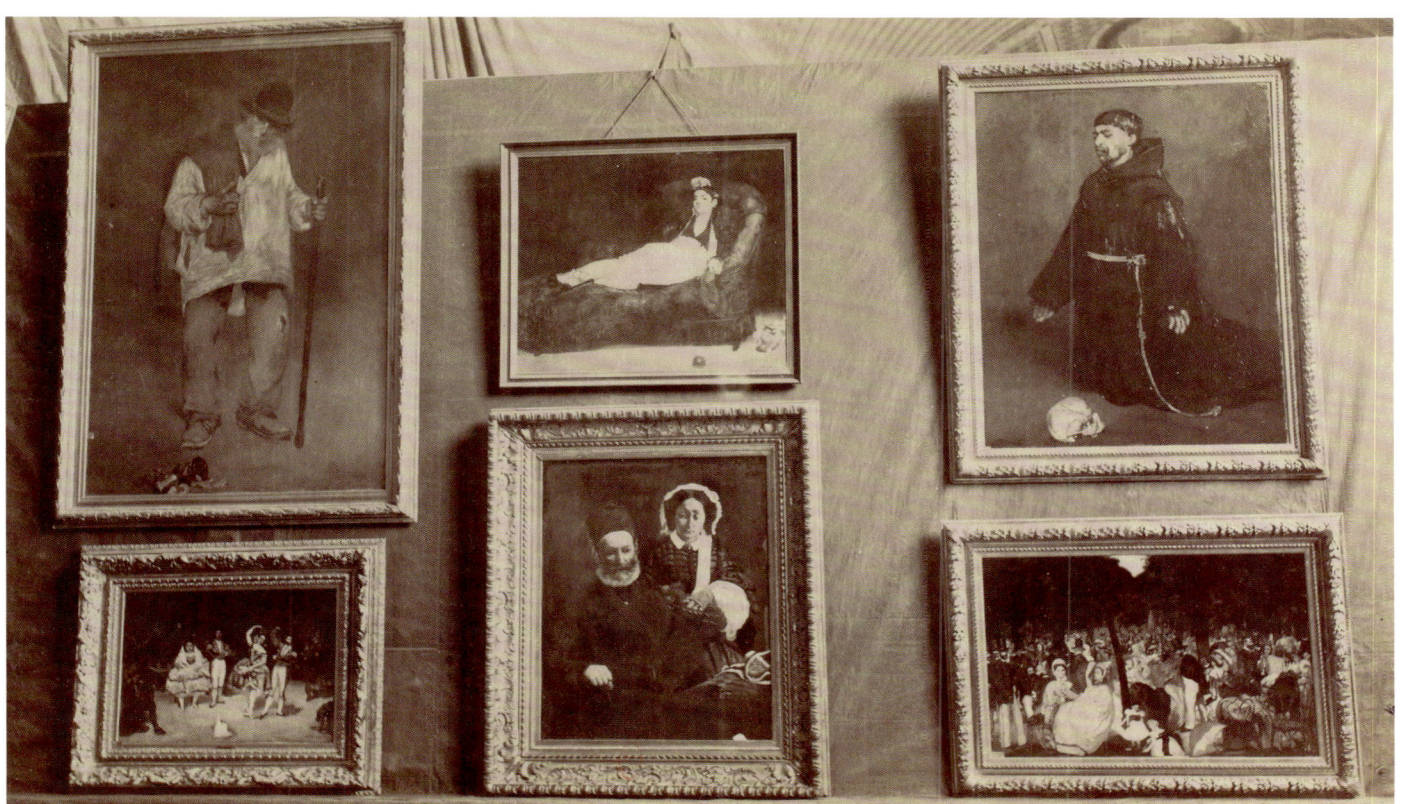

Fig. 9. Anatole Godet, *Retrospective exhibition of the work of Édouard Manet, École des Beaux-Arts, January 6–8, 1884.* Photograph, fol. 5. Bibliothèque Nationale de France, Paris

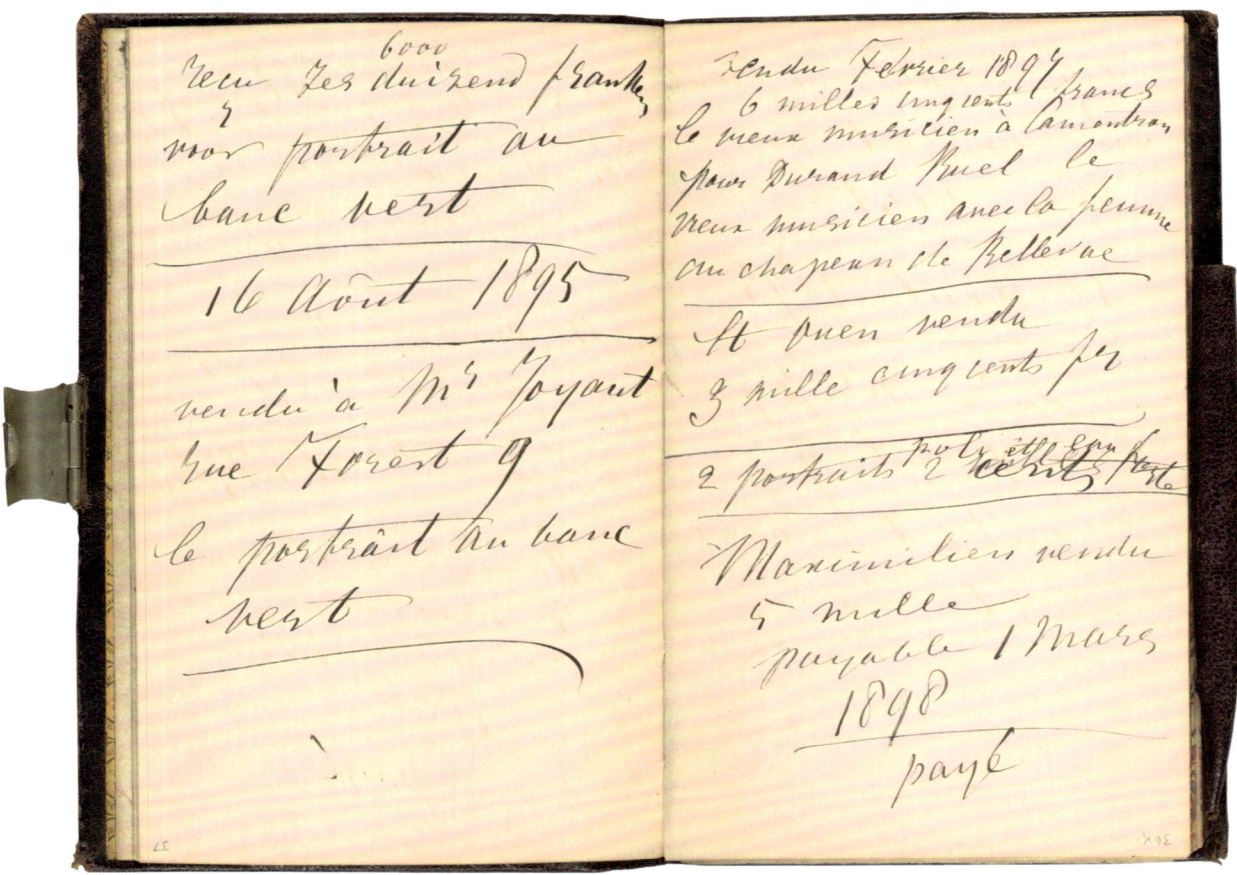

Fig. 10. Suzanne Manet, Carnet de comptes, fol. 36v–37r, 1892–1900. The Morgan Library & Museum, New York (MA 3950.2:2). Purchased as the gift of Mrs. Charles Engelhard and children in memory of Mr. Charles Engelhard, 1974

they were working on their landmark monographs, Léon was the last surviving family member to have known Manet. Julie was only four when her uncle died. The archives he inherited, notes he made on Manet's life, his inventory of the studio, and personal recollections shared with scholars still form a core part of primary source material available about the artist.[95] Though never a recognized member of the Manet family, Léon and the archives he held and created were essential to telling the story of Manet's artistic greatness and centrality to art history.

As with all things related to the Manet family, their keeping of Édouard's legacy is full of things left said and unsaid—unknown facts and true behaviors that will never be known. Yet, despite this, the family ultimately succeeded in supporting and celebrating Édouard's art. Manet was extraordinarily famous by the time of Léon's death in 1927 and firmly canonical by the time Julie died in 1966. Images of Eugénie, Gustave, Eugène, Suzanne, Berthe, and Léon are part of the canon of modern art. With this exhibition and catalogue, their roles will now be understood as more than just models or relatives, but rather as the providers of a powerful catalytic mixture of inspiration, support, and love.

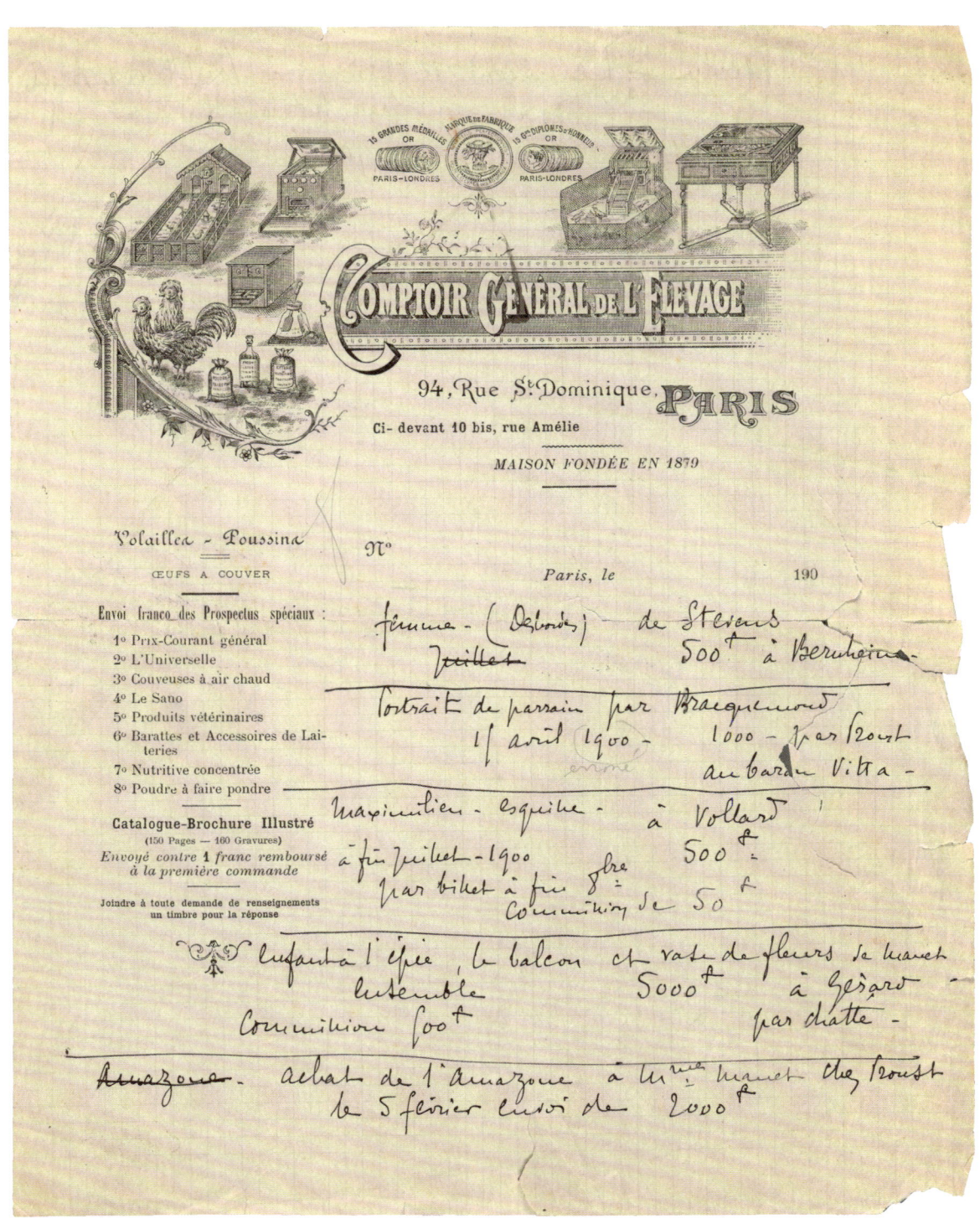

Fig. 11. Léon-Édouard Koëlla, known as Léon Leenhoff, Receipt for the sale of Manet paintings that likely includes forgeries, about 1905–10. The Morgan Library & Museum, New York (MA 3950)

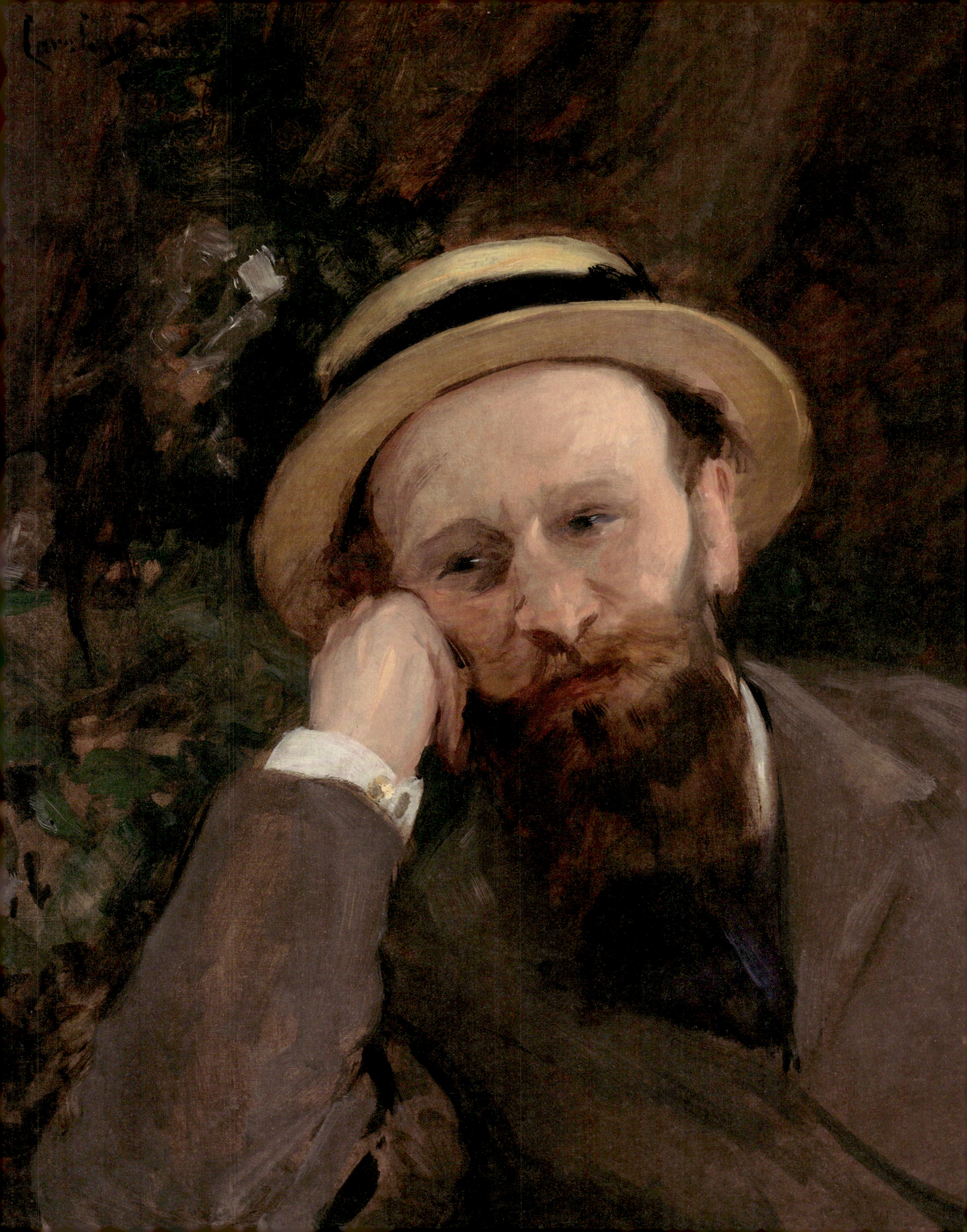

Paris is A Mother

HILTON ALS

The story goes that Auguste Manet, a lawyer who lived by the clock and not in dreams, was fed up with his teenage son Édouard, born in 1832, who had no interest at all in the law, despite the fact that a number of men on Auguste's side of the family had made great careers for themselves supporting Justice.

Édouard (fig. 12) had other things on his mind; often he went with his maternal uncle to the Louvre, that arsenal of dreams, where he could stock up on fantasies made real by the artist's hand. Maybe he would be an artist, too. But Auguste had other plans, made other plans. A career in the navy, a career as a European colonizer—that would set Édouard right. So, in 1848 or so, Auguste packed Édouard off to Brazil on a boat called *Havre et Guadeloupe*, and just imagine that son of the haute bourgeoisie with his foulard in the damp air having no clear idea of what he had done to deserve being sent away, but internal journeys are always worth it: how could he not think of home living so far away, and of course some of those memories must have been of his art-loving mother, Mme Manet— Eugénie-Désirée Fournier Manet—because for so many sons memory is a mother anyway.

Born in 1811 to a French family that had recently returned to Paris after making its fortune in Sweden, Eugénie was named after a queen of Sweden; the youngest of four, and the only girl, Eugénie was the goddaughter of a royal ascendant couple, her godfather being Charles Bernadotte, the French Napoleonic maréchal who became the crown prince of Sweden a year before Eugénie's birth. (Bernadotte never learned to speak Swedish, even after taking the throne in 1818; he ruled Norway and Sweden until his death in 1844). That detail about Eugénie's early life has always struck me as interesting—her proximity to pomp and circumstance, but all slightly off-kilter because of Charles's obstinacy, his refusal to learn a language that would take him away from his native France even as he lived and ruled elsewhere. Édouard's parents, like parents everywhere, had their own reality in the world of one another. Even though Auguste seems to have taken no pleasure in social life, he likely allowed receptions to be hosted at his home twice a week because it was expected of a well-salaried civil servant; that was part of the job. Eugénie, on the other hand, delighted in parties, receptions; a lover of music, she had a fine voice, and part of what makes Édouard's portrait of his mother so extraordinary is that you can hear her silence in it and her watchfulness in all that black—Manet black, which stirs the soul to reflection (fig. 13).

Opposite: Fig. 12. Carolus-Duran, *Édouard Manet*, 1876. Oil on canvas, 63.5 × 45.4 cm. RISD Museum of Art, Providence

Overleaf: Fig. 13. Detail of Édouard Manet, *Madame Auguste Manet* (cat. no. 1)

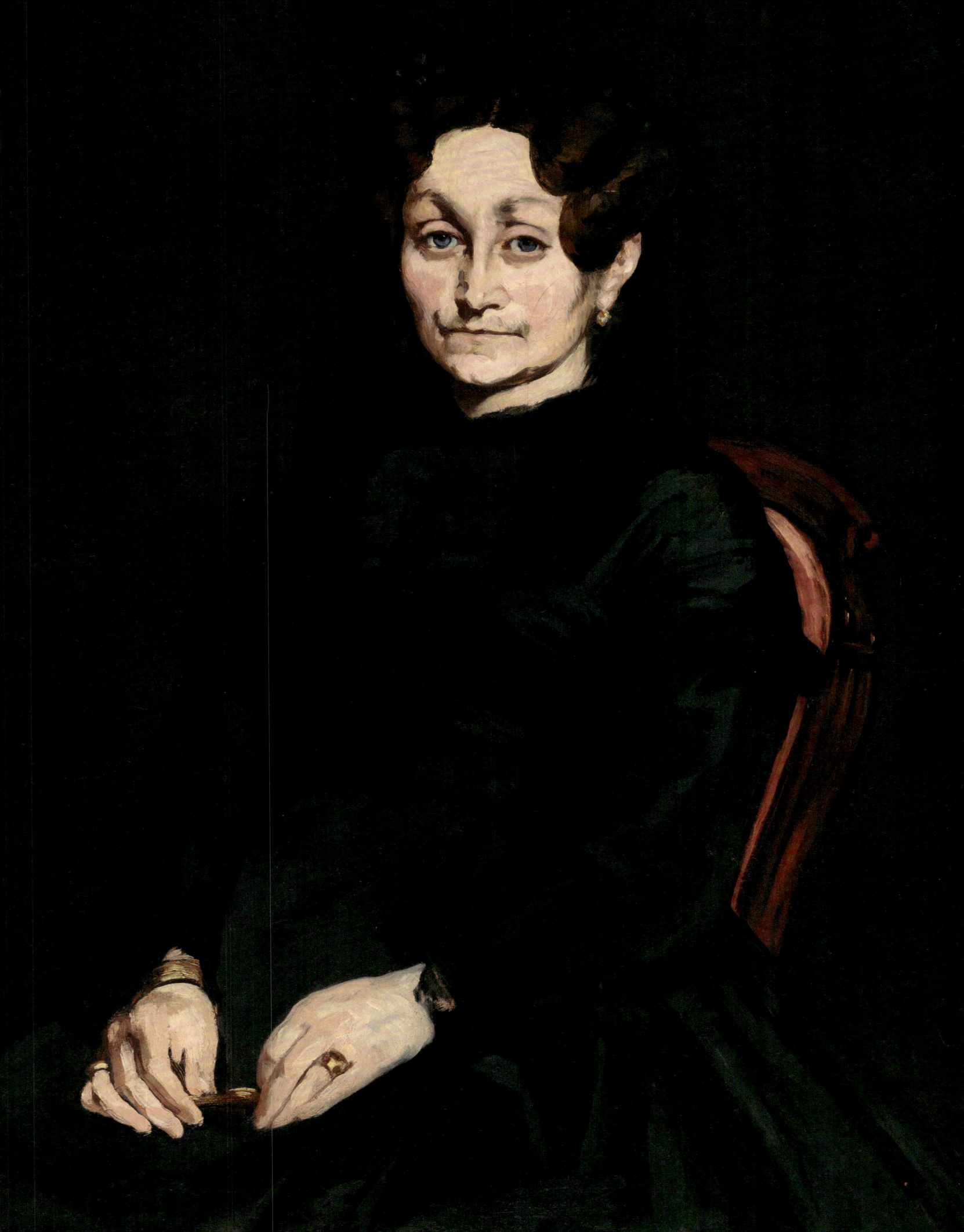

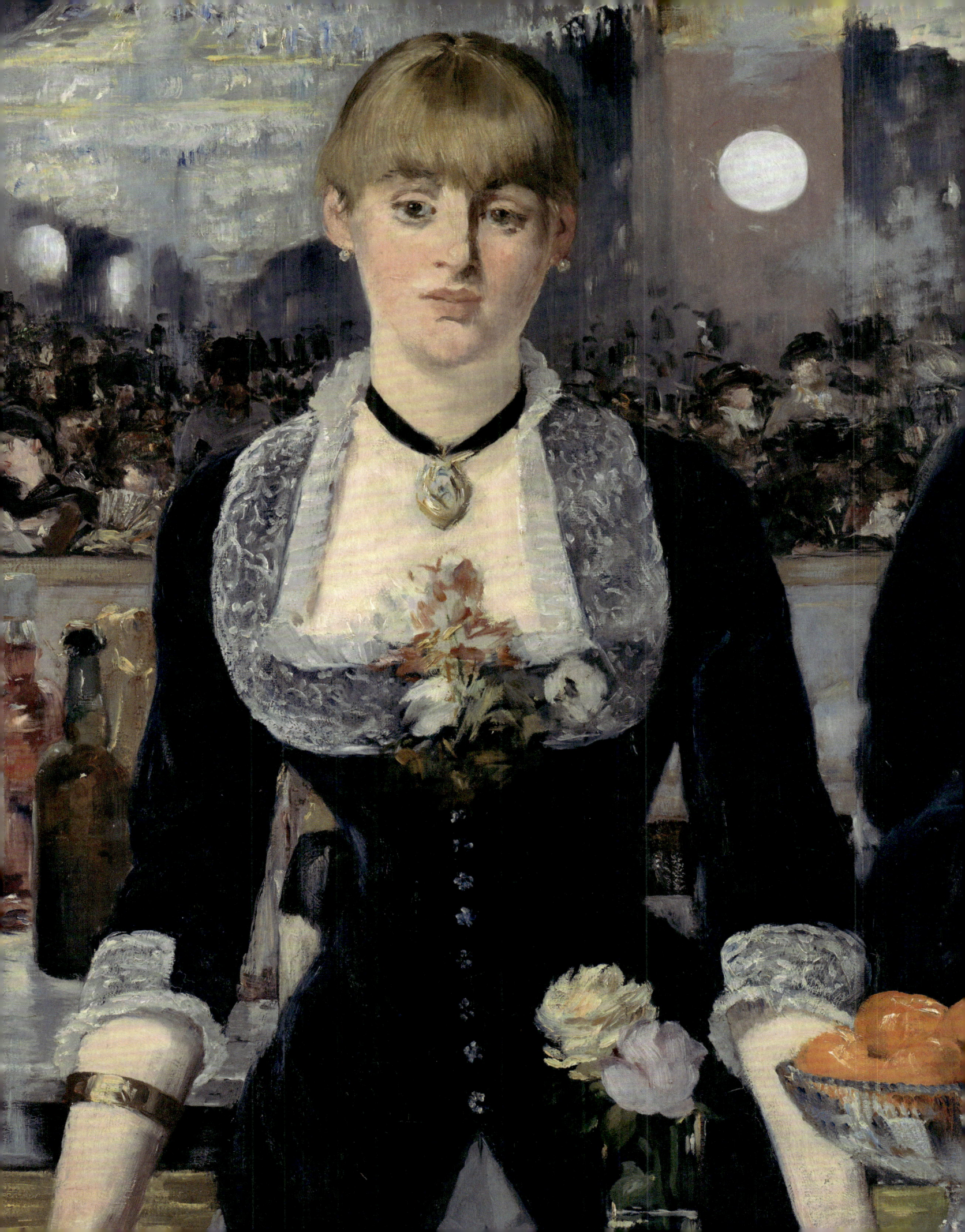

Back then, women were supposed to be a lie, to aspire to a kind of female minstrelsy—"correct" behavior that belied who they were, what they were. Eugénie had the soul of an artist, but how to reconcile that with "position"? Imagine what women had to give up then without even knowing it. No secondary school education until 1850 or so, no French version of Mrs. Pankhurst to argue for their rights, but British feminists felt French women were different anyway, that, culturally speaking, their sisters across the Channel had power behind the throne, and I wonder if that wasn't the case with Auguste and Eugénie; her great vivacity no doubt added some uplift to their fine surroundings, with its pillows and rugs and correctness. (But it seems not to have affected all the Manet sons. One of the younger brothers, Gustave, went into the family business so to speak and also ended up with a career in law.)

Still, there was Eugénie's Édouard, with his love of art, and I think Mme Manet is not inseparable from those glorious showy women who mean so much to us in *Le Déjeuner sur l'herbe* (1863, see fig. 84) not to mention the barmaid who is silent and resolute in *A Bar at the Folies-Bergère* (1882, fig. 14) and *Olympia* (1863, fig. 15). Why count Mme Manet among these women? These show business creatures who no matter what the day seem to live at night, and for pleasure, in paintings that act as a kind of stage for their theatrical and theatricalized personalities? I think it has something to do, for sure, with their belief in their right to life—as much as the artist has to his imagination. Manet got to these women, to his fabled realism about time and place, through a funny sort of apprenticeship. After returning from Brazil to Paris, Auguste suggested that since Édouard loved art so much, he might enroll at the École des Beaux-Arts; it was run by the Académie des Beaux-Arts, itself part of the bureaucratic Institut de France, a government founded and funded grouping of France's many official *academies*. But academic precision was not Manet's thing. When he was eighteen Manet turned down his father's suggestion and does not seem to have even tried to be admitted to the prestigious École. Instead, he apprenticed himself to Thomas Couture, an artist who made big historical paintings such as *The Romans in Their Decadence* (1847), and imagine Manet at eighteen stepping into that scene. Couture had an outsized ego ("I pride myself in the belief that I am the only truly serious artist of our epoch"), but Manet had reality. It's been reported that Couture once admonished a model for not striking a more Roman pose, and Manet reportedly said, "We are in Paris. We intend to stay here." The "here" would become the capital of the nineteenth century. When Manet was a young man, industrialization was just around the corner, and the sky had new vistas to contemplate—new houses, new roads—which meant that life had to shape itself to its changes, to say the least. He had no real role models to follow, so, looking around, he saw that Paris itself contained multitudes and could be one model and its citizens another. He stayed with Couture for six years.

Manet became himself through resistance and by looking at and accepting the world around him—a world that had nothing to do with justice triumphing or the rendering of "correct" forms in a drawing or painting—*as it was*. Manet's genius is built on seeing the world not as French power imagined it—all those pictures of Paris, of Marianne leading the French Republic—but *as it was*. To see *Maman* as she was, to see the barmaid as she was, to see Olympia as she was or might have been, was to use fact for what it could do: provide fodder for the imagination. Édouard's mother was a fact of Paris, a fact of her gender, and the fact of what her son saw in her formal blackness: a woman who, like Manet's other women, gave the ever-yearning artist everything and nothing, just like modern life itself.

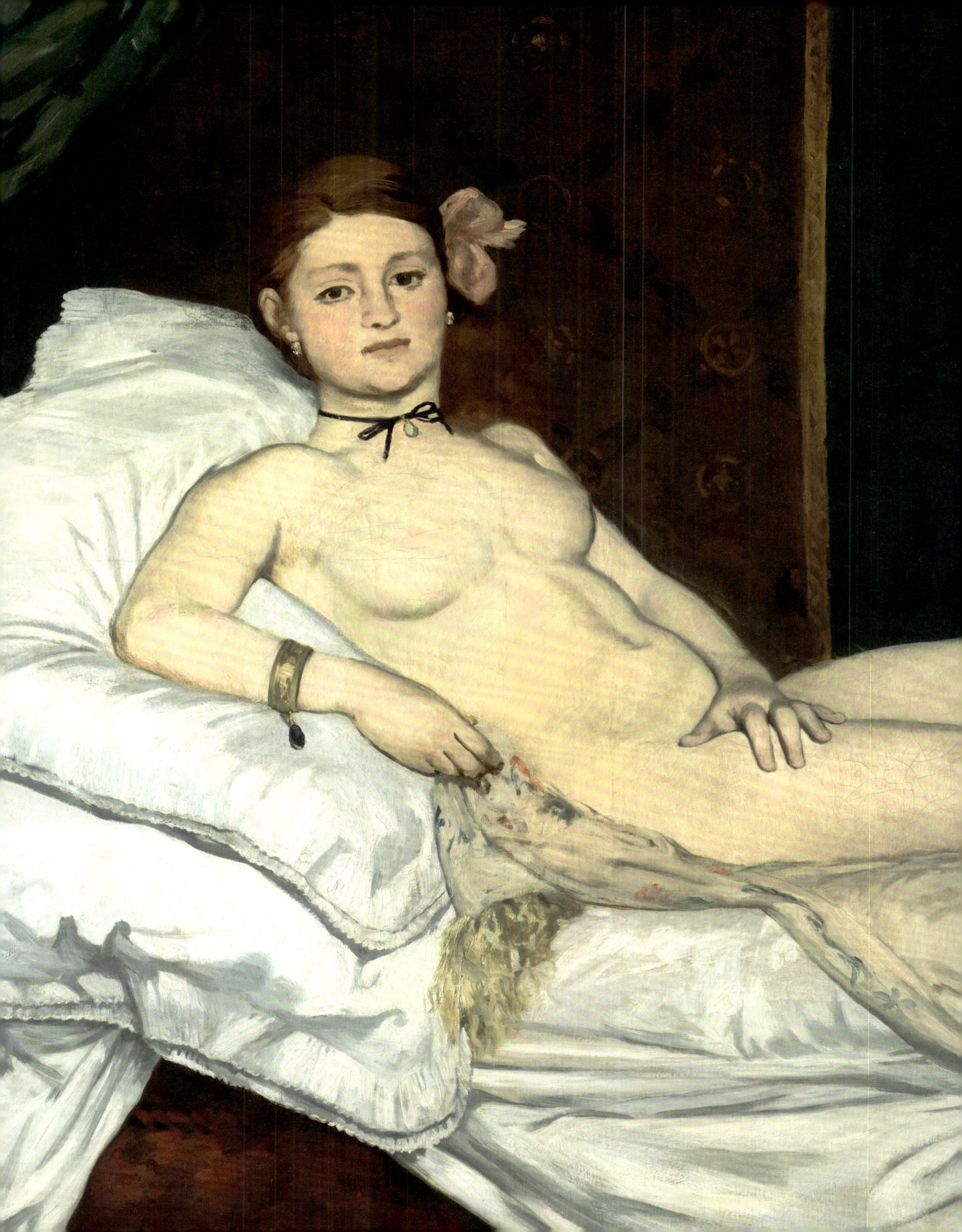

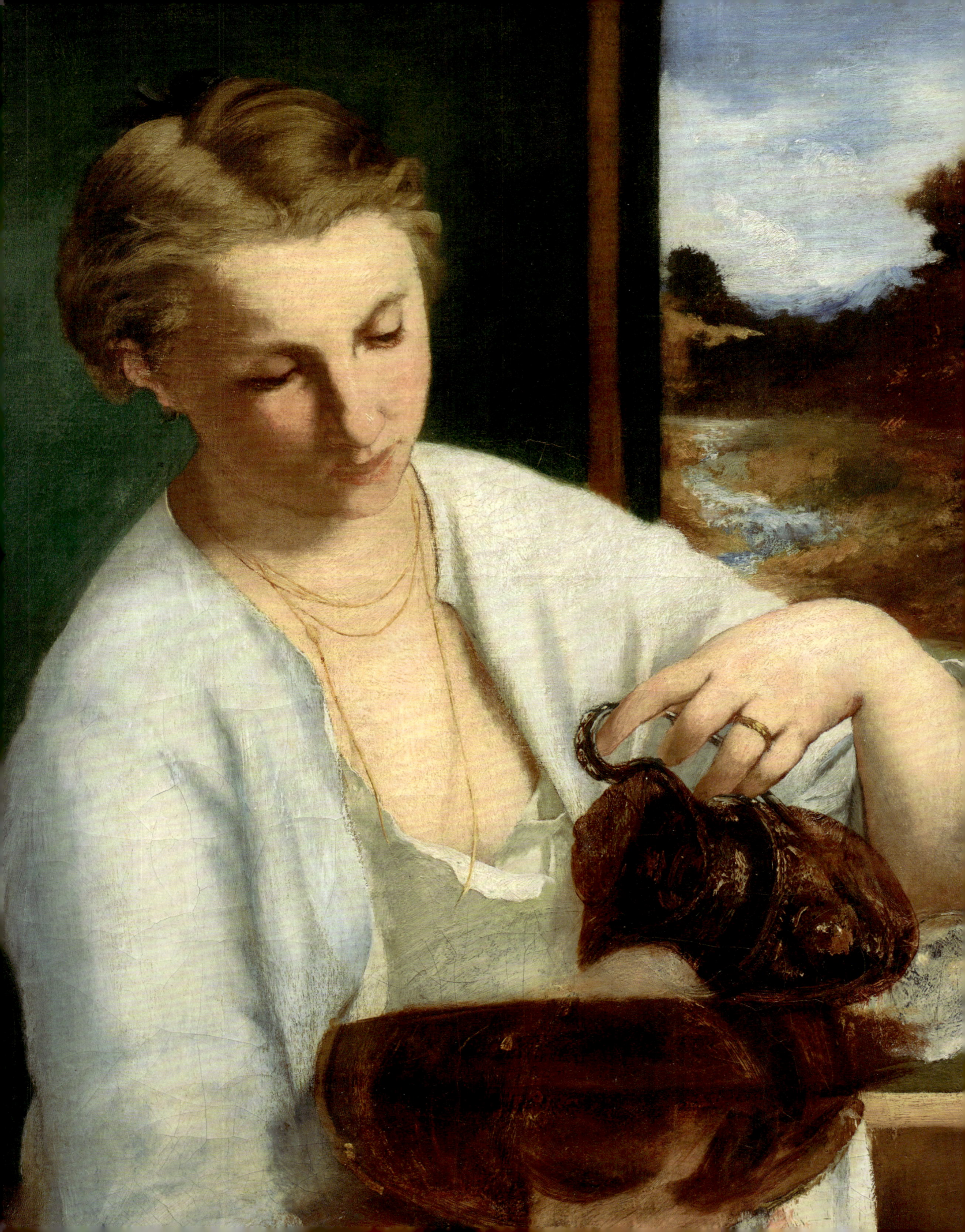

Suzanne Leenhoff: Manet's Early Inspiration

JULIET WILSON-BAREAU

From his earliest years in Thomas Couture's studio, Édouard Manet set himself two goals: to produce art that both engaged with and rivaled the Old Masters and to create major compositions for successful display at the Paris Salon. This essay traces some of his efforts from roughly 1858 to 1862 to simultaneously fulfill both those goals—and the ways in which the family, particularly Suzanne, was part of that effort. In Couture's atelier, the singular focus of all of the students was, of course, to be admitted to the juried exhibition at the center of the nineteenth-century art world—and ideally to be celebrated. Although he bristled against his training with Couture, Manet nonetheless stayed in the studio for six years.[1] His resentment of his teacher was not enough to dampen his ambitions to show at the Salon.

His other training ground was, of course, the incredible collections of art available in Paris. As a registered copyist at the Louvre, he had direct access to works by Titian, Veronese, Rubens, and others. The Old Masters were at this doorstep. In the early 1850s, however, he traveled to the Netherlands and Italy—and possibly elsewhere in Europe—where he could see works beyond the French capital.[2] Finally, starting in 1858, he gained access to the print collection of the Bibliothèque Nationale (then the Bibliothèque Imperiale),[3] where he saw albums of engravings after works in famous public collections around the world and also a range of series of prints made after notable private collections like the "Recueil Crozat" and the famed but dispersed Orléans collection. The Bibliothèque also installed permanent displays of engravings in a newly renovated display area for prints.

Manet made many direct copies on paper and in oil of works by the Old Masters. These include the portrait of Jacopo Tintoretto and his copy of Titian's *Madonna of the Rabbit*. However, to just copy these Old Master works was not enough to fulfill his ambitions. He had to create and innovate by having an artistic conversation with these sources—and to do this he needed a living model. Suzanne Leenhoff was that model right from the start. Suzanne, the former family piano teacher and the artist's future wife, was a critical link between art historical sources and Manet's ambitions to create a major composition for the Salon.[4] His frequent choice of her as a model—and her complicity in the matter—relates not only to their emotional and physical attachment to one another but may also reflect her familiarity with the work of artists' models. An under-analyzed fact about Suzanne is that she came from a family of developing visual artists: her brothers, Ferdinand and Rudolf Leenhoff, and her brother-in-law sculptor Joseph Mezzara, who married Suzanne's sister Mathilde in 1856, among others.[5] In the orbit of Mezzara and his students, which included Ferdinand, she could have had direct experience with being an artist's model prior to posing for Manet. She may not have viewed posing nude as scandalous but rather as just another role necessary to the artistic process.

By focusing on Manet's many Old Master-inspired depictions of Suzanne made between the late 1850s and 1862—across a series of drawings, fragmentary paintings, and finished compositions—one can trace his quest to satisfy the goals of both rivaling the Old Masters and becoming a triumph at the Salon. He seems to have created and planned

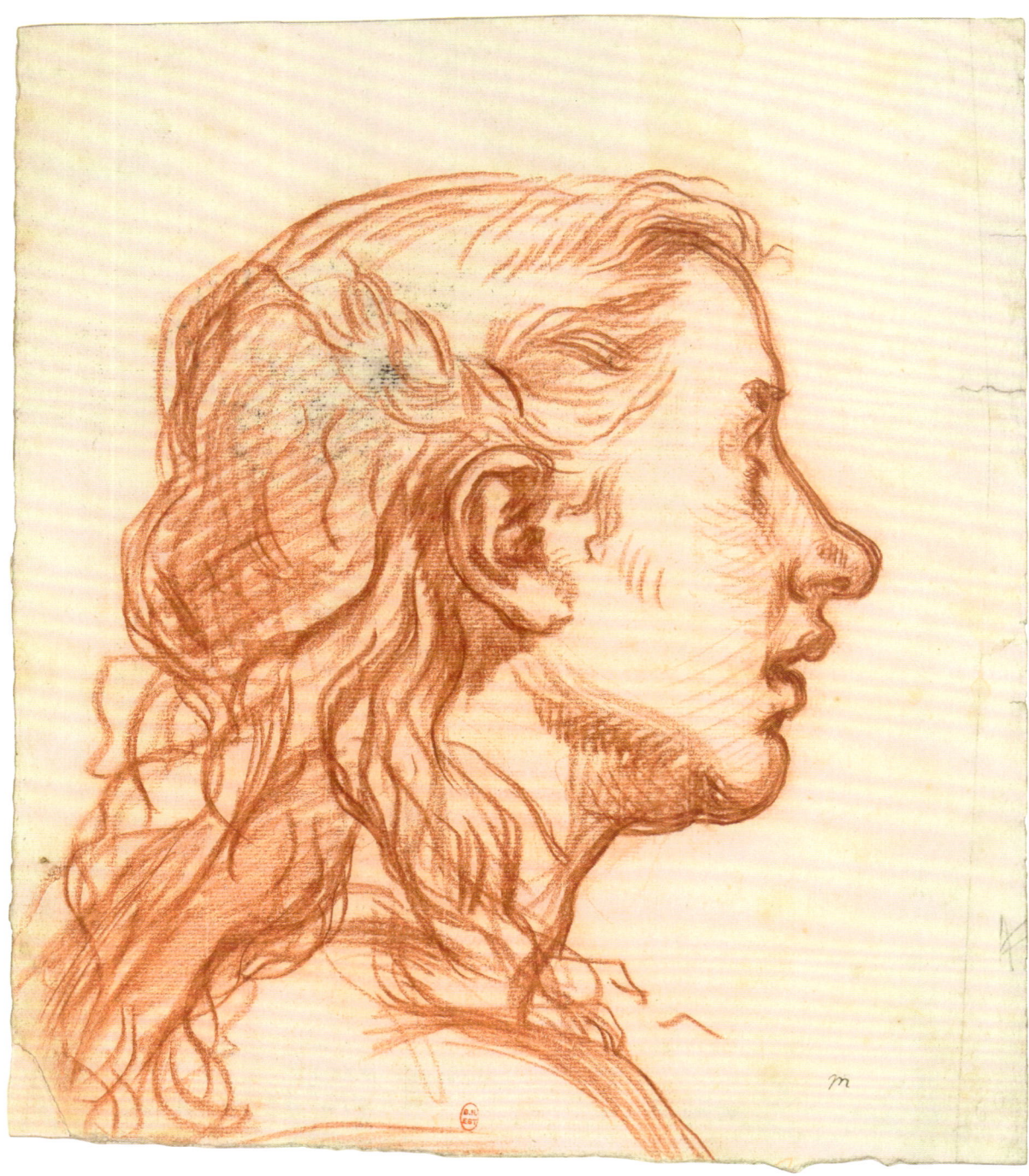

Fig. 16. Édouard Manet, *Head of a Young Woman in Profile,* 1859–61. Red chalk with traces of charcoal, 30 × 25.5 cm. Bibliothèque Nationale de France, Paris

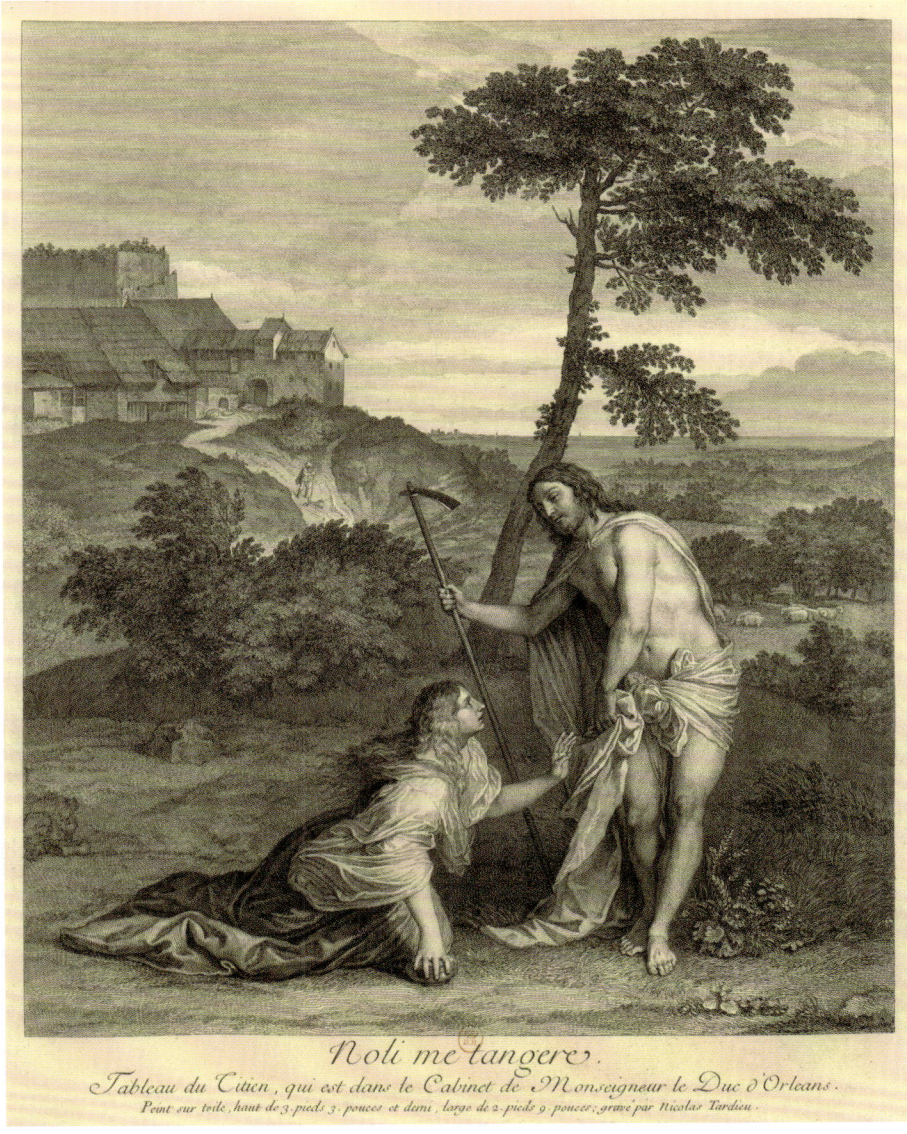

Fig. 17. Nicolas Henri Tardieu after Titian, *Noli Me Tangere*, 1729. Engraving, 43.6 × 34 cm. Bibliothèque Nationale de France, Paris

for many large compositions to fulfill these ambitions, but most of them were never finished. Instead, he cut out fragments from them, sometimes specifically creating discrete titled paintings. In other cases, the fragments were posthumously marketed and sold as distinct works. All along the journey, Suzanne was by his side as model, muse, and ultimately wife then widow.

The first steps in Manet's practice involved the creation of sketches and preparatory drawings on paper. Suzanne appears across a range of drawings related to the Old Masters, some of which can be tied to specific sources and others for which the inspiration is obscure. For example, consider the image of her in profile in *Head of a Young Woman in Profile* (fig. 16), which seems to be based on the engraving from the "Recueil Crozat" (fig. 17) after Titian's magnificent *Noli Me Tangere* (about 1514; National Gallery, London). The Titian shows Mary Magdalene in the garden at Christ's feet, and Manet has seized on the Magdalene's profile, which is facing in the same direction as the engraving.[6] Suzanne also appears in a series of drawings where she is cast in the role of a bather (figs. 18, 19).[7]

From these diverse drawings, Manet started to build composite compositions—first planning them on paper and then in oil. A composite drawing in the Museum Boijmans Van Beuningen in Rotterdam known as *The Finding of Moses* (fig. 20) consists of several joined sheets of paper and is

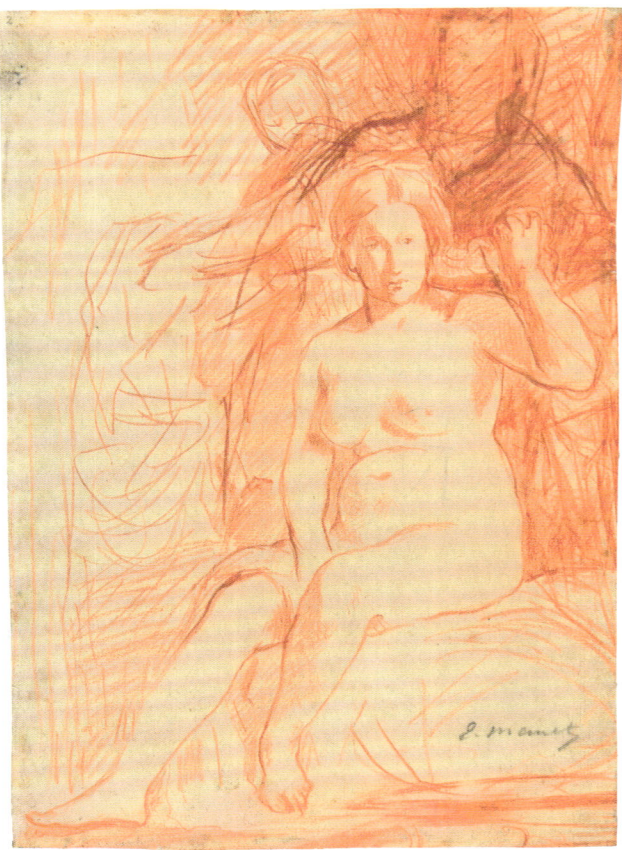

Fig. 18. Édouard Manet, *Seated Nude*, 1858–60. Red chalk on buff paper, 28 × 20 cm. The Art Institute of Chicago

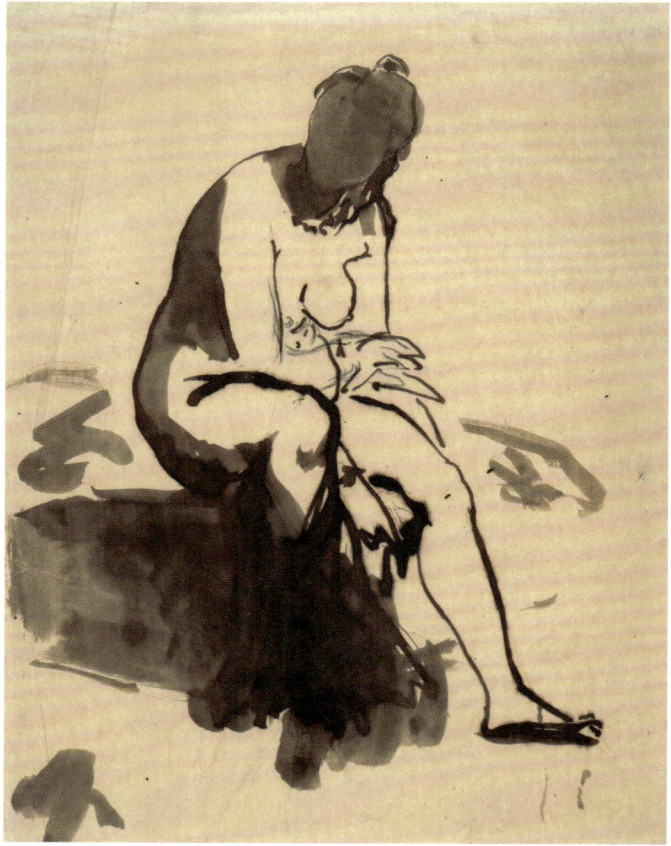

Fig. 19. Édouard Manet, *After the Bath*, 1860. Wash drawing, 26.7 × 20.3 cm. Private collection

squared for transfer. Peter Meller—who wrote the most authoritative work on Manet's Italian sources—links this figure (clearly posed by Suzanne) to a preparatory drawing for Raphael's *Fire in the Borgo* fresco in the Vatican, which is in the Albertina in Vienna.[8] The Rotterdam drawing is clearly a *modello* for a larger canvas that Manet was developing. Antonin Proust, Manet's close friend and one of the first to publish recollections about the artist, recalled, "In the rue Lavoisier [the artist's studio from late 1856 until 1859], Manet had begun a large painting, *The Finding of Moses*, which he never finished."[9]

Perhaps the clearest guide available to understanding Manet's earliest ambitions to create large canvases based on the Old Masters—and specifically the Moses scene remembered by Proust—is the oil study in Oslo for *Surprised Nymph/Moses Saved from the Waters* (cat. no. 5). With a range of figures set in a landscape, the oil sketch demonstrates a "mix-and-match" approach that Manet brought to his Old Master sources. Many of the figures can be linked to specific pieces. For example, the twisting figure at left recalls an image identified by Meller as a copy after an engraving of

a lost Giulio Romano painting and also recalls a figure in Titian's *Concert champêtre* (see fig. 85).[10]

Further evidence of Manet's sources comes from two fragments left behind after the artist was unable to complete the complex composition as one comprehensive whole. These two additional canvases—one a fragmentary sketch and one a finished painting sent for exhibition—isolate subjects that Manet started to address both in the Rotterdam drawing and in the Oslo study and *Surprised Nymph* (see fig. 1), which Proust recalled he cut from the canvas. In both works, Suzanne poses in the role of a biblical heroine.

Of all the paintings of Suzanne, *Surprised Nymph* is the most studied. It has been linked to works showing the heroines Susanna and Bathsheba and may resemble the antique sculptures of bathers that Manet passed every time he visited the Louvre.[11] Its x-radiograph also reveals a complex series of underpaintings that corroborate Proust's recollections and verify it was once part of a larger, more complex canvas that resembles the Oslo oil sketch.[12] Although *Surprised Nymph* did not represent the ultimate large-scale Salon painting that Manet perhaps hoped it

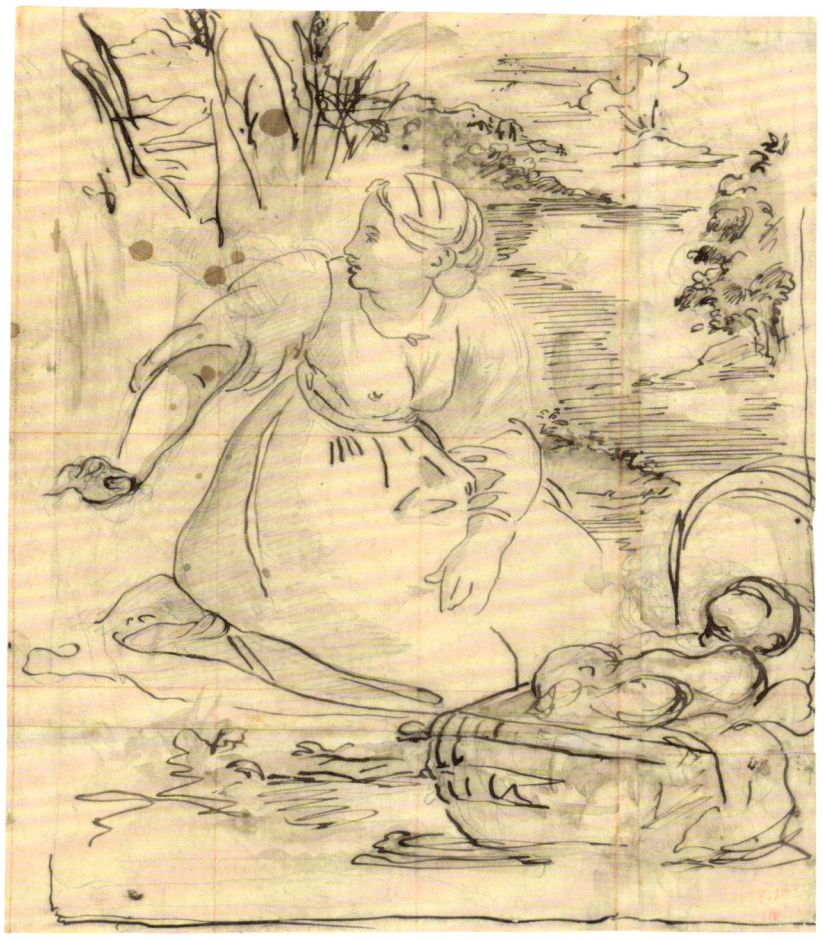

Fig. 20. Édouard Manet, *The Finding of Moses*, about 1858–60. Pen and sepia ink with wash over graphite, squared with red chalk, on joined sheets of laid paper, 33.3 × 28 cm. Museum Boijmans Van Beuningen, Rotterdam

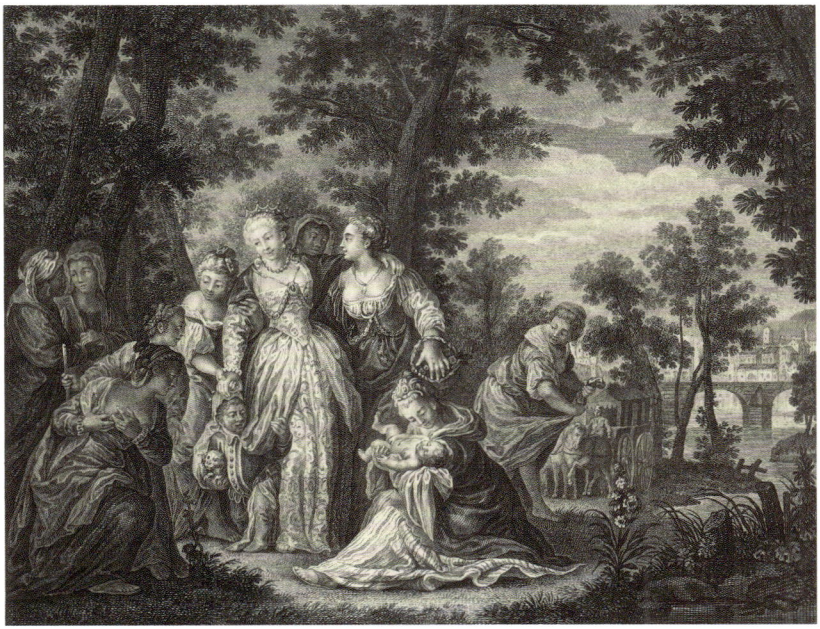

Fig. 21. Jean Louis Delignon after Paolo Veronese, *Moses Saved*, about 1786–1808. Etching and engraving, 41.7 × 28.7 cm. British Museum, London

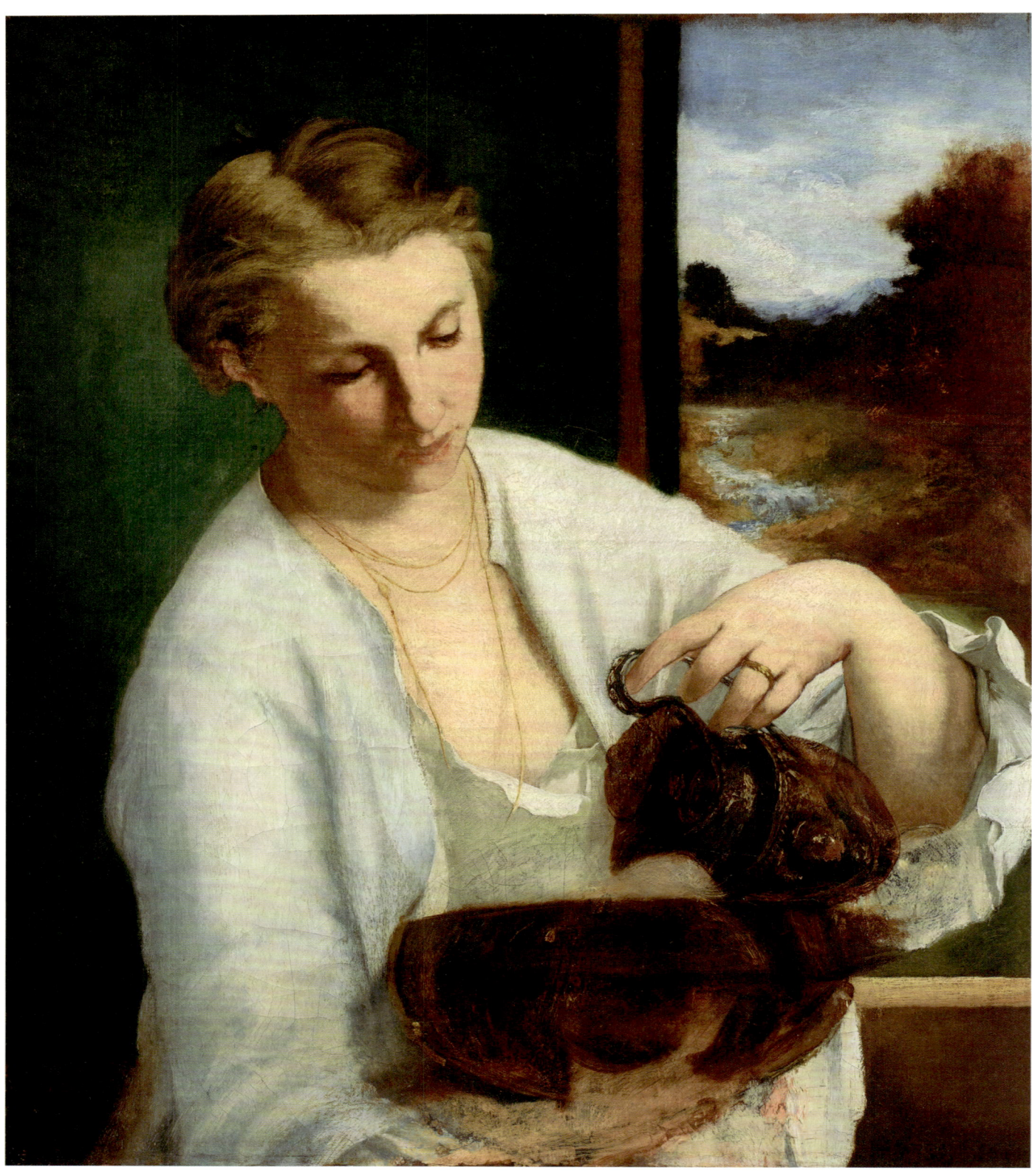

Fig. 22. Édouard Manet, *Woman with a Jug (Suzanne Leenhoff, later Manet)*, 1858–60. Oil on canvas, 61 × 54.5 cm. Ordrupgaard, Copenhagen

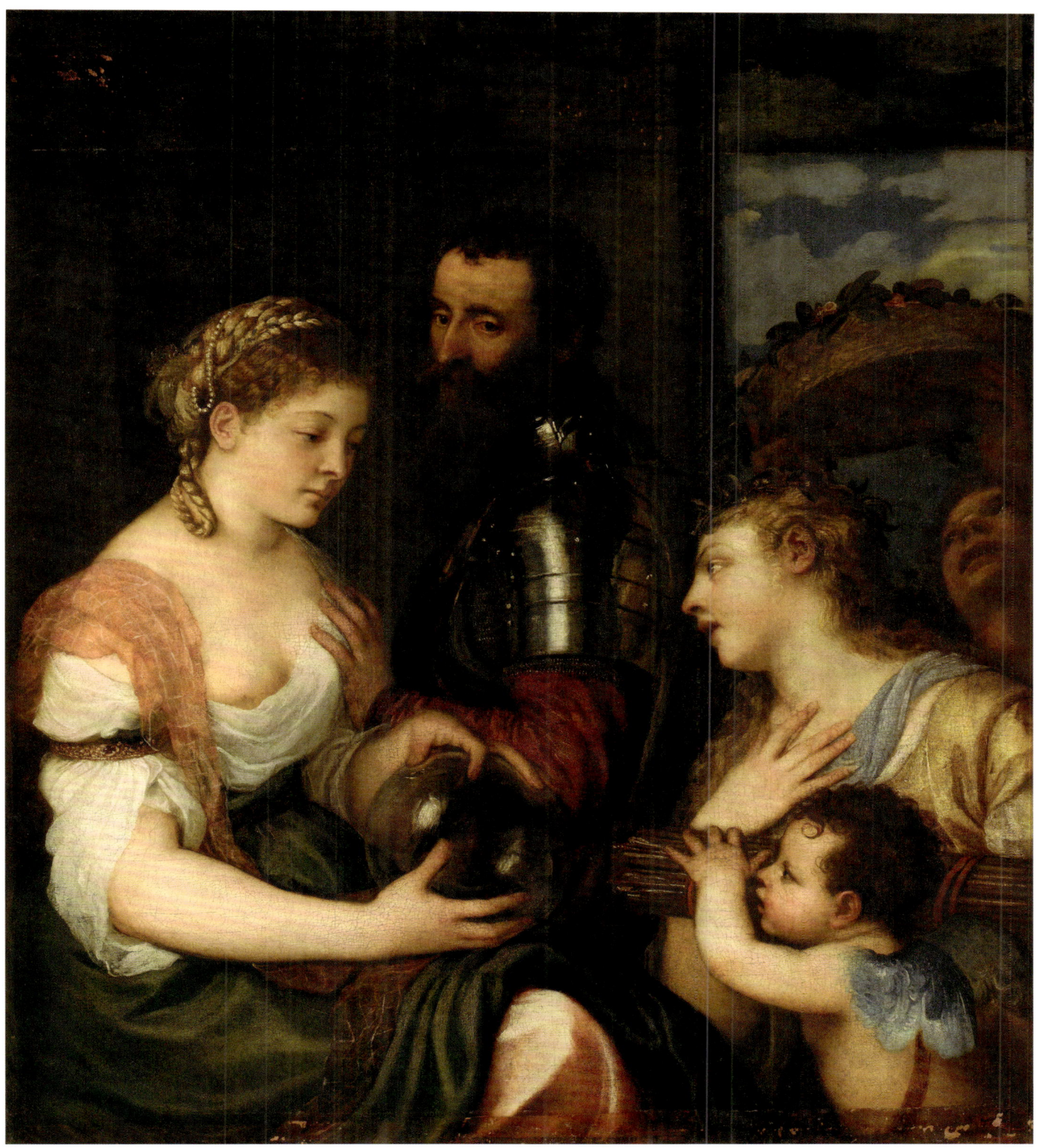

Fig. 23. Titian, *Allegory of Marriage*, about 1530–35. Oil on canvas, 123 × 107 cm. Musée du Louvre, Paris

would become, he did send the painting to be exhibited in St. Petersburg, Russia (although with a now-missing addition of a satyr figure in the corner and under the title *Nymph and Satyr*). The artist valued it highly. In 1871–72 in his own studio, he set its price equivalent to that of the monumental *Old Musicians* (1862; National Gallery of Art, Washington).[13]

Moses Saved (cat. no. 4), which came to light only relatively recently, is little studied. This image of Suzanne does not seem to be primarily based on the Veronese painting of this subject that was in the Louvre (and is now on deposit at the Musée des Beaux-Arts de Lyon) but rather on a print after another version of the work that had been part of the dispersed Orléans collection, which had been long exhibited in the Palais Royal (fig. 21). Suzanne's pose and the pose of the faceless child clearly mirror the central figure in the print. However, Manet never developed this depiction into a finished composition that survives—although a vignette in the print *Les Gitanos* (1862) bears some resemblance.

In this way, *Moses Saved* recalls a better-known fragmentary canvas for something that was probably part of another ambitious but unfinished work intended for the Salon: *Woman with a Jug (Suzanne Leenhoff, later Manet)* (fig. 22). What one cannot see in reproduction is the completely ragged edges of *Woman with a Jug* clear physical evidence that it is a fragment that was likely cut out of some huge Salon composition. Suzanne is posing in a way and in a setting that seems to reference Titian's *Allegory of Marriage* (fig. 23). She also wears, quite prominently, what appears to be a wedding band on her finger—although this was certainly painted years before her marriage to the artist. She is more modestly dressed than Titian's woman, and Manet has edited out the armored figure. Instead, the Titianesque Suzanne appears directly in front of an open window. Her dress—and the fact that she is pouring liquid out of a jug rather than holding a symbolic glass orb—recalls some of the Dutch art available for study in the Louvre, perhaps something similar to Gerrit Dou's *The Dutch Cook* (fig. 24). The Dutch source may have been a *clin d'oeil* at his model's nationality. The surface of *Woman with a Jug* obscures an even more complex engagement with the Old Masters. Technical analysis reveals that there is significant underdrawing related to another major work that Manet could encounter at the Louvre: Veronese's *Wedding Feast at Cana* (1563). There are many architectural elements that seem to be transcribed from the *Feast at Cana,* suggesting that this fragment of a larger composition obscures yet another early attempt at a monumental Old Master–inspired canvas.[14]

Perhaps Manet's expression of his appreciation for his model—and later his wife—is clearest when considering two canvases, one little known and one well known, alongside each other. *The Salamanca Students* (fig. 25) was the first work Manet exhibited publicly. It was shown at the Société des Amis des Arts in Boulogne in 1860. The story comes from *L'histoire de Gil Blas de Santillane*, a French picaresque novel by Alain-René Lesage. The episode depicted is from the very beginning of the novel where the protagonist addresses the reader. He tells the story of two students traveling to Salamanca who happen upon a stone marked with an epitaph stating that the interred soul—rather than the interred body—of a man is below. One student dismisses the epitaph, while the other thinks it is worth exploring and possibly trying to free the interred soul. The curious student starts digging and lifts the stone. His efforts are rewarded when he finds a leather purse full of money and a note stating that whoever had enough wit to understand the inscription deserves to be the heir to this fortune.[15] In essence,

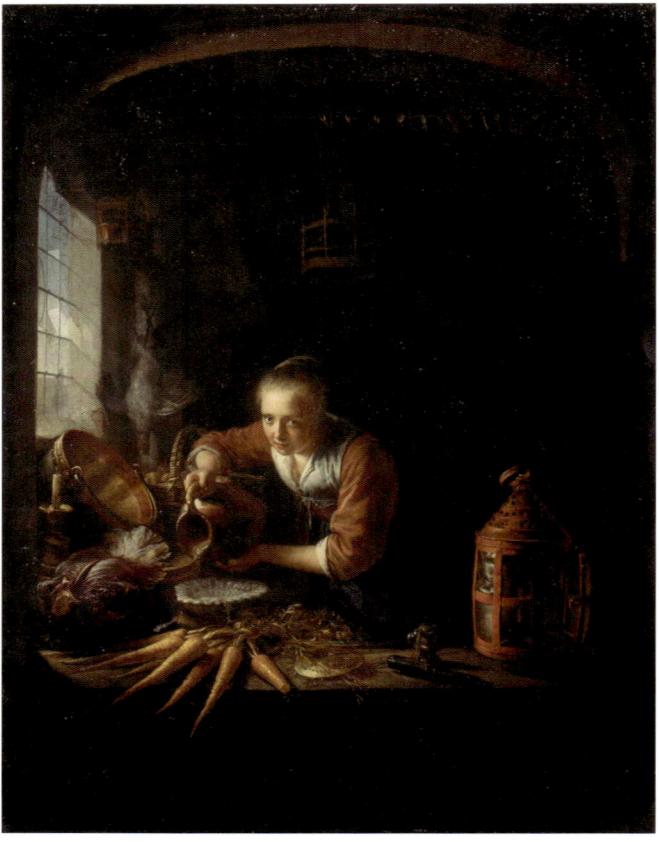

Fig. 24. Gerrit Dou, *The Dutch Cook*, 1647. Oil on panel, 36 × 27.3 cm. Musée du Louvre, Paris

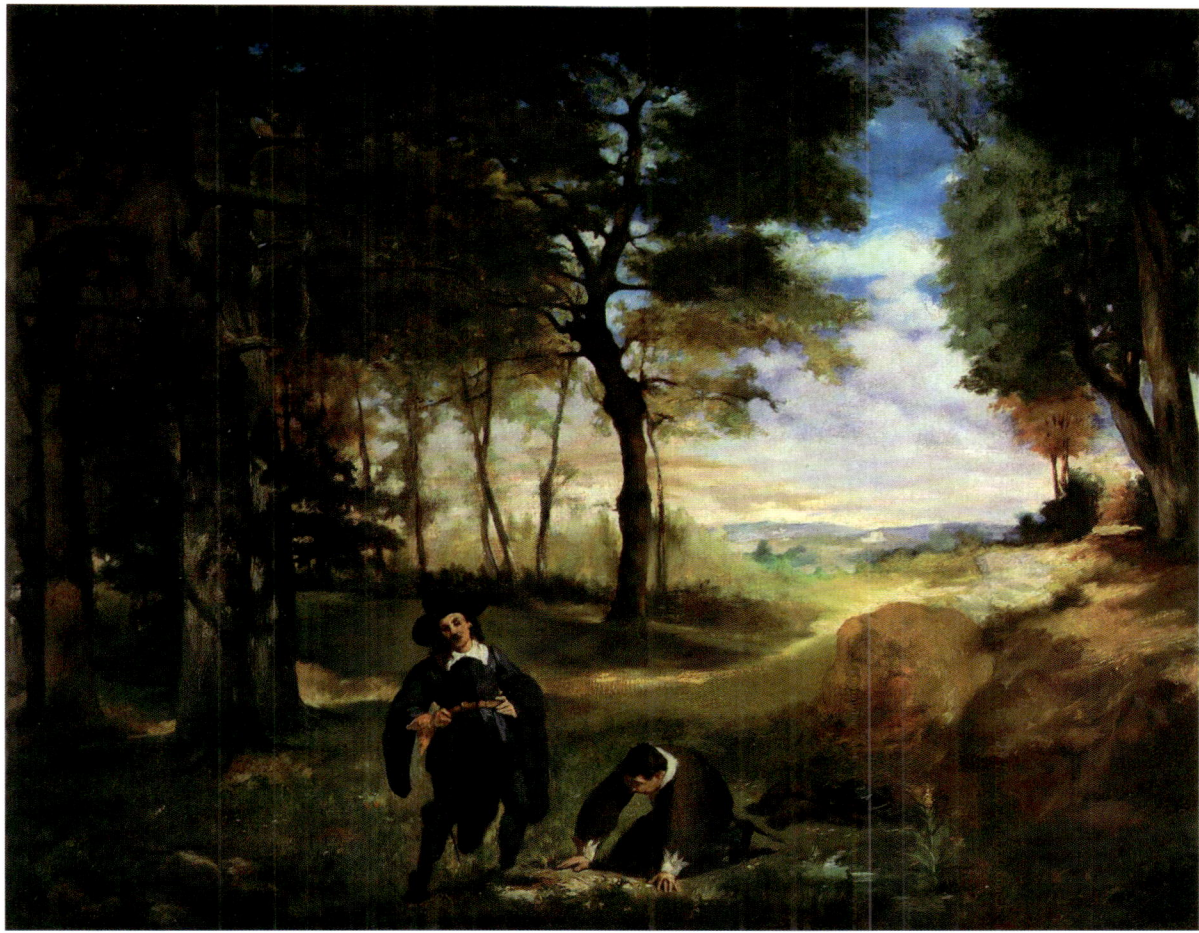

Fig. 25. Édouard Manet, *The Salamanca Students*, 1860. Oil on canvas, 72.7 × 92.6 cm. Pola Museum of Art, Hakone

the student was rewarded with treasure for his intelligence, curiosity, and hard work. The landscape in which the students appear is reminiscent of the Old Masters, but also resembles the landscape near Gennevilliers, the ancestral lands of the Manet family.[16]

The landscape that Manet creates for *The Salamanca Students* is very similar to the one whose original title was *Paysage*, i.e., *Landscape–Saint-Ouen*—now known as *Fishing (La Pêche)*, a title that was invented by Duret for his 1902 catalogue of Manet's work (cat. no. 6). For Manet, the two landscapes were full of personal significance, as allegories of himself and his aspirations. In *The Salamanca Students*, exhibited in 1860 in Boulogne, the young student is rewarded for his persistent and thoughtful curiosity, while in the possibly slightly later view of the *Landscape–Saint-Ouen*, Manet himself appears as an equal and modern rival to Rubens, accompanied by his muse, model and (future) wife, in the costumes and a setting that integrate engravings after

Rubens and his second wife on their estate with a view of Gennevilliers from the Isle of Saint-Ouen on the Seine, the place-name used by Suzanne for the work that originally hung in Eugène Manet's apartment, but was exchanged with him and later sold by her as *Saint-Ouen*. Suzanne, who began her enduring relationship with the artist above all as his model, became his wife and his life-long and cherished companion whose own independence, sense of humor, and devotion to music chimed with all that Manet held dear.

Note from the author: This essay is the result of a spinal injury (in July 2023) that marked the end of my direct participation in the project to explore Manet's family relationships and his art. Diana Greenwald kindly put together a text based on my initial presentation and our informal conversations at an inspiring roundtable in Boston and then later, in London, after I had returned home. While very grateful for Diana's help, I deeply regret that I have been unable to do more than continue to offer advice and share ideas with my colleagues as new contexts appeared and continue to appear even as this catalogue goes to press.

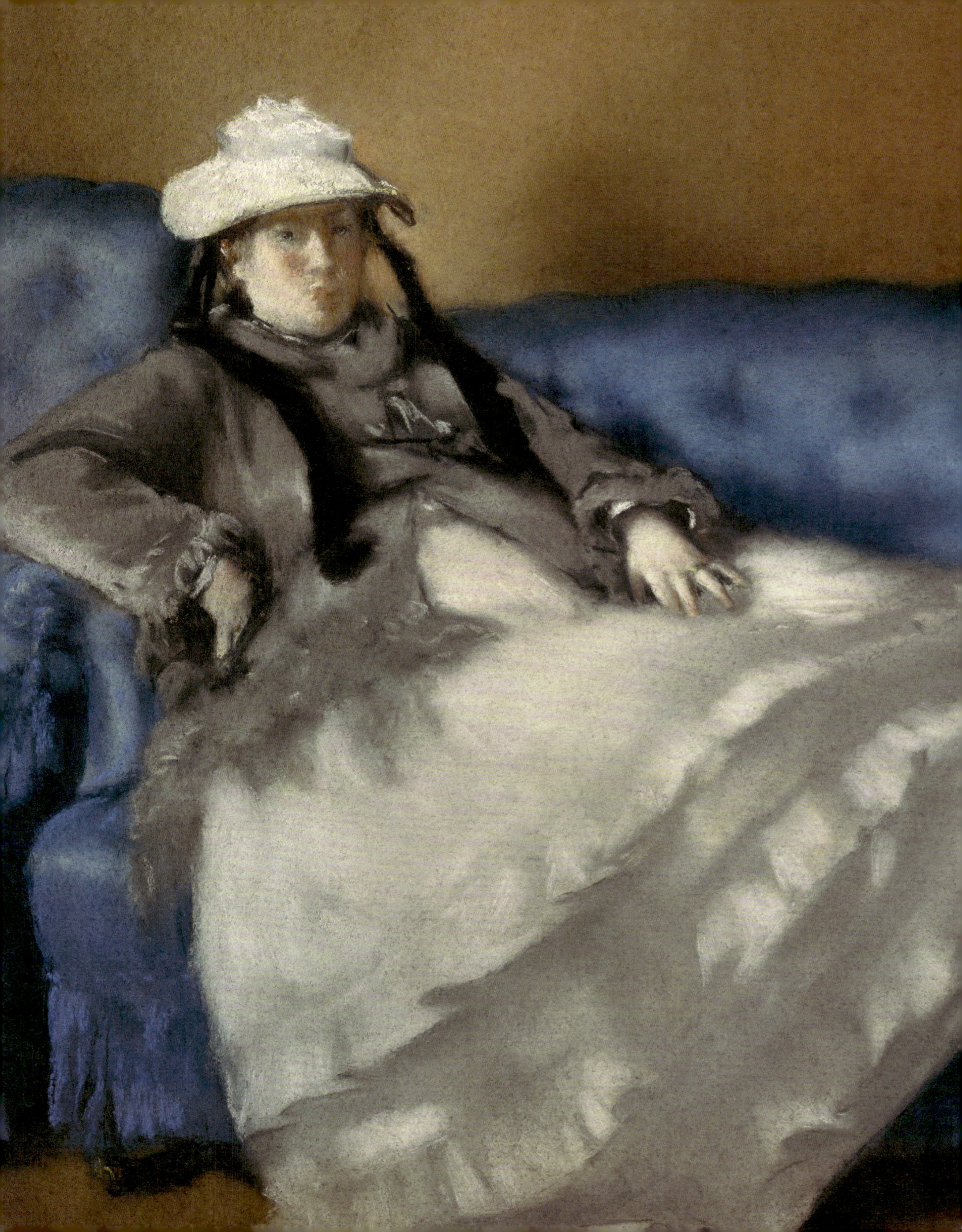

Suzanne: The Private Portraits

EMILY A. BEENY

A photograph, a book

The photograph, punched through with pins, is creased, scuffed, faded (fig. 26). Its subject, in profile, offers the camera a slight self-conscious smile. Her features are soft. Her toilette is simple: hair combed back from her temples, braided and pinned; a dark dress with a square neckline. She wears no jewelry. Here is Suzanne Leenhoff Manet (1829–1906), aged about thirty-eight, immediately recognizable from her husband's portraits. For it is through the lens of these pictures that we see her, and because of them that we remember her. Over the thirty-four years of their relationship, Manet painted his wife more frequently than any other woman. She was a patient unpaid model, inspiring more than a dozen paintings and many more works on paper. Born into an artistic family in Zaltbommel and trained as a pianist, Suzanne arrived in Paris in 1847, joining the Manet household as a piano teacher two years later.[1] She was pushing twenty; Édouard was seventeen. Unmarried, she bore a son, Léon, in January 1852.[2] Although his paternity remains uncertain, this boy's godfather was the young painter, who married Suzanne on October 28, 1863.[3] Their union produced no children—there is, indeed, some reason to believe it was chaste—but was evidently marked by a deep mutual affection.

In a letter dated October 6, 1863, the poet Charles Baudelaire shared Manet's "most unexpected news" with the journalist Étienne Carjat: "He is leaving tonight for Holland and will bring back *his wife*. He nevertheless made certain excuses. It would appear that this wife is beautiful, very kind, and a great artist. So many treasures in a single female—isn't it monstrous?"[4] Others did not see Suzanne in quite the same light. After meeting her for the first time, the artist's cousin Ambroise Adam sneered, "I saw the young bride, who is 27 years old but looks 30 and is quite 'solid'—even at the piano. She has talent as a musician, but as a Dutch woman, she is the shape and size characteristic of her country."[5] Similar swipes at Suzanne's foreignness and figure pepper the correspondence between Marie-Joséphine Cornélie Morisot and her daughter Berthe, while the attitude of Manet's own mother toward Suzanne, with whom Eugénie lived for almost two decades, today appears tinged with classist suspicion—and, perhaps, resentment of a darker and more private kind.[6]

The profile photograph, though, presents a woman of placid temperament and modest habits, the same woman we meet in Manet's portraits. Housed at the Morgan Library, this object belongs to an archive amassed by Manet's biographer Adolphe Tabarant. Tracing key events in the painter's career and critical fortunes, the archive offers incidental testimony to Suzanne's life. The art she made, as a performer in an age before recorded music, has vanished, but here are tokens of friendship and admiration, letters and visiting cards, books dedicated to her by their authors, funeral announcements and registers, a small, informal account book, bound in dark blue leather and filled, in her impatient hand, with a jumble of French and Dutch. Covering a period from 1892 to 1900, the book is loosely organized, with lists of artworks consigned or sold alongside lists of household expenses, from rent and groceries to train tickets. Upon his death in 1883,

Manet left his wife mostly debts; his paintings were her great inheritance, and the sale of his studio contents was meant to make her fortune.[7] But the 1884 auction, mounted—against the advice of Suzanne's mother- and sister-in-law—at the Galerie Georges Petit was a spectacular commercial failure, leaving the widow in straitened circumstances, scraping by on the sale of individual works for the rest of her life.[8]

A visitor to Suzanne's home in the late 1880s offered a vivid account of the situation:

> "[. . . The] walls were covered with pictures. Above the piano, we saw the Olympia. . . . Other pictures and pastels made up an admirable ensemble. Sad amid these memories, Mme Manet went from one to the next talking to us of the dearly departed. . . . When we asked . . . if she ever thought of letting a few pictures go, she replied, her eyes full of tears, 'It's as if I had to sell my children!'"[9]

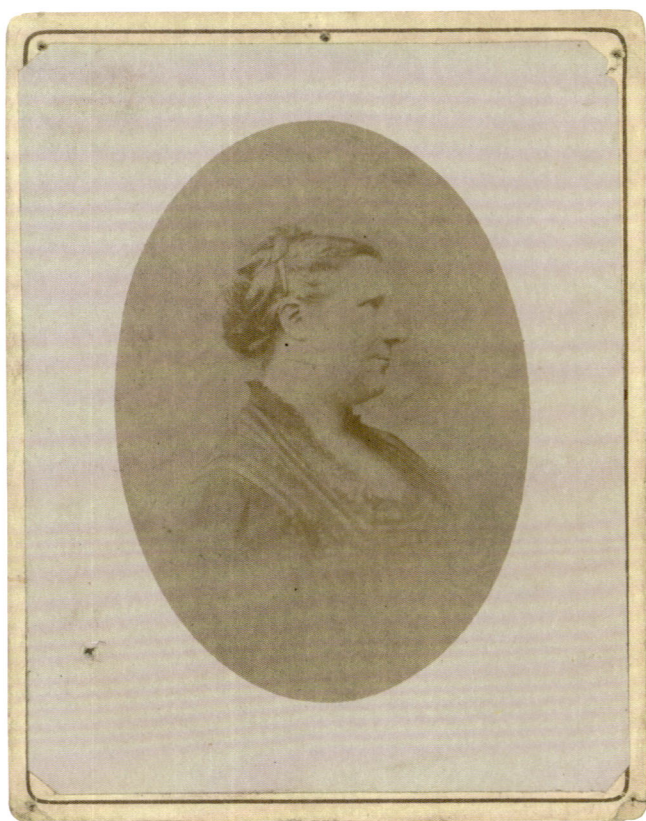

Fig. 26. Unidentified photographer, *Suzanne Manet*, about 1865–68. Photograph mounted on cardboard, 7 × 10 cm. The Morgan Library & Museum, New York (MA 3950). Purchased as the gift of Mrs. Charles Engelhard and children in memory of Mr. Charles Engelhard, 1974

But sell them she would. A decade after the studio sale, Suzanne faced the specter of eviction from her home in Gennevilliers. One by one, paintings from a group she had surely never meant to part with—portraits of herself by her husband—began to appear in the little account book: "ik met de kat," "pastel," and "moi chapeau noir manteau gris" in the spring of 1894; "portrait au piano" that fall; "le portrait au banc vert" the following summer; and, finally, "Saint Ouen" in the winter of 1897.[10] These private paintings tell two stories: one of the life Suzanne had shared with their author, and the other of her lonely survival.

The first to go

These were not the first "Suzanne pictures" to sell: in the 1870s Manet himself had sold a pair of important plein-air scenes for which she had posed,[11] and the early *Surprised Nymph* (fig. 1), modeled by a blushing nude Suzanne, went with his studio contents in 1884.[12] The only proper portrait sold to date, however, seems to have been *Reading* (cat. no. 11) a serene likeness of Suzanne in white,[13] her wedding band prominently displayed, which Manet likely painted around 1865, reworking the composition and adding the figure of Léon reading at right a decade or so later.[14] The artists John Singer Sargent and Ernest Duez "discovered" this work on an 1885 visit to Suzanne and helped broker its sale to the American heiress Winaretta Singer. As Duez reported to this collector, "We've found a portrait of [Madame Manet] dressed all in white in a white room. It's enchanting. . . . She reluctantly agrees to let it go. But then she is obliged to, since her situation is not bright."[15]

Suzanne had just been disinherited. Upon her death in January 1885, the painter's mother, Eugénie, left everything—including an annuity that would originally have gone to Édouard—to her granddaughter, Julie Manet.[16] Since her husband's death, Suzanne had been living with her mother-in-law in a flat at the home of Julie's parents, Berthe and Eugène Manet, in the rue de Villejust. Now she decamped for Gennevilliers, where the family's cousin and attorney Jules Dejouy provided her with a little house, free of rent, in the rue de la Croix-des-Vignes. It was there that she sold *Reading*—for 3,500 francs, according to Duez—and there she would remain until the death of her benefactor in early 1894. Dejouy left half his property to his goddaughter, Julie Manet, stipulating that Suzanne should have use of the house for five years. When the land at Gennevilliers was apportioned to the various heirs, however, the plot on which Suzanne's home stood did not fall to Julie, throwing her aunt's occupancy into question. Suzanne wrote to Berthe in March of that year, voicing

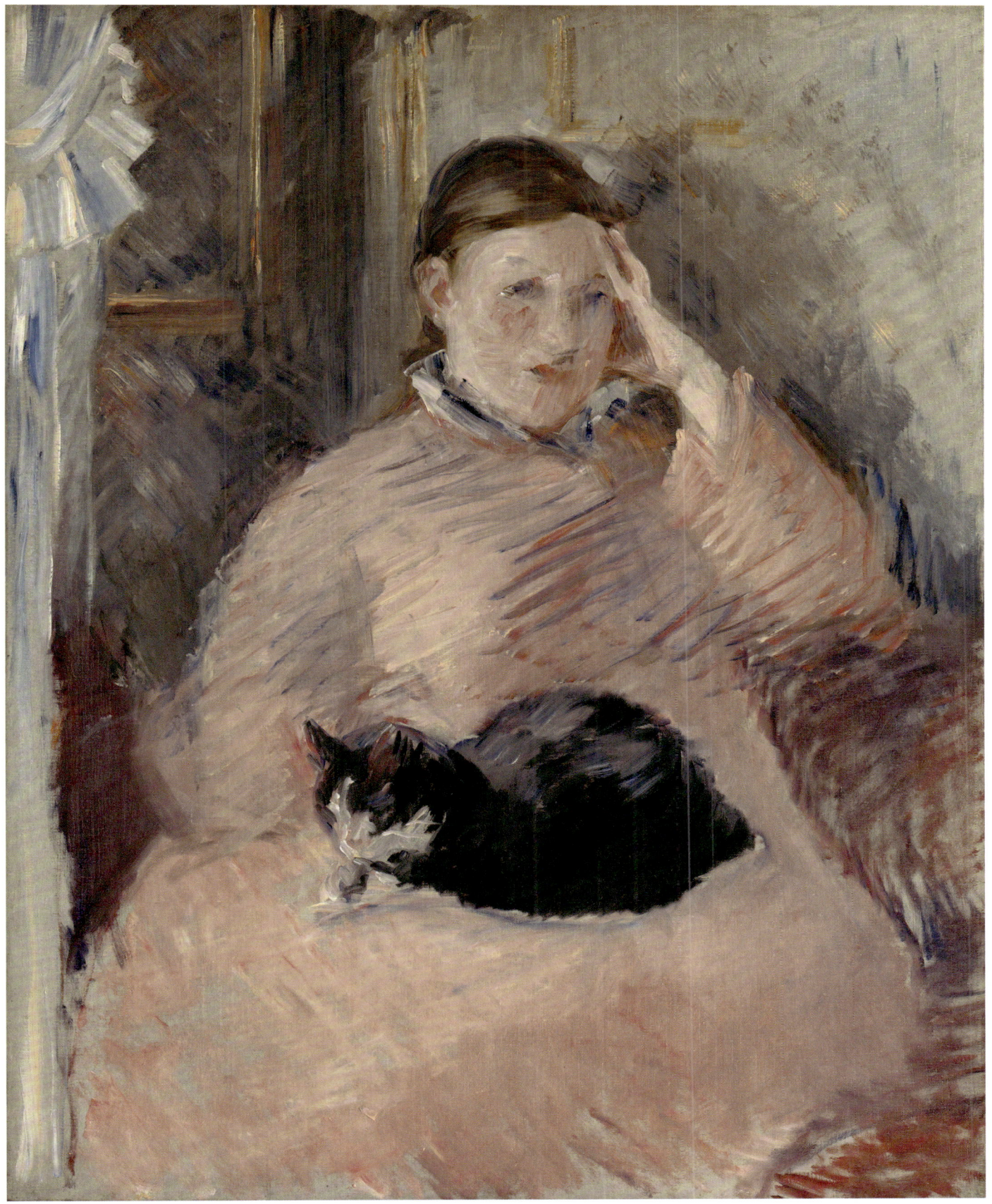

Fig. 27. Édouard Manet, *Woman with a Cat*, about 1880–82. Oil on canvas, 92.1 × 73 cm. Tate Gallery, London

distress at the prospect of moving again, and Berthe offered to pay the new owner rent, allowing her sister-in-law to remain.[17] In the end, though, Suzanne would pack her belongings again, moving first to an apartment in the Boulevard Voltaire at Asnières and finally to another, in the rue Saint-Dominique back in Paris.[18] It was in the wake of Dejouy's death that Suzanne began to sell her own portraits in earnest.

". . . ik met de kat . . ."

In a white and gold paneled room—bourgeois, correct, somewhat austere—a woman sits, head in hand, cat in lap, bathed in light from an unseen window (fig. 27). This is an intimate work: the sitter wears a housecoat, her hair is unpinned, her expression, careworn; brisk, unblended strokes of blue lend the scene a peculiar immediacy. Abandoned unfinished, the canvas invites us to watch Manet paint his wife. This picture appears on a page in Suzanne's account book from the spring of 1894. There she recorded a series of transactions with the modern art dealer Ambroise Vollard, including this one: "March 10 me with the cat—100 [francs] paid."[19]

The painting's date has proved elusive.[20] Both Suzanne's melancholy posture and Manet's impatient handling point to the artist's final years, a time of illness and frustration. Some specialists have situated this picture in the summer of 1880, which the family spent at Bellevue, where Manet took an ineffectual bathing cure to treat the worsening symptoms of syphilis.[21] But others have placed it in the final year of Manet's life, after his return to Paris from another unsuccessful rest cure, at Reuil. The white and gold paneling, however, may belong to Eugénie Manet's apartment at 49, rue de Saint-Pétersbourg, shared with Suzanne and her husband. Manet seldom painted there, but dwindling mobility might easily have compelled him to do so in the fall of 1882. Within a year, the apartment stood empty. After the horror of his final sickness and the sorrow of his death, the artist's family moved out.

By the time Vollard came calling eleven years later, Suzanne had moved house twice and was again on the brink of losing her home.[22] Vollard took special notice of her portraits, later listing those he saw: "Madame Manet in white on a blue sofa, a portrait showing her in a conservatory, and another from the Camondo collection today in the Louvre. . . . Added to this, all the things we used to call sketches, today the pride of museums, such as . . . Madame Manet in pink, a cat on her knees."[23] The "sketches" held particular interest for Vollard—not least because they could be gotten on the cheap; in 1894 he was still something of a "bottom feeder" finding his way in the market.[24] Paying modest prices,

Vollard picked up a number of unfinished works from Suzanne that spring, subsequently selling several, including the portrait with a cat, to Edgar Degas, who exchanged for this picture a pastel of his own valued at 500 francs.[25] For the artist-collector, unfinished works had a different appeal, offering a window onto the working process of his friend and sometime rival. The subject of this particular unfinished painting, though, also held a special fascination for Degas, who acquired not one but at least two pictures of Manet's wife.[26]

". . . pastel . . ."

The second of them was a pastel, most likely the work for which Suzanne recorded a payment of 1,200 francs on April 10, 1894, from the dealer Alphonse Portier (fig. 28).[27] Degas would trade for it with Portier against 2,000 francs worth of his own work.[28] Although Suzanne did not record a subject or a title, the identity of the buyer and the comparatively high price favor identification with the work that wound up in Degas's possession: Manet's most carefully finished pastel.[29] Apparently just returned from an outing, in an ensemble of white, black, and gray, Suzanne rests her feet on a blue sofa. Its brilliant color matches her eyes. Manet's velvety handling, spare composition, and precise use of color recall the work of Jean-Étienne Liotard, the eighteenth-century master of the medium.[30] Suzanne displays her wedding band. Here, in the eyes of her husband, she is beautiful.

The critic Arsène Alexandre would later compare Degas's excitement about the acquisition of this work to that of a "young man on the subject of his first romances."[31] As in the case of the unfinished portrait with a cat, his interest in this picture was surely in part technical—Degas was, after all, the great pastellist of the age—but his peculiar fascination with Suzanne predated his real engagement with pastels: he had painted her himself in about 1868 (see fig. 45).[32] The story—as told by Degas to Vollard—is now well known.[33] Degas paints a double portrait of Suzanne playing the piano and Manet listening. Degas presents this work as a gift to his friend, who, evidently displeased with the depiction of his wife, slices off the right half. Seeing what Manet has done to his picture, Degas snatches it back. In retaliation, Manet demands that Degas return a small still life.[34] Degas extends the sliced canvas at right, intending to "restore" Madame Manet, but, by the time the two artists reconcile, Manet has already sold his still life to a collector. Degas keeps his mutilated canvas, with Suzanne still missing.

Viewed in this light, Degas's acquisition of the two "Suzanne pictures" looks like an attempt to fill a quite literal

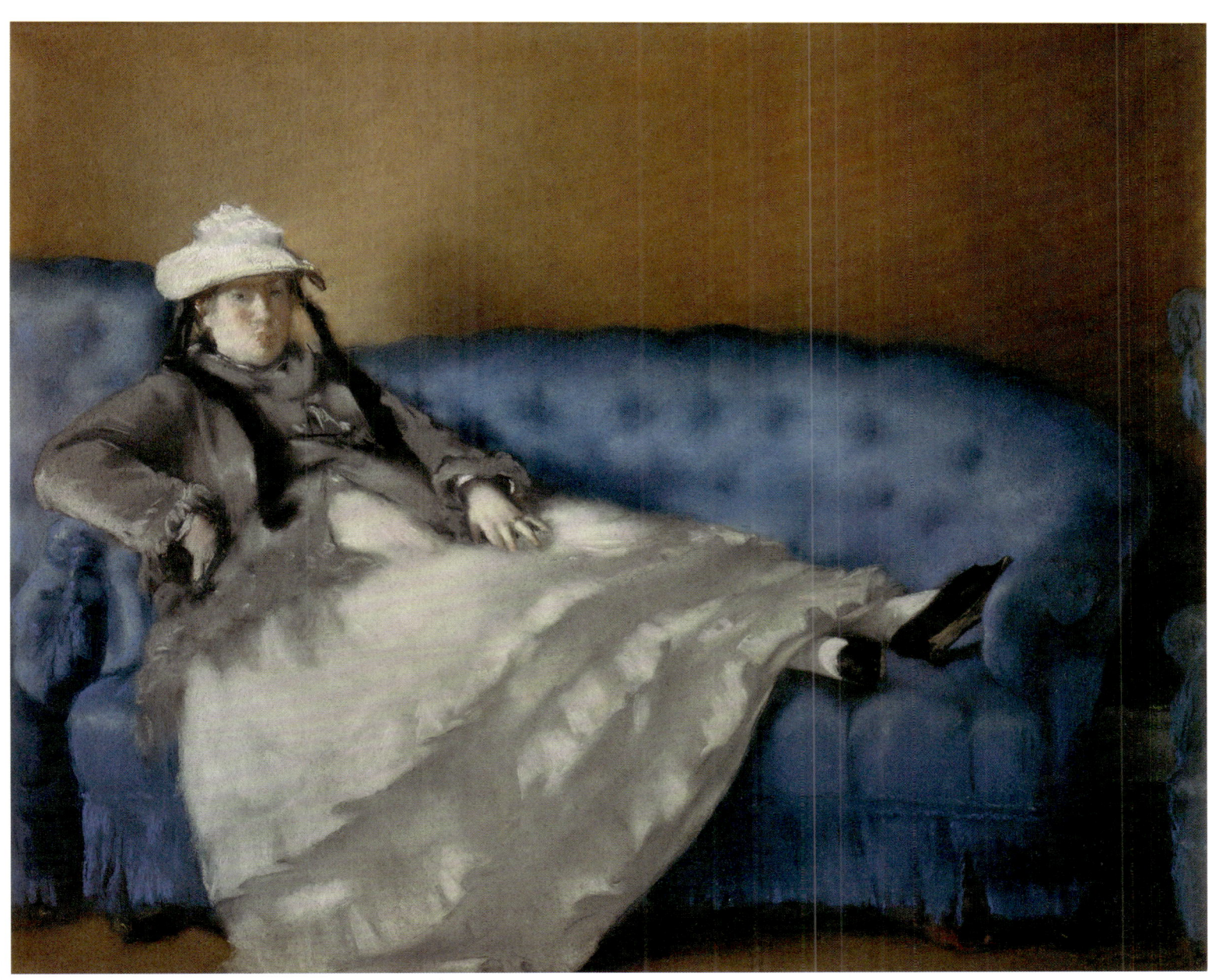

Fig. 28. Édouard Manet, *Madame Édouard Manet on a Blue Sofa*, 1874. Pastel on brown paper mounted on canvas, 49 × 60 cm. Musée d'Orsay, Paris

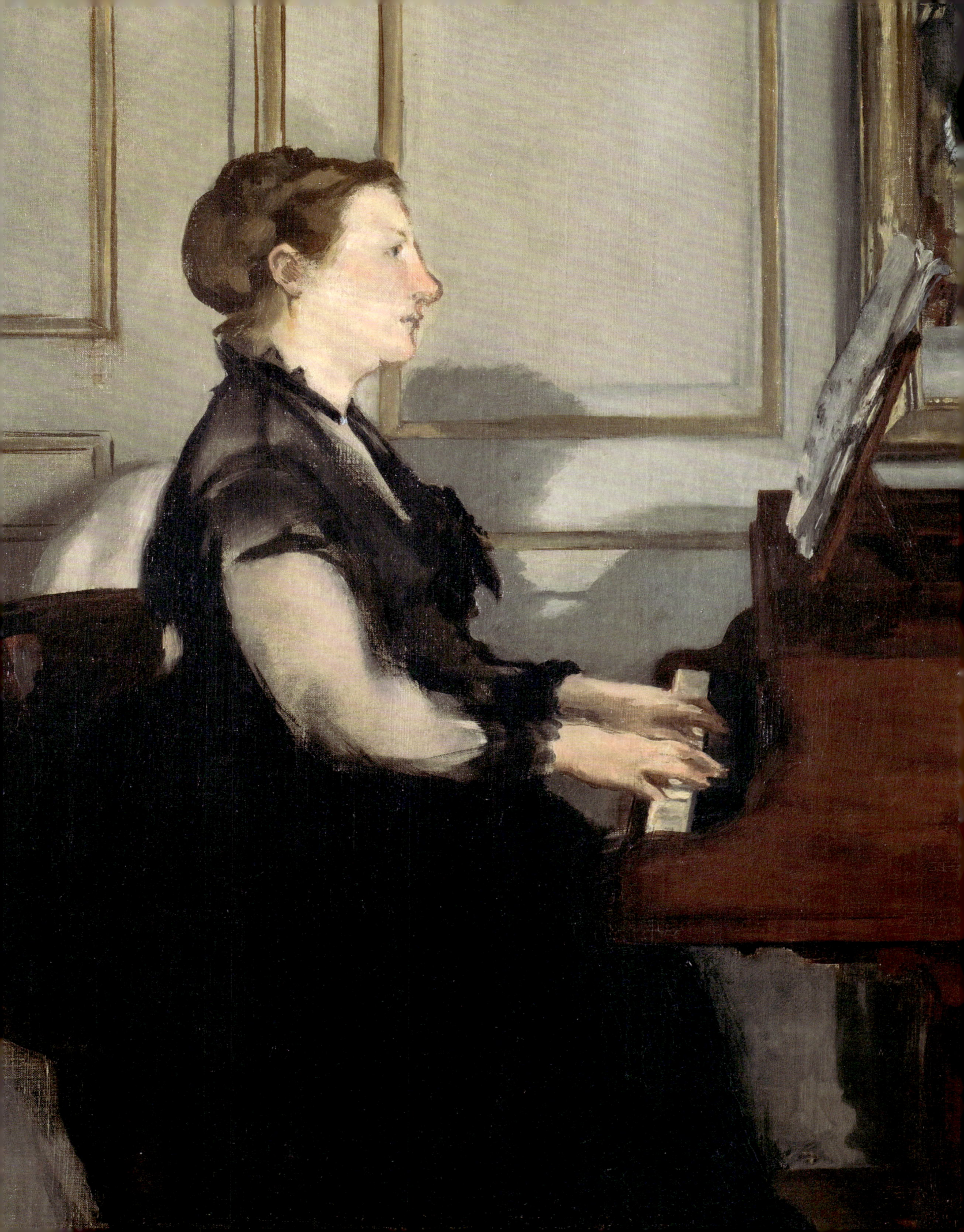

void. Given his interest in these works, it might seem strange that he did not seek out the widow herself. Although his social life was less active in later years,[35] Degas remained in contact with Suzanne's sister-in-law, Berthe, and presumably could have purchased these pictures more cheaply without an intermediary. Did he and Suzanne get along? Had she taken his way of depicting her in the double portrait as an insult? Degas may well have avoided Gennevilliers for another reason, namely, his disapproval of the way Suzanne was handling her husband's legacy. He was not entirely wrong to worry. On one visit, Vollard rescued a rolled-up scrap from Manet's unfinished *Execution of Maximilian* (about 1867–68; National Gallery, London); Léon had cut up the canvas to make it more saleable, apparently without objection from Suzanne. Vollard brought the scrap to Degas, who reconstituted the remains of the composition, proclaiming "Méfiez-vous de la famille [Beware of the family]."[36]

Here begins the trope of Suzanne as a foolish woman who misunderstood her husband's work and abused his legacy. Art historians cannot help but regret some of the decisions she made: slicing up Manet's sketchbooks to sell individual sheets, colluding with a dealer to conceal photographic evidence of retouching, and so on.[37] When confronted about reworked paintings in a prominent collection, she would admit to Julie—with a "nonchalance hollandaise"—that she had authenticated at least one doubtful work.[38] But the whiff of bigotry conveyed by this phrase—penned by a daughter of the affluent sixteenth arrondissement, the niece who came into a fortune at the same moment her aunt lost her home—should perhaps encourage us to suspend judgment. What Suzanne did, she did to survive, and, as this mesmerizing pastel indicates, the understanding that she and her husband shared was of a different order. Manet's defacement of Degas's double portrait might suggest that he knew how others saw his wife and that he wished to protect her from their chilly regard. Degas might buy as many portraits of Suzanne as he could get his hands on, but would he ever really see her?

"... moi chapeau noir manteau gris ..."

Next, in May 1894: an unresolved sketch, half-length, in three-quarter profile (cat. no. 14). The subject is dressed to go out, with a parasol tucked beneath her arm and one inchoate hand drawing on (or off?) the glove of the other. Evidently scraped down, reworked, and abandoned unfinished, the subject's face is just barely recognizable as Suzanne's. The corresponding entry in her account book indicates this work was part of a larger transaction with Vollard comprising

drawings, sketches, and scraps. It reads, simply, "me, black hat, gray coat 60 [francs]."[39] She sold herself cheap.

"... portrait au piano ..."

Six months later, a carefully finished—and highly personal—picture followed: Manet's only portrait of his wife at the piano,[40] sold to the dealer Maurice Joyant for 5,000 francs (fig. 29 and cat. no. 9).[41] With her eyes on the score and her fingers fluttering over the keys, Suzanne draws a melody from the instrument: Chopin, perhaps, a particular specialty;[42] or Wagner, often played for Baudelaire;[43] possibly Haydn, a favorite of her husband's;[44] or, indeed Emmanuel Chabrier, a family friend as well as a composer, who would dedicate his "Impromptu in C Major" to Suzanne in 1873.[45] Of course, Manet had first encountered his future wife as a piano teacher, and, from the beginning, he introduced her to his friends as a musical artist.[46] She auditioned twice for the Paris Conservatory,[47] but whatever professional ambitions she may have harbored were cut short by the birth of Léon and then by her marriage into the Manet family. A respectable bourgeois lady could not go on the stage, but Suzanne continued to perform for discerning audiences in the private setting of Eugénie's drawing room.

Paneled in white with gold trim, this room provides the setting for Suzanne's portrait at the piano; the mirror at right reflects a mantel with the clock presented to Eugénie and Auguste Manet upon their wedding by her godfather, the French-born king of Sweden.[48] The room offers an impeccably Parisian frame for the pointedly Dutch Suzanne, dressed in black and posed like a lady at a virginal in a seventeenth-century genre scene.[49] Eugénie entertained her own friends on Tuesdays and those of her three sons on Thursdays: Baudelaire and Degas, Émile Zola and Henri Fantin-Latour, Zacharie Astruc and Pierre Puvis-de-Chavannes, the Morisot family and Stéphane Mallarmé. In letters and book dedications, Eugénie's guests paid tribute to Suzanne—a "great pianist" who "played like an angel"—alongside other musicians of talent, including her close friend the violinist Fanny Claus, the pianists Chabrier and Palmyre Meurice, and the guitarists José Bosch and Lorenzo Pagans.[50] Inscribing a copy of *L'Après-midi d'un faune*, illustrated by her husband and published in 1876, Mallarmé offered Suzanne a poem:

> The faun would dream of a chaste wedding ring
> Amidst the nymphs in the wood, if only he knew to listen
> At the drawing room door when the grand piano sings
> Like your spirit, shifting from grave to tender.[51]

This playful verse captures something magical in Suzanne's talent. It may also gesture to her past life, as a nude nymph in her husband's work, and to the more emotionally complicated fact that her husband still spent his days surrounded by nymph-like models in a world beyond the drawing room door.

Various observers—even diligently feminist ones—have treated this painting as proof that Suzanne was, to put it bluntly, fat, effectively endorsing Marie-Joséphine's and Berthe Morisot's nasty assessments of her appearance in the early 1870s.[52] But the picture itself betrays no such censoriousness and might be best understood as a rejoinder to the Degas portrait that Manet destroyed. As many scholars have remarked, Suzanne's husband essentially picked up where the sliced canvas leaves off, replacing the white gown with a black one. He evidently used the profile photograph today at the Morgan Library as a guide (see fig. 26). One imagines him pinning it to his easel, following the contours of his wife's features with patient precision. Transformation was plainly not the goal: Manet neither flattered nor mocked his subject. To capture her appearance was enough. The resulting work conveys the kind of beauty that the artist's friend and colleague Giuseppe de Nittis later attributed to Suzanne:

> Not that she was very pretty. But she had something particular, the grace of goodness, of simplicity, of a candid spirit, a serenity that nothing could alter. One sensed in even the slightest thing she said the deep love she had for that charming *enfant terrible*, her husband."[53]

Two years after the sale of this portrait to Joyant, a long list of expenses appears in Suzanne's notebook: rent, tickets, a wine merchant's bill, and so on. At the top of the page, she noted the source of funds used to cover these costs: "paid with the money from the portrait at the piano."[54]

". . . le portrait au banc vert . . ."

Possibly still dearer to Suzanne than her portrait at the piano was a later likeness sold in summer 1895.[55] It is the last in a series of canvases showing the sitter in the same outfit, with a gray coat and black hat, all probably posed in about 1876. First, the unfinished, somewhat ruined canvas was sold to Vollard in February 1894 (cat. no. 14). Second, a frontal bust-length portrait,[56] also unfinished, with pentiments above the sitter's head revealing the original position of the hat and a pair of horizontal lines at right (fig. 30) pointing the way to the final work in the series (fig. 31). Here, the lines take on

more solid form in a green garden bench on which the subject and her black hat sit, side by side, surrounded by hot-house plants. Wearing a serene expression and an ensemble of gray silk taffeta, Suzanne rests her hands in her lap, her wedding band gleaming.

Both painter and sitter were evidently pleased with the picture. Tabarant tells us it hung in the couple's bedroom in the rue de Saint-Pétersbourg and in Suzanne's subsequent bedrooms in the rue de Villejust, the rue de la Croix-des-Vignes, and the Boulevard Voltaire.[57] Newly installed at this final address and evidently struggling to live off a modest bequest left to her by Berthe, Suzanne finally sold the garden bench portrait to Joyant in August 1895.[58]

The bench itself was a studio prop, first recorded in Manet's rue d'Amsterdam atelier in April 1876.[59] Suzanne seldom visited this professional sphere, and so the portrait may record a rare moment shared in the studio, probably connected with the genesis of a considerably larger and more public-facing work: *In the Conservatory* (fig. 32).[60] Shown at the Salon of 1879, that picture portrays an enigmatic encounter between an elegant young woman and her dapper companion in a winter garden setting. The models were Monsieur and Madame Jules Guillemet, close friends of the Manets, and, according to Tabarant, Suzanne visited the studio regularly during their posing sessions.[61] Though the Salon picture is signed and dated 1879, while the portrait of Suzanne bears the date of 1876,[62] the former was already well underway by the end of 1877,[63] and the two projects might easily have overlapped.

The similarities between these compositions—their backdrops and benches, the women in dark dresses and three-quarter profile—have invited all sorts of comparisons between the artist's depictions of his friend's wife and his own. Suzanne is often cast in these assessments as a kind of dumpy disappointment in comparison with the pert, slender Madame Guillemet, whose particular beauty was more typical of the women whom Manet painted in the 1870s and 1880s. He was plainly not immune to their charms; today one hardly knows what to make of a story relayed by De Nittis:

> "One day [Manet] was following a pretty young girl, slender and chic, when suddenly, his wife joined him and said with a smile, 'This time I've caught you at it.' 'Oh my!' he replied, 'I thought it was you.' Now, Madame Manet perhaps a bit stout, a placid Dutch woman, had nothing about her of the dainty Parisienne. She told the story herself, with her open-hearted smile."[64]

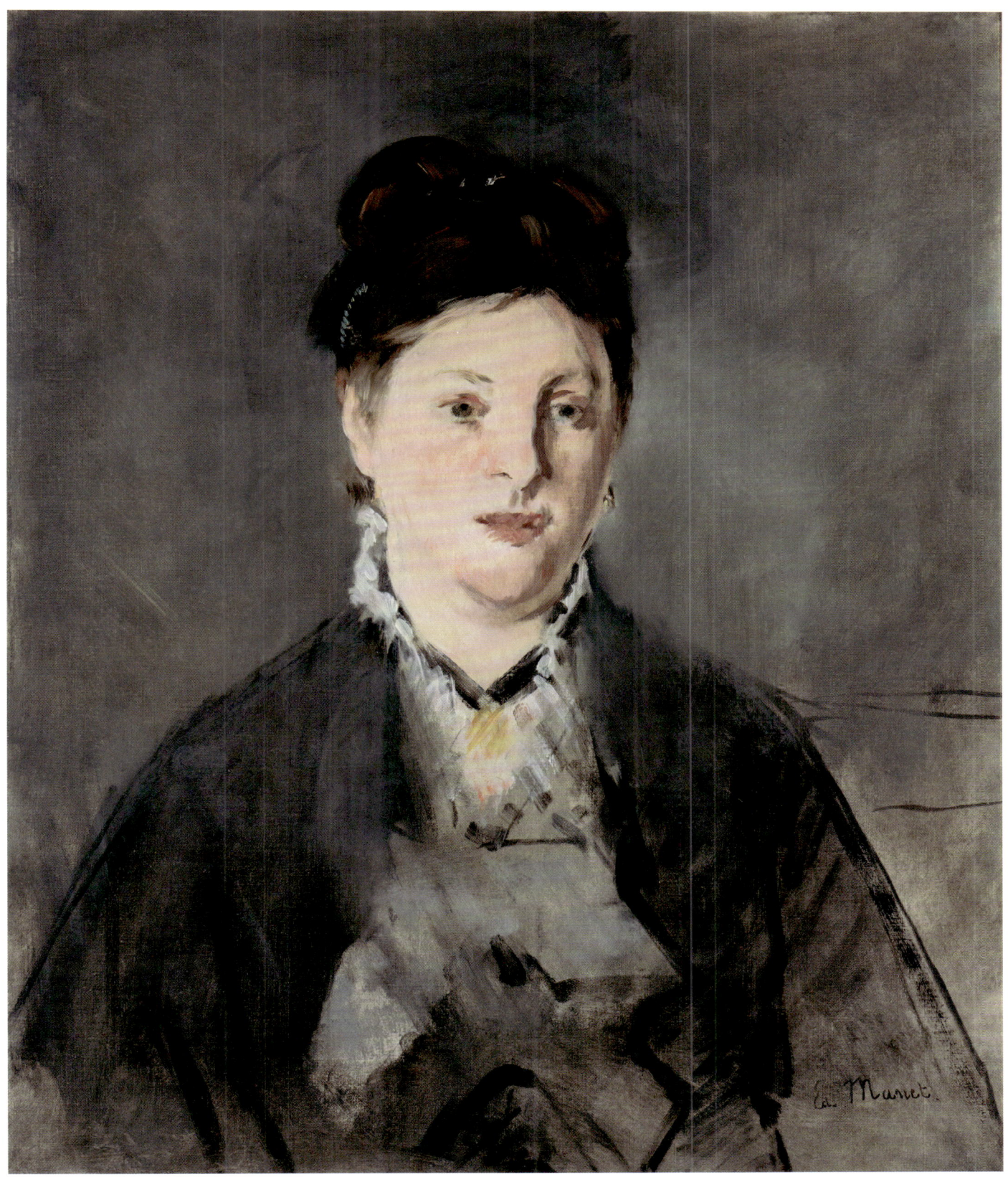

Fig. 30. Édouard Manet, *Madame Manet*, 1874–76. Oil on canvas, 60.6 × 50.8 cm. Norton Simon Art Foundation, Pasadena. Gift of Mr. Norton Simon

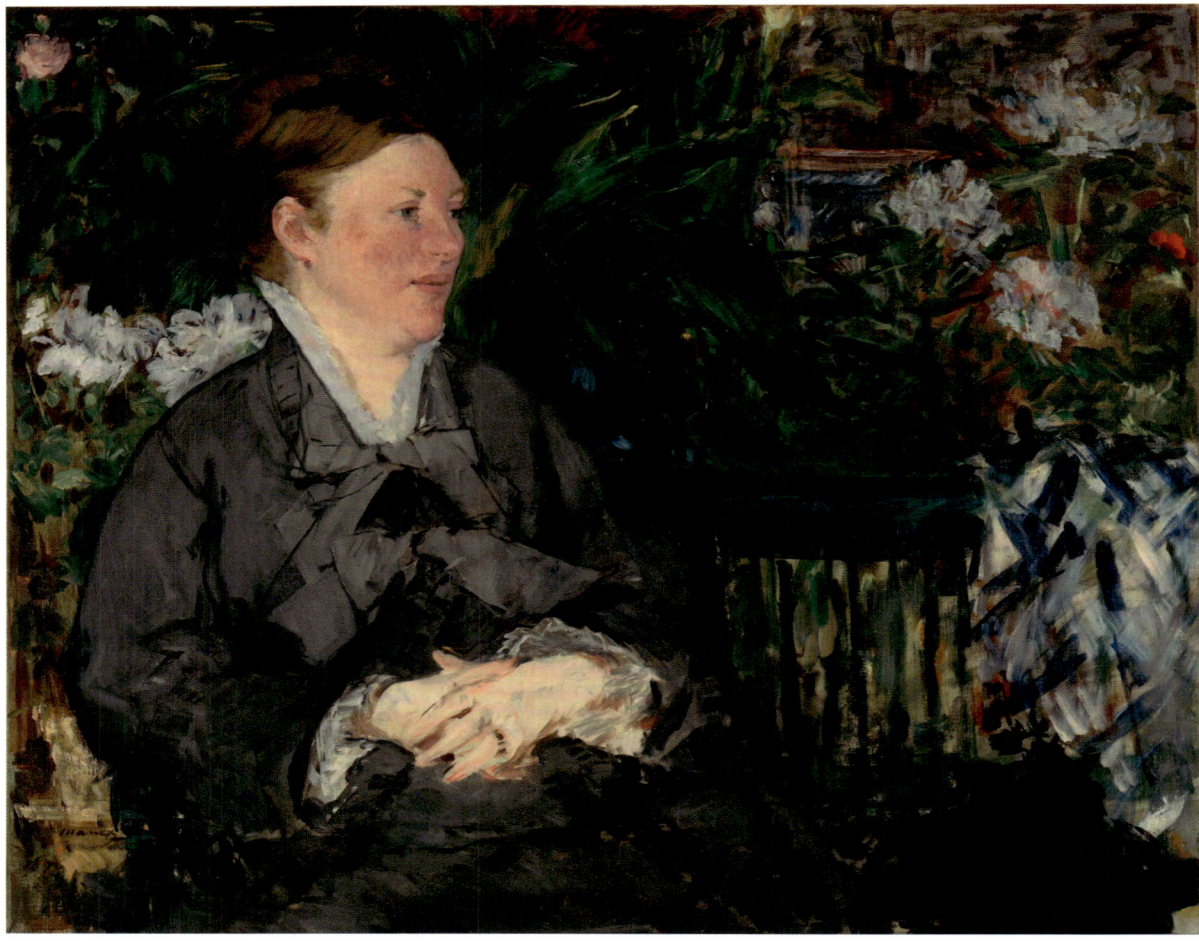

Fig. 31. Édouard Manet, *Madame Manet in the Conservatory*, 1879. Oil on canvas, 100 × 81 cm. Nationalmuseum, Oslo

Manet's wandering eye was evidently something of a private joke within the couple, even if he was, as De Nittis insisted, "faithful despite all appearances."[65] Fidelity, of course, has many definitions. Manet might flirt with his pupil, Eva Gonzalès, and send playful, teasing notes to his pretty young sitter Isabelle Lemonnier; he might even conduct a more intimate relationship with the demimondaine Méry Laurent, as his use of the informal "tu" in their letters seems to suggest.[66] But the garden bench portrait, hung in the couple's bedroom, indicates that he shared something different and deeper with Suzanne, the companion of his whole adult life. Much of the background greenery, like the bench and the shawl tossed over it, appears to have been painted at top speed, but the treatment of Suzanne's head is another matter. Described in exquisite, painstaking detail, here is a

likeness worthy of Hans Holbein, at once tender and matter-of-fact. Before parting with it in 1895, Suzanne commissioned a copy (fig. 33), probably from her nephew, the sickly, eccentric Sunday painter Édouard Vibert (1867–1899).[67] Until her death, it hung in her bedroom, marking the place of the lost original.

"... Saint Ouen ..."

The last of the "Suzanne pictures" to go was also among the first painted and not a portrait in the strictest sense of the word but a landscape, today known as *Fishing* (cat. no. 6).[68] Here both Suzanne and her husband appear in fancy dress, playing the roles of Peter Paul Rubens and his young wife, Helena Fourment, in a dreamscape freely adapted from the

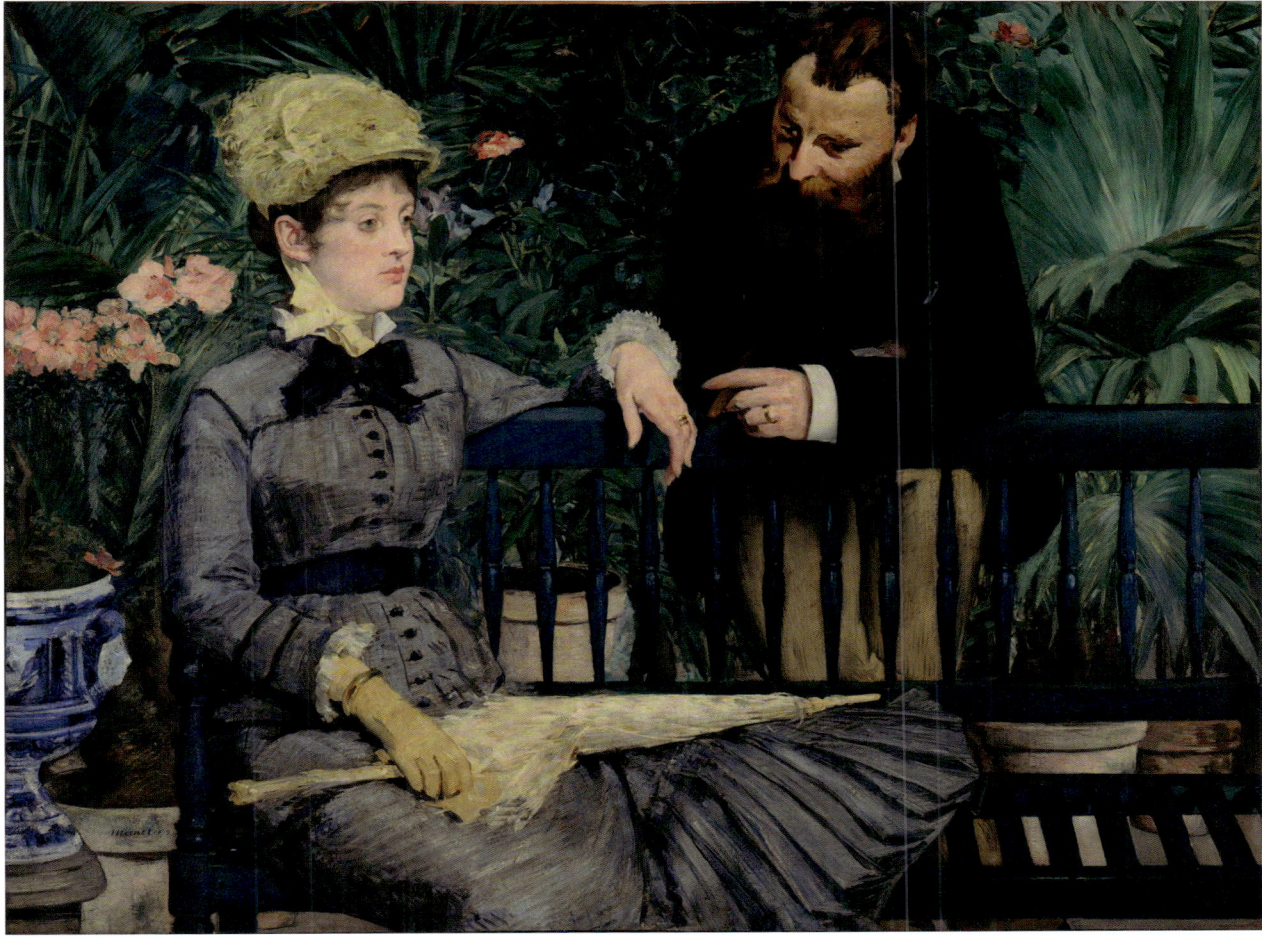

Fig. 32. Édouard Manet, *In the Conservatory*, 1877–79. Oil on canvas, 115 × 150 cm. Staatliche Museen zu Berlin, Nationalgalerie

Flemish master.[69] Suzanne, her arms demurely folded, stands at lower right beside Manet, who, with a grand seigneurial gesture, indicates the landscape beyond: probably a stretch of Gennevilliers still belonging to the Manet family, across the river from the Île Saint-Ouen.[70] "All this," he seems to say, "is ours." Of course, it was, and it wasn't, as Suzanne's precarious widowhood would prove, but the pictorial universe—if not the literal real estate—encompassed in this gesture would be shared with, and ultimately bequeathed to, Suzanne.

Distinguishing this work from other portraits, Suzanne wears no wedding band. The picture may date to the year between the death of Manet's disapproving father and the couple's marriage.[71] It was likely presented to the painter's mother and came to Suzanne following Eugénie's death,[72]

when the artist's widow decamped for Gennevilliers, where she would live not far from the setting for this scene. The fact that the property depicted did not actually belong to Suzanne ultimately meant that she would lose the picture, too. The painting's sa e, to Gaston-Alexandre Camentron, possibly acting as agent for the famed Impressionist dealer Paul Durand-Ruel, appears on a page in her notebook under from February 1897: "St Ouen sold 3 thousand five hundred fr."[73] Once again, before giving up the picture, Suzanne had her nephew copy it. Léon later passed the copy off as an origina , perverting his mother's desire for a keepsake into an act of forgery.[74] The incident contributed to Suzanne's reputation as something less than a connoisseur of her husband's work, an undeserving custodian of her own image.

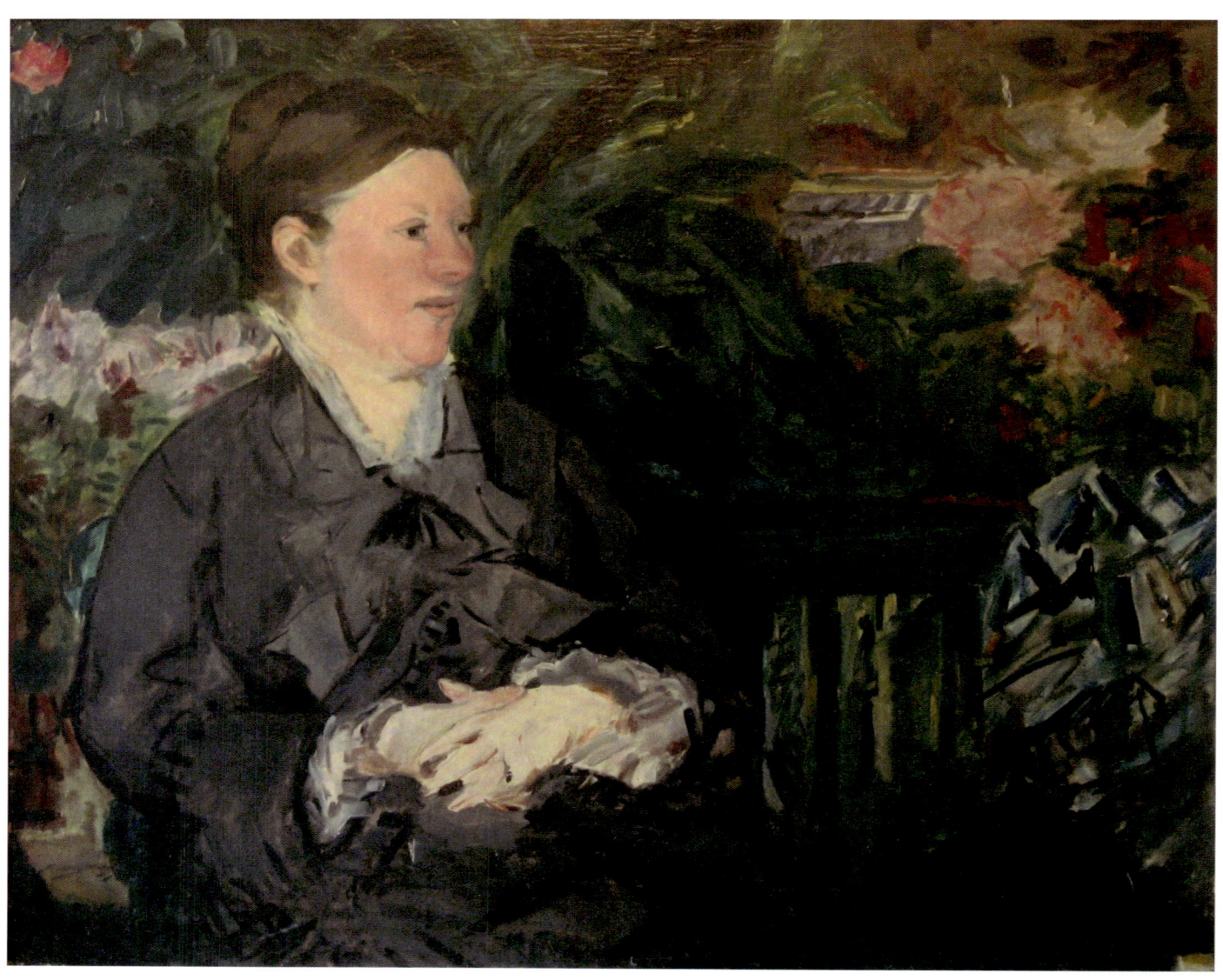

Fig. 33. Attributed to Édouard Vibert, *Madame Manet in the Conservatory*, about 1879–95. Oil on canvas, 100.5 × 81.5 cm. Private collection

"Your husband, Édouard"

Though Manet spent his days in his studio and at cafés, he and Suzanne were seldom parted for longer periods of time, rendering written correspondence for the most part unnecessary. Hence, of the various documents in the Tabarant archive, a sheaf of letters from the painter to his wife is perhaps the most precious. Written on tissue-fine paper and carried out of the besieged city by hot-air balloon, these chronicle the unraveling of Paris, surrounded by Prussian troops, in 1870–71.[75] At the outbreak of the Franco-Prussian War, of course, many Parisians left the city. Sending his family off to stay in the Atlantic Pyrenees, Manet enlisted in the National Guard alongside Degas and other artists. They would stay and fight.

Writing in September, he reassured Suzanne that he would move her pianos out of their apartment for safekeeping in case of fire.[76] He told her all the trees were being cut down, and furniture burnt in the fields.[77] In October he told her of sleeping on straw at the front lines and of the gradual disappearance of milk and meat from shops. He told her of a smallpox outbreak and the ruinous price of potatoes. He wrote, "I looked for your photograph a long time, my dear Suzanne. I finally found the album in the sitting room table, and I can look at your sweet face."[78]

In November he told her of friends killed and taken prisoner. He told her of a neighbor's cat abducted and eaten. He thanked her for the wool socks she had knit for him, describing them as "delicious."[79] In December, he told her of a battle, with mortars whizzing past, and of young Prussian prisoners, weary of the fight.[80] He worried that she might be in need of money and urged her to ask his mother for help.[81] He told her of the cold in a city with nothing left to burn, and on Christmas Day, he wrote, "I can never get used to coming home to this sad apartment. . . . I have your portrait hanging in every corner of my bedroom. So, I see you every morning and night. . . . Your husband, Édouard."[82]

Here, we glimpse what these portraits actually meant to the two people involved in their making. Hanging in the empty apartment on the rue de Saint-Pétersbourg in the loneliest months of Manet's life, they afforded him some of the same solace they would offer his widow decades later, in her little house at Gennevilliers, in her apartments at Asnières and in Paris, as she added up her grocery bill and made it to the next day: reminders of a deep, shared understanding; a hand in the darkness, a face known by heart.

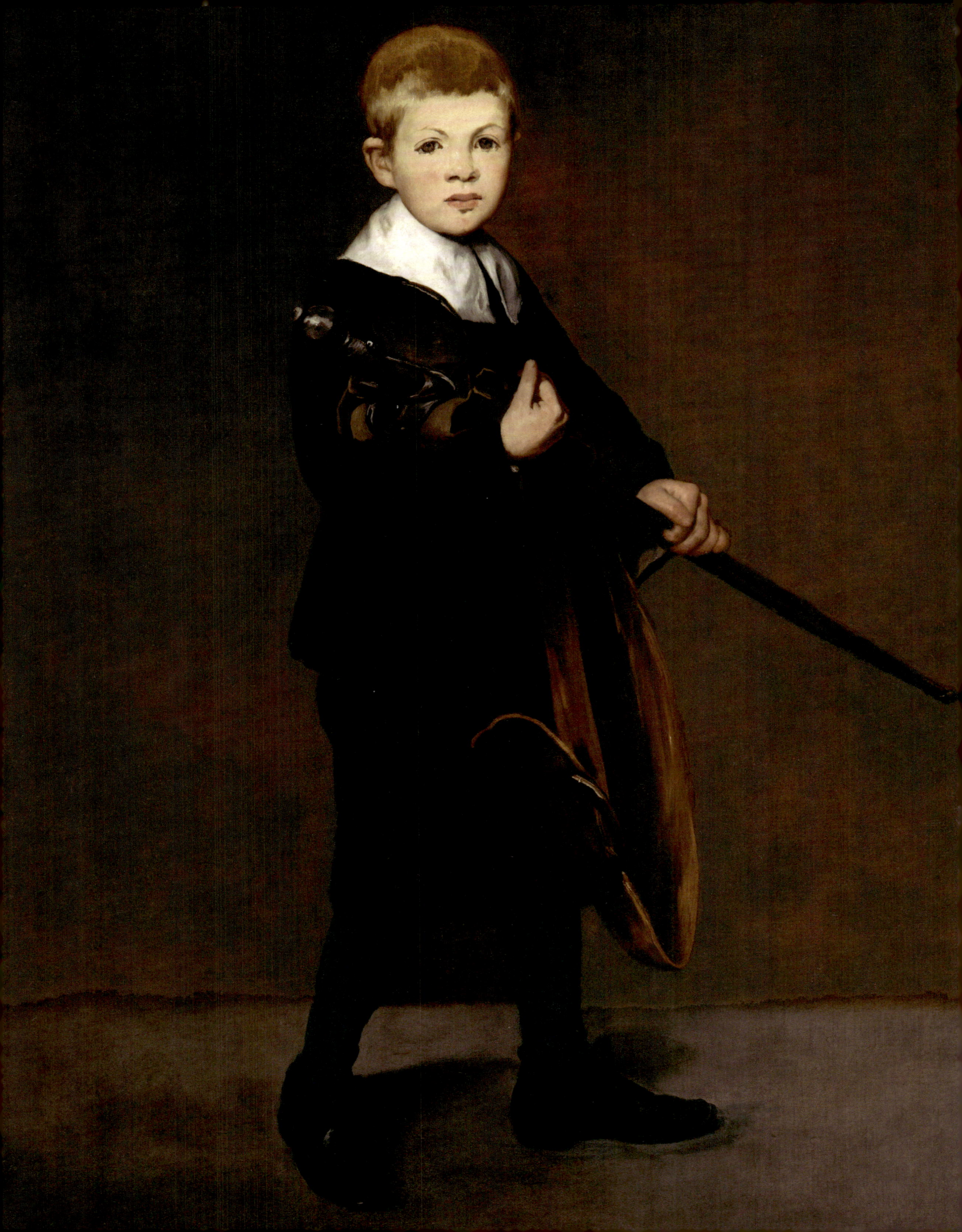

Léon Leenhoff:
Model Across Media

KATHRYN KREMNITZER

Throughout the 1860s, Manet reprised his own oil paintings in watercolor to realize them in etching, a practice he repeated for several of his most accomplished, controversial, and personal canvases in the early decade of his career.[1] Some of the most comprehensive examples of this cross-media iterative process feature Léon Koëlla, better known as Leenhoff, who was the son of Manet's wife, Suzanne, and also possibly the artist's half-brother (see fig. 63).[2] Whether a biological relation or not, Léon was part of Manet's immediate family, one of his most frequent models, and a key decision maker in the organization of his estate and the subsequent cataloging and dissemination of his work after his death. Léon posed for Manet eighteen times in paintings that date between 1859 and 1872, several of which the artist also realized in watercolor and etching.[3] Manet's early working method—from painting, through intermediary watercolors, and probably photography, to etching—materializes the artist's interest in Léon as a model across media. Taking an object-based look at several paintings, watercolors, and prints featuring Léon allows one to glimpse a cross-media practice that Manet advanced to resolve and reimagine his subject, someone who was at once familiar, available, and adaptable. Manet returned to Léon again and again in different guises— first in costume to evoke centuries past and later in genre scenes that verge on portraiture. He appears in works intended for the Salon and in those that never left the studio. He is in oil on canvas, watercolor, and etching. While we may never know whether it was Léon's proximity, physical characteristics, personality, or pliability that made him one of Manet's most frequent and favored models, the material

record of works produced by the artist attest to his interest in, and even care for, the boy that would grow up to take on an important administrative role in documenting and dispersing the artist's estate.

This essay begins with Léon's earliest appearance in Manet's oeuvre and will focus on key examples related to two early paintings in which he features: *Spanish Cavaliers* (1859–60, cat. no. 2) and *Boy with a Sword* (fig. 34). It concludes with a discussion of how Léon, whose posing for Manet served as a vehicle for artistic experimentation, became responsible for recording that evolving oeuvre following the artist's death. The archive that Léon helped create includes key clues about how Manet understood the relationship of his subjects depicted across media, and how those works were exhibited, collected, and received in relation to one another.

Manet first posed Léon around 1859, when he was seven years old, as a boy carrying a tray in the foreground of a painting known as the *Spanish Cavaliers* that together with another canvas, *Spanish Studio Scene* (see fig. 77), may have been part of a larger scene inspired by Velázquez's much-admired *Las Meninas* (1656; Museo del Prado, Madrid). The figures in this invented studio scene, some posed by members of Manet's own family, were repositioned from another painting he first copied at the Louvre and then translated across watercolor and etching. Manet painted a version of *The Gathering of Gentlemen*, then attributed to Velázquez and known as *Réunion de portraits (Gathering of Portraits)*, that he called *The Little Cavaliers* and signed "Manet d'après Vélasquez [sic]" (fig. 35).[4] Manet's painting is

Fig. 34. Édouard Manet, *Boy with a Sword*, 1861. Oil on canvas, 131.1 × 93.4. The Metropolitan Museum of Art, New York. Gift of Erwin Davis, 1889

65

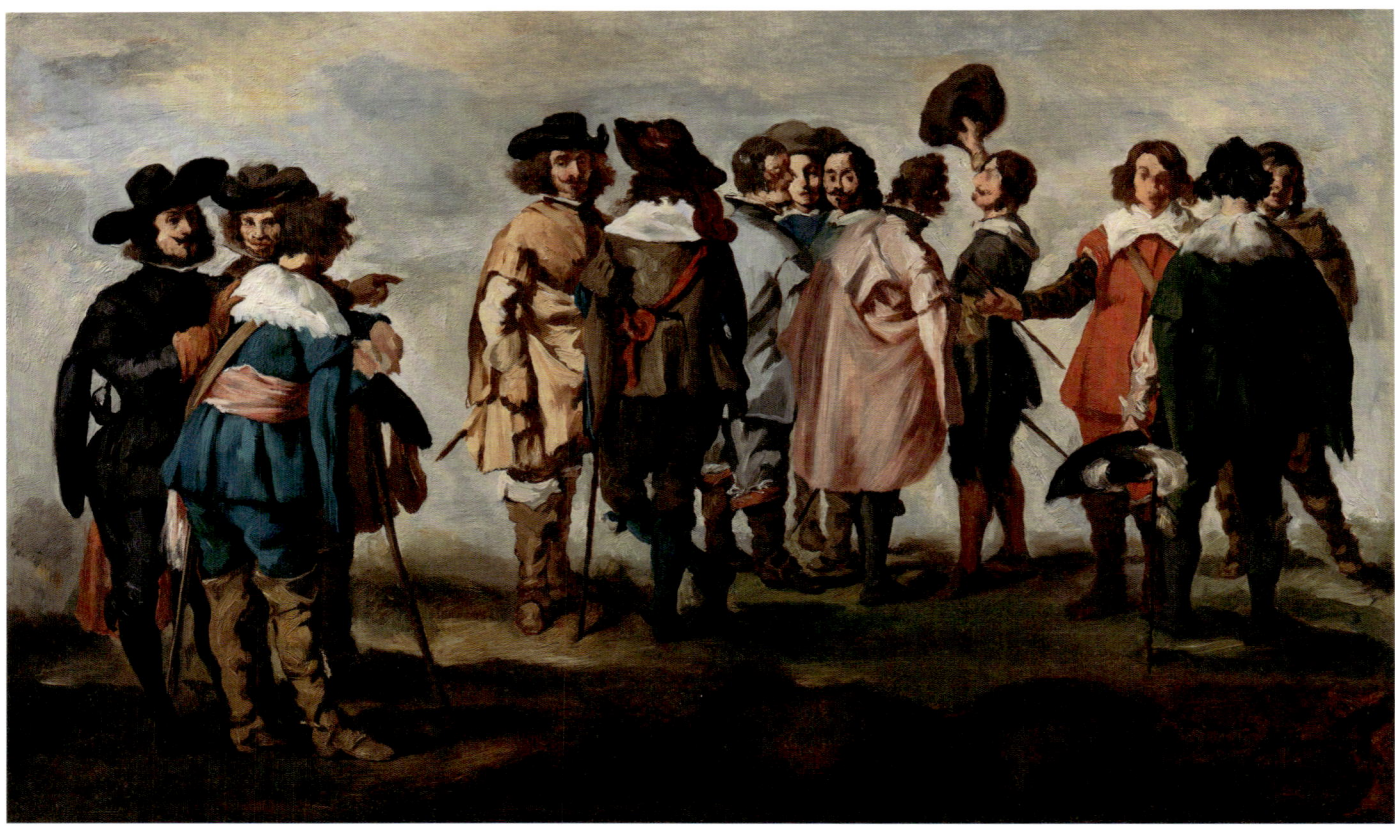

Fig. 35. Édouard Manet, *The Little Cavaliers*, about 1860. Oil on canvas, 45.7 × 75.6 cm. Chrysler Museum of Art, Norfolk. Gift of Walter P. Chrysler, Jr.

undated, and, though he renewed his registration as a copyist at the Louvre on July 1, 1859, the register that would have recorded his request for permission to make the copy is missing.[5] Manet also realized this composition as an etching, his first, across three states, which he exhibited and published on several occasions during his lifetime.[6] Manet exhibited an impression in the prints section of the Salon des Refusés in 1863 (no. 674, *Les Petits cavaliers,* d'après Vélasquez [sic.]), alongside other Spanish-inspired works.[7] Manet also worked up a first state impression of the etching in watercolor, probably around 1862. Whether he considered the watercolor-etching to be a finished product or an intermediary step in elaborating later states of the print is difficult to know, as he subsequently reworked the copperplate extensively.[8] However, the evolution of this composition across media, from Manet's spirited transcription of a painting at the Louvre through his own interpretations in etching

and with watercolor, marks the beginning of a significant working process he repeatedly undertook from painting, through watercolor, to etching in this pivotal first decade of his career. These early composite scenes, inspired by Old Master precedents, informed such triumphant compositions as *Music in the Tuileries* (see fig. 4), a gathering of Manet's own friends and family, including Léon, that also features a self-portrait, an homage no doubt to Velázquez.

Although it is not known exactly how the *Spanish Cavaliers* and *Spanish Studio Scene* relate, and whether they once formed part of a larger whole, it *is* clear that the boy carrying a tray in the foreground of the former, posed by Léon, held the artist's attention.[9] Manet extracted this figure at almost the same scale in watercolor (fig. 36), maintaining the painting's orientation, and reversed in etching, realized first in pure etching (fig. 37). He used a progressively darker aquatint in the second, definitive state (fig. 38) and in a third somewhat

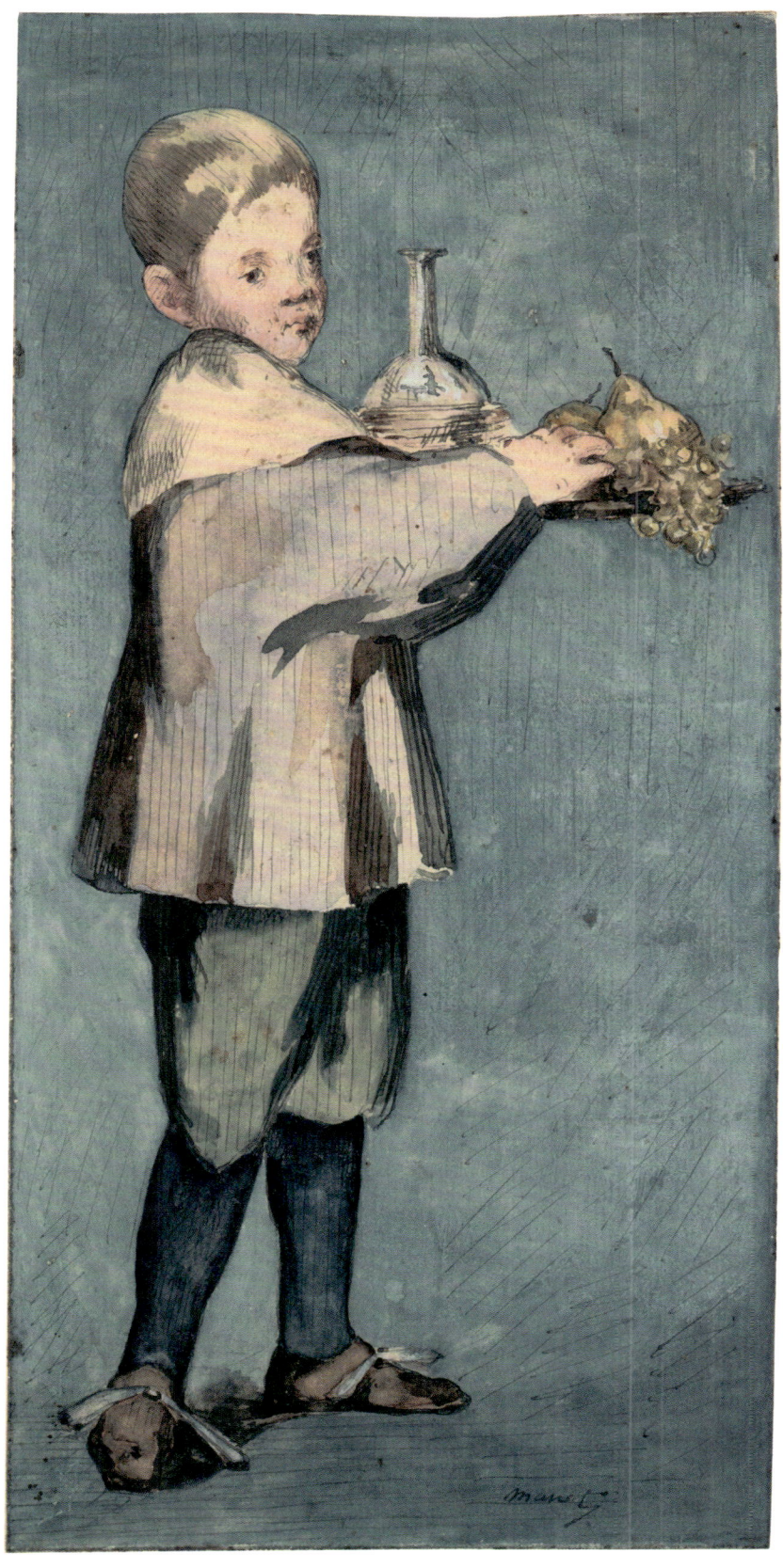

Fig. 36. Édouard Manet, *Boy Carrying a Tray*, 1860–61. Watercolor over graphite on paper, image: 10 × 20.5 cm; sheet: 21.4 × 11.4 cm. The Phillips Collection, Washington, DC, 1922

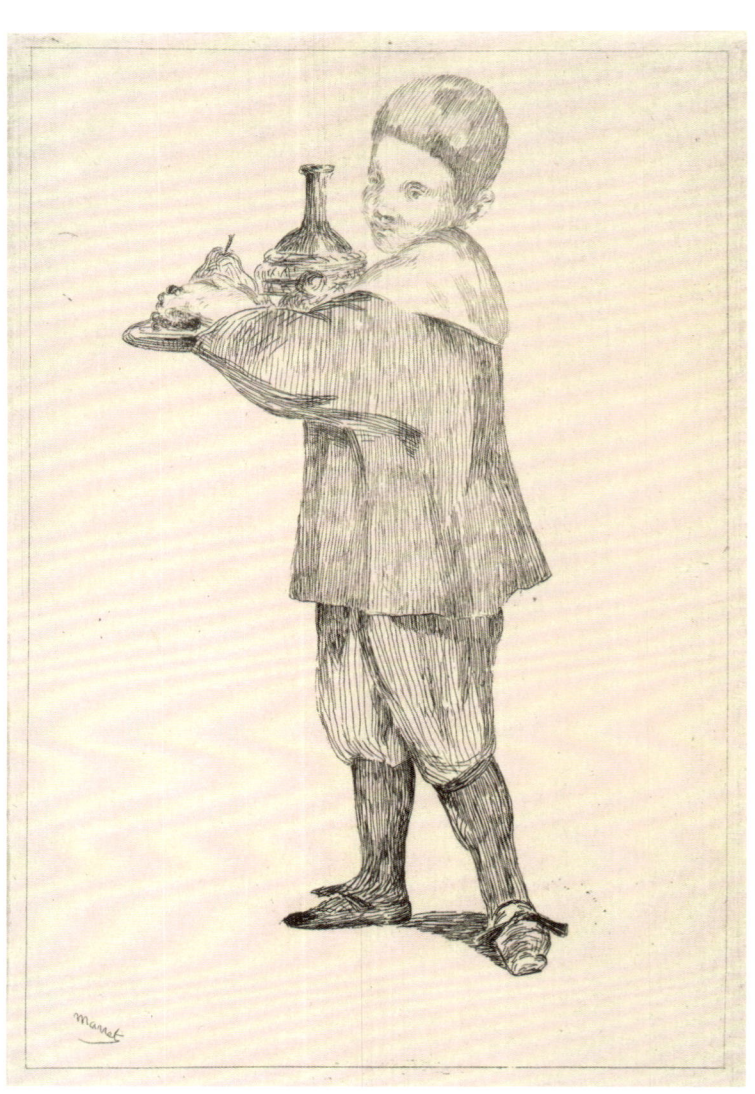

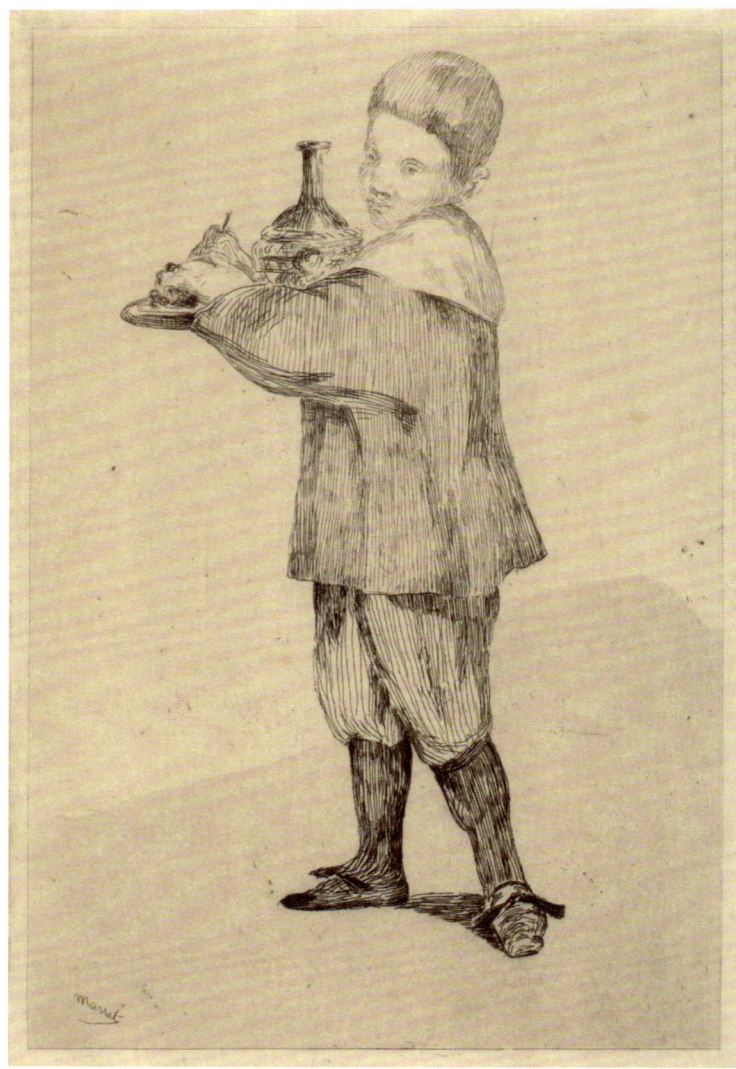

Fig. 37. Édouard Manet, *Boy Carrying a Tray*, 1862 or 1867–69. Etching, first state, image: 22.2 × 14.6; sheet 24 × 15.8 cm. New York Public Library

Fig. 38. Édouard Manet, *Boy Carrying a Tray*, 1862. Etching and aquatint, second state, image: 22.2 × 14.5; sheet 46.7 × 29.8 cm. The Art Institute of Chicago

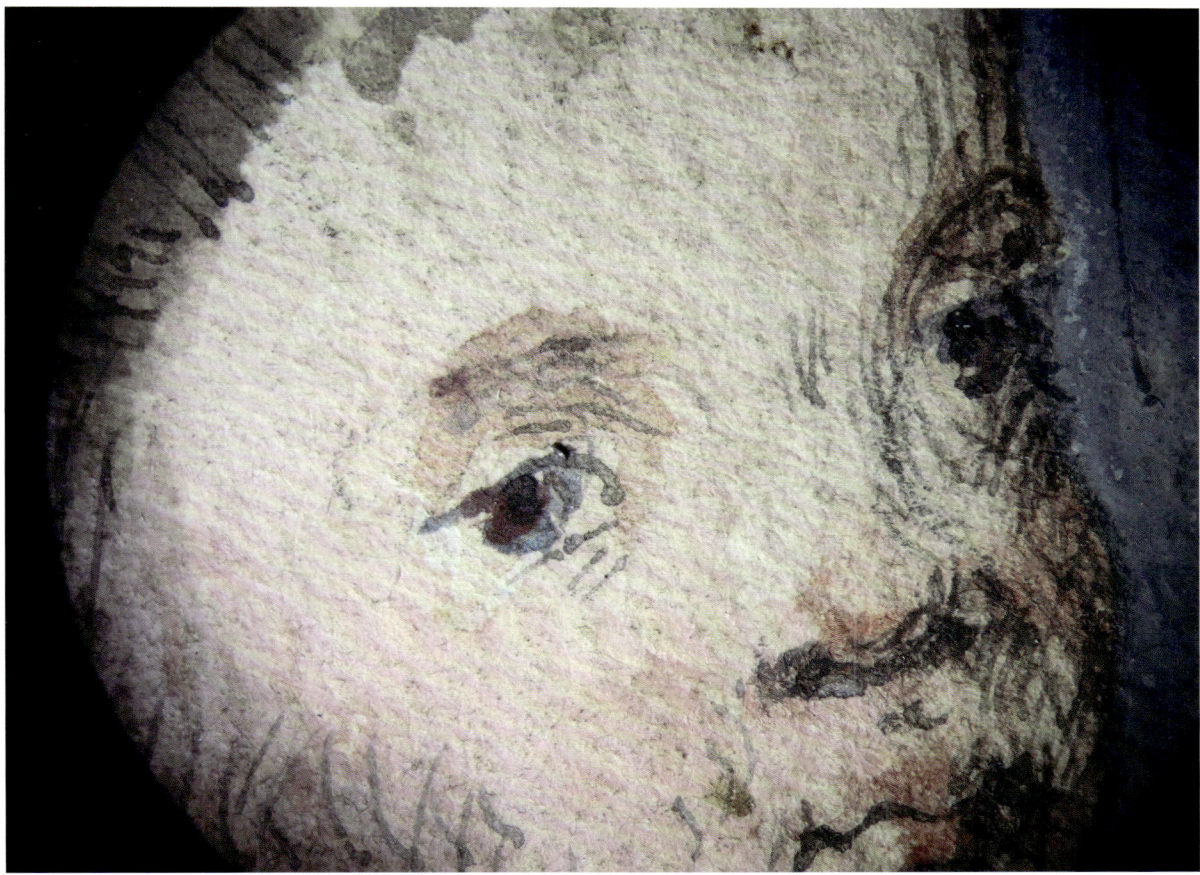

Fig. 39. Detail of *Boy Carrying a Tray* (fig. 36), showing possible underdrawing around the eye

defective state. The prints measure slightly larger than the watercolor. The plate is signed *Manet* in the lower left, but the etching was never published during the artist's lifetime.

Manet included a variation on the boy carrying a tray nearly a decade later in *The Balcony* (see fig. 6). Here, Léon appears in the shadows behind fellow artist and family friend—and, later, relative by marriage—Berthe Morisot, violinist Fanny Claus, and painter Antoine Guillemet. Manet, however, did not include Léon in a watercolor study for the painting, suggesting he was added during the development of the canvas.[10] Adding Léon in Spanish costume perhaps reinforced the influence of Spanish sources: Velázquez, Francisco de Zurbarán, and Francisco de Goya's *Majas on a Balcony* (see fig. 76). This last image had been on view at the Louvre in King Louis Philippe's Spanish gallery from 1838 to 1848, after which it was held by his son Antoine, Duke of Montpensier, and circulated as an etching. Interestingly, Léon figures in a similar pose holding a tray in a painted sketch of Manet in his studio by fellow artist and friend Henri

Fantin-Latour; whether borrowed from one of Manet's compositions or painted from life, from memory, or some combination, Léon's appearance here lends a sense of veracity to the scene, as if he were a reliable and regular witness to, if not participant in, studio sessions.

In the watercolor, the boy is taken out of the studio and placed against a blue-green background; in addition to a tapered drinking vessel, he also balances a pear and a bunch of grapes on his tray. Firsthand study of the watercolor reveals important findings about Manet's medium and order of operations on the sheet that suggest the care with which he realized the composition anew.[11] Although it was not possible to determine if the dry media observed was graphite or black chalk, underdrawing was visible in select areas, especially under magnification—for example, around the eye (fig. 39), at the edge of the collar, and outlining his calves. Those lines that look like graphite to the naked eye—for example, in the contours of the grapes, in the boy's shirt and shoelaces, and in the artist's signature—appeared aqueous

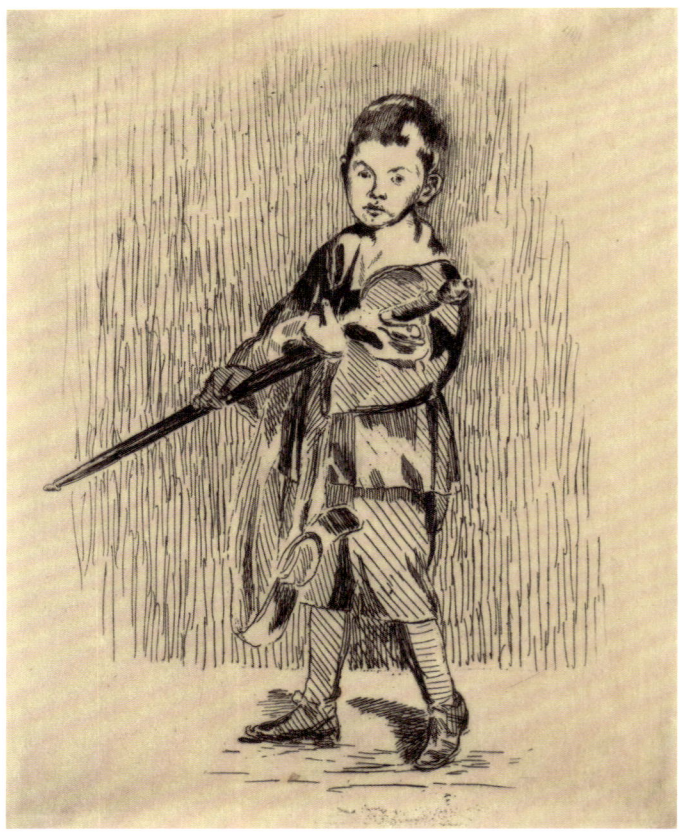

Fig. 40. Édouard Manet, *Boy with a Sword Turned to the Left I*, 1861–62. Etching, first state, 33.9 × 22.7 cm. Nationalmuseum, Stockholm

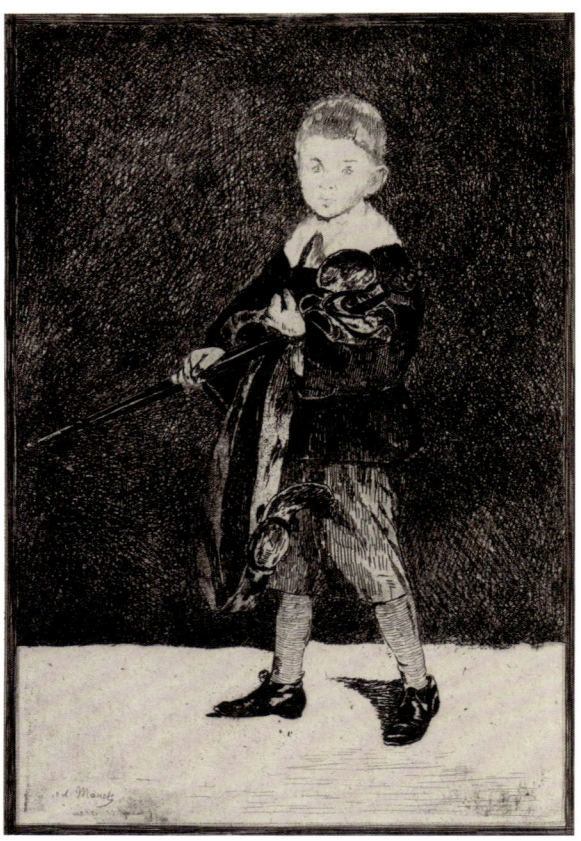

Fig. 41. Édouard Manet, *Boy with a Sword Turned to the Left III*, 1862. Etching and aquatint, 31.8 × 22.9 cm. Museum of Fine Arts, Boston. Katherine E. Bullard Fund in memory of Francis Bullard

under magnification, suggesting they were done directly in watercolor. Manet outlined much of Léon's face and costume in blue ink, which reinstates rather than establishes contours on top of the watercolor, confirming that the composition was worked up from an initial drawing in dry media, through layers of wash, and, finally, reinforcements in ink to refine outlines. This process attests to a careful and deliberate working method that suggests the piece, which Manet signed in watercolor with a brush, was more than an intermediary working study and rather realized to reconsider the composition in another medium, anticipating its reinvention as an etching.

Manet followed a similar trajectory from painting through etching for a subsequent composition, *Boy with a Sword* (see fig. 34), painted in late 1861 in his studio on the rue Guyot, in which Léon posed in seventeenth-century Spanish dress with a sword borrowed from the painter Charles Monginot. Only a single impression from the first tentative state is known, printed on thin paper, unsigned

and undated, and previously in the collection of Philippe Burty and Edgar Degas (fig. 40). He realized the composition in etching across four plates, preserving the painting's orientation in the first three plates, referred to as *Boy with a Sword Turned to the Left I–III* (fig. 41), and reversed in the final fourth, called *Boy with a Sword Turned to the Right* (fig. 42). Manet may have used this trial proof to make an ink drawing on papier calque, which was more likely traced from a photograph of the painting to help translate the image from canvas to copperplate.[12] The drawing, whose present whereabouts are unknown, was first owned by Manet's only official student, Eva Gonzalès, and, following her death, her husband, Henri Guérard, an accomplished printmaker with whom Manet collaborated and who collected the artist's work in his own right. Manet tried the composition again on a second plate, which he also abandoned after a few trial proofs, for a third plate, signed *éd. Manet* in the lower left corner, probably with an eye toward Alfred Cadart's 1862 publication *8 gravures à l'eau-forte par Édouard Manet*, then in preparation.

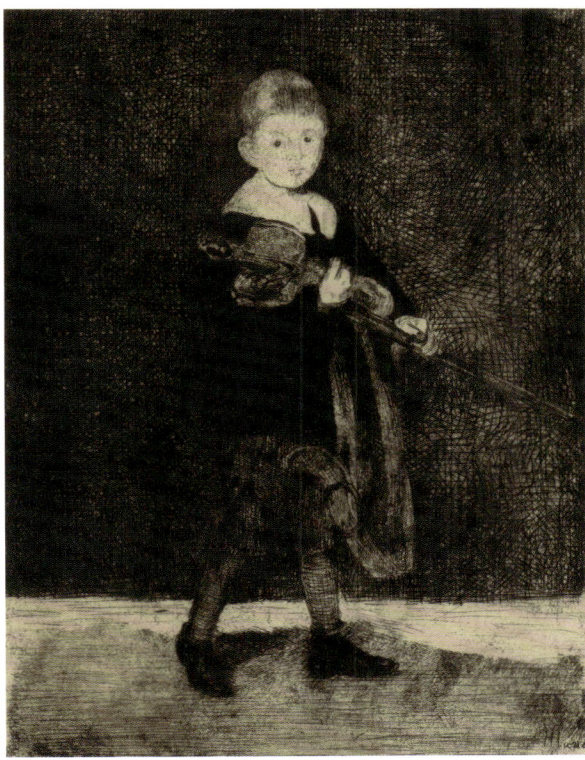

Fig. 42. Édouard Manet, *Boy with a Sword Turned to the Right*, 1862. Etching and aquatint, image: 27.4 × 20.6 cm; sheet: 51.5 × 35 cm. Bibliothèque Nationale de France, Paris

Boy with a Sword was ultimately excluded from *8 gravures*, but a number of impressions exist on the same Hudelist paper that was used for that edition as well as the collection of fourteen etchings printed for friends on the occasion of Manet's marriage to Suzanne in 1863.[13] Manet worked this third plate across four states, relying on nuanced tonal values rather than strict delineation to define the costume and accessories: the first and the second states were realized in pure etching with no sense of background except for a shadow behind the boy's left foot. In the third state, Manet added linear elements to define the compositional space and pictorial plane, including an angled spray of diagonal lines behind Léon to suggest a wall and a shadowy set of lines in front of the figure to establish the floor, together with a light aquatint, all of which are contained by a few faint lines to frame the image. In the fourth state, the background is almost entirely black, thanks to denser cross-hatching and a heavier aquatint that almost completely obfuscate the boy's jacket and sword, leaving his face, collar,

and hands in stark contrast against an imposing field of lines. The framing lines in the fourth state were also widened and darkened to dramatic effect. Manet etched a fourth and final plate, reversing the orientation so Léon is facing right, from which a unique proof exists.

In the 1880s, Léon switched from being the subject of the artist's many depictions across media to becoming responsible for the visual recording of those works in yet another medium: photography. In his notes, Léon writes that after Manet's death in 1883, he hired Fernand Lochard, "photographe connu des artistes" and supplier of photographic equipment, to photograph works remaining in the artist's studio, at 77, rue d'Amsterdam, a few blocks from Lochard's shop at 39, rue Laval, and other select locations.[14] These silver albumen photographs were intended to illustrate a corresponding inventory, numbered 1 to 327, ahead of the artist's posthumous exhibition at the École des Beaux-Arts in January 1884 and subsequent sale the following month (fig. 43). The photographs were trimmed to the subject, laid onto cards, and bound into albums. The primary set consists of four volumes compiled in no discernible order—one at the Bibliothèque Nationale de France and three at the Morgan Library—that once belonged to the scholar Adolphe Tabarant.[15]

Léon's register, with preliminary notes in graphite and ink, ahead of the 1884 exhibition and sale establishes the order in which the photographs should be considered; the albums must be read in tandem with the register and vice versa. Separately, Léon hired the fine art photographer Anatole Godet (with whom Manet had worked during his lifetime to have select paintings photographed) to record the exhibition installation. Taken together as invaluable archival records, the Lochard photographs document how Manet's works looked at the time of his death before several were posthumously restored or reworked to increase their salability. Godet's photographs, in turn, document how Manet's works were presented to the public. It is worth noting that works on paper, in addition to paintings, were posthumously photographed by both Lochard and Godet. These photographs testify to the importance of the works on paper for Manet and his circle. They were documented and displayed alongside, and on equal footing with, oil paintings, and included multiple states of prints. The inventory, photographs, exhibition, and sale were arranged by friends and family who had firsthand knowledge of Manet's working practice. They knew how his work could be best presented and considered for posterity.

While several of the works discussed above were included in the posthumous exhibition and therefore

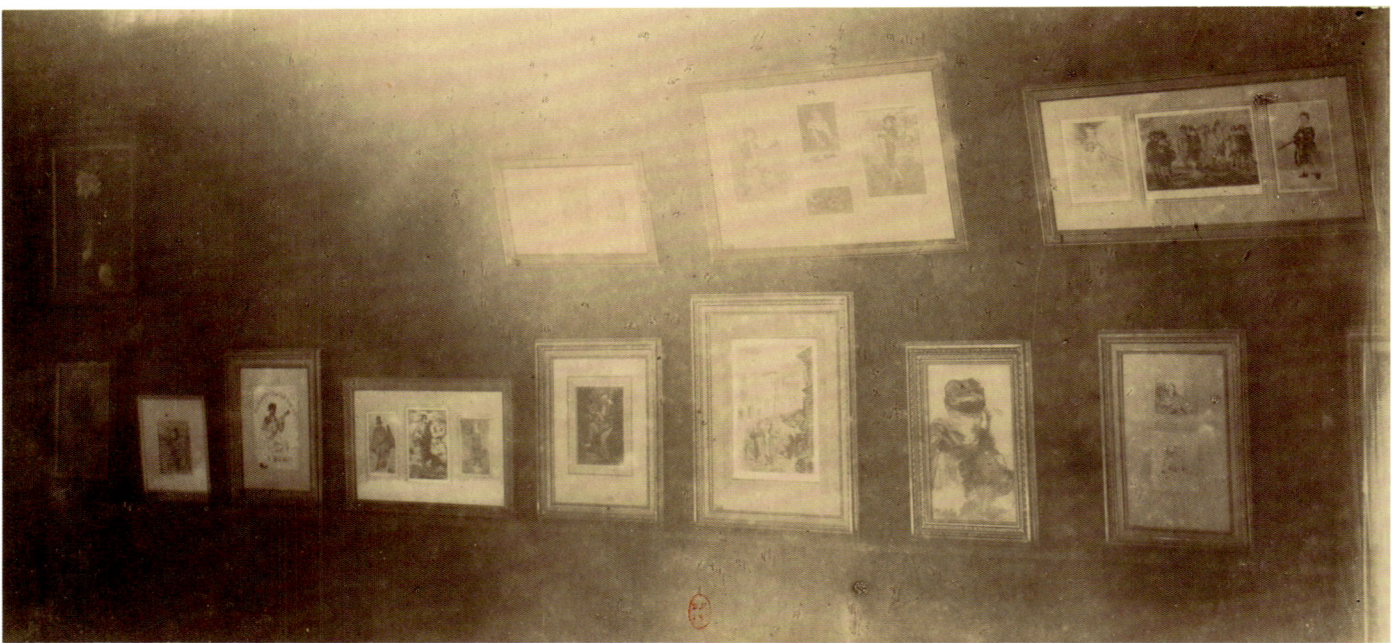

Fig. 43. Anatole Godet, Retrospective exhibition of the work of Édouard Manet, École des Beaux-Arts, January 6–8, 1884. Photograph, fol. 16. Bibliothèque Nationale de France, Paris

photographed by Godet as installed, select works were specifically and idiosyncratically framed and photographed by Lochard ahead of the exhibition. This presentation attests to the ways in which the works were encountered and enumerated within Manet's oeuvre. For example, a third state impression of the *Little Cavaliers* etching was shown in a frame flanked by an impression from the third state of the third plate of *Boy with a Sword Turned to the Left* and a counterproof of the second plate.[16] That *Boy with a Sword* was shown in different states speaks to an appreciation of the uniqueness of each impression and the comfort with which contemporary audiences engaged with an image in multiples and across media. Lochard photographed these composite arrangements, including a second state impression of *Boy Carrying a Tray* that was shown together with impressions of the *Absinthe Drinker* and *Les Gitanos* (*The Gypsies*).[17]

Annotations in various hands, most notably Léon's, on the Lochard photocard with the photograph of *Boy with a Sword Turned to the Left* speak to the composition's realization across media, as well as particulars related to the provenance, exhibition, and photographing of specific works (fig. 44). Notably, the etching is described as, "Portrait de Léon Leenhoff tenant une vieille épée/Grave d'après le tableau/La planche n'est pas encore retrouvée."[18] The painting, which was already in a private American collection (Erwin Davis, who bequeathed it to the Metropolitan Museum of Art

in 1889), is noted as *Peinture en Amerique* and was therefore excluded from the retrospective exhibition and subsequent sale. The etching is noted to have been included in the exhibition but held back from the sale, *reserve*. In his register, Léon notes that the etching of *Boy with a Sword* (no. 201) was signed, unframed in the studio, photographed on October 21 with numbers 304 (etching of *Little Cavaliers*) and 302 (etching of *Boy with a Sword*), and measured 48 by 35 cm. In addition to the register and annotated photographic archive, Léon transcribed a selection of Manet's letters, notes, accounts, address book, agenda, and other recollections about particular paintings that he then assembled for Étienne Moreau-Nélaton ahead of the scholar's 1926 catalogue of the artist's works.[19]

From model to manager, Léon played a pivotal role in Manet's early career and posthumous reception in a way that bridged personal and professional relationships. Perhaps most important, his register and annotations on the Lochard photocards suggest a clear understanding of the relationship between Manet's paintings, watercolors, and prints. Their coequal status in his recording of the artist's oeuvre further suggests the importance of seeing Manet's work together, across media. This working across media should inform an understanding of his art in conversation, rather than disparate and unequal parts divided along material classifications. As Manet told his friend the journalist Antonin Proust, "I must be seen whole."[20]

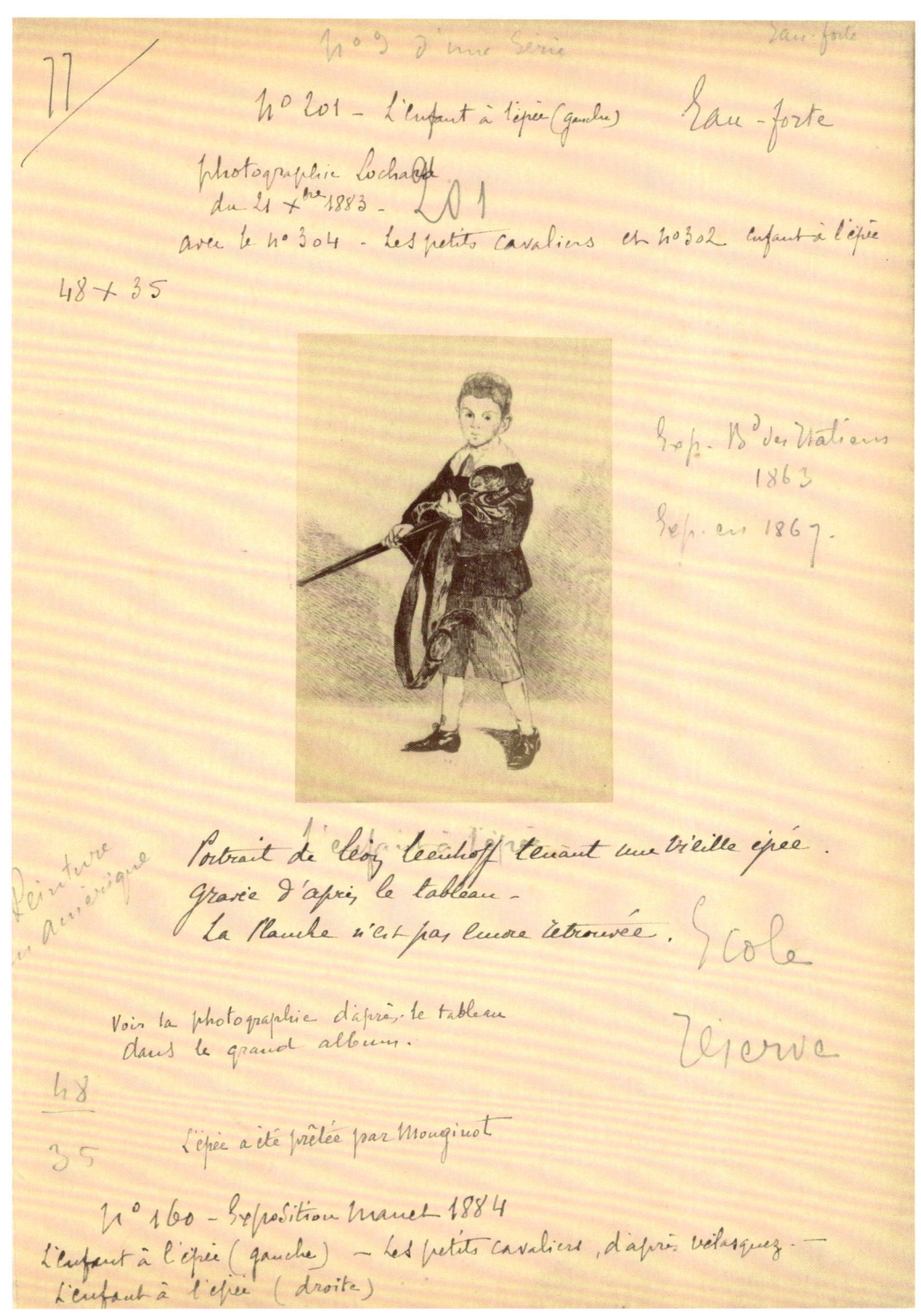

Fig. 44. Fernand Lochard, *Boy with a Sword Turned to the Left*, in Album of photographs of the work of Édouard Manet, about 1883, vol. 2, 77r. The Morgan Library & Museum, New York (MA 3950 1:1–3). Purchased as the gift of Mrs. Charles Engelhard and children in memory of Mr. Charles Engelhard, 1974

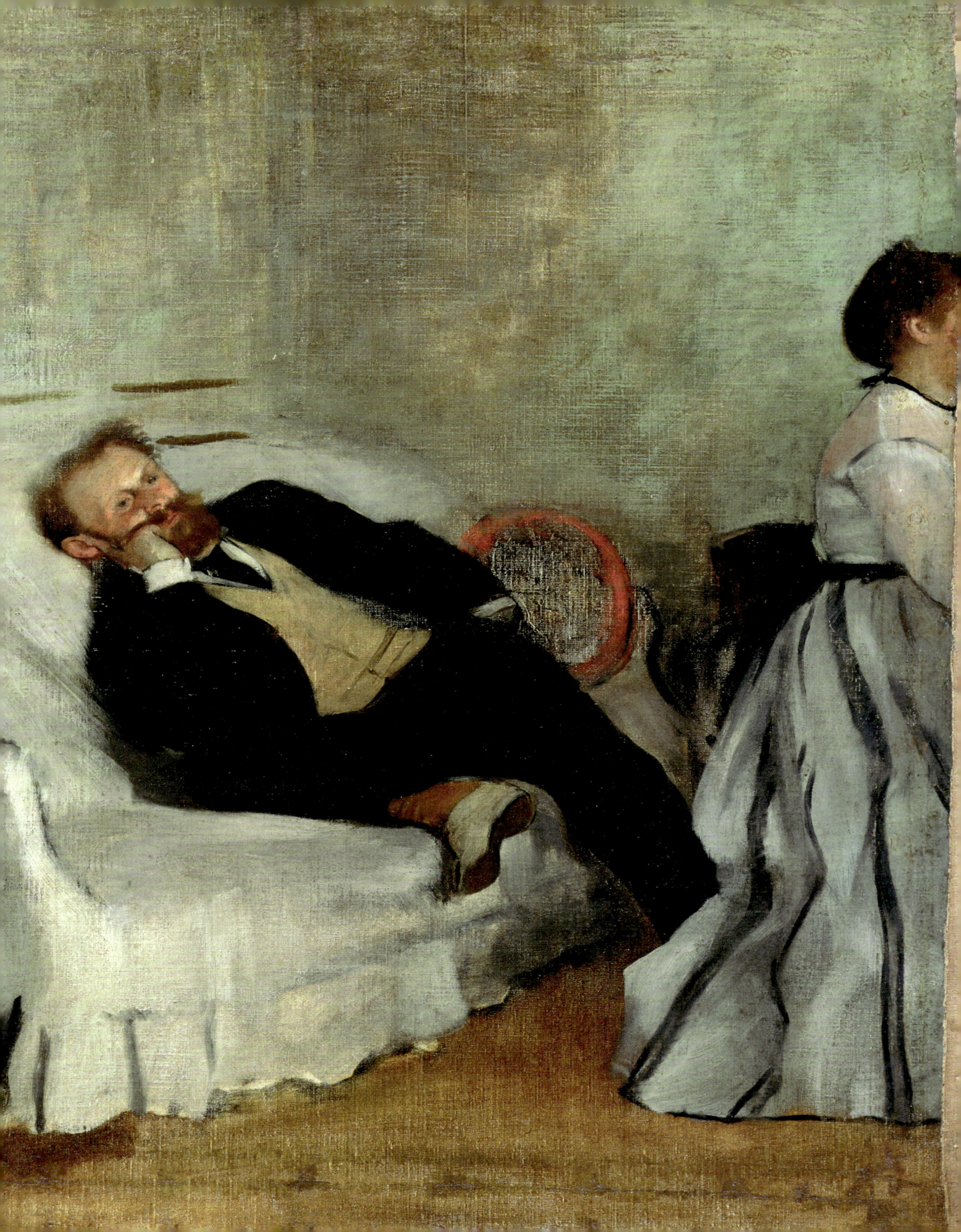

Cut Paintings, Illegitimate Children, and Two Exceptional Artists: Edgar Degas and the Manet Family

ISOLDE PLUDERMACHER

Born only two years apart at the beginning of the July Monarchy (1830–48), Édouard Manet (1832–1883) and Edgar Degas (1834–1917) came from similar backgrounds.[1] Both were the eldest sons in bourgeois Parisian families (Manet's father was a judge, Degas's, a banker) and each was expected to follow in his father's footsteps. But both abandoned studying the law and convinced their families to let them pursue careers in art.[2] Their family wealth made it possible for them to be classically trained in painting in the studios of recognized artists who encouraged them to study the Old Masters.[3] The two seem to have met at the Louvre in the early 1860s in front of Velázquez's *The Infanta Margarita*, which Degas was engraving directly on a copper plate. Early in their careers, the two artists also had studios in the same neighborhood. Manet occupied a studio on rue de la Victoire from 1858 to 1861,[4] on the same street as the headquarters of Degas's father's business[5] and just a few blocks from Degas's atelier at 13, rue Laval in 1859. The deep connection between Manet and Degas—a mix of friendship, admiration, and rivalry—has been the subject of extensive research and a recent exhibition.[6] This essay, however, is the first to focus on how this singular relationship relates to Manet's family life. Studying three episodes of contact between Degas and the Manet family—the creation and slashing of a painting, a trial about the paternity of an illegitimate child, and Degas's active collecting of Manet's works after Édouard's death—can reveal how there were significant intersections between their personal lives and their artistic creations.

The Cutting Out of *Monsieur and Madame Édouard Manet*

Manet was famous for his ability to speak with women.[7] This is in contrast to Degas, who was notably uncomfortable with women and remained single all his life. Degas had, however, special relationships with the wives of some of his close friends.[8] This included Suzanne Manet, with whom he shared a deep love of music. She was a talented pianist and, along with Manet, she was one of the few close friends invited to take part in the Monday music sessions organized by Degas's father in his home in rue Mondovi.[9] It was presumably friendship with Manet and his wife that inspired Degas to create the double portrait *Monsieur and Madame Édouard Manet* (fig. 45). Painted around 1868, the portrait's complex material history reflects not only the chaotic nature of the relationship between Manet and Degas but also—I believe—Manet's sensitivity about the public image of his marriage with Suzanne. The painting shows Suzanne playing the piano, while behind her, Édouard listens, halfway reclining on a sofa covered in white. The scene's composition recalls *Young Woman at the Piano* (fig. 46), which Frédéric Bazille painted for the Salon of 1866 and was refused by the jury.[10] Degas's work evokes a scene from the musical evenings organized by the Manets every Thursday at 49, rue de Saint-Pétersbourg, where Édouard and Suzanne had lived with the painter's mother, Eugénie, since 1866. Degas was a regular guest, and he probably gave this painting to the couple as a thank you for their courtesy.[11]

Fig. 45. Edgar Degas, *Monsieur and Madame Édouard Manet* (detail), 1868. Oil on canvas, 65 × 71 cm. Kitakyushu Municipal Museum of Art

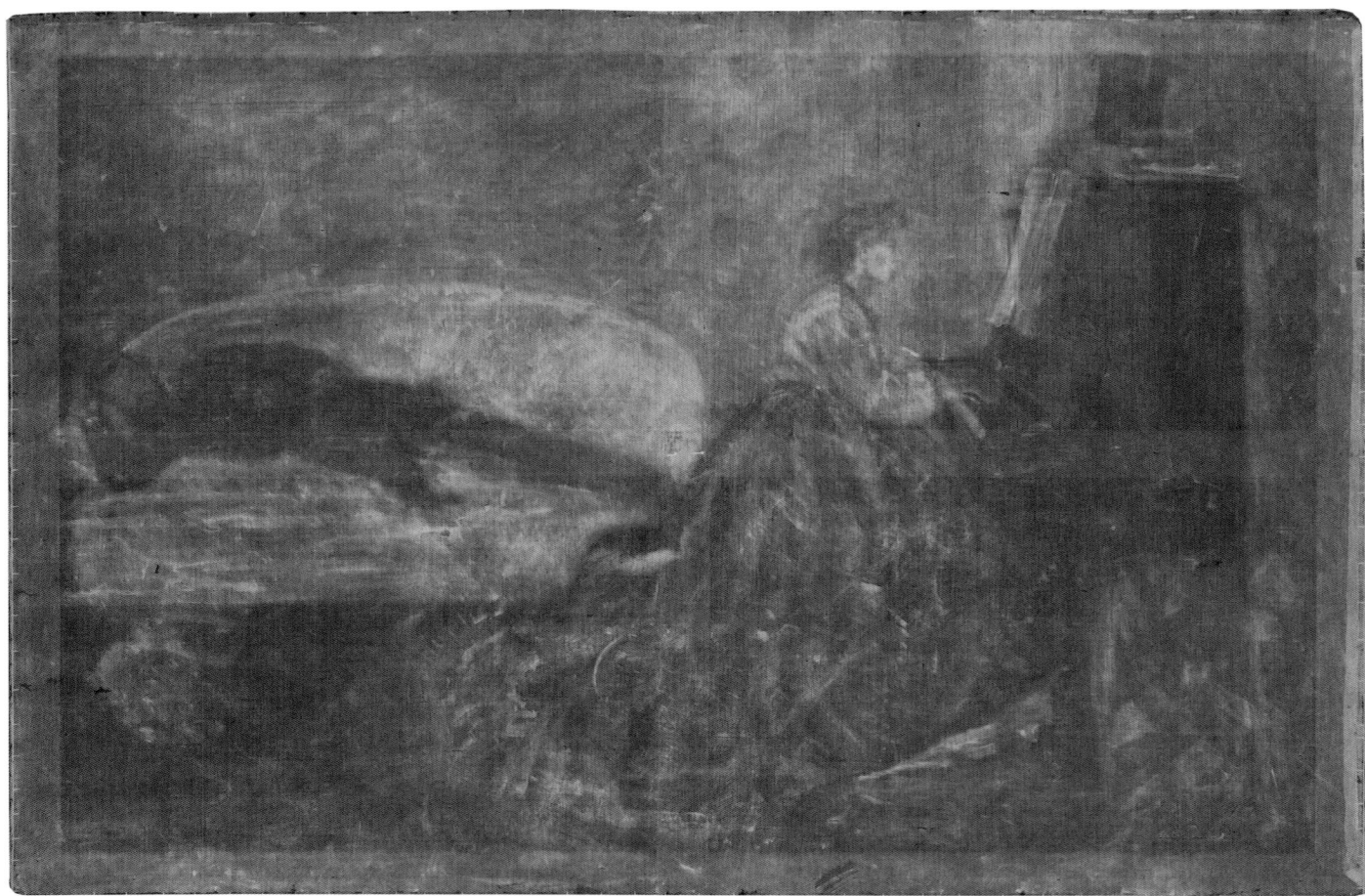

Fig. 46. Frédéric Bazille, X-ray of *Ruth and Boaz* showing *Young Woman at the Piano*, 1865–66. Oil on canvas, 138 × 202 cm. Musée Fabre, Montpellier

Manet first hung the painting in his home.[12] Then, for murky reasons, he cut the canvas vertically, removing Suzanne's profile and her hands placed on the keys. In so doing, Manet did not intend to transform the double portrait into two separate portraits[13] but rather to remove any recognizable features of his wife's face. He left only her "chestnut hair raised in a bun, revealing the ear."[14] Degas discovered this act of great symbolic violence one day when he visited the Manets: "The blow it did to me when I reviewed my study with Manet . . . he will remember many years later— I left without saying goodbye, taking my painting with me."[15]

Manet's motives for this radical gesture, which led to his "most serious quarrel" with Degas, remain mysterious.[16] The most commonly cited explanation, which comes directly from Degas, is that Manet found his wife's image was "made too ugly [*trop enlaidie*]" and that he "coldly suppressed" her.[17] Artist and critic Jacques-Émile Blanche proposed a psychological reading of Manet's motives, suggesting that the

"figure was cut off from the canvas for being unflattering, driven by the *weakness* [emphasis added] of the husband."[18] Blanche later described how Manet's relatives disapproved of his cutting the canvas: "Mrs. Berthe Morisot, as well as the other members of the Manet family . . . resented Édouard when (out of *revenge?*) [emphasis added], he cut off the part where Degas had painted Madame Édouard Manet at the piano in the double portrait of the husband and wife."[19]

While Manet did not reveal his motives, he produced a work that constitutes a response in the form of a correction to Degas's painting.[20] *Madame Manet at the Piano* (fig. 47 and cat. no. 9) takes place in the same setting. Across both works, one can see the light paneling with gilded edging and the sofa covered in white from the living room of 49, rue de Saint-Pétersbourg. Suzanne is seated at the piano wearing a dress that shows her arms through transparent sleeves, just like Degas's canvas. Her face is painted strictly in profile, a

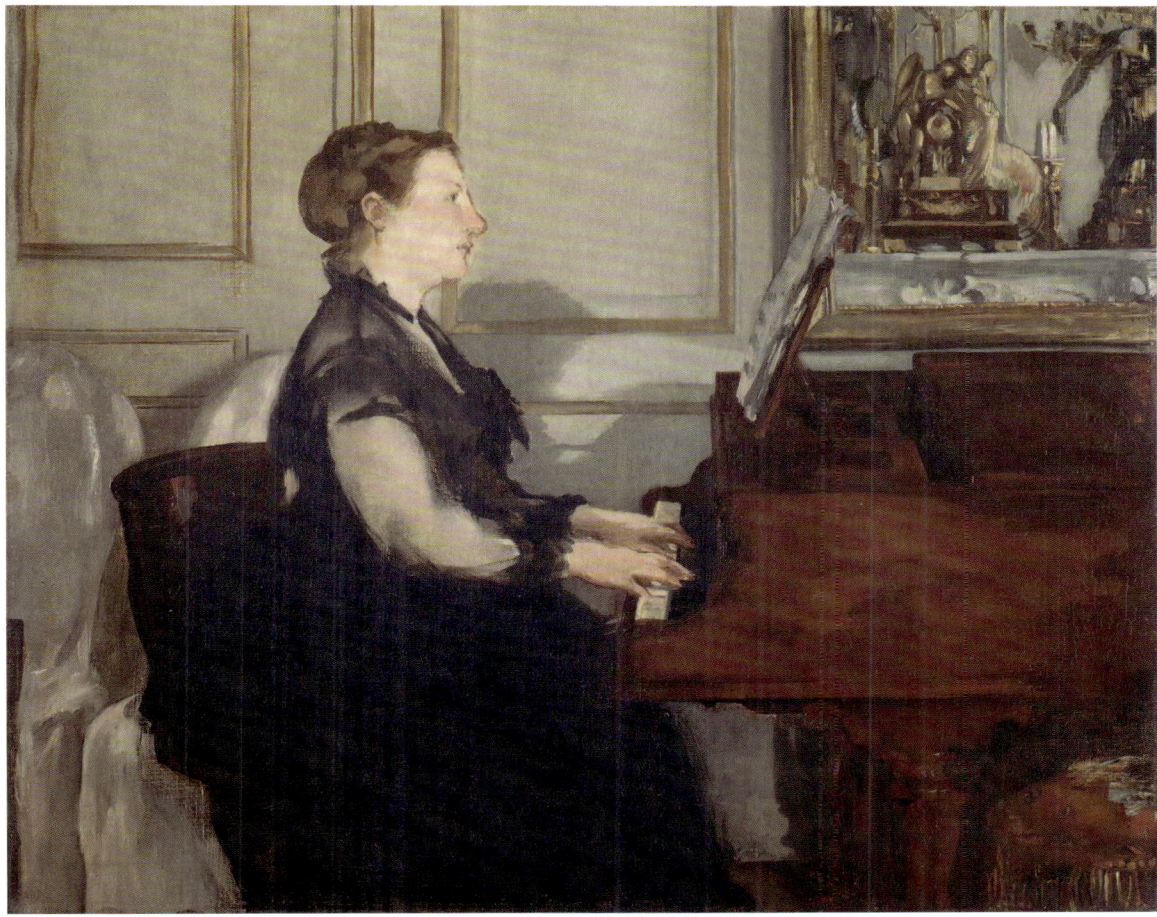

Fig. 47. Édouard Manet, *Madame Manet at the Piano*, about 1868. Oil on canvas, 38.5 × 45.6 cm. Musée d'Orsay, Paris (cat. no. 9.)

perspective that does not really show her to greatest advantage—her prominent nose is slightly red at the tip and her neck is thick. Apart from one youthful drawing inspired by Titian (see fig. 16), Manet was careful to flatter Suzanne by showing her in frontal or three-quarter view, poses highlighting the softness and roundness of her face.[21] It is, therefore, likely that Manet did not appreciate Degas's choice of showing her in profile.

The most notable difference between the two paintings is Manet's choice to represent Suzanne alone, while Degas showed the Manet couple. There may lie the deepest object of the dispute. Before its mutilation, Degas's image was both the only portrait of Suzanne and of the Manet couple painted by the brush of an artist other than Manet himself. Furthermore, Manet painted himself and Suzanne side by side only once, in *Fishing* (cat. no. 6). Wearing fashionable seventeenth-century costume and set in a fantastical Rubenesque landscape, Manet's painting of himself and Suzanne is

distant from the realism of Degas's painting. Degas's work may have outraged Manet with its revelation of a moment of realistic intimacy shared by the couple in their living room. It does not, in fact, show the broader sociability of a musical Thursday soirée but rather focuses on the specific connection between husband and wife.

Despite his mother's hosting evening gatherings, Manet's apartment was principally an intimate domestic space. This contrasted with his studio, which was a place of sociability, in addition to being a place of creation. There, he frequently received friends and colleagues, palette in hand. If his atelier did not appear as such in all of his works, he designed the staging of most of his paintings there—including *Émile Zola* (1868; Musée d'Orsay, Paris), which gives the impression of having been painted in the writer's home. Manet himself appears in a studio at the center of the group in several collective portraits by artists who were among his admirers, such as Henri Fantin-Latour and Frédéric Bazille.[22]

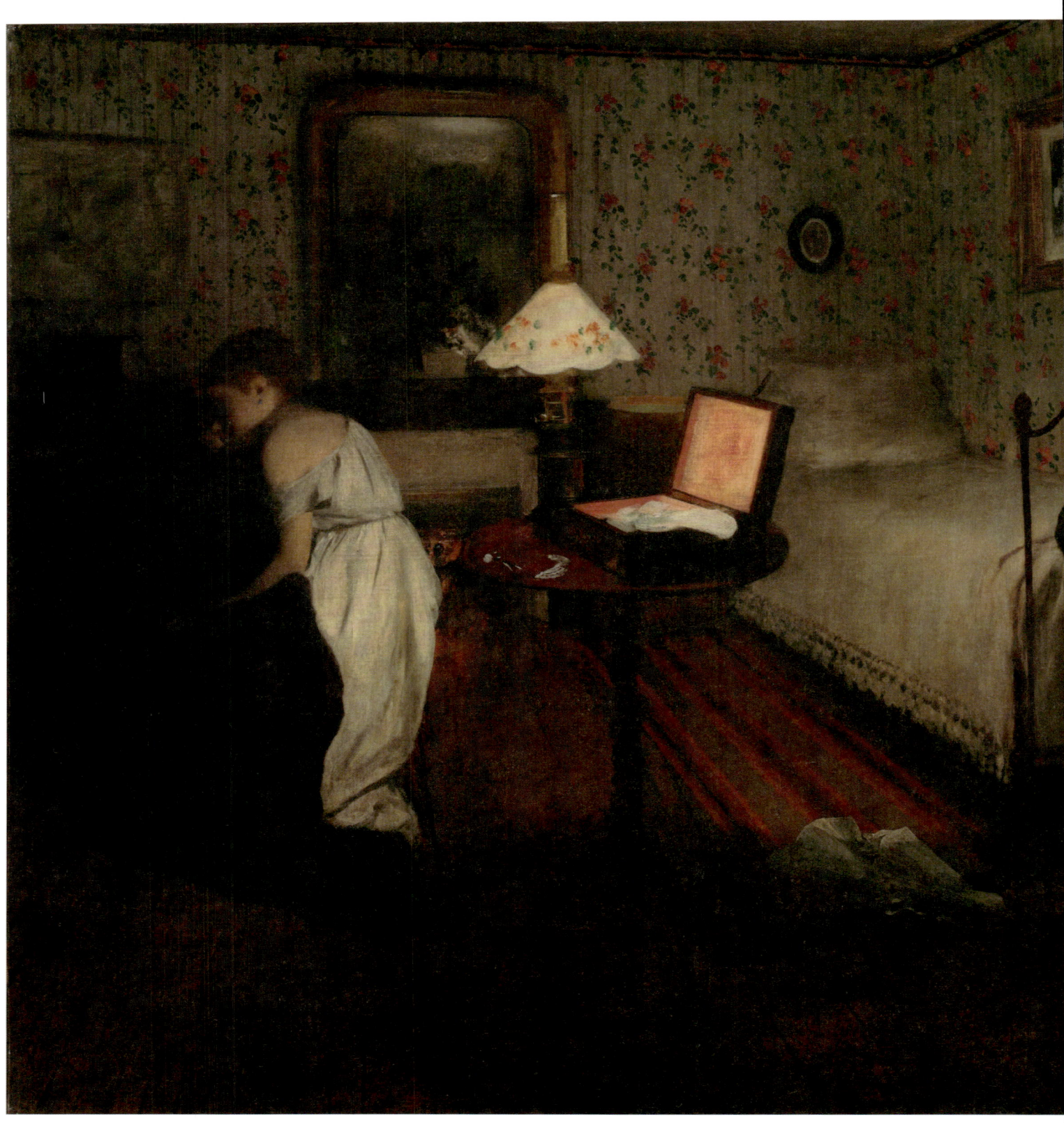

Fig. 48. Edgar Degas, *Interior*, 1868–69. Oil on canvas, 81.3 × 114.3 cm. Philadelphia Museum of Art, The Henry P. McIlhenny Collection in memory of Frances P. McIlhenny, 1986

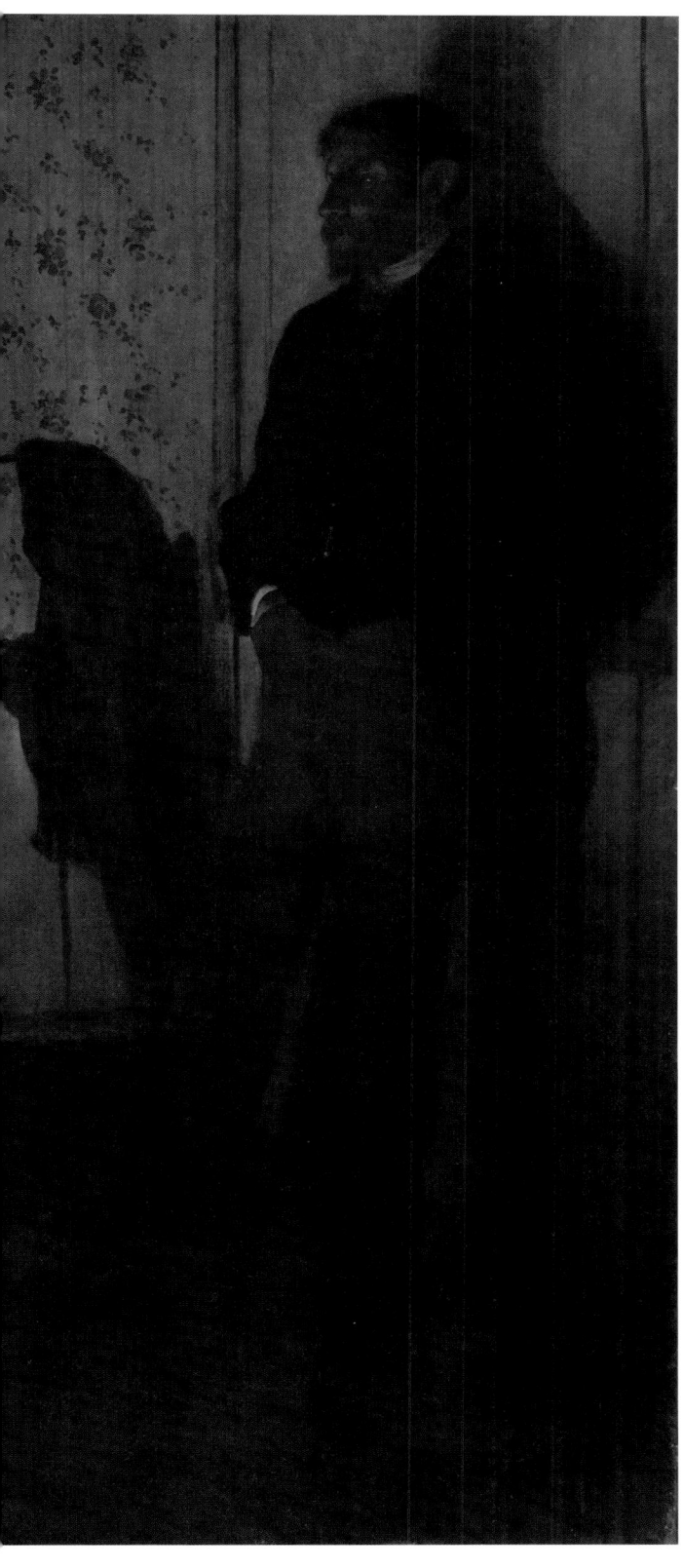

Significantly, Suzanne almost never visited the studio, and her sphere—the r Parisian apartment—rarely appeared in his work.[23] It only served as a setting for family portraits not intended for public exhibition. *Madame Manet at the Piano,* for example, remained in Manet's personal collection. It was exhibited for the first time at the 1884 posthumous exhibition at the École des Beaux-Arts.[24]

The intimacy of Degas's double portrait is also perceptible in the preserved part of the painting. Indeed, Manet appears in a strange pose, quite unconventional for a portrait, that critics have variously described as "curled in a ball," "half-lying," or "slumped on a sofa."[25] His right elbow rests on his folded right leg, his cheek rests on his right hand, his left hand is slipped into his pocket, and we can see his left leg stretched out behind Suzanne's striped skirt. After Manet's death, this posture struck people who were close to the artist as "an attitude strangely habitual to him. Those who knew Manet well cannot look without pain upon this picture; it is something more than a likeness, it is as if you saw the man's ghost."[26] It offers a visible counterpoint to Manet's carefully cultivated public persona, showing him at home only in the company of his wife, whose gentle and reassuring personality tempered his restless nature.[27]

Manet willingly posed for his artist friends, Degas included. (We know of around ten drawings and several engravings by Degas representing Manet alone, in different clothes, places, and attitudes.) If Manet chose to leave this part of the painting ntact, we can assume that the image of him Degas captured did not make him uncomfortable, unlike that of Suzanne. To the extent that the painting of Suzanne has disappeared, we can only hypothesize about what it originally looked like. Her face was likely more expressive than the perfectly posed neutrality in her husband's *Madame Manet at the Piano.* The "distortion of the features of his dear Suzanne"[28] that Manet could not tolerate in the double portrait was therefore not necessarily related to her physical attributes but may have been about Degas's ability to capture the intimate emotion she felt as she interpreted the music.

Degas's image of Suzanne may have seemed like a breach of a possessive right that the artist may have thought of as belonging exclusively to a husband: to depict the image of one's wife. This link between marital status and the right to representation can be seen in the portraits of Berthe Morisot, who was Manet's favorite model from 1869 to 1874. Morisot modeled for him in poses revealing their close friendship and working relationship. When she married his brother Eugène in 1374, Manet stopped painting her, as if her status as a wife made her inaccessible as a model.

Therefore, what may have most perturbed Manet about *Monsieur and Madame Manet* was Degas's ability to capture a moment of domestic intimacy between husband and wife. Specifically, it is an intimacy related to Suzanne's playing the piano—the very talent that brought her into the Manet family's employ and then to Édouard.[29] In some ways, therefore, Degas placed the couple's origin story on display—one that involves the fact that Suzanne worked for the Manets before marrying into the family. It is also an indirect evocation of the origin of their romantic relationship—of the initial seduction—which may have developed around the practice of music. Degas's painting, however, does not show Manet under the spell of his musical wife. Even though Moreau-Nélaton describes Manet as "intoxicated by the enveloping perfume of the melody" played by his wife, "the incomparable pianist," Manet seems somewhat bored or indifferent.[30] He is relaxing on the sofa in an almost lascivious posture reminiscent of the *Barberini Faun*.[31] The way in which a relationship between a man and woman is depicted in this painting even recalls Degas's most disturbing image of a couple: *Interior,* also known as *The Rape* (fig. 48). Painted around the same time, both paintings show a man with a hand in his pocket, staring at the back of a woman.[32] *Interior* is filled with tension and fear, and *Monsieur and Madame Manet* likely showed a complicated mixture of marital intimacy, boredom, and emotion. Painting him alongside his wife, Degas was able to pierce the artist's carefully cultivated public persona and reveal a profoundly private moment. Manet apparently did not like it.

Léon Leenhoff, Paul Achille Legrand, and the Case of Two Godfathers

A study of the links between Manet and Degas and their families must include Léon Koëlla, better known as Léon Leenhoff, Suzanne's son, who was presented in public as her younger brother. He was also Édouard Manet's godson. When he was about fifteen—around the time Degas completed *Monsieur and Madame Édouard Manet*—Léon started working for Degas's father as a stock exchange clerk, probably on the recommendation of Édouard or Suzanne.[33] This first job marked an important stage in Léon's life, a transition from the little boy seen in works from the late 1850s to mid-1860s to the confident dandyish young bourgeois man in *Luncheon in the Studio* (see fig. 7).[34] This passage to adulthood and employment with the De Gas family also coincided with, Tabarant contends, Léon being told "in his

ear" that "his so-called sister, Suzanne, was actually his mother," even before he requested a replacement birth certificate that revealed as much.[35] Considering their closeness to the Manets and the fact that they employed Léon, it is possible that the De Gas knew about this secret.

Just a few years after Léon learned about his own murky parentage, the Manet family structure found an echo of sorts within the De Gas family thanks to the misadventures of Edgar's younger brother, Achille De Gas (1838–1893). Achille was a man whose presence, elegance, and brief time in the navy made him more like Manet than his own elder brother. The mood of an early Degas portrait of Manet (fig. 49) in wash is strikingly similar to the mood of Degas's depiction of Achille in *A Cotton Office in New Orleans* (fig. 50),

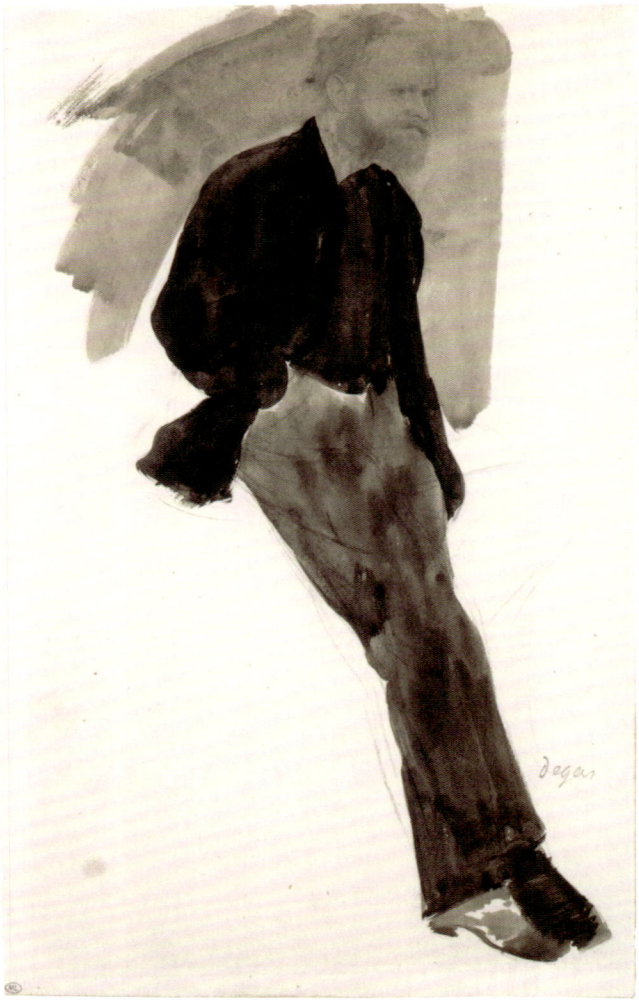

Fig. 49. Edgar Degas, *Édouard Manet*, about 1868. Graphite and India ink wash on paper, 35 × 20 cm. Musée d'Orsay, Paris

Fig. 50. Edgar Degas, *A Cotton Office in New Orleans* (detail), 1873. Oil on canvas, 73 × 92 cm. Musée des Beaux-Arts, Pau

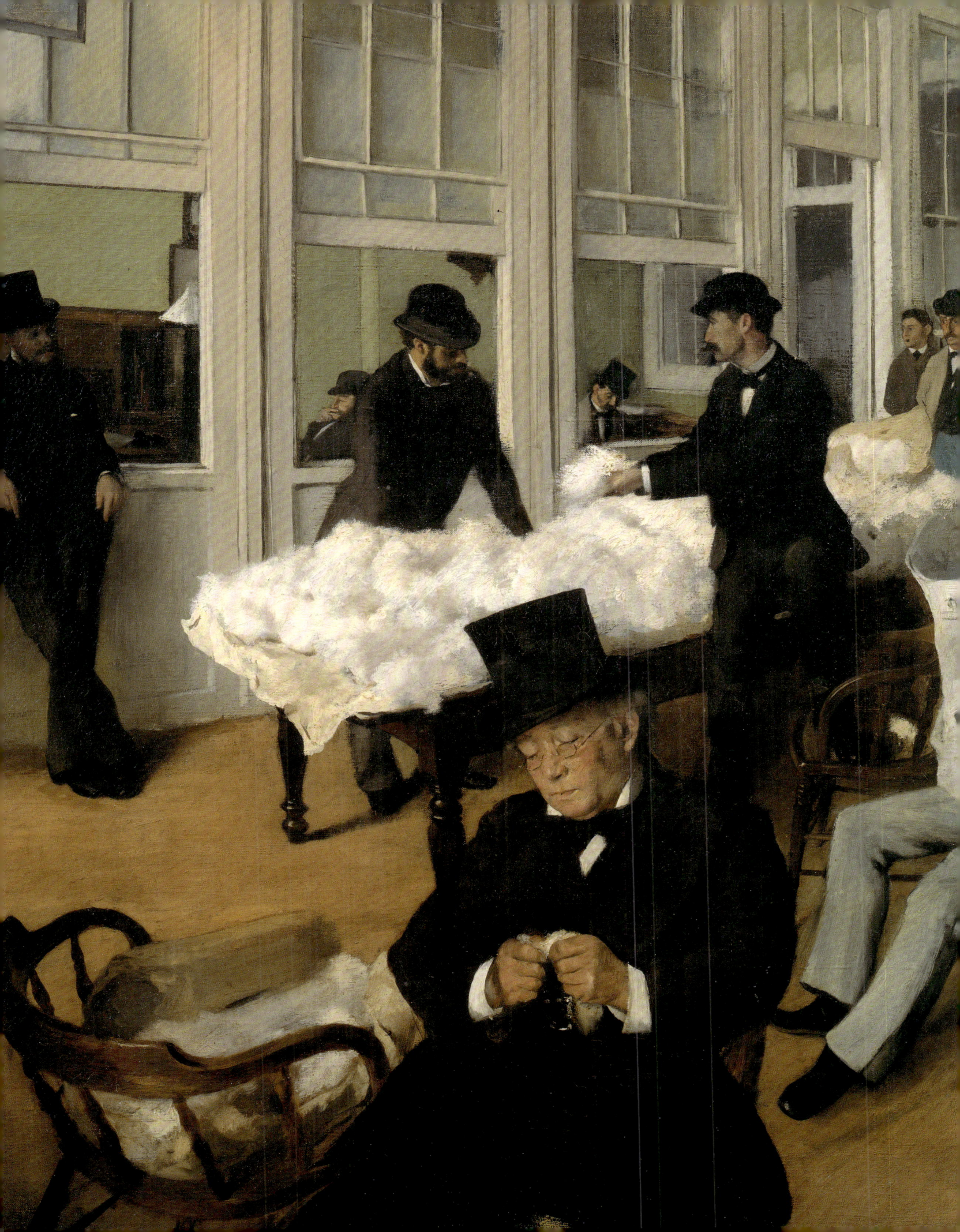

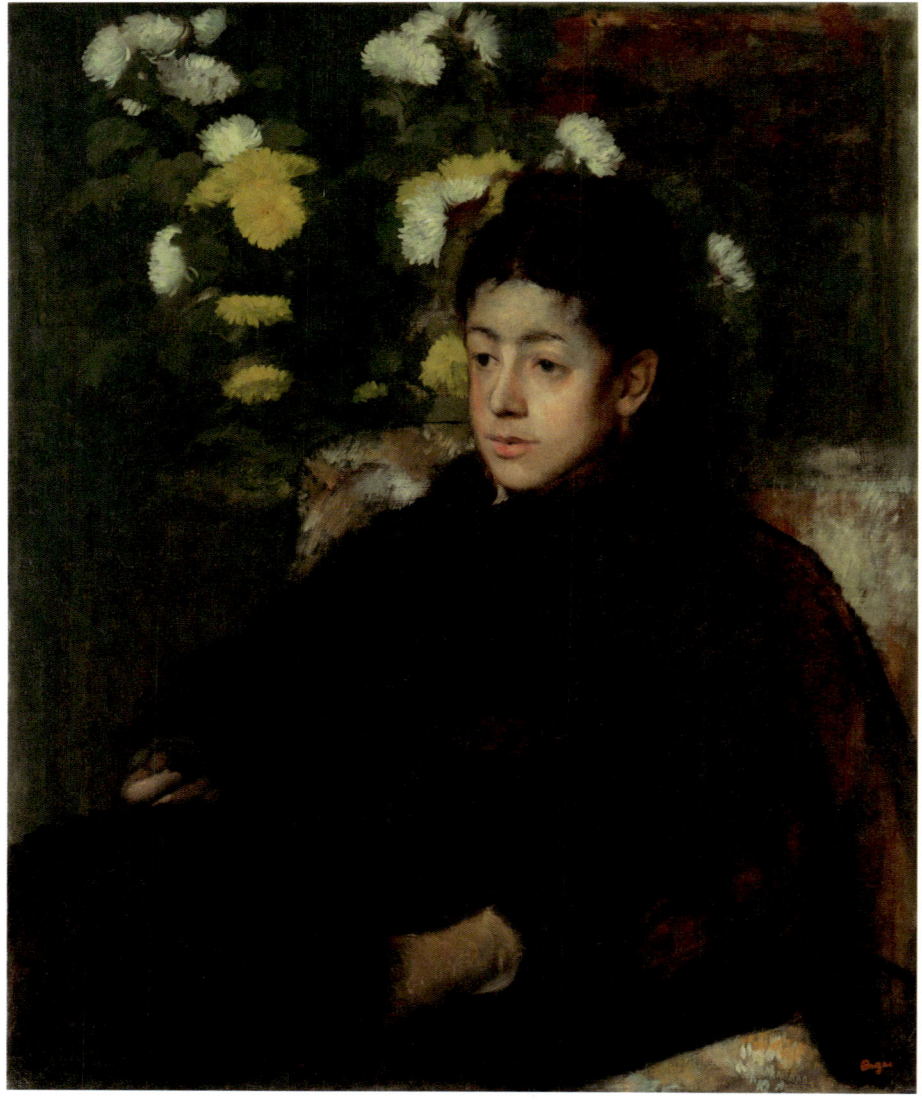

Fig. 51. Edgar Degas, *Mademoiselle Malot*, about 1877. Oil on canvas, 81 × 65 cm. National Gallery of Art, Washington

which he executed during his only stay in the city, between October 1872 and March 1873. A dandy carelessly leaning against a counter, indifferent to the bustle of those around him, Achille expresses through his posture a certain distance vis-à-vis the cotton activity occupying other members of his family. For a period, Achille divided his time between Paris and Louisiana, where he and his brother René created an import-export company in New Orleans in 1866. During this time, he had an affair with a young woman named Augustine Malot, previously a dancer in the *corps de ballet* of the Paris Opéra, whom Edgar portrayed at least five times (fig. 51).[36] On July 2, 1874, Augustine gave birth to a baby boy. The Register of Vital Records specifies that the child, named

Paul Achille, was the son of "Augustine Thérèse Malot, 27 years old, proprietor and unmarried."[37] Although it is stated that the child was born of an "unknown father," Achille De Gas, "thirty-five years old, banker residing in Paris, 28, rue de la Victoire," is a signatory of the declaration of birth. Two successive entries are added to the register in the margin of that declaration. The first indicates that Augustine Malot legally acknowledged the child on July 21, 1874, at the city hall of Paris's seventeenth arrondissement.[38] The second indicates that a man named Georges Victor Legrand, whom Augustine Malot married on September 10, 1874, legally recognized the child on October 23 of the same year. The little boy died a few months later, on March 22, 1875, in the absence of Georges and Augustine, who had gone to Algeria.[39]

The paternity of little Paul Achille is more complex than what is revealed by the Register of Vital Records, as would soon come to light following an incident on August 22, 1875. That day, in front of the Paris stock exchange, Achille De Gas was publicly attacked by Georges Legrand, the husband of his former mistress, who hit him on the head with a cane. Achille retaliated by firing three shots from a revolver, wounding Legrand slightly. Arrested by the police, transferred to Mazas prison, then released on bail, Achille appeared before the Paris criminal court in September 1875. The trial attracted a crowd of curious people, as the incident made the headlines of both the French and international press. The quarrel between the men was a result of a mutual hatred fed by jealousy, disputes about money, and a sense of honor. The trial revealed many details about Achille's private life. The public learned that he was the biological father, as well

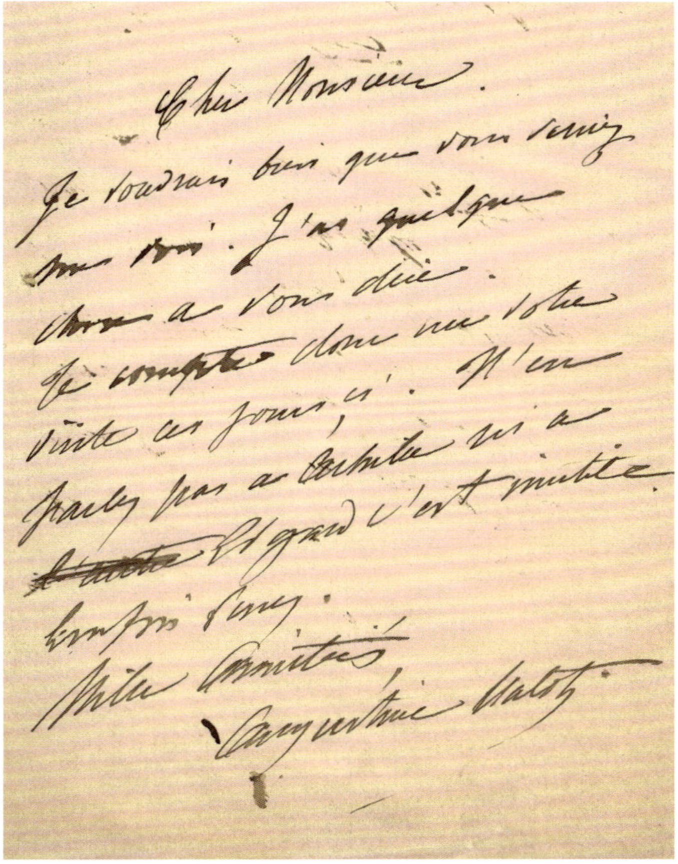

Fig. 52. Augustine Malot to Édouard Manet, about 1874. The Morgan Library & Museum, New York (MA 3950). Purchased as the gift of Mrs. Charles Engelhard and children in memory of Mr. Charles Engelhard, 1974

as having been named the godfather of little Paul Achille, who had died a few months earlier. They also learned that Legrand had only legally recognized the child as his own to please his wife Augustine, when he thought she was dying.[40] Achille had set up an insurance policy of 25,000 francs for his natural son, payable to his mother when he reached majority. Upon the child's death, several payments were made: Achille gave Augustine a sum of 2,000 francs, while an insurance premium of 800 francs was collected by Legrand. The reporting on the relationship between Augustine and Achille was the first time the Degas name was associated publicly with the world of dance and the opera, in the form of a liaison between a banker and a dancer, the image so emblematic of Edgar Degas's later works.

The incident seems to have affected Manet more than one might expect. He attended the highly publicized trial. As one journalist remarked: "When we arrived, we saw the room of the 9th chamber absolutely full. There were, however, few well-known people: we only notice Mr. Manet."[41] Why did Manet insist on being present? First, he knew two of the protagonists. He was friendly with Achille, and a letter preserved at the Morgan Library reveals that Manet was also close to Augustine Malot. This letter (fig. 52), addressed to Manet by the young woman on an unknown date (necessarily before Augustine's marriage, since she signs it with her maiden name) contains the following words written in a nervous script: "Dear sir, I would like you to come to see me. I have something to tell you. I'm counting on your visit these days. Do not talk to Achille or the other Edgard [sic], it is useless. Do come. A thousand regards. Augustine Malot."[42]

This missive testifies to how Manet played the role of trusted confidant who could conceal information from the De Gas brothers. It also suggests that Manet had previously paid one or more visits to the young woman whose home on the rue de Chazelles was next to his studio on the rue Guyot. Could this mysterious revelation be related to her future motherhood? And was her choice to confide in Manet linked to his family situation? The complex relationships surrounding baby Paul Achille was reminiscent of aspects of Léon's particular situation. The choice to give Paul Achille his natural father's first name as a middle name—as well the decision to name the natural father as the child's godfather—is particularly interesting in light of the fact that Léon's full name was Léon Édouard and Édouard Manet was named his godfather. The circumstances of Legrand's recognition of Paul-Achille are notable. Unsure of the boy's paternity, he legitimized him two months after his marriage to Augustine. She was gravely ill. His recognition likely allayed her concerns for her son's

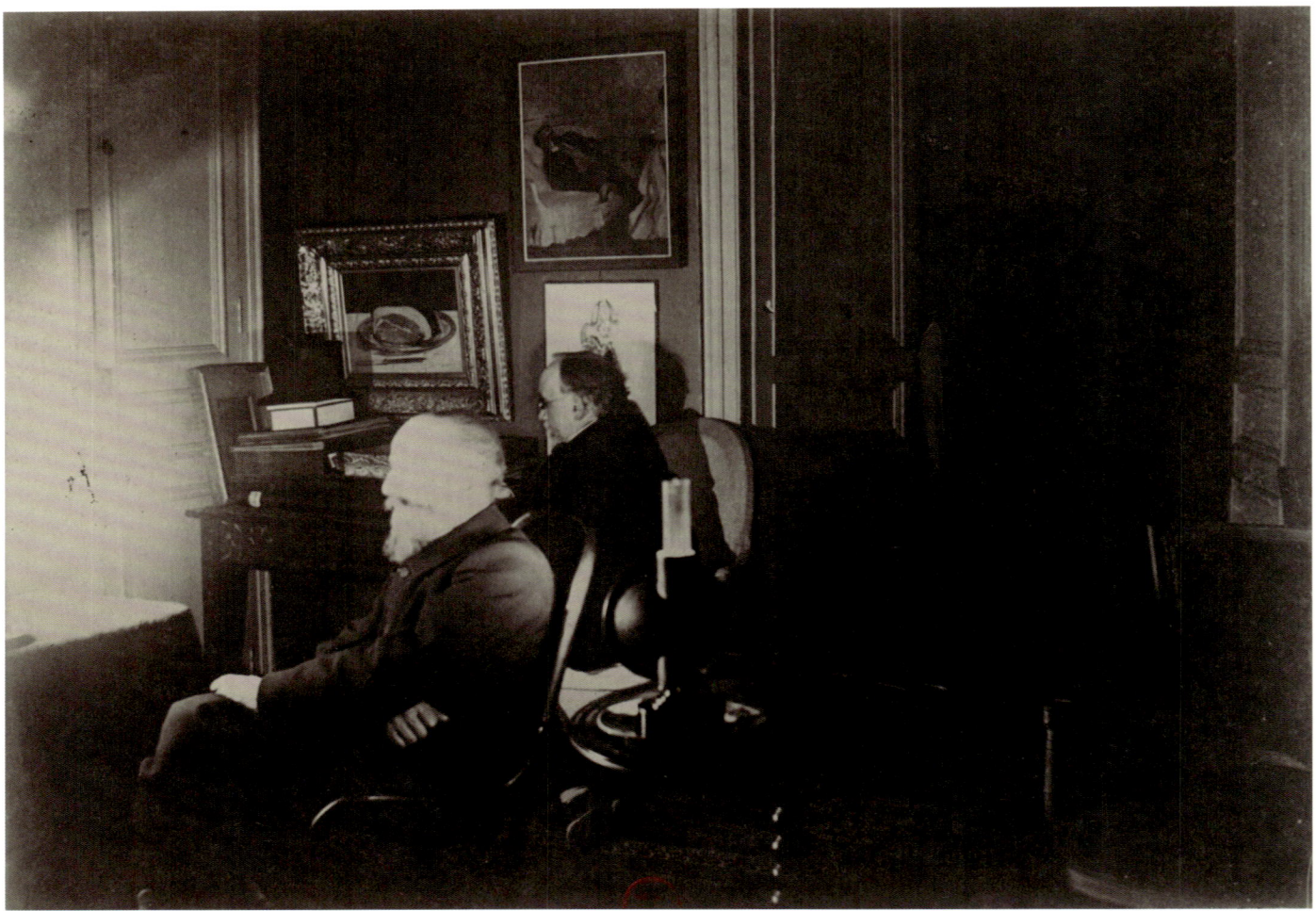

Fig. 53. Edgar Degas, *Self-Portrait with Paul Albert Bartholomé*, in the Salon of Degas, showing the portrait of Édouard and Suzanne Manet (fig. 45) on the wall, 1895. Contretype, 8.9 × 12.9 cm. Bibliothèque Nationale de France, Paris, Département des Estampes et de la Photographie

future. Regardless of paternity, a husband could easily recognize his wife's natural child. Manet could have done this for Léon and reassured Suzanne about his future. The failure to legitimize Léon suggests a compelling reason—perhaps a family secret—for not undertaking this simple but important act.

One can observe that the two artists did not seek to erase the presence in their work of people whose uncertain status could disrupt the family order. Léon Leenhoff is thus one of Manet's favorite models, from early childhood to adulthood, while Degas represented Mademoiselle Malot on at least five occasions—a frequency of depictions second only to certain members of his family. These portraits, produced in various media always show her in an identical pose, suggesting that Degas was able to create—almost obsessively—several variations within the same mold. One of these works *Portrait of a Woman* (1877; Detroit Institute of

Art), was probably reworked several years later. It shows the model with aging features, as if the artist had projected forward in time—imagining the future of his brother's former mistress, who had left such a public mark in the history of the De Gas family. With one exception, Degas kept all of his portraits of Malot until his death. This choice suggests that he did not consider the presence of his model as disgraceful or disturbing the family order. A drawing of her was bequeathed to Jeanne Fèvre, the artist's niece, who sold it in 1934 noting the identity of the young woman and her talent as a dancer at the Opéra.

"Never Get Married"

In the case of Mademoiselle Malot, one wonders if Degas's attachment to her portraits can be explained by the attachment he felt toward the model. The same question arises for Suzanne Manet. Although little is known about the nature of their relationship, Degas remained in touch with Suzanne after Manet's death. She sometimes acted as an intermediary for people who wanted to meet the famed, aging, and occasionally socially awkward artist.[43] Stating his deceased friend "was greater [*plus grand*] than we thought," Degas was at Manet's funeral and participated in the banquet organized at Père Lathuille's by Léon Leenhoff to honor the late artist.[44] Most important, through his activities as a collector, Degas posthumously continued this relationship with Manet. Images of Suzanne became a notable feature of Degas's exceptional collection.

First and foremost, there was his own destroyed painting, taken back from Manet following the latter's mutilation of the canvas. It appears hanging on the wall of his living room in an 1895 photographic self-portrait (fig. 53) where he poses alongside his friend, the artist Albert Bartholomé. In a studied staging, the cut double portrait of the Manet couple appears just above Degas's head; it is flanked by two other Manet works from his collection.[45] The fragmentary canvas was tightly framed.[46] The lower and right edges were folded so Suzanne's face is barely visible and her presence is reduced to "a piece of skirt."[47] This painting was probably hung not long before the photo was taken because it was around the same time that Julie Manet describes how she discovered this portrait of her late "Uncle Édouard" in Degas's salon.[48] At some point between 1895 and 1906,[49] Degas had "a piece of straight canvas added, with the intention of repainting the missing half of Madame Manet."[50] This project—described as an attempt to "*rétablir Madame Manet pour lui rendre son portrait*" (roughly translated as restoring Madame Manet to return her to her portrait)—was never completed.[51] The painting, as we know it today, was in his studio when he died in 1917.[52]

Perhaps because of his ambition to *rétablir* Suzanne in his own painting, Degas acquired several of Manet's works depicting his wife, including two oils, one pastel, and one drawing.[53] The drawing, acquired after Manet's death, was described in his handwritten notes as "Naked woman" (likely for a *Suzanne*, see fig. 19).[54] Degas also almost certainly owned *Study for Moses Saved from the Waters* (cat. no. 4). Having only recently reappeared on the art market, this painting is not mentioned in Degas's handwritten notes about his collection.[55] However, it appears in the 1927 estate sale of René De Gas, who probably inherited it from his brother

under the title "Maternity Study."[56] Either because of an error on the part of art experts or as a result of family lore, the painting was marketed in that sale as a work by Degas instead of Manet. This portrait of Suzanne posthumously reunited the two artists in an unexpected way, to the point of confusing them as the maker of the work.

The two other images Degas owned of Suzanne echo Manet's famed *Olympia*—though without the explicitly erotic energy—and were acquired around 1895 (fig. 54).[57] The first is a "sketch [*ebauche*]" where Suzanne is "seated, in a pink dress . . . with a black cat on her lap"[58] (see fig. 27) and the second is a pastel where Suzanne, lying on a blue sofa, wears a "white dress, a white country straw hat, and a black bow" (see fig. 28).[59] In his description of this work, Degas identifies the "interior and furniture of the small salon of the rue de Saint-Pétersbourg."[60] This was the same room that is the setting for the mutilated *Monsieur and Madame Manet*, with the same sofa, though here devoid of its white cover. This pastel also hung in 1895 in Degas's salon, not far from the slashed image.[61] In that position, it served as a stand-in or a response to the destruction: Suzanne has taken Manet's place lying on the sofa.[62] Perhaps the jubilant prospect of such a rapprochement was the cause of Degas's almost lusty eagerness to acquire the pastel.[63] The art critic Arsène Alexandre remembered having seen Degas "agitated like a young man about his first love . . . of the fear of seeing this ravishing pastel of *Madame Manet on a Blue Sofa* escape from him."[64] Perhaps, in this commentary, there is a hint of another motive for Manet's "revenge" against Degas's picture; he may have been aggravated by his friend's possible attraction to Suzanne.[65]

Another cut painting constitutes an important piece of the enigma of the relationship between Manet, his wife, and Degas: *The Execution of Maximilian* by Manet (1867–68; National Gallery, London). The work was in fragments, because, as Degas mentions in his notes about his collection, "This painting remained long rolled in Gennevilliers at Mme Manet's home, was cut and sectioned, in all probability by Leenhoff, her brother."[66] It is unclear if Degas was referring to one of Suzanne's artist brothers—Ferdinand and Rudolf—or to Léon, who continued to be called her brother even after she legally recognized him as her son.[67] Regardless of which Leenhoff was guilty, Degas confided to Vollard about the cutting of this canvas: "What a misfortune, can you believe it, they dared to cut this painting! It was the family that did it! Never get married."[58] This was the lament of an old bachelor accustomed to mending works cut by Manets.

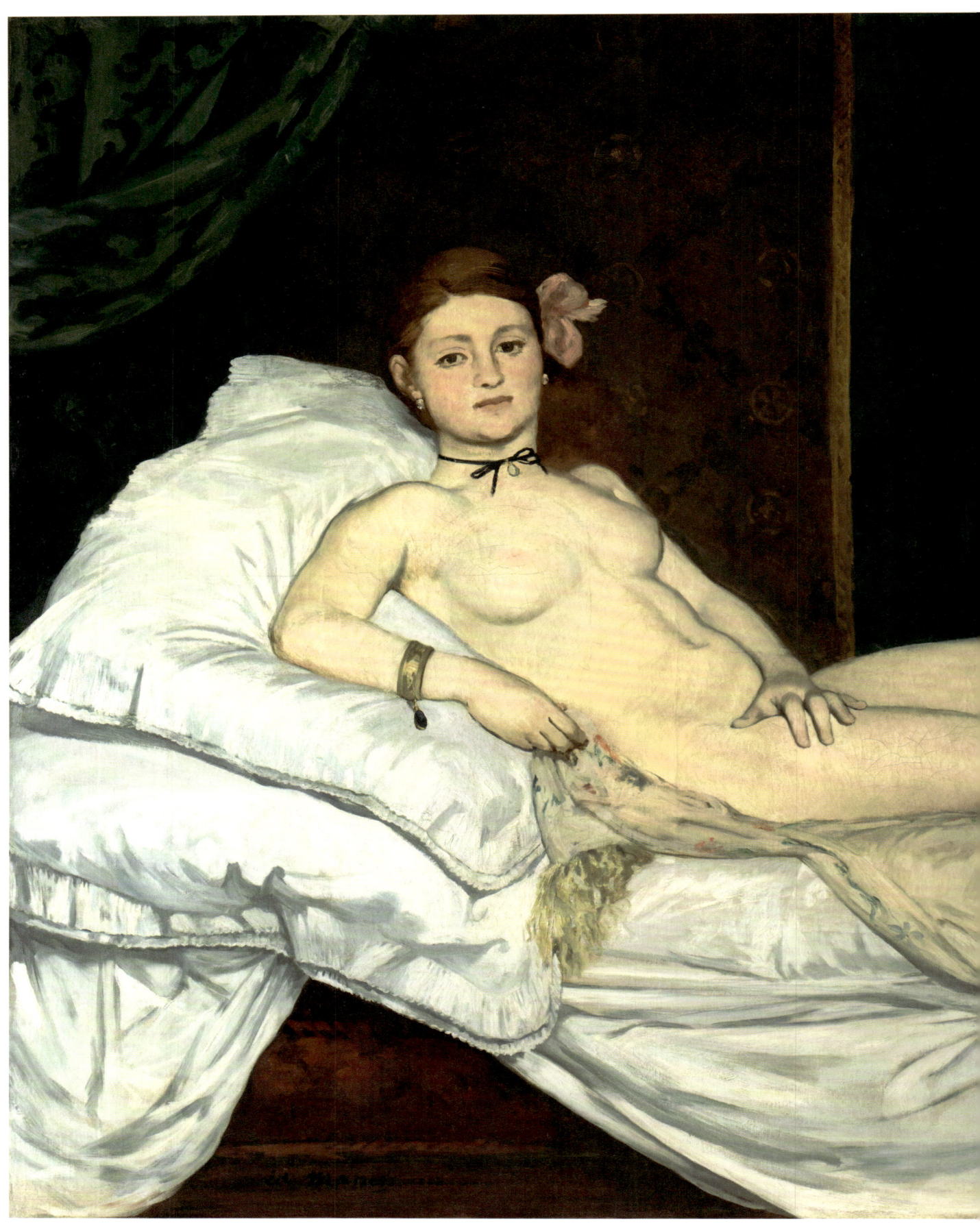

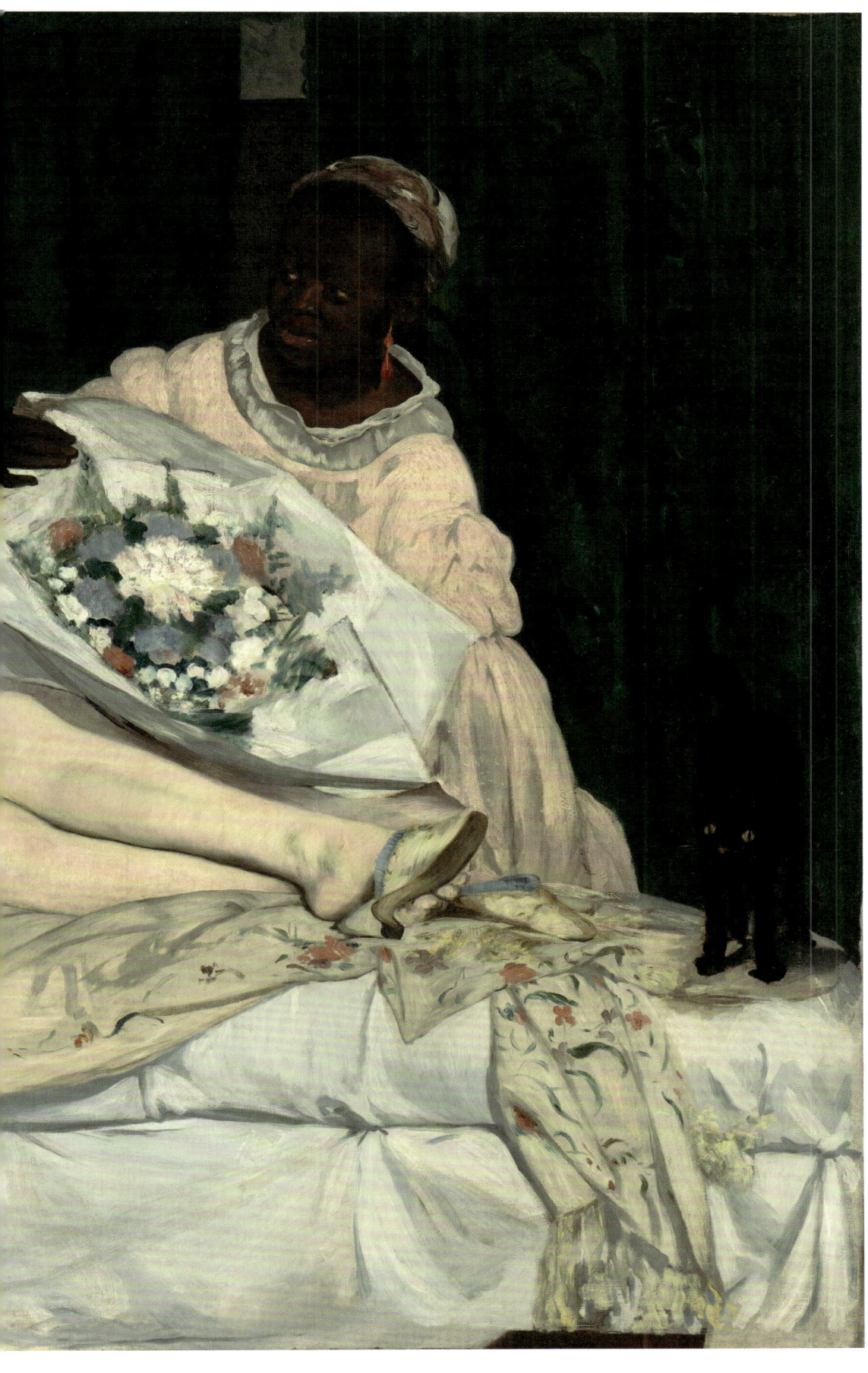

Fig. 54. Édouard Manet, *Olympia*,
1863. Oil on canvas, 130.5 × 191 cm.
Musée d'Orsay, Paris

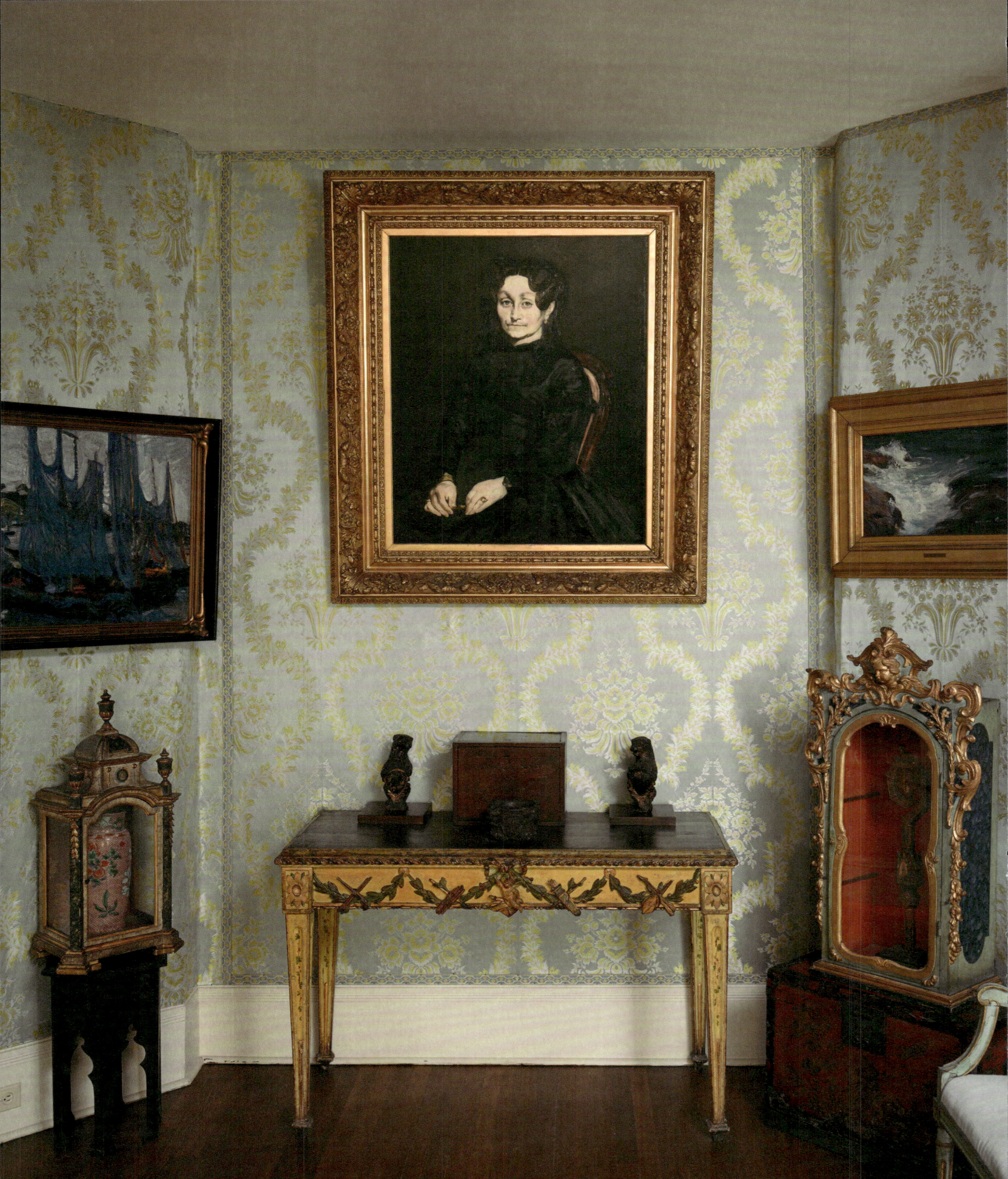

Madame Auguste Manet and the Painting of Modern Life

NANCY LOCKE

When Émile Zola was creating his twenty-volume Rougon-Macquart cycle of novels about modern French society and its range of problems, he wrote in his notebook, "Histoire naturelle et sociale d'une famille au XIXe Siècle [The natural and social history of a family in the nineteenth century]."[1] The key to Zola's sweeping exposé of modernity was not alcoholism, prostitution, speculation, or another specifically modern iteration of a social problem but the complex history of a family. Although the "painting of modern life" (so named by Charles Baudelaire) is often thought of as the painting of various subjects deemed to be modern—cafés, boulevards, suburban leisure—perhaps it would be better conceived as painting in which the modern family is central. Family members populate the work of Édouard Manet, from the inclusion of his brother and brother-in-law in *Le Déjeuner sur l'herbe* (see fig. 84), to the artist's own appearance with his wife-to-be, Suzanne Leenhoff, and her son, Léon, in *Fishing* (cat. no. 6). In fact, painting the modern and painting the family seem to be, for Manet, one and the same.

Madame Auguste Manet (cat. no. 1) shows Eugénie-Désirée Fournier (1811–1885) as a widow. It is Manet's most concentrated representation of his mother, who had already posed for the double portrait *Monsieur and Madame Auguste Manet* (cat. no. 3). In this essay, I propose to look at *Madame Auguste Manet* as exemplifying Manet's vision of the painting of modern life. Described by Bernard Berenson as "a colossal thing" but not much discussed in the Manet literature, the painting can properly be seen as possessing the essential qualities that characterize Manet's art as a whole.[2] I will also look at the exhibition history of the painting in the early

twentieth century, at the time when Berenson acquired it on behalf of Isabella Stewart Gardner.

In *Madame Auguste Manet* Eugénie appears in widow's black; Manet's father had passed away on September 25, 1862. The fact that she wears some simple gold jewelry and the veil is behind her head rather than covering her face, allows the viewer to surmise that at least a year had passed since his death. During the first year of mourning for widows, *le grand deuil austère*, face and hair were to be covered, and no jewelry was to be worn; during the next six months, pieces made of jet were permissible.[3] Eugénie's black belt buckle typifies the jet accessories worn by widows in the second year of mourning. Her black dress, with its hint of sheen and its understated trim, also signals mourning after the first six months, as shinier fabrics would have been avoided.[4] The dress otherwise exemplifies the fashions of the 1860s, with its sloping shoulder, high waist, and full skirt.

Eugénie's coiffure also suggests that the portrait was made some time after the first six months of high mourning, as it would have been proper for a widow to cover her hair completely during that time. In the portrait, rows of curled hair above her ears and parallel with her cheekbone can be seen out in front of the black veil that drapes onto her shoulders. According to Léon, Eugénie continued to wear her hair in the style fashionable in the 1830s and 1840s.[5] One can see a similar hairstyle on Maria Amalia of Naples and Sicily, who became Queen of France during the July Monarchy, in her portrait by Franz Xaver Winterhalter (fig. 55).[6] Comparing *Madame Auguste Manet* with the more formal, but bloodless, portrait of the queen by Winterhalter reveals just how

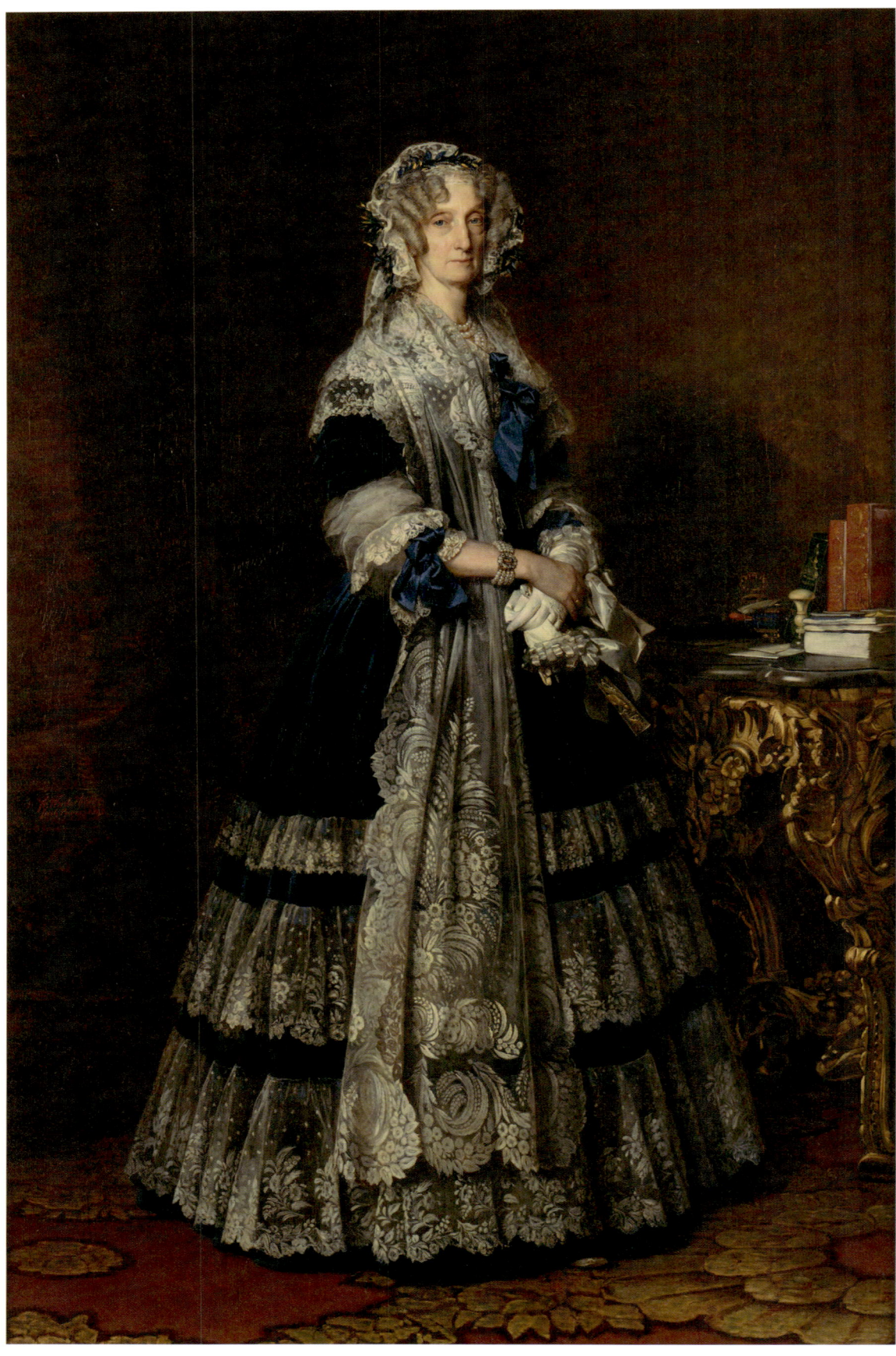

Fig. 55. Franz Xaver Winterhalter, *Maria Amalia of Naples and Sicily, Queen of France*, 1842. Oil on canvas, 215 × 140 cm. Château de Versailles et de Trianon, Versailles

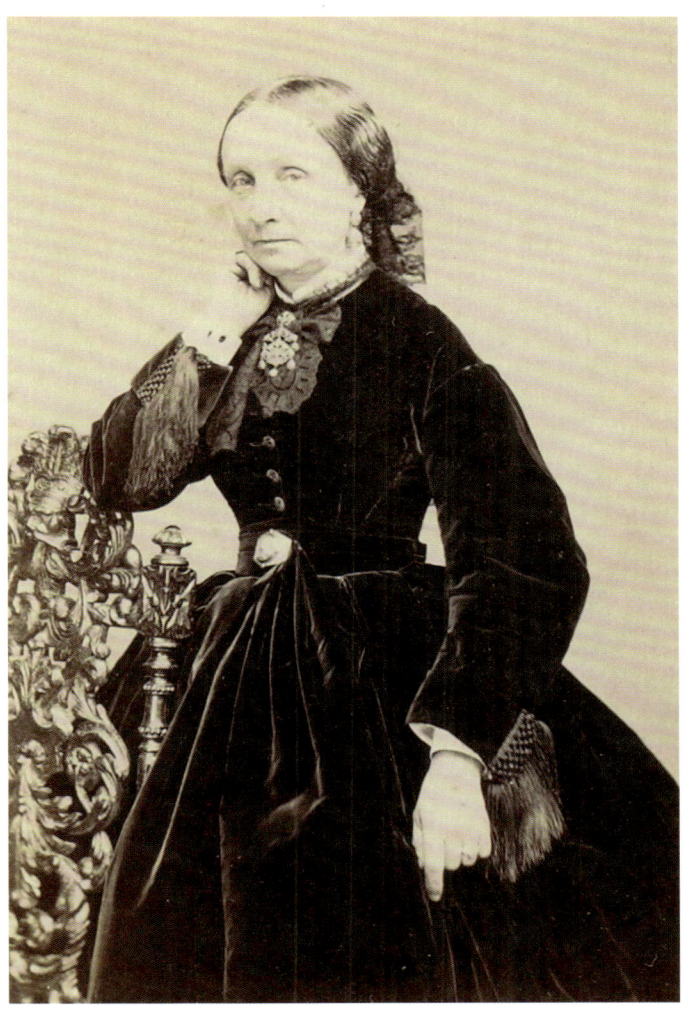

Fig. 56. Charles Amédée Barenne, Eugénie-Désirée Fournier (Madame Auguste Manet), from *Album of Cartes-de-Visite Portraits Belonging to Édouard Manet*, about 1857–62. Carte-de-visite, 9.2 × 5.6 cm. Bibliothèque Nationale de France, Paris

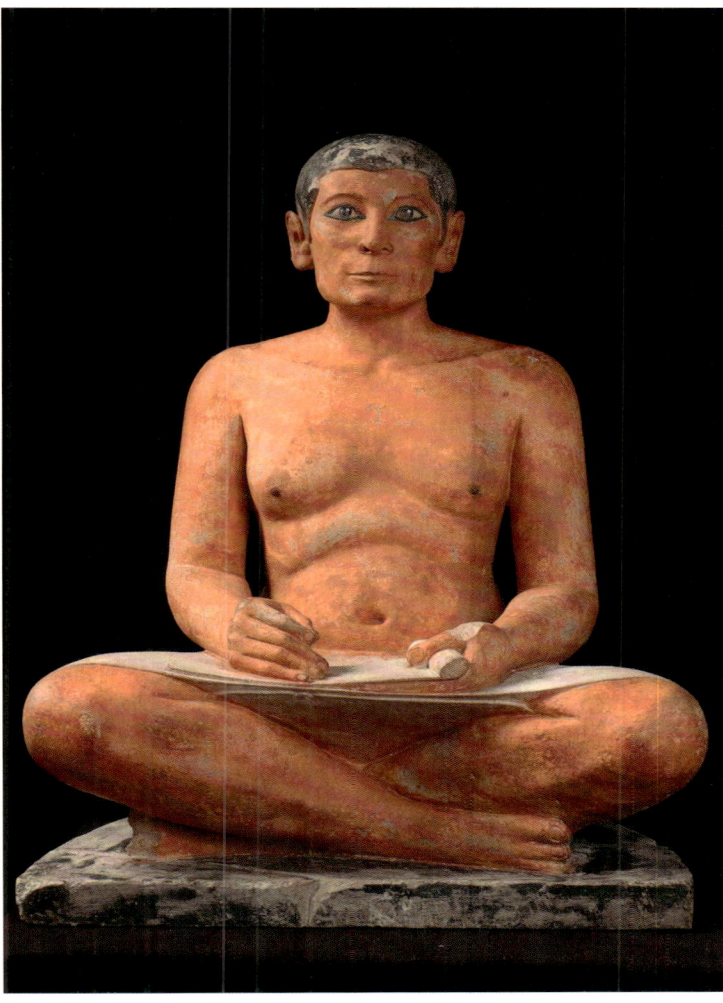

Fig. 57. Egyptian, Saqqara-Nord, *Seated Scribe*, 2620–2500 BCE. Limestone with alabaster, rock crystal, and copper, 53.7 × 44 × 35 cm. Musée du Louvre, Paris

powerful, and indeed startling, Manet's painting becomes when the viewer comes face to face with it.

It is the arresting gaze of Madame Auguste Manet that remains one of the painting's most forceful elements. Her figure is life-size, and Manet silhouettes the light color of her face and hands against her black dress, black veil, and dark background. Her expression resembles the one she displayed in a carte-de-visite portrait in an album belonging to Édouard Manet; the photograph had probably been taken a few years earlier (fig. 56).[7] The subtle turn of her head, the straight line of her lips, the softness of an older woman's jawline, all are quite similar between painting and photograph. Yet, the expression that might be described as pensive in the carte-de-visite, lightened by the slight over-

exposure of the face in relation to the black velvet dress worn in the photograph, takes on more gravitas in Manet's imposing painting. Manet's painterly handling of every facial feature—the creases at the corners of her mouth, the cleft in her chin, the arch of her eyebrows, and the emphatic shadows around her eyelids—not only accentuates shadows that are minimized in the photograph but also emphasizes the fleshiness of the sitter. As is often the case with Manet's figural subjects, there is a slight asymmetry in his approach to Eugénie's eyes. Manet positions the eye on the viewer's left just a bit higher than the eye on the right; the more spherical left eye looks out more forcefully in the viewer's direction, whereas the right eye appears more receptive to the viewer's gaze. Manet allows traces of the hairs of the brush to imitate eyebrows or the downy hair on the sides of the face and to call attention to the painterliness of the work as a whole. No wonder Berenson wrote to Isabella Stewart Gardner, the "drawing is of the surest, the touch most vigorous," and compared it to the *Seated Scribe* in the Louvre, an Old Kingdom ancient Egyptian sculpture of a figure with a similarly serious expression, hands in lap (fig. 57).[8] Berenson's comparison of Manet's oil painting to an ancient sculpture of the somber scribe might accentuate the starkness of each, but it also brought home the indelible modernity of Manet's figure.

When one hears the word "modernity," what often comes to mind is an image emanating from somewhere else, like something seen in an advertisement or a poster, or the latest hemline or dress style from a designer or couturier. Manet loved clothes and was acutely aware of fashion, but I do not think he thought of modernity that way. Modernity, for Manet, is not merely glimpsed in a magazine or a shop window; modernity is the here and now, and we bear the imprint of it the way we inevitably reveal the march of years on our faces and bodies. For Manet, we are social beings, and we intersect with modernity, wittingly or unwittingly. Eugénie dons a black veil, black dress, and black belt because she is in mourning—gone is the white bonnet with wide blue ribbon she wore in the double portrait; in *Madame Auguste Manet* there is no white collar or brooch, no full white sleeve like the one that she sported in the portrait alongside her husband. Is she pushing the boundaries of propriety with her gold bracelet and the hint of color in her drop earrings? Perhaps—it is hard to imagine that every widow adhered to period etiquette one hundred percent of the time. Is her hairstyle more 1840s than 1860s? Yes, but she was probably not the only elegant woman in her early fifties clinging to a hairstyle that harkened back to the way she wore her hair in the early years of her marriage. An 1860s dress with an 1840s hairstyle was simply how some of us lived now; that, too, was modernity.

The poet and critic Baudelaire had already written about the modernity of mourning attire in his "Salon of 1846" when he noted that his own contemporaries wore black: "Is it not the necessary garb of our suffering age, which wears the symbol of a perpetual mourning even upon its thin black shoulders?"[9] Baudelaire advocated for artists to find "modern beauty and modern heroism" in contemporary life rather than in the historical subjects that occupied most artists at the annual Salons.[10] He expressed disappointment that when artists did set out to paint contemporary life, they often "contented themselves with public and official subjects." "However," he observed, "there are private subjects which are very much more heroic than these."[11] Like Zola's

description of his novelistic project, Baudelaire's intimations of the "painting of modern life" in 1846 point toward representations of mourning and of private subjects. Madame Auguste Manet in mourning—dressed in black from head to toe, and no longer accepting many social invitations—would seem to be the emblem of a Baudelairean modernity.[12] "We are each of us celebrating some funeral," he asserted.[13]

Manet exhibited a *Portrait of Mme M . . . . . .* when he held his solo exhibition on the Avenue de l'Alma during the 1867 Exposition Universelle, and Léon Leenhoff maintained that this work was the portrait of Manet's mother.[14] *Madame Auguste Manet* stayed in the family during the lifetimes of Eugénie, who died in 1885, and Suzanne Manet, who died in 1906. In 1909 Léon sold the painting to a dealer in London, from whom Bernard Berenson purchased it on behalf of Isabella Stewart Gardner in 1910.

Gardner had been interested in acquiring a painting by Manet, and the museum's archives include an article describing the portrait of Manet's mother that Berenson had clipped and sent to the collector (fig. 58).[15] The article from *The Nation* was inventoried by the museum as concerning the exhibition of the painting at the Imperial International Exhibition, or World's Fair, at the White City in London in 1909. The painting exhibition at that fair was, in fact, quite limited and not a Salon-style national or international survey.[16] The article Berenson sent to Gardner actually describes an exhibition in February and March of 1909 called "Fair Women," held at the Royal Academy (the New Gallery, 121 Regent Street, London). This exhibition, held by the International Society of Sculptors, Painters and Gravers, included works by the Spanish artist Francisco de Goya, eighteenth-century British artists like Thomas Gainsborough and Sir Joshua Reynolds, Victorian artists including John Everett Millais and George Frederic Watts, society painters such as François Flameng and Giovanni Boldini, woodblock prints by Kitagawa Utamaro and Suzuki Harunobu, and nineteenth-century French artists from Jean-Baptiste-Camille Corot to Gustave Courbet, including Impressionists Pierre-Auguste Renoir, Berthe Morisot, and Mary Cassatt. It was well covered in the French and British press.[17] Critics in fact produced some lucid and perceptive commentary on Manet's striking work, and for students of Manet who are accustomed to the insults lobbed at him during his lifetime, it is satisfying to read these more reasoned critiques. A look at this substantial body of criticism illuminates the context for Berenson and Gardner's purchase in 1909.

Most critics had at least a few words to say about the way the portrait exemplified Manet's "realism," even if just to cept his Eve of St. Agnes, though what it is doing in a collection of Fair Women, it is hard to say. His few portraits of a later period, though of no great importance, are painted with a knowledge and a freshness that make many near canvases look muddy and fumbling, while in one, the portrait of his daughter, there is a bunch of flowers so delicate and subtle in handling that, by comparison, the more ambitious details of other painters seem vulgar and crude. For Millais was accomplished technically, if he often fell away from his own high standard. Studies by Leighton, careful but uninspired, early portraits by Watts, of Lady Holland and Ellen Terry as a girl, complete the work of any note by British artists of their generation. It has so little in common with anything else in the gallery that you might think it was there solely to prove how slight was its effect upon the art of England or the art of the world.

It is another thing with the contemporaries of these men in France, who also believed in the return to nature which the Pre-Raphaelites preached, but did not know how to practise. Courbet stood in no need of Primitives, or of anybody, to show him the way to nature. He used his own eyes and would have been the last to content himself by substituting a new convention for an old. Only one of his pictures is exhibited, Jeunes Fille cueillant des fleures but in it you have an example of pure realism, of nature studied for herself, and you find that robust quality which only this intimate, intelligent study of nature will give. The young girl is solidly and vigorously painted, but she stands to one side as if trying to efface herself, and not distract attention from the mass—the avalanche—of flowers filling the rest of the canvas, put down in all their delicacy and fragility of form, in all their vividness and tenderness of color, but with a breadth that shames the tedious little photographic details of the Pre-Raphaelites. This is really a study of nature, not an inventory; and though the picture is not so typical of Courbet as some of his more famous canvases, it explains what "going to nature" and "realism" meant to the school of which he was the prophet.

A Whistler hangs beside the Courbet, and a second fills a centre in the same gallery. This is the Symphony in White No. III, too often seen of recent years to need description. It has artistic interest, apart from its own beauty, as the first picture he exhibited as a Symphony, and marks, therefore, his complete emancipation from Courbet. The other Whistler is The Gold Girl, the portrait of Connie Gilchrist, who, with her skipping rope, was a music-hall celebrity. I have never thought it one of Whistler's finest compositions, and it was never quite finished. The difficulties for a painter, so dependent on his model, were great, for he wanted to show the dancer in the art of skipping, and succeeded really only in rendering arrested movement. But the lines of the lithe girlish figure are of the utmost grace, the folds of the curtain behind her carry out most wonderfully the curves of the rope, while the golds of this curtain and the girl's dress, just broken by the effective little touches of red in the handles of the rope, make as beautiful a harmony as he ever created. There is, however, a heaviness in the background, which, together with the failure to suggest action in the figure, just keeps it from being the masterpiece it ought to be. But both these pictures explain the aims and achievement of the painter who was destined to be a stronger influence during the last half-century even than Courbet.

There is only one Manet, the portrait of his mother, a half-length, not exhibited, I am told, since 1867. It is an extraordinary performance, a piece of realism if there ever was one. The mother, elderly but not yet old, is sitting, her hands in her lap. She wears black, her hair is black, and is arranged in tight puffs on either side of her face in the fashion for elderly ladies of her day, and over it is the black cap the Frenchwoman of her age and class is still so likely to wear. Her face is plain, the eyes prominent, the beginning of a black moustache on the upper lip. Thus she was seen in life, thus you see her on canvas, and by the sheer strength of the realism and the vigor of the painting, she is so alive, so abounding in vitality and character, that the near portraits fade into phantoms. She has the supreme beauty of ugliness that you find in some Rembrandts—not a Fair, but a Real, Woman, whom you would not exchange for a whole gallery full of modern attempts at prettiness or eccentricity.

I dwell upon these three men because there is no question—to me—that they have had more effect upon art than any artists of the last century.

In the Sculpture Hall, space has been made for a fine show of Alfred Gilbert's work. The collection is representative, including some of his most distinguished portrait busts, statuettes, part of the tomb for the Duke of Clarence, jewelry, and official badges, chains, and seals. In fact, an excellent opportunity is given for the study of the work of the most distinguished English sculptor. The effort has also been made to get together a characteristic collection of the work of Charles Conder, who died shortly before the show opened. Conder had a charming decorative sense within certain limits. He could decorate a fan delightfully, his silk panels were dainty, he painted shawls, even dresses with a graceful gaiety. But his charm was chiefly in his color and in the quality he got from the silk upon which so much of his work was done. But most of the pictures now exhibited are of figure subjects and reveal his weakness as a draughtsman, especially when he attempted to draw or paint the nude.

N. N.

The Ways and Means Committee would have found it hard to explain any smaller liberality than has been displayed in revising the art tariff. Against the present virtually prohibitive tax, every hand has been turned save only that of the Philistine who believes that every expensive thing is a luxury, and therefore ought to be discouraged. Travel and wider familiarity with the great public and private collections of our own country have taught Americans the use of beautiful things and broken the older backwoods philosophy of art, which fitted so neatly into the Republican scheme of protection. We may now hope to be enriched by the wonderful treasures of the eye which Mr. Morgan and other connoisseurs have stored up in Europe. But even if the greatest American collections abroad are not brought in, tourists will increase their purchases, and art dealers' imports will increase. Only in modern works will the inflowing current continue to flow shallow, unless Congress yet sees the absurdity of taxing contemporary foreign artists in the hope of aiding home talent.

Ralph Nevill's "French Prints of the Eighteenth Century" (The Macmillan Co.) is a good elementary handbook of the subject and something better; for it is agreeably written and contains much of anecdotal interest. A plea for the work of the école galante is really needed in English. Lady Dilke did much to reveal the essential seriousness of this apparently frivolous art, but the average Briton, or for that matter, American, finds it hard to overcome certain racial misgivings. It is not that the Briton objects to the occasional naughtiness of the French designers (he gladly collects far naughtier prints made in England), but he is morally perturbed before a naughtiness that presents itself with such charm and taste. As a matter of fact, the austere collector may readily enough ignore that minority of salacious subjects, and find an enjoyment both keen and innocent in the delightful invention and workmanship of the rest. To depict the society of the waning ancien régime the engravers provided a peculiarly appropriate technique—an engraving first fully executed in etching, and always preserving the freshness and informality of the sketch. Then the color printers devised difficult methods to reproduce the gouaches of Lavreince and others. In comparison with the French color printing, that of England is puerile. Only that of Japan surpasses it. To all these matters Mr. Nevill is a cicerone, both competent and vivacious. He provides, beside a text of a very informatory sort, a select catalogue of the more important prints, including summary notices as to states, sale prices, etc. Fifty plates add to the usefulness of the book. We could wish that more attention had been paid to the book illustrators, Gravelot, Marillier, and others. From poor or imperfect copies of eighteenth century books, prints quite as meritorious as those

[handwritten note in left margin:] This is the picture I want you to buy. I had not seen this article when I wrote this morning. B.B. Apr. 10 09

Fig. 58. "Art: A Show of Fair Women, London," *Nation* 88, March 25, 1909, no. 2282, p. 313, with Bernard Berenson's note to Isabella Stewart Gardner. Isabella Stewart Gardner Museum, Boston

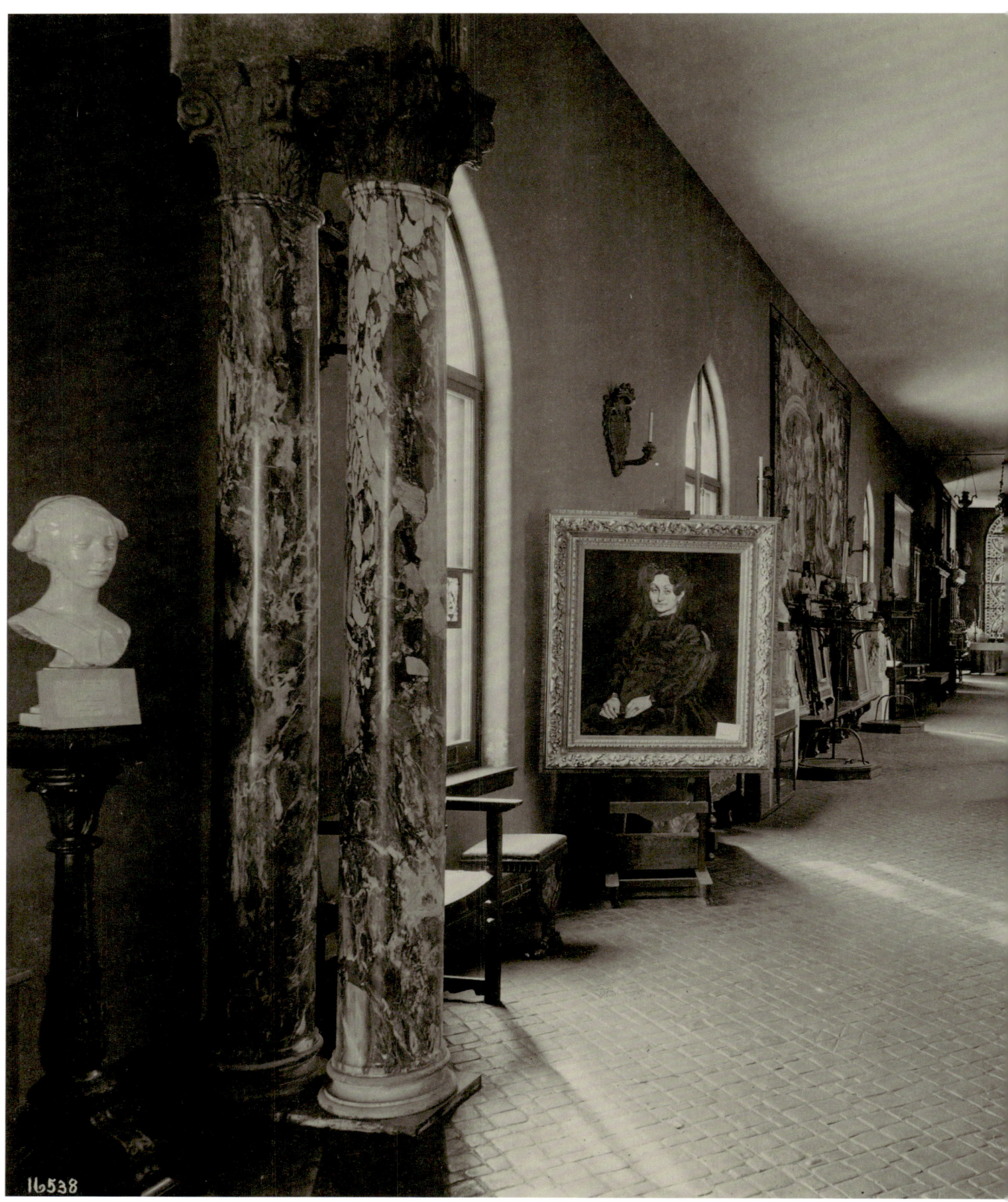

Fig. 59. Thomas E. Marr & Son, Long Gallery, 1910. Isabella Stewart Gardner Museum, Boston

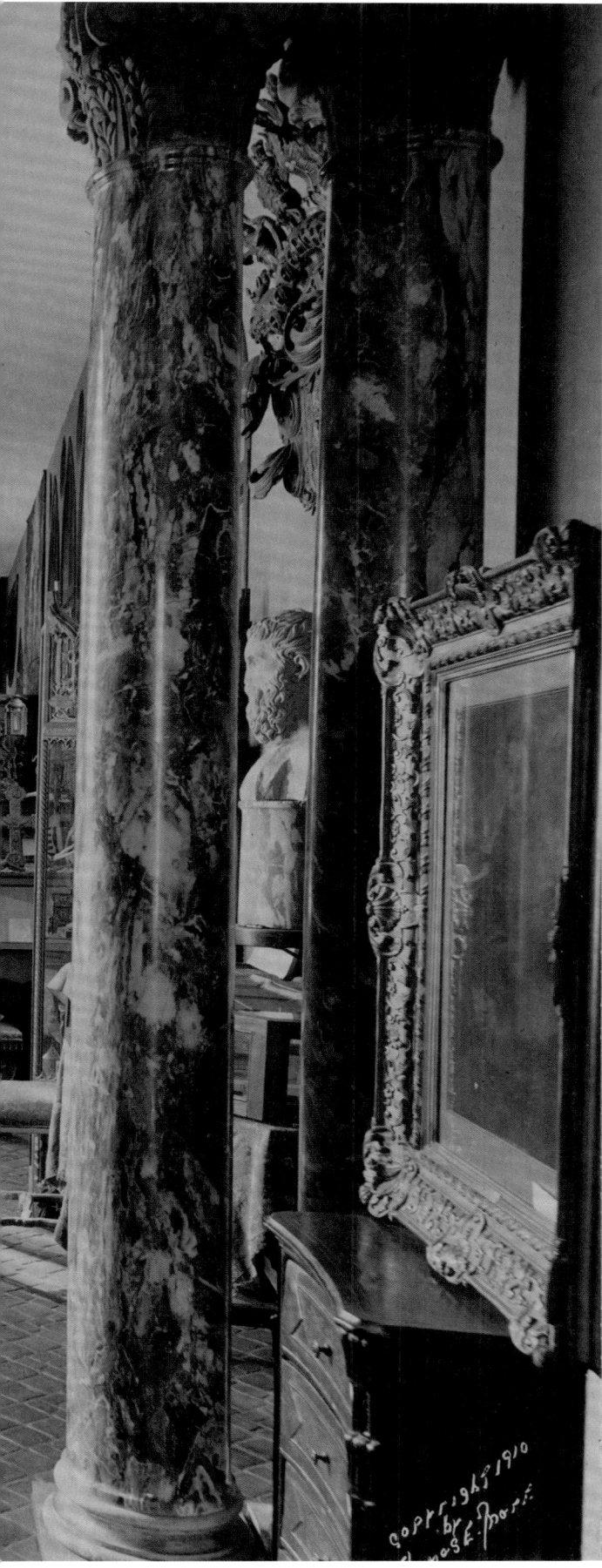

note his unflinching approach to his model's age. Egan Mew in the *Bystander* expressed approval that the exhibition title "Fair Women" had not been taken "in any narrow sense. The splendid 'Madame Manet mère,' and many another picture, possesses that beauty of the spirit which has not in the past been connected with the generic title," even if the *Times* critic thought that "in the presence of the Manet . . . the visitor will not unduly press the word 'Fair.'"[18] Other critics connected Manet's technique with Eugénie's age. Laurence Binyon, for instance, wrote in the *Saturday Review*, "And in Manet's portrait of his mother, so admirable in its decisive brush-drawing, its tender severity, how rawly the yellow-white of the face and hands stares from the surrounding black! It is extraordinary that it should seem so much alive, when all the bloom of life has been flayed off."[19] The critic writing for the *Manchester Courier* was not far from Binyon.

> Of Whistler's contemporaries, and the group of artists who have been loosely described as 'Impressionists,' Manet must surely hold high rank. The 'Portrait de Madame Manet *mère*'. . . is a masterpiece of psychological portraiture with its fluent drawing and simple yet convincing colouring. Manet indulged in no half-measures. . . . He was concerned only with the essentials, and this lady, grave and sedate, almost speaks from the frame. It is not surprising . . . that this great painter should have exercised a powerful influence on the art of the time.[20]

A notion of Manet's influence also appears in the *Athenaeum*, which noted the modern artists' "real aloofness from the fashionable prettiness of the moment" and the modern movement's "paramount value of sincerity." The critic singled out Manet's "audacious excursion into the flesh painting of the very tones of the black dress."[21] The *Art Journal* critic Frank Rinder, after discussing portraits by Reynolds and Gainsborough, proclaimed:

> After these portraits, that of his mother, by Édouard Manet, is prose; yet what pure, broad, intrepid, salutary, incisive prose. . . . Who will dare to traverse the avowal of this unheralded master, *'je ne me suis pas trompé de métier'* [I did not choose the wrong profession]? Could sheer, honest, weighty thinking in paint—hardy feeling, too—be carried farther? This is a signally beautiful instance of art not losing its inspiration among its conventions and artifices. Whistler breathed his 'Mother' on to canvas . . . Manet's 'Mother,' inimitable in the manipulation of paint, is frankness beautified.[22]

With both the *Art Journal* and the *Athenaeum* singling out Manet's handling of paint to represent flesh, it is noteworthy that Roger Fry in *Burlington* launched into a detailed exploration of tone and value in the composition. Fry wrote:

Then, again, how interesting to see Manet taking up Goya's idea of emphasis at the point where he left it, and pressing it to such fierce conclusions as in his great portrait of his mother! The logic of it is overpowering in its precision. His conception of colour demanded the utmost breadth of the lighted planes, and his idea of character and form the utmost relief consistent with that. In fact he required in paint a relief analogous to that attained by Donatello—flat in the higher planes and sharp in its transition to the *fond* [background]. Such a relief demands at once the utmost force and the utmost subtlety, and Manet establishes it so convincingly that for the sake of a colour opposition he can actually afford to discount it in the flat black mass of hair plastered on the brow. A masterpiece of painting, but hardly of technique; for it threatens to be but a wreck in the near future.[23]

Fry is mistaken about the color of Madame Manet's hair, a rich brown in distinctive rolls, not a "flat black mass," but he brilliantly lays out the painting's main formal wager: that light-colored flesh tones could stand sharply against a sea of black and serve to heighten the gravity of his sitter's presence. It is quite likely that Berenson encountered some of this English criticism, rich in keen observations of the painting's distinctive effects, when he traveled to London.

The article that we know that he read and sent to Isabella Stewart Gardner, however, appeared in the American periodical *The Nation*. In it, there is both a straightforwardness and a thoroughness about the description of Manet's painting. *The Nation*'s critic in London wrote:

There is only one Manet, the portrait of his mother, a half-length, not exhibited, I am told, since 1867. It is an extraordinary performance, a piece of realism if there ever was one. The mother, elderly but not yet old, is sitting, her hands in her lap. She wears black, her hair is black, and is arranged in tight puffs on either side of her face in the fashion for elderly ladies of her day, and over it is the black cap the Frenchwoman of her age and class is still so likely to wear. Her face is plain, the eyes prominent, the beginning of a black moustache on the upper lip. Thus she was seen in life, thus you see her on canvas, and by the sheer strength of the realism and the vigor of

the painting, she is so alive, so abounding in vitality and character, that the near portraits fade into phantoms. She has the supreme beauty of ugliness that you find in some Rembrandts—not a Fair, but a Real, Woman, whom you would not exchange for a whole gallery full of modern attempts at prettiness or eccentricity.[24]

This writer demonstrates a real sensitivity to Madame Manet's age and class as well as an appreciation of the artist's inclusion of facial hair and Eugénie's old-fashioned hairstyle. For this writer, it is the vitality and character of Manet's sitter that stand out most; Madame Manet is a real woman, not a confection. The author of this vivid account of *Madame Auguste Manet* at the "Fair Women" exhibition turns out to be Elizabeth R. Pennell (1855–1936), an American writer based in London.[25] She was a travel and food writer, an art critic and scholar of James Abbott McNeill Whistler, and a biographer of Mary Wollstonecraft. The social circle she entertained along with her husband, artist Joseph Pennell, included Aubrey Beardsley, Whistler, Henry James, Oscar Wilde, and George Bernard Shaw—many of whom were Gardner's friends; Joseph Pennell sent her a letter in 1906 related to his own studies of Whistler.[26] The review Berenson clipped was signed "N.N.," no name, and there is no reason to think that Berenson or Gardner would have known that the author was a woman, much less one whose social world was progressive when it came to thinking about gender. Nevertheless, it is worth underlining a couple of points. On one level, Pennell's piece very much aligns with the other critics who emphasized Manet's candor about representing an older woman; on another level, she used language that spoke directly to the major concern on Berenson's mind. As Berenson wrote to Gardner from London on March 30, 1909: "I have the hope of getting you something that I have been looking for for years, something that will connect the Degas with the Pollaiuolo, something that is perhaps more overwhelming, more colossal than either."[27] Pennell's observation that in her view, nearby portraits "fade into phantoms" next to the Manet seemed to be just what Berenson was looking for on Gardner's behalf.

When *Madame Auguste Manet* first went on view in Fenway Court, Gardner placed the painting on an easel in the Long Gallery on the third floor (fig. 59). The museum-going public took notice, as the *Boston Journal* reported:

Two hundred persons, the full number of ticket holders admitted in any one day, were at the museum of Mrs. John L. Gardner's palace in the Fens yesterday . . . Manet's portrait of his mother, the most recent addition to Mrs. Gardner's collection of masterpieces, drew particular attention. Mrs. Gardner obtained possession of the painting in Paris only a short time ago, after her agents had been seeking it for years. Specimens of his work are rare in this country.[28]

Angled away from the wall, illuminated mostly by natural light pouring in from the museum's central courtyard, the painting faced visitors as they walked the length of the gallery. With the easel raising the life-size figure above the level of the chairs, Eugénie met viewers at what was arguably the optimal height for a Manet figure painting—at eye level.

Madame Auguste Manet takes its place alongside Manet's most memorable modern-life paintings that also featured a powerful gaze at the viewer, like *Le Déjeuner sur l'herbe* (see fig. 84) and *Olympia* (see fig. 54). Unlike those paintings of Victorine Meurent, however, the portrait of Manet's mother invokes death and mourning. The scholar Jean Clay wrote of one of Manet's portraits of Berthe Morisot in mourning: "Something like a portrait *from* death—already substituted for the death it foreshadows. An image in the future perfect tense, where mourning begins: I paint while knowing that this portrait will survive you; I paint what you will have been."[29] Manet's portrait of his mother represents not only a stage in her mourning for her husband but also a memorial to her, of her—a private person who, as Baudelaire would argue, was more heroic and modern than any number of more public figures Manet might have painted. The artist's attention to the signs of her age and mourning attire, well noted by London critics in 1909, means that the portrait was seen as more than a likeness. *Madame Auguste Manet* remains intimately tied to Eugénie's widowhood and, as such, exemplifies the private, familial side of Manet's vision of the painting of modern life.

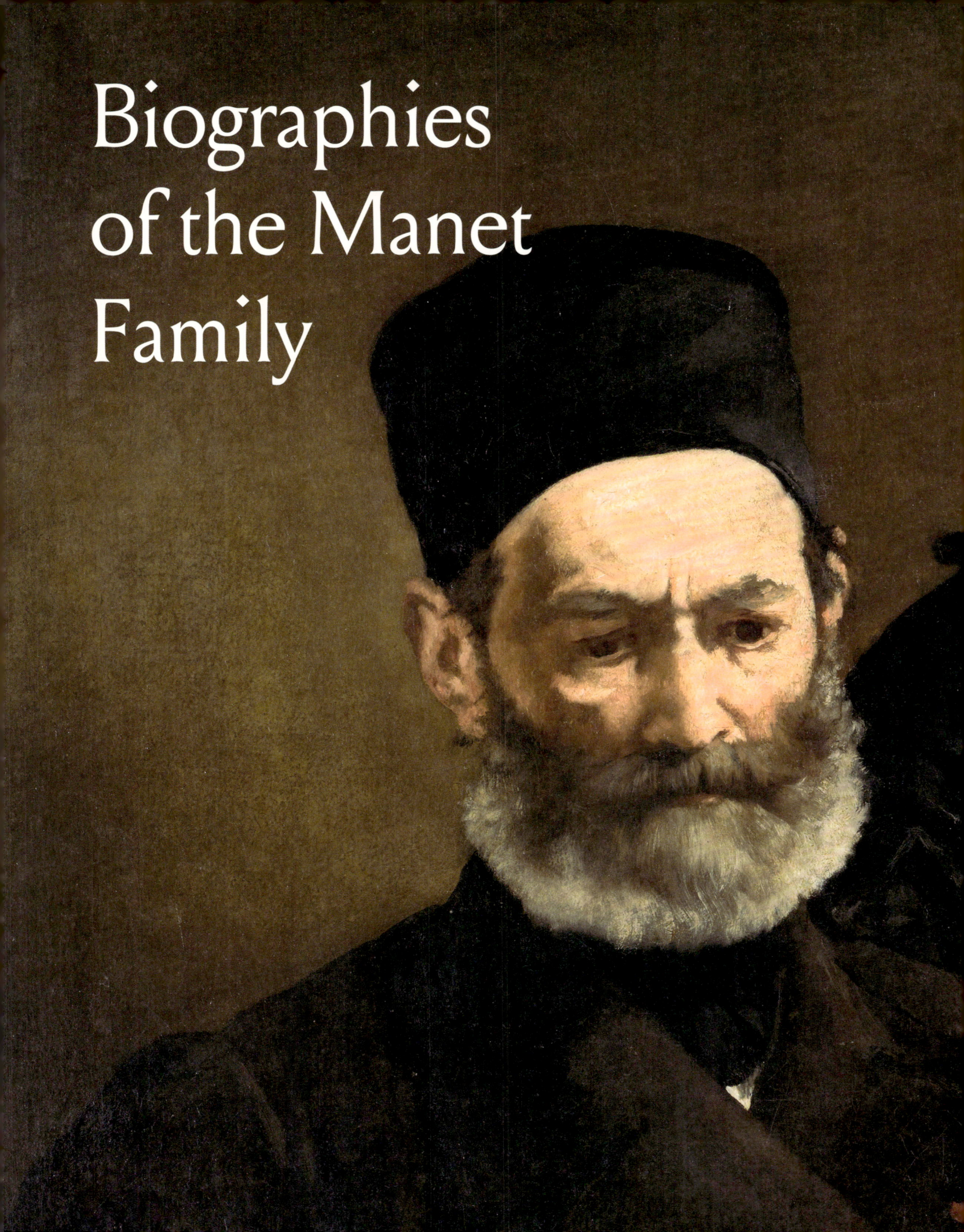

Biographies
of the Manet
Family

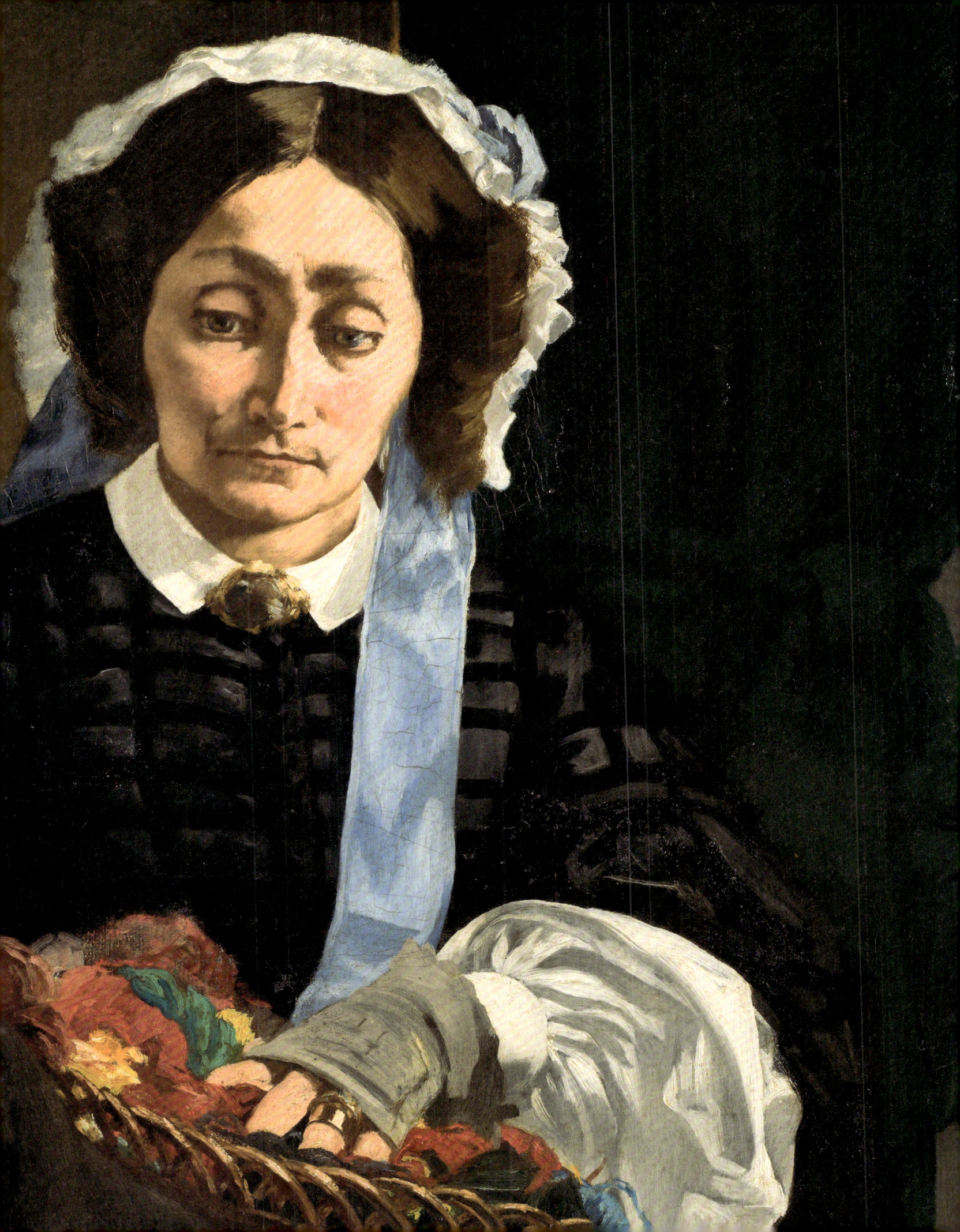

Family Tree

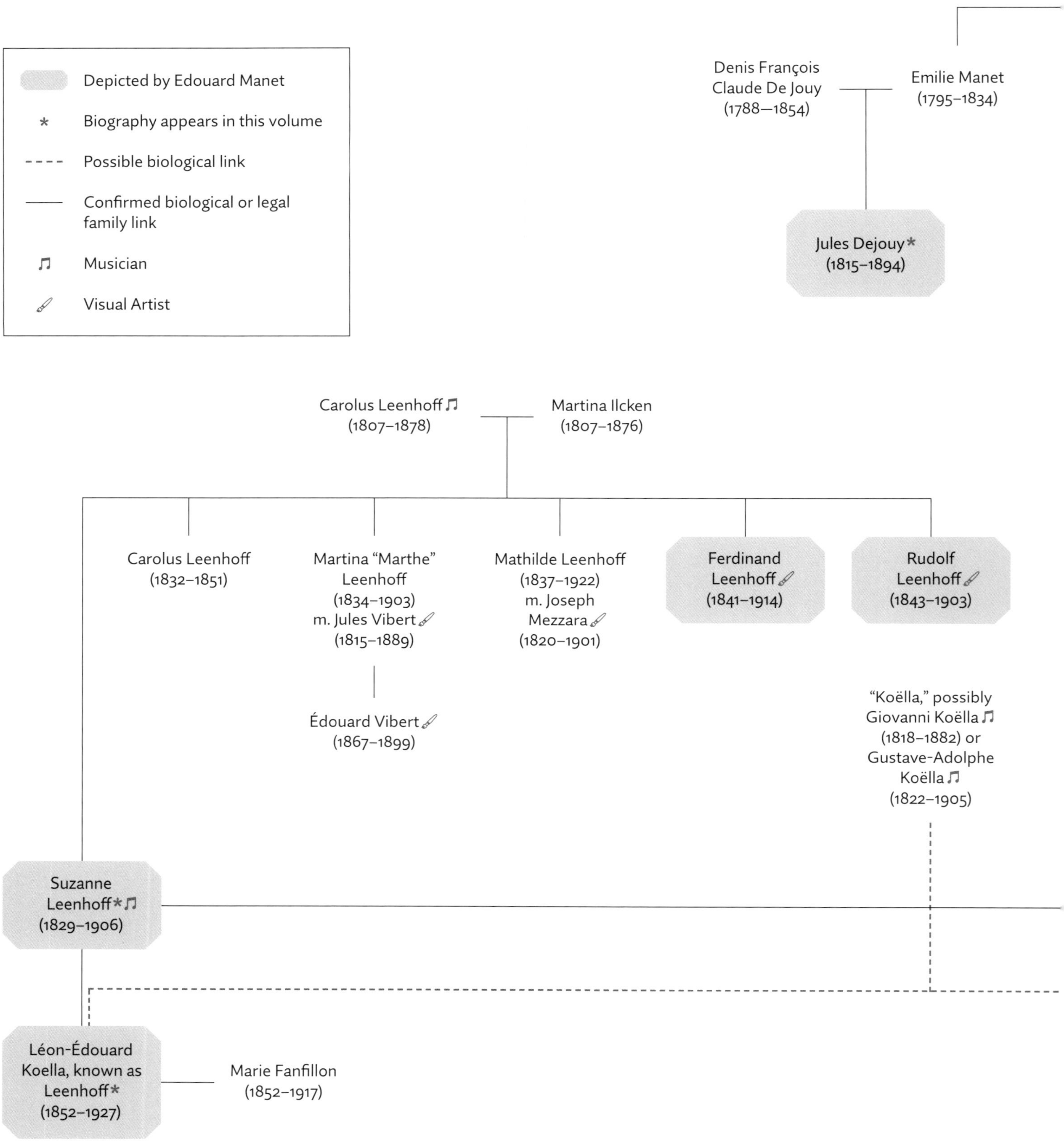

Legend

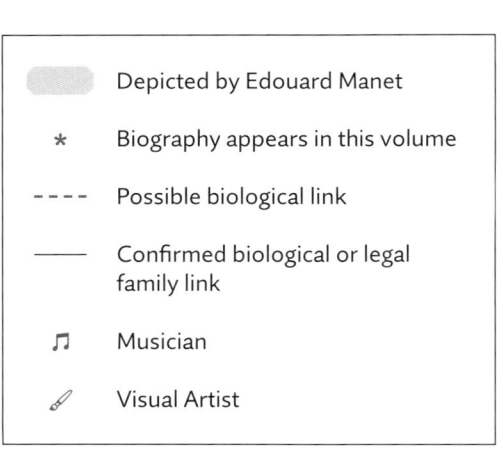

Depicted by Edouard Manet

*   Biography appears in this volume

- - - -   Possible biological link

———   Confirmed biological or legal family link

♫   Musician

🖌   Visual Artist

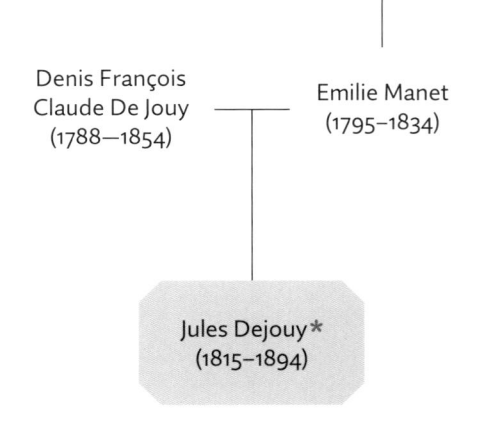

Denis François Claude De Jouy (1788—1854) — Emilie Manet (1795—1834)

Jules Dejouy* (1815–1894)

Carolus Leenhoff ♫ (1807–1878) — Martina Ilcken (1807–1876)

Carolus Leenhoff (1832–1851)

Martina "Marthe" Leenhoff (1834–1903) m. Jules Vibert 🖌 (1815–1889)

Édouard Vibert 🖌 (1867–1899)

Mathilde Leenhoff (1837–1922) m. Joseph Mezzara 🖌 (1820–1901)

Ferdinand Leenhoff 🖌 (1841–1914)

Rudolf Leenhoff 🖌 (1843–1903)

"Koëlla," possibly Giovanni Koëlla ♫ (1818–1882) or Gustave-Adolphe Koëlla ♫ (1822–1905)

Suzanne Leenhoff * ♫ (1829–1906)

Léon-Édouard Koella, known as Leenhoff * (1852–1927) — Marie Fanfillon (1852–1917)

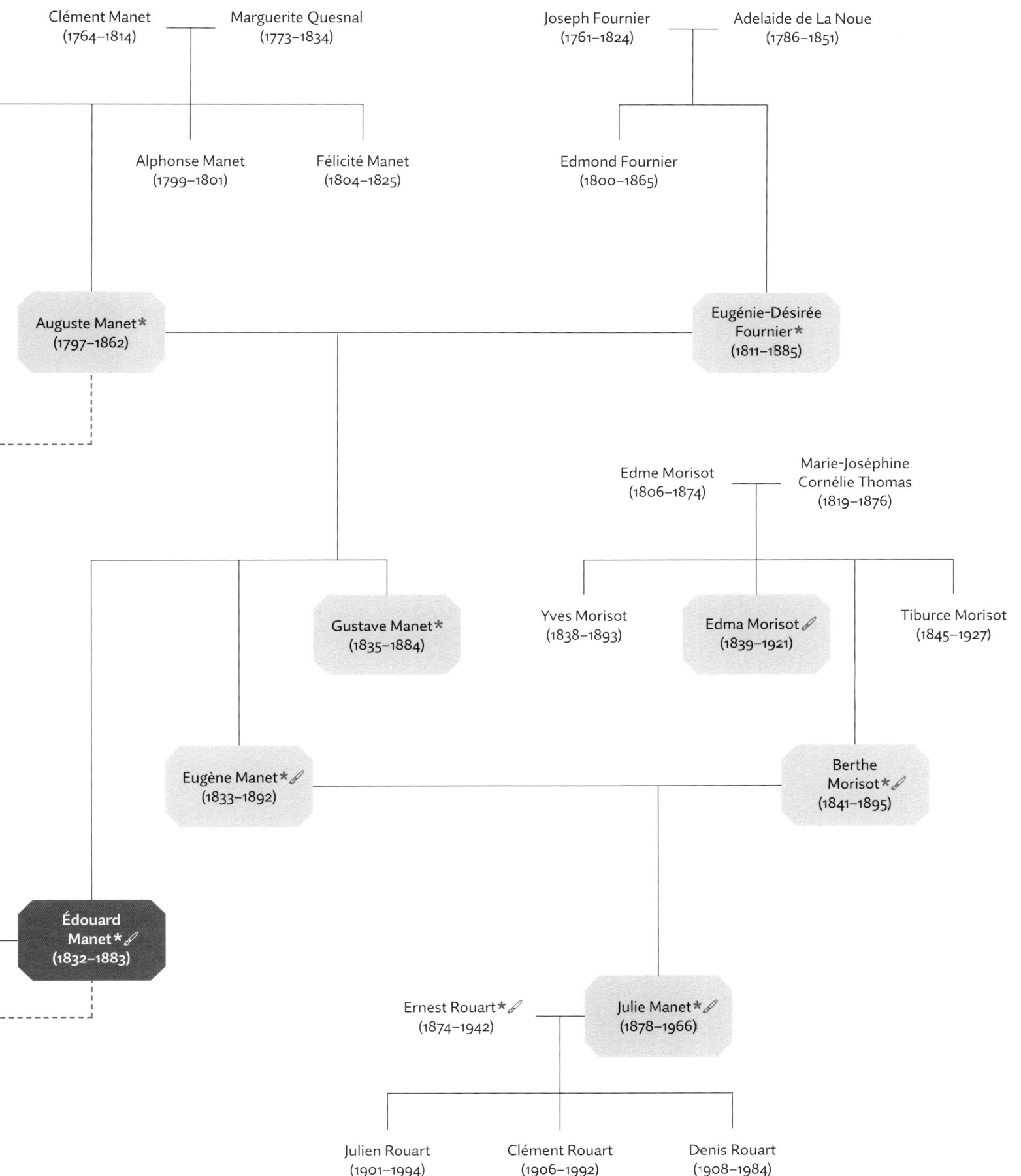

Clément Manet
(1764–1814)

Marguerite Quesnal
(1773–1834)

Joseph Fournier
(1761–1824)

Adelaide de La Noue
(1786–1851)

Alphonse Manet
(1799–1801)

Félicité Manet
(1804–1825)

Edmond Fournier
(1800–1865)

Auguste Manet*
(1797–1862)

Eugénie-Désirée
Fournier*
(1811–1885)

Edme Morisot
(1806–1874)

Marie-Joséphine
Cornélie Thomas
(1819–1876)

Gustave Manet*
(1835–1884)

Yves Morisot
(1838–1893)

Edma Morisot
(1839–1921)

Tiburce Morisot
(1845–1927)

Eugène Manet*
(1833–1892)

Berthe
Morisot*
(1841–1895)

Édouard
Manet*
(1832–1883)

Ernest Rouart*
(1874–1942)

Julie Manet*
(1878–1966)

Julien Rouart
(1901–1994)

Clément Rouart
(1906–1992)

Denis Rouart
(1908–1984)

Auguste Manet (1797–1862)

Auguste Manet was born into a family that had, for more than a century, been prosperous landowners in Gennevilliers, a then-rural and now-suburban town about six miles from the center of Paris (fig. 60).[1] Auguste's father, Clément, a former judge, was a significant property holder in the community and its mayor. Auguste followed a predictable and respectable path: he studied the law and then, after clerking, worked for the Ministry of Justice, where he moved up quickly through the ranks.[2]

On January 18, 1831, he married Eugénie-Désirée Fournier (1811–1885), who came from an equivalently wealthy but slightly more eccentric background that included commercial and diplomatic connections to Sweden.[3] She was nineteen years old, and he was thirty-three. With a dowry from the Fournier family, income derived from landholdings

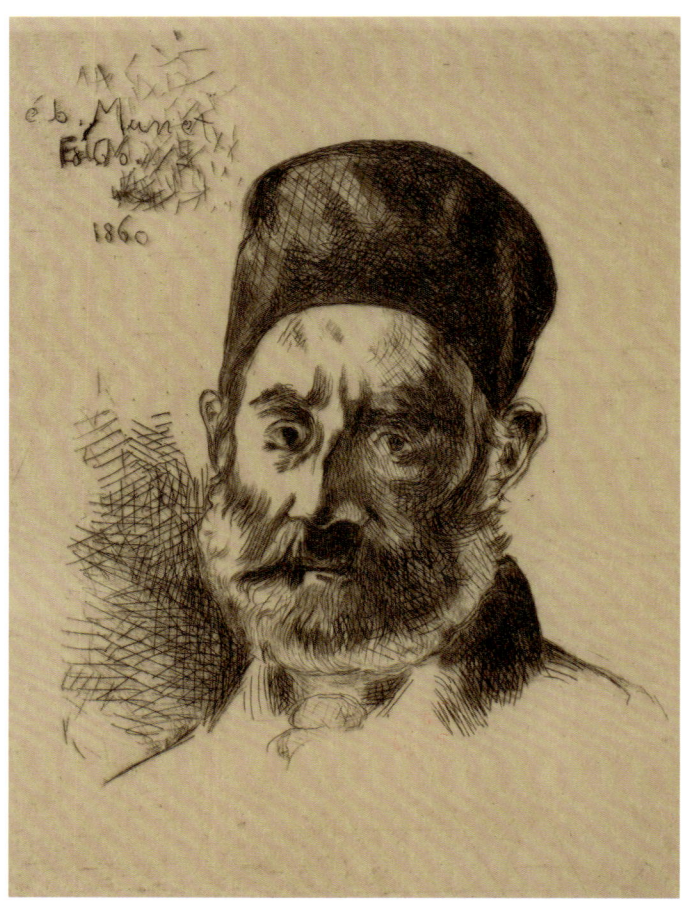

Fig. 60. Édouard Manet, *M. Manet, the Artist's Father*, 1860. Etching and drypoint, 20.6 × 23.8 cm. Nationalmuseum, Stockholm

in Gennevilliers and other investments, and his salary from the Ministry of Justice, Auguste was able to provide a comfortable upper-class life for his family.[4] His eldest son, Édouard, was born in January 1832 in their Paris home at 5, rue des Petits-Augustins (now rue Bonaparte), almost exactly a year later. It was a good year for Auguste; he was also awarded the *Legion d'honneur*, France's highest civil order of achievement, in the same month.[5] His two younger sons were born in 1833 and 1835. In January 1841, he became a judge at the Tribunal de la Première Instance, a lower-level court that heard civil and criminal matters. Serving as a civil judge, he would have heard cases about disputed paternity, wills, divorce, and copyright.[6] From there, however, his career stagnated—he would remain at that rank for the next two decades.[7]

Auguste has often been portrayed as stern and demonstrably disappointed in his eldest son's lack of academic talent and interest in the arts.[8] The artist's close friend Antonin Proust described Auguste's reaction to his family's suggestion that Édouard be allowed to study drawing: "[He] took this advice very badly."[9] When it became clear Édouard would never study the law, Auguste encouraged him to join the navy. After a failed first attempt at the naval officer's exam, Édouard went on a monthslong trans-Equatorial voyage to Brazil in December 1848.[10] In the artist's letters from this time, there is evidence of genuine affection for Auguste, suggesting the latter was an attentive father.[11] After Édouard's return from Brazil, Auguste, perhaps grudgingly, supported his son's decision to become an artist.[12]

During Édouard's trip to Brazil, a new person joined the Manet family household: Suzanne Leenhoff, a Dutch pianist hired by the family in 1849 to teach the younger Manet boys to play the piano.[13] Her employment presumably lasted until 1852, when she gave birth to her son, Léon-Édouard Koëlla—or at least until she was too visibly pregnant to work.[14] Auguste was possibly Léon's father, although this has not been confirmed. If Auguste had fathered Léon while Suzanne was employed in his household, it would be a serious crime, made even more disgraceful by his position as a judge.[15]

In the decade after Léon's birth, Auguste's health deteriorated. He was suffering from tertiary syphilis, a late-stage progression of the venereal disease, and became paralyzed in 1857.[16] He stopped reporting to his chambers. In an 1859 request for Auguste to retire, Eugénie wrote: "I beg you to consider the weakness of this poor, miserable man. If you had heard, Minister, the cry that escapes from his chest and the expression of pain permanently on his face—even though he has had every possible treatment."[17] Édouard depicted his father for the first time (cat. no. 3) just a couple of years before he died of syphilis on September 22, 1862.[18]

DIANA SEAVE GREENWALD

Eugénie-Désirée Fournier (Madame Auguste Manet, 1811–1885)

Born in Paris on February 11, 1811, Eugénie-Désirée Fournier (fig. 61) was the daughter of Joseph Antoine Ennemond Fournier (1761–1824) and Adélaïde Elisabeth de La Noüe (1779–1851).[19] Her older brother Edmond was born in Gothenburg, Sweden, where their father had worked as a merchant and served as vice consul of France.[20] By virtue of her father's work and relationship with Charles Bernadotte, a French marshal who became Crown Prince Charles XIV John of Sweden, Eugénie was the goddaughter of the king of Sweden. On January 18, 1831, Eugénie married Auguste Manet (1796–1862), who became head of the personnel division at the Ministry of Justice, then a civil judge at the Tribunal de première instance.[21] Édouard, their first child, was born on January 23, 1832; Eugène followed on November 21, 1833; and Gustave on March 16, 1835.

Eugénie's father died in Bretigny, in the southern suburbs of Paris, when she was thirteen, and she lost two brothers quite early: Édouard Karl Fournier (1801–1830), a lieutenant in the First Regiment of Cuirassiers garrisoned at Tours, was killed in a duel at age twenty-nine, and another who died in childhood.[22] Her eldest brother, Edmond Fournier (1800–1865), pursued a military career and became an artillery captain and colonel; his last position was as director of the province of Constantine, Algeria.[23] Back in Paris, Edmond lived directly across the street from the Manets in the rue des Petits-Augustins (now rue Bonaparte), and he encouraged the artistic talents of young Édouard. Having faithfully served the Orléanist government of King Louis-Philippe, his politics were likely at odds with the republican views of the Manet family.[24] After the death of the Fournier mother in 1851, Edmond argued with Auguste Manet, probably over the handling of her estate.[25] He retired to Pontcelles, no longer on speaking terms with the Manets. When his son Edmond, who was the same age as Édouard Manet, was killed in the battle of Sevastopol in 1855 and the

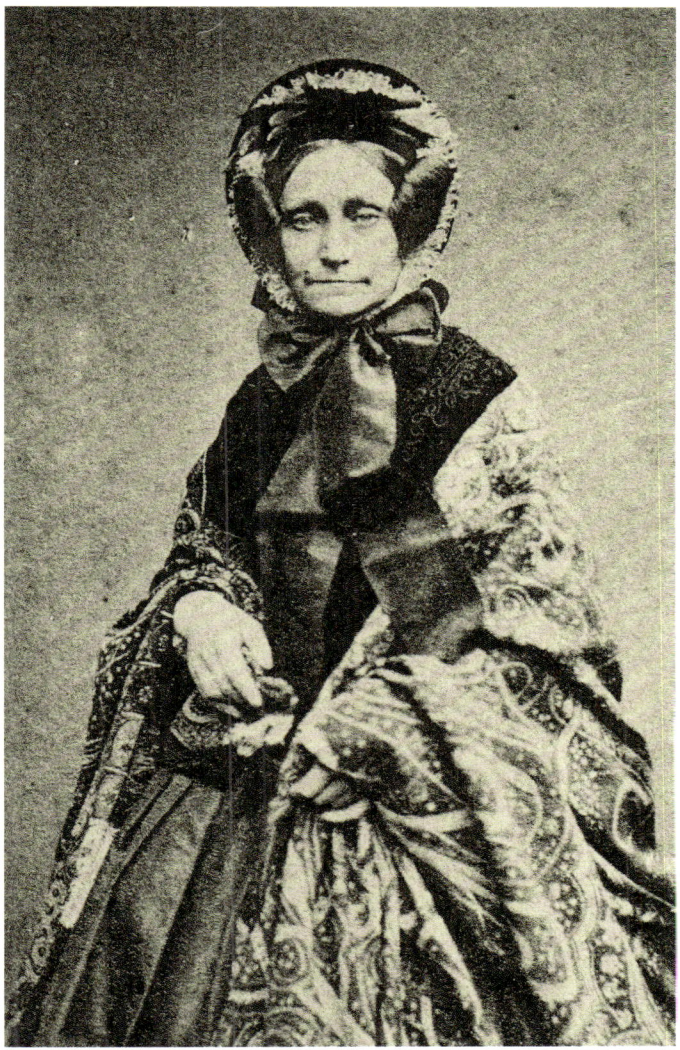

Fig. 61. Étienne Carjat, *Eugénie-Désirée Fournier (Madame Auguste Manet)*, from Étienne Moreau-Nélaton, *Manet raconté par lui-même* (Paris, 1926), vol. 1, fig. 54, before 1863. Bibliotheque National de France, Paris

artist offered condolences, Edmond senior referred to the division between Manet's parents and himself as one that "cannot be healed."[26]

The estate of Eugénie's mother was sizable: it included a four-hundred-acre working farm in Marolles-en-Hurepoix (Essonne) and rents from properties in Paris, Brussels, and Kortrijk, Belgium.[27] The fact that Eugénie's parents obtained a legal separation of property in 1802 attests to the extent of their wealth and the need for Eugénie's mother to inherit and maintain title to properties under her own name. The legal proceeding, rare in the nineteenth century, resembles the modern prenuptial agreement, even though it could be secured after marriage. Eugénie's considerable inheritance allowed her to subsidize Manet's solo exhibition at the Avenue de l'Alma in 1867; records show that she loaned him more than 18,000 francs toward the exhibition.[28] Eugénie also gifted Manet and Suzanne Leenhoff 10,000 francs at the time of their marriage in 1863, although she had it written into their marriage contract that she could ask for the return of the money if Édouard predeceased her with no children.[29] After Édouard's death, she indeed asked for the return of the money—suggesting she did not think Léon was Édouard's son.[30]

Eugénie sang at musical evenings at the Manet home, and she was invited to sing at other gatherings in their social circle. She received her own friends on Tuesdays and her sons' friends on Thursdays; Léon recounted an impressive list of writers, artists, and government officials who frequented the Thursday soirées.[31] After the death of Auguste, Eugénie moved in with Édouard, Suzanne, and Léon. She lived and vacationed with them until Édouard's death in April 1883.[32] Eugénie then moved in with her son Eugène and his wife, Berthe Morisot, in their newly constructed home at 40, rue de Villejust (now rue Paul Valéry).[33] She suffered a stroke in July 1883 and passed away on January 8, 1885.[34] She was buried at Montmartre Cemetery next to her husband. Like many widows of means, she purchased the grave concession at the time of his death in 1862.[35]

NANCY LOCKE

Suzanne Leenhoff (Madame Édouard Manet, 1829–1906)

Suzanne Leenhoff was born in Delft, the Netherlands, on October 30, 1829, eldest child of Martina Adriana Johanna Ilcken and musician Carolus Antonius Leenhoff (fig. 62). The couple had six more children. In 1840 the family moved to the small town of Zaltbommel, where Carolus was offered the position of bell ringer of the local church. Suzanne learned piano from her father,[36] and her talent came to the attention of Franz Liszt when he was passing through Zaltbommel in 1842. The composer may have suggested that Suzanne be sent to Paris to continue her musical training.[37]

In 1847 the Leenhoff family—except for Carolus—moved to Paris, where Suzanne's paternal grandmother lived and where their artistic aspirations could flourish.[38] In fact, almost all of the siblings would turn to art.[39] Suzanne contin-

ued her piano studies but twice failed the entrance exam of the National Conservatory.[40] Beginning in the late 1840s, she gave private piano lessons, and that is how she met the Manet family, when she was hired to teach the painter's younger brothers.[41]

In the spring of 1851, Suzanne became pregnant. Her teaching career ended when she gave birth to Léon-Édouard Koëlla on January 29, 1852. Suzanne's mother publicly asserted that the child was hers, and Suzanne always presented Léon as her younger brother. She did not officially recognize him as her own child until 1900.[42] In July 1852, Manet visited the Rijksmuseum in Amsterdam. One wonders if the painter accompanied Suzanne to the Netherlands to introduce her newborn to her father, who was still living there. If Suzanne did not accompany the painter, he may

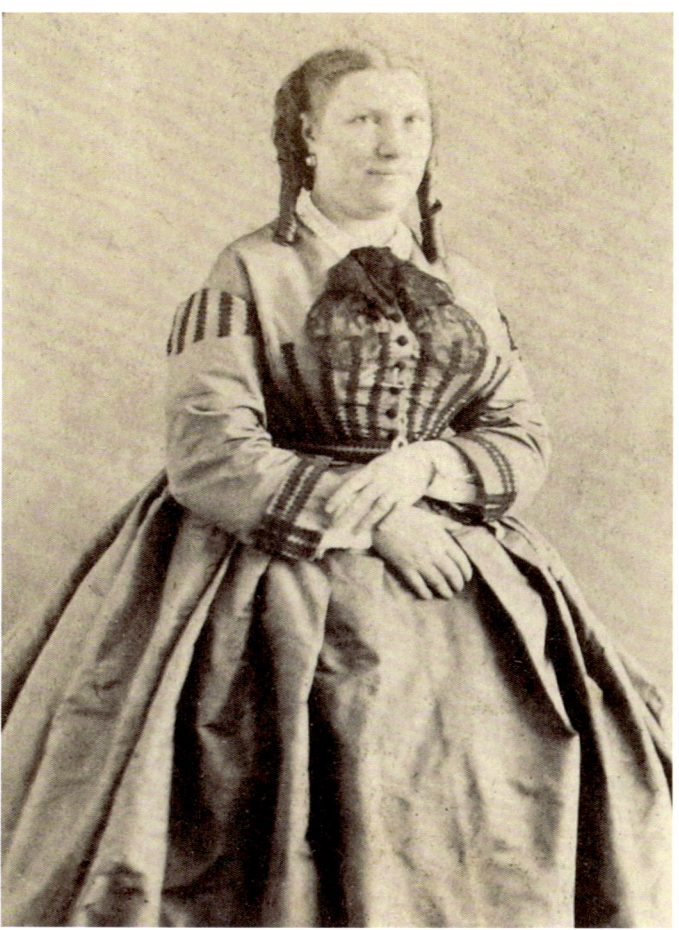

Fig. 62. Unidentified photographer, *Madame Édouard Manet (Suzanne Leenhoff)*, from *Album of Cartes-de-Visite Portraits Belonging to Édouard Manet*, about 1870. Carte-de-visite, 9.2 × 5.6 cm. Bibliothèque Nationale de France, Paris

have nonetheless assured Carolus that he was taking care of his daughter.

In 1860, Suzanne likely settled with Manet in the rue de l'Hôtel-de-Ville. This liaison and cohabitation, however, was kept secret even from those in Manet's inner circle until the couple's marriage in Zaltbommel on October 28, 1863.[43] Upon their return from the Netherlands as a married couple, the Manets lived at 34, Boulevard des Batignolles before moving in with the painter's mother at 49, rue de Saint-Pétersbourg. There, Suzanne—alongside her mother-in-law—co-hosted the family's Tuesday and Thursday evening salons, though Eugénie seems to have been the family's primary hostess. Despite Suzanne and Édouard's hopes to expand their family, Léon remained Suzanne's only child.[44]

Having officially become Madame Manet, Suzanne socialized alongside her husband. She was present at parties at the homes of writer Paul Meurice and his wife, Palmyre; of Jules Michelet and his wife, Athénaïs; at the Morisots, and many other friends' homes. Her talents as a pianist were called upon during these evenings. A guest recounted one such occasion at the house of the painter Giuseppe de Nittis: "The evenings were very cheerful. . . . Very good music was made there. Madame Manet, the painter's wife, a tall and heavy Dutchwoman, would play classical pieces, her exceptionally beautiful hands running over the keyboard with a lightness and a feeling so little suggested by her appearance that it was enchanting."[45] In private, too, the musician delighted her husband, whose "daydreams are often lulled by the melodies of his wife."[46] This continued throughout their lives together. During the painter's therapeutic stay at Bellevue in 1880, when Manet missed the social life of the capital, Suzanne "played him sonatas that delighted him."[47]

The illness and then death of the painter in 1883 were a painful ordeal for his wife: "Her pain is extreme and her devotion was great," as wrote Berthe Morisot to her sister. The struggle over Manet's estate was another trial to endure. After Édouard's death, Eugénie—the painter's mother—was iron-willed, even cruel, with her daughter-in-law. In fact, Suzanne inherited debts payable to her mother-in-law.[48] From then on, Suzanne lived in poverty in a house in Gennevilliers provided by Jules Dejouy, Manet's cousin. "I live as I can, from almost nothing. I always feel I have such a great well of sorrow, that anything unpleasant that happens to me moves me very little, and nothing surprises me anymore,"[49] she wrote to Morisot. Suzanne lived surrounded by Manet's paintings. One visitor described how "her apartment was made up of several rooms whose walls were covered with

pictures." These included *Olympia* (see fig. 54) and "other paintings and pastels forming an admirable ensemble." She was "sad in the midst of these memories . . . telling us about her dear departed [husband]."[50]

Suzanne lived on the meager income she got from renting the land she had inherited, a bequest from Berthe Morisot, and from the sale of Manet's works.[51] Manet's friend Antonin Proust helped her sell paintings, sketches, drawings, and prints on the best terms possible to dealers or collectors, though some of them were unscrupulous and took advantage of the impoverished widow. In 1895, Suzanne left Dejouy's dilapidated house in Gennevilliers and moved into an apartment in the nearby town of Asnières. Proust's support remained essential, and it seems that it was through him that Suzanne benefited, at least after 1900, from an "annuity" paid by the baritone and collector Jean-Baptiste Faure.[52] Suzanne Manet died on March 8, 1906, in her son Léon's apartment at 94, rue Saint-Dominique in Paris.

SAMUEL RODARY

Léon-Édouard Koëlla, known as Léon Leenhoff (1852–1927)

The complexities of the Manet family revolve around Léon-Édouard Koëlla, who was known as Léon Leenhoff for much of his life (fig. 63). Two things are certain. First: he was the son of Suzanne Leenhoff (1829–1906), Édouard Manet's future wife. Second: he was born out of wedlock. While his maternity is sure, his paternity is unknown and will likely never be known. Three possible fathers have been proposed: Édouard himself, a traveling musician with the last name Koëlla—the last name on Léon's birth certificate—and Édouard's father, Auguste. There are myriad arguments for and against these candidates.[53] Regardless, Léon was publicly presented as Suzanne's youngest brother rather than her son.[54]

He knew nothing of his complicated family status until his adolescence. Léon lived with Suzanne and Manet after their 1863 marriage—and likely even before. He knew they were his godmother and godfather, as is written on his 1855 baptismal certificate, and definitively learned Suzanne was his biological mother after obtaining a replacement birth certificate in 1871.[55] Despite that shock, he spoke positively about his upbringing: "In the Manet and Leenhoff families, I always said 'godmother' and 'godfather' . . . in society, they were my brother-in-law and sister. A family secret of which I never learned the last word, having been pampered and spoiled by both of them . . . We lived happily, the three of us; above all, I lived happily . . . Therefore, I had no need to question my birth."[56]

Léon was also one of Manet's most frequent models. Between the 1850s and his last appearance in the early 1870s, he appears in as many as eighteen extant oil paintings and a range of pastels, watercolors, and prints.[57]

By the 1870s, he was working at the Paris Bourse as a clerk for the financial firm owned by the family of artist Edgar Degas.[58] Although he had disappeared from Manet's work by the middle of the 1870s, Léon remained part of the

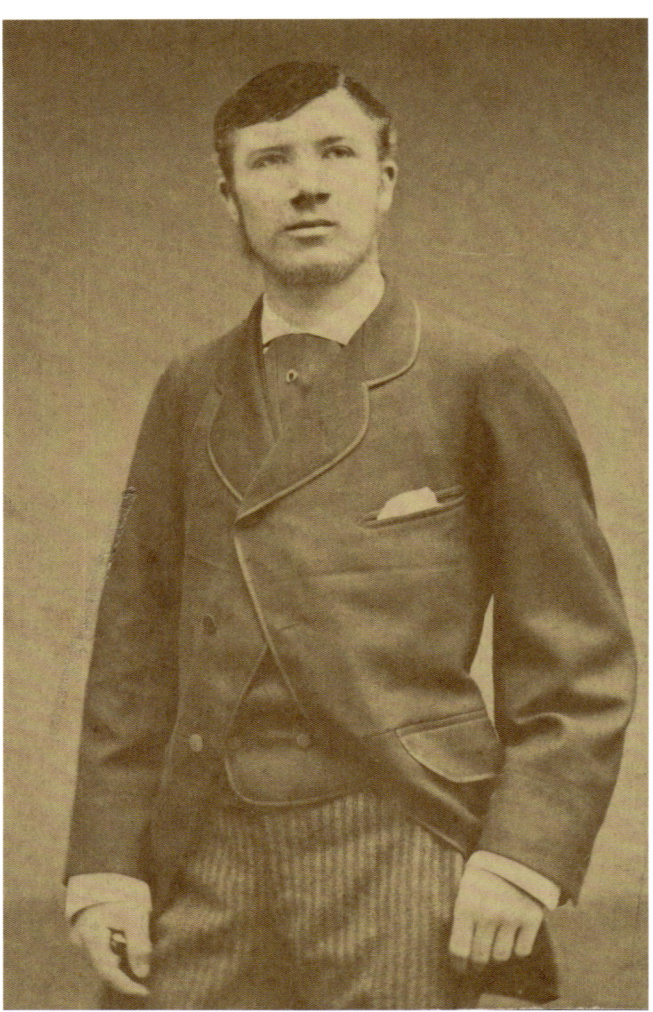

Fig. 63. Unidentified photographer, *Léon Koëlla, known as Léon Leenhoff*, 19th century. Carte-de-visite, 9.2 × 5.6 cm. The Morgan Library & Museum, New York (MA 3950). Purchased as the gift of Mrs. Charles Engelhard and children in memory of Mr. Charles Engelhard, 1974

household. According to available accounts, he was genial and well liked.[59] He helped care for Édouard as the artist's tertiary syphilis worsened and was present during his painful final days.[60] In his will, Manet recognized Léon and his position in the family as best he could: "I appoint Suzanne Leenhoff, my lawful wife, as my universal legatee. In her last will, she will leave everything I have left to her to Léon Koëlla, called Leenhoff, who has given me the most devoted care; I believe my brothers will find these arrangements perfectly natural."[61] Though his status was unclear, Manet clearly felt—and believed his two brothers would understand—that Léon was part of the family. Suzanne only officially recognized Léon as her son with a civil act in 1900.[62] Of course, by then he was forty-eight years old, had married five years earlier, and was running a poultry business.[63]

Léon dedicated himself to the preservation of Manet's memory and was an essential part of the team that organized the posthumous exhibition and sale of Manet's art.[64] His register of the works left in the artist's studio and corresponding photographs are a comprehensive, invaluable inventory.[65]

Despite a shared dedication to Édouard's legacy, cracks between Léon and the legitimate Manet family started to show following the artist's death. The artist's mother wrote scathingly about Suzanne and Léon's claims to the Manet estate.[66] As time went on, Léon and his mother fell into financial difficulties. As a result, they started to sell the works of art by Manet that were still in their possession.[67] These later sales—first by mother and son and then by Léon after Suzanne's death in 1906—present some problems for the provenance of Manet's works. They included increasingly unfinished works that were likely significantly retouched and were possibly copies.[68] Julie Manet, the last remaining legitimate heir, was scandalized and distressed by this treatment of her uncle's artworks.[69]

During the last decade of his life, Léon was the most important source of information and archival material for foundational texts written about Manet by Adolphe Tabarant and Étienne Moreau-Nelaton. Each author's archives—preserved at the Morgan Library and the Bibliothèque Nationale, respectively—are full of manuscript material and notes provided by him. Despite this centrality to the telling of the Manet story, Léon remained an enigmatic figure on the fringes of the family, even in death. In 1917, Léon asked for his recently deceased wife—and, by implication, for himself—to be buried in the Manet family plot. Julie Manet and her husband, Ernest Rouart, denied his request.[70]

DIANA SEAVE GREENWALD

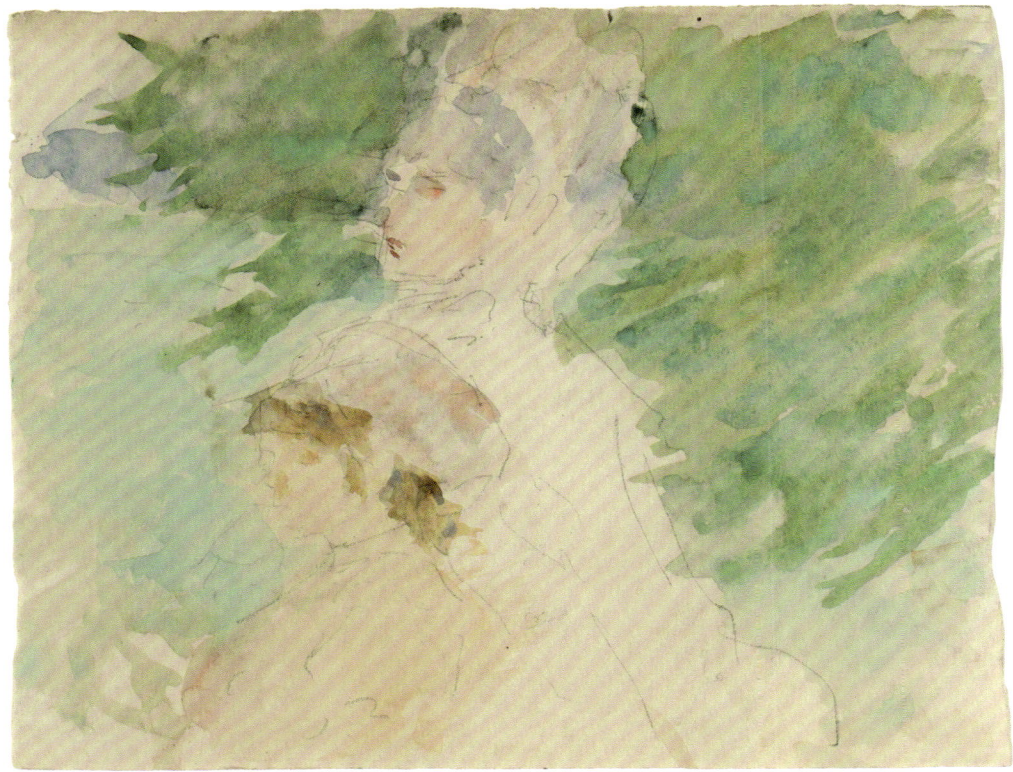

Fig. 64. Eugène Manet, *Julie Manet with Her Nanny*, 1883–84. Watercolor and graphite on paper, 12.7 × 16.5 cm. Private collection

Eugène Manet (1833–1892)

Eugène Manet was a younger brother of Édouard Manet and the husband of Berthe Morisot. An amateur artist who painted throughout his life but never exhibited his own work, he devoted himself to ensuring that his wife had uninterrupted time in the studio and opportunities to show her paintings.

As teenagers in 1849, Eugène and Gustave began taking piano lessons with Suzanne Leenhoff, a Dutch musician living in Paris whose extended family included numerous artists.[71] Thirteen years later, Édouard and Suzanne married. Eugène remained close with the couple, modeling for some of his brother's most significant works. He first appeared in *Music in the Tuileries* (fig. 4) and three years later posed for *Le Déjeuner sur l'herbe* (fig. 84) alongside Suzanne's brother Ferdinand Leenhoff and painter Victorine Meurent. Édouard painted him again with Suzanne a decade later in *On the Beach*.[72] The subjects of some of Eugène's own drawings and pastels suggest that he may have accompanied Édouard when his brother painted away from the studio.[73]

In September 1868, Morisot began posing for Édouard. Morisot's mother, acting as chaperone, accompanied her daughter to his studio. If not there, Eugène met his future wife when she, her sister Edma, and their mother became regular guests at the Thursday evening soirées hosted by the Manets' mother, Eugénie.[74] The two families became close, and, in the summer of 1874, they vacationed together on the Normandy coast in Fécamp. Eugène and Berthe married in December of that year. Henceforth, when Berthe painted outside, she was frequently accompanied by Eugène, who painted alongside her. Berthe's opinion of her husband's artwork is unknown, but Eugène once did suggest, "I wouldn't mind at all if you were to compliment me a bit on my painting."[75] Eugène's works were more loosely drawn than Morisot's, but because they painted the same subjects and used the same materials, some are almost indistinguishable from each other.[76] Their daughter Julie was born in 1878 and soon became the favored model for both (fig. 64).

Eugène encouraged his wife's Impressionist colleagues. Eugène, Édouard, and their younger brother Gustave were all close with Claude Monet. In the mid-1870s, when Monet suffered financial difficulties, they each advanced him funds for the purchase of his paintings.[77] After running into Mary Cassatt, in 1882, Eugène told his wife of Cassatt's request to paint her and their daughter, Julie, together.[78] Berthe presumably refused, but that may have prompted her later that same year to paint her first self-portrait, with Julie.[79] Berthe also made seven paintings of Eugène, five of him with Julie. She wrote to Edma, who had often posed for her, "The poor man has taken your place."[80]

Edgar Degas invited Eugène to show with the Impressionists in 1877.[81] Because Édouard refused to participate in the exhibitions, preferring to seek recognition at the Salon like the artists in his wife's family, this invitation from Degas may have been his attempt to further link the Manet name with the Impressionists. It could, however, also speak to Degas's desire to encourage his friend to continue painting.

Eugène also devoted himself to assisting his wife. So that she would concentrate on her painting, he once suggested, "Keep visitors out, see people only at night, and lock your door when you are working."[82] When Berthe was in Nice with Julie, he retrieved her works from their rented country home, took them to be framed, and delivered them for inclusion in the upcoming Impressionist exhibition in Paris. He arrived as the paintings were being installed, writing to his wife, "Everyone was delighted to see me, especially because I have come for the purpose of exhibiting your works."[83] Despite his encouragement, Berthe was most concerned with her brother-in-law's response. "What does Édouard say of the exhibition as a whole?" she asked. "Has he been there?"[84]

When Édouard died in 1883, Eugène purchased a grave in the Passy cemetery, where he, Berthe, and Suzanne would also be interred.[85] Shortly thereafter, Eugène and Berthe moved into their new purpose-built house on the rue de Villejust. The following year, Eugène and Gustave Manet served on the committee organizing the memorial exhibition of Édouard's work. In the subsequent auction of Édouard's paintings, Eugène and Berthe purchased eight for their home. "Here I am with a whole gallery," Berthe wrote to her sister. "Our future inheritance from Madame [Eugénie] Manet has been eaten into, but no matter, one can only laugh."[86]

Eugène kept a journal when the family traveled to the Netherlands and to Gorey on the isle of Jersey in 1885–86,[87] and in 1889 he published a somewhat autobiographical novel, *Victimes!*[88] In October 1891, to achieve their desire to see "themselves in a beautiful setting before dying,"[89] they purchased a seventeenth-century château, le Mesnil-Saint-Laurent in Juziers, twenty-five miles northwest of Paris. Eugène died six months later and Berthe was soon forced to rent it to pay for its upkeep.[90] One of Eugène's final hopes, which may have been prompted several years earlier by his friendship with gallerist Theo van Gogh, was to organize an exhibition of Berthe's work. Her first and only lifetime solo exhibition, it opened five weeks after Eugène's death.

BILL SCOTT

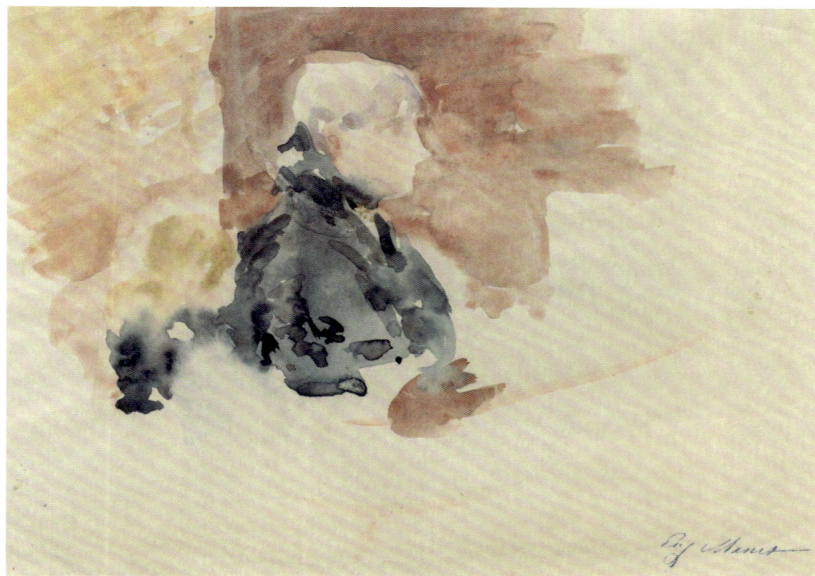

Fig. 65. Eugène Manet, *Berthe Morisot and Her Daughter, Julie Manet,* 1885. Watercolor and graphite on paper, 19.1 × 27.3 cm. Private collection

Berthe Morisot (Madame Eugène Manet, 1841–1895)

Berthe Morisot was a leading figure among the Impressionists and, at the start, the only female member of the group. She and Édouard Manet—colleagues and friends—inspired each other's work. As Manet's sister-in-law, she further reinforced his informal connection with the Impressionists.

As teens, Berthe and her two sisters, Edma (1839–1921) and Yves (1838–1893), took private drawing lessons arranged by their mother, who wanted to present their pictures to their father as a birthday present. Highly motivated, Berthe and Edma requested a more challenging teacher. For the next three years, Joseph-Benoît Guichard taught them in his own studio and at the Louvre, where, accompanied by their mother, the sisters copied paintings by Titian and Veronese. But when they asked to paint outdoors, Guichard encouraged them to go to Jean-Baptiste-Camille Corot. Under Corot's rigorous supervision, they copied his own landscape paintings in his studio before working en plein air with him and later with his protégé Achille-François Oudinot. Berthe also studied sculpture with Aimé Millet and was inspired by the sketch-like plein-air works of Léon Riesener, a favorite of Edgar Degas, Henri Fantin-Latour, and Pierre-Auguste Renoir.[91] Berthe and Edma both had landscape paintings accepted in the 1864 Paris Salon.

Morisot was introduced to Édouard Manet in 1868 and a few weeks later began posing for the seated figure in his large canvas *The Balcony* (see fig. 6).[92] She continued to show her work at the Paris Salon but ceased when she aligned herself with the Société Anonyme Coopérative des Artistes Peintres, Sculpteurs et Graveurs, organized by Renoir, Claude Monet, Camille Pissarro, and Alfred Sisley—later known as the Impressionists. She had ten works in the group's first show, in 1874, and would go on to participate in seven of their eight exhibitions. At the end of that year, Morisot married Manet's younger brother, Eugène, who, like Edma before him, became her frequent painting companion (fig. 65). He posed for her seven times, five of them with

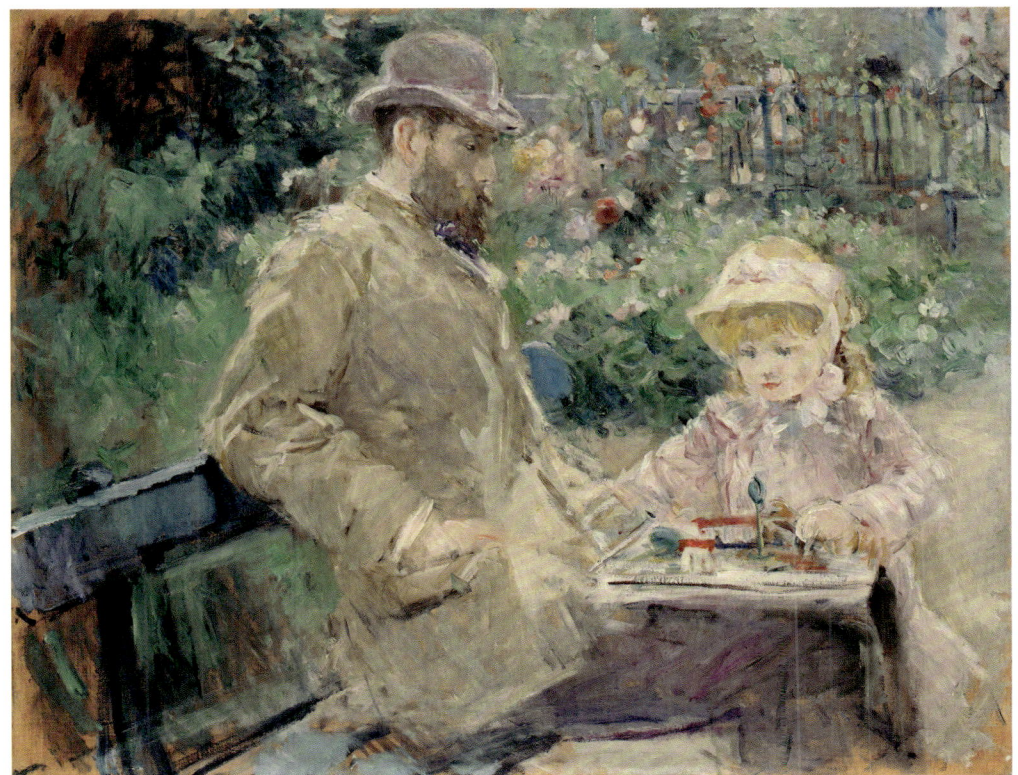

Fig. 66. Berthe Morisot, *Eugène Manet et sa fille dans le Jardin de Bougival*, 1881. Oil on canvas, 73 × 92 cm. Musée Marmottan-Monet, Paris

their daughter, Julie, born in 1878. The first painting she made of them together (fig. 66) was included in the 1882 Impressionist exhibition. It was the only portrait of her husband that she showed in her lifetime. Although he was Morisot's strongest advocate, she was annoyed by his reluctance to pose. "At once it becomes too much for him," she wrote.[93]

Besides Eugène, Morisot's preferred models were Julie, her sisters, her nieces, and several close female friends. She also hired young women recommended by other artists to pose in elegant dresses she acquired specifically for the purpose. One model recalled, "She would have me meet her [in the Bois de Boulogne] at half past six in the morning. At nine, her 'effect' was finished, and we returned to her home for a cup of coffee."[94] Morisot had always worked without making preparatory sketches or studies. But after seeing Renoir's drawings on an 1886 visit to his studio, she began to draw and to spend more time reworking her canvases. In addition to participating in the Impressionist exhibitions, she showed her work in London, New York, Brussels, Antwerp, and Paris. She had only one solo show, in 1892 at the gallery Boussod, Valadon et Cie in Paris. Forty paintings dating from 1872 to 1892 were presented together with pastels, watercolors, and drawings. Eugène had died just weeks before the opening, and she and Julie soon thereafter moved from the family home on the rue de Villejust to a smaller apartment on the rue Weber, closer to the Bois de Boulogne, where they painted together.

Throughout her life Morisot devoted herself to keeping Manet's work, even more than her own, at the forefront in the eyes of artists and the public. When she acquired his *Lady with Fans*,[95] she wrote to Edma, "I am in love with it. . . . I shall not let it go except to the Louvre, and if this does not come to pass in my lifetime, it will in [Julie's]."[96] She also acquired several family portraits, including Manet's *Study for Music in the Tuileries*, the only work of his for which Eugène had posed that she and Julie owned.[97] Manet gave her two of the ten portraits he painted of her, and she purchased a third at auction in 1894.[98] At the same sale, a painting of hers, first sold in 1880 when it was displayed in the fifth Impressionist exhibition, was acquired by the French government.[99] Exhibited in the Musée du Luxembourg, it was the only work of hers to be acquired by a museum in her lifetime. The evening before her death, she wrote to Julie with suggestions for the dispersal of some of her canvases. She asked her daughter to give a painting each to Edma, to Renoir, and to Monet. And for Degas, who had amassed an extraordinary art collection, she requested, "Tell M. Degas that if he founds a museum, he should select a Manet."[100]

BILL SCOTT

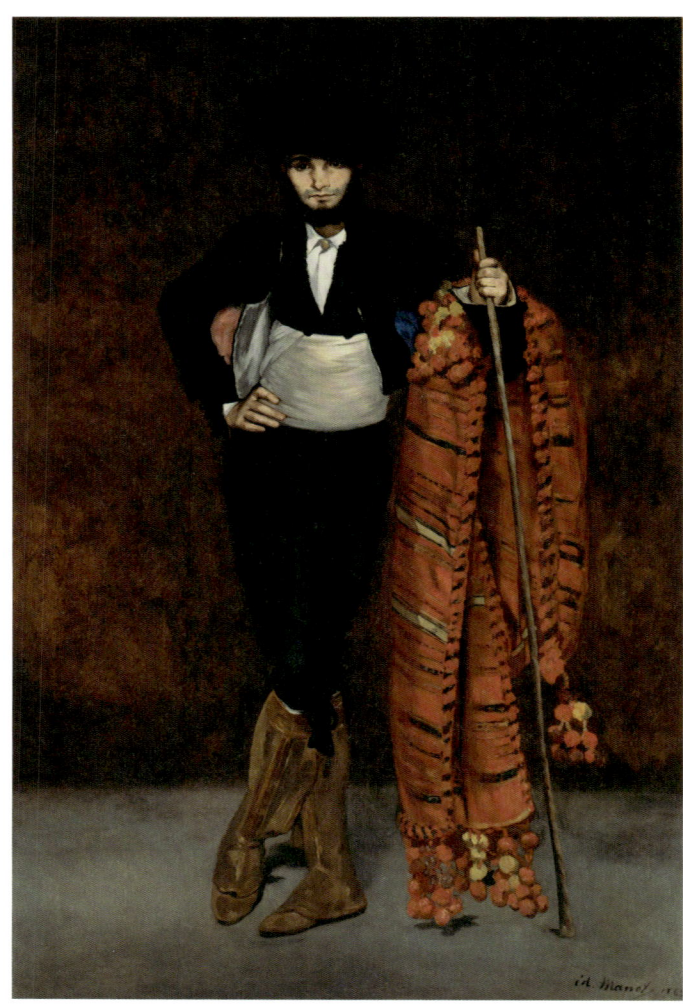

Fig. 67. Édouard Manet, *Young Man in the Costume of a Majo*, 1863. Oil on canvas, 188 × 124.8 cm. The Metropolitan Museum of Art, New York. H. O. Havemeyer Collection, Bequest of Mrs. H. O. Havemeyer, 1929

Gustave Manet (1835–1884)

Gustave Manet was born on March 16, 1835, the last of Auguste and Eugénie Manet's three sons and the younger brother of Édouard and Eugène. The details of his life are the least known of the Manet brothers and though further research is required to determine if Gustave made art himself, it is well known that he was involved with Édouard's art and the art world.[101] He came the closest out of the Manet children to follow in their father's footsteps by becoming a lawyer; although Gustave's political disposition and views as a Radical Republican—left-wing views

Édouard shared—would steer him toward politics. Unlike today's definition of radicalism as an extremist ideology, Radical Republicanism in nineteenth-century France was a moderate center-left position.[102]

Gustave and his brothers served in the National Guard during the Franco-Prussian War (1870–71) and stayed in Paris during the Prussians's siege of the city. His disappointment with the French government's decision to capitulate to Prussia and the resulting peace treaty is evident in his letters to his mother, where he called it a disgrace. Having opposed the violence of the subsequent Paris Commune (March–May 1871), he worked with other like-minded Republicans to attempt to broker a peaceful solution. Gustave introduced Édouard to Georges Clemenceau, the French statesman and future prime minister, whom the artist painted around 1879–1880.[103] Gustave became Inspector General of Prisons, and served as a municipal councillor for Paris's eighteenth arrondissement in 1876 and 1878 after being successfully elected with the backing of Clemenceau.[104] At the end of his life, Gustave was working as a municipal councillor in the south of France.[105]

Gustave supported his brother's art in several ways, most notably as a model. He can be found along with several family members and friends in *Music in the Tuileries* (see fig. 4). He also posed for Édouard's landmark 1863 *Young Man in the Costume of a Majo* (fig. 67).[106] In this painting he is wearing the same trousers and bolero jacket worn by Victorine Meurent in *Mademoiselle V . . . in the Costume of an Espada* (1862, Metropolitan Museum of Art, New York). Gustave likely served as a model, along with his older brother Eugène, in *Le Déjeuner sur l'herbe* (see fig. 84). It is believed that the reclining male figure in the right side of the painting is a composite of the two men. Antonin Proust, a lifelong friend of the Manet family, said the figure has Gustave's dark hair and Eugène's "finer features."[107]

Though not a professional artist himself, Gustave was part of the Manets' broadly creative social group and was a regular feature of the gatherings Eugénie Manet hosted for her own friends on Tuesdays and for Édouard and his many notable friends on Thursdays.[108] He was even the first member of the Manet family to meet Claude Monet. Early in their acquaintance, Monet apparently asked him whether he was related to the artist Édouard Manet who—to the frustration of both artists—had a similar signature. To this Gustave answered simply: "He is my brother."[109] Eventually all the Manet brothers would become close friends with Monet, and Gustave served as the witness to Monet's marriage to Camille-Léonie Doncieux in 1870.[110]

Though Gustave is the most obscure of the three Manet brothers, available sources—including his simple response to Monet—suggest that he was frank, terse with his words, and stoic. His letters to his mother during the war were written from a political perspective and lacked the sentimentality expressed freely in Édouard's.[111] This does not, however, mean he was not close to his family. Gustave was at his brother's side, along with medical personnel, during the operation to amputate Édouard's gangrenous foot at the end of the artist's life, and he kept nearby family members informed during the procedure.[112] The surgery was not successful, and Édouard died eleven days later on April 30, 1883. Gustave led his brother's funeral procession along with Eugène and their cousin Jules Dejouy.[113] Gustave also played a part in shepherding his brother's legacy, working alongside other family members to organize a posthumous retrospective exhibition of the eldest Manet's work.[114]

Gustave died on December 18, 1884, shortly after his eldest brother. He was in Menton, a seaside town in the south of France, where he had moved to treat his own poor health.[115] In another blow to the Manet family, Eugénie would die soon after Gustave in January 1885. The one possible consolation amid all this tragedy is that Eugénie was not cognizant of her youngest son's death prior to her own passing.[116] Claude Monet sent a letter to Eugène after having read of Gustave's death in the newspaper. He wrote, "I am very shocked, and greatly aggrieved, for we were old acquaintances, old friends."[117]

ADRIENNE CHAPARRO

Jules Dejouy (1815–1894)

Édouard Manet's first cousin and close friend, Anatole Jules Dejouy, was almost a generation older than the artist (fig. 68). He had a long and successful career as a lawyer at the Paris court of appeals. Manet named Dejouy executor of his will, and his cousin also helped organize the 1884 exhibition and sale of works after the artist's death.

Jules, as he was called, was the son of Denis François Claude De Jouy (1780–1854) and Emilie Manet (1795–1834), the sister of Manet's father Auguste. Dejouy's father, a wealthy businessman and property owner in Paris, became the mayor of Gennevilliers, where the Manets owned extensive property and where Jules was born.[118] Jules's grandfather, Jean-Baptiste François Noël Dejouy (1753–1814) was a judge in the civil and criminal tribunals of Seine-et-Marne,

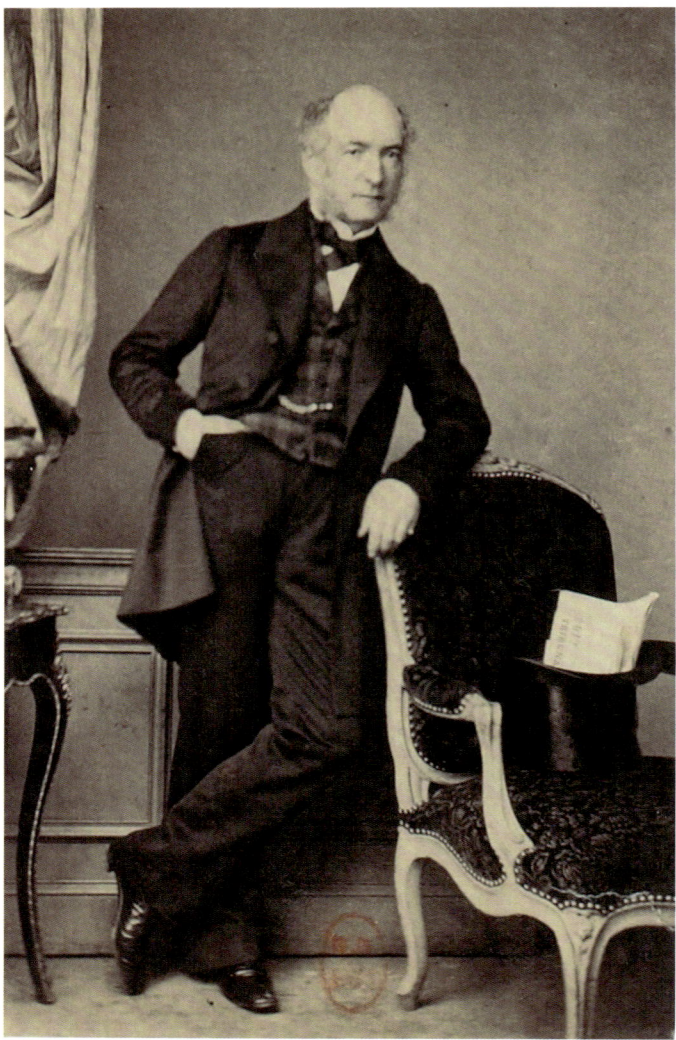

Fig. 68. Franck, *Jules Dejouy*, from *Album of cartes-de-visite Portraits Belonging to Édouard Manet*, about 1857–70. Carte-de-visite, 9.2 × 5.6 cm. Bibliothèque Nationale de France, Paris

a lawyer at the *parlement* (appeals court) of the *ancien régime*, and a banker authorized to transmit papal bulls and other official documents from the Roman Curia.[119] Dejouy married his cousin, Marie Geneviève Quatremère (1825–1847), at Saint-Sulpice in Paris on April 27, 1847.[120] The union lasted less than seven months; Marie Geneviève died in Rome, November 23, 1847, at age twenty-two. Dejouy remained an unmarried widower for the rest of his life.[121]

Jules took his oath of service as a lawyer on November 7, 1836.[122] When he became a lawyer at the Paris court of appeals in 1849, there were 27 *cours d'appel* in France.[123] The appeals courts represented a second degree of judicature

that reexamined judgments from the first-degree courts like the Tribunal de première instance (where Manet's father served as a civil judge), and the Tribunal de Commerce, which handled commercial cases.[124] Dejouy specialized in business law; one of his biggest clients was the insurance company Urbaine.[125] Appeals assigned to Dejouy dealt with myriad issues, including contested wills, mortgages and fore-closures, and separation of properties.[126] He also acted as counsel to the communes around Paris.[127] Dejouy some-times argued in courts outside the capital, but other than one year as a substitute in the public prosecutor's depart-ment, he spent his fifty-five-year career at the Paris court of appeals.[128] He also mentored younger lawyers, including Manet's youngest brother Gustave, who became the Inspec-tor General of Prisons, and Léon Gambetta, who held a variety of governmental positions in France's Third Republic, including Prime Minister.

When Manet's friend, the writer Émile Zola, wrote his novel *La Curée (The Kill)*, a story of corruption and specula-tion during the vast renovation of the city of Paris under Georges-Eugène Haussmann, he asked Jules Dejouy for examples. Zola's preparatory dossier for *La Curée* includes notes he took from Dejouy's explanations of the inner work-ings of city expropriation, and how landlords and financiers profited from it.[129] For example, Zola's notebook reads: "Examples of expropriation (Dejouy). Boulevard du Prince Eugène (Dates). Surveying agents. *Agents of expropriation.* Theft of the Compagnie Immobilière/exemption of 2 years of rent."[130] The lawyer's explanation of how speculators in league with the surveying agents could buy up properties in advance of the city's actions—then inflate claims of rents due to obtain maximum compensation from the city—helped Zola create the character of Aristide Saccard, who becomes an assistant surveying clerk at the Paris Hôtel de Ville.[131] A common tactic, noted as "exemption of 2 years of rent," was for the speculator to buy a building slated for demolition, then raise the rents on paper while actually offering tenants an off-the-books discount such as two years' free rent. The speculator then quoted the higher rent figure when the city assessed the building's value to pay. Zola's Aristide quickly picks up on this trick and uses it to build his over-leveraged real estate empire.

Zola's notes from Dejouy include the example of the Boulevard du Prince-Eugène.[132] Now called the Boulevard Voltaire, the sprawling Haussmannian project included a case that went through nine years of litigation, with two appeals handled by Dejouy.[133] In the penultimate chapter of *La Curée*, the impending path of the Boulevard du Prince-Eugène prompts Aristide to persuade his wife to sign over her title to an affected property on the rue de Charonne; the resulting indemnity is central to the novel's dramatic conclusion.

In 1888, after decades of service in the appeals court, Dejouy was elected to the Conseil de l'Ordre des avocats, an elite administrative council of twenty-four members overseeing all tribunals and appeals courts.[134] In the winter of 1892, the jurist suffered an attack of some sort, and became paralyzed.[135] He died in Paris on March 9, 1894, two days after his seventy-ninth birthday.[136] His obituary in *Le Droit* called him one of those "ancestors who had accustomed us to watching them defy the years," and noted that he had become "one of the best known and most sympathetic figures in the judicial world."[137]

NANCY LOCKE

Julie Manet (Madame Ernest Rouart, 1878–1966)

Julie Manet, the only child of Berthe Morisot and Eugène Manet, was raised in a world of artists and writers. She became her mother's favorite model, and her uncle Édouard also painted her when she was little (fig. 69). She accompanied her parents when they painted outdoors. In the Tuileries Garden in Paris, when Julie was six, Morisot was delighted when her daughter "saw pink in the light and purple in the shadows."[138]

The family lived in the two-story ground floor apartment in the building constructed by Berthe and Eugène on rue de Villejust. The salon where they entertained also served as Morisot's studio. By age nine, Julie was painting with her parents in the studio, their garden, or in the Bois de Boulogne, the large park close to their home. When Julie's cousin Paule Gobillard, eleven years her senior, decided to become a painter, Morisot accompanied her to the Louvre, where they drew together from Old Masters paintings.[139] Julie also started making pencil and watercolor copies after photographs of works by Titian and François Boucher as well as after her own portrait by Pierre-Auguste Renoir, which had been recently commissioned by her parents. Mostly, she made copies of the seventeen oil paintings by Édouard Manet hanging in their house (fig. 70).[140]

After her father's death in 1892, her mother moved them to a smaller apartment on rue Weber, closer to the Bois de Boulogne. Julie began writing a journal, which

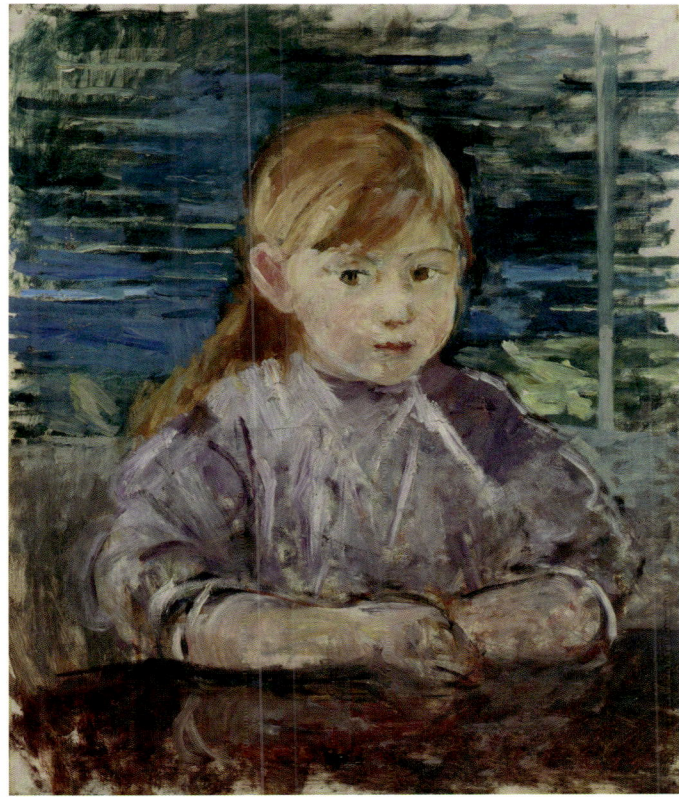

Fig. 69. Berthe Morisot, *Fil'ette en mauve*, 1383. Oil on canvas, 57.2 × 47 cm. Cathy Lasry

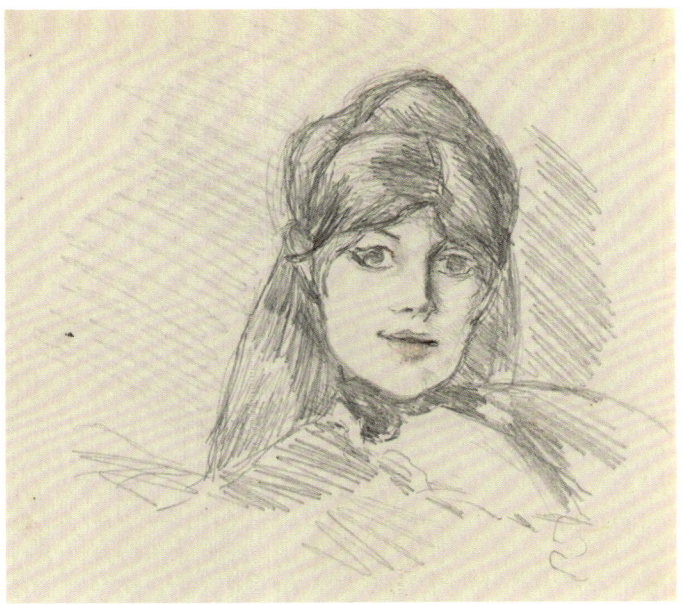

Fig. 70. Julie Manet, Copy of Édouard Manet, *Berthe Morisot étendue* (1873), about 1896. Graphite and colored pencil on paper, 26.7 × 20 cm. Private collection

included descriptions of her daily activities, the unexpected death of her mother in 1895, and a detailed account of the presentation of more than 395 works by Morisot at the Galerie Durand-Ruel in 1896. Renoir and Stéphane Mallarmé served as guardians to Julie, an orphan at sixteen. It was they who, together with Edgar Degas and Claude Monet, arranged and installed the memorial exhibition for Morisot.[141]

Thereafter, Julie lived with her cousins Paule and Jeannie Gobillard (also recently orphaned) in her childhood home on the rue de Villejust. In 1897, encouraged by Degas, she met Ernest Rouart, a young painter he was mentoring.[142] Three years later they married in a double ceremony with Jeannie and poet Paul Valéry. Just as Julie had posed for close to one-third of Morisot's paintings, she began to pose frequently for Ernest.

Throughout her life Julie was devoted to preserving her mother's memory. At nineteen, she copied Veronese's *Le Calvaire* in the Louvre, as Morisot had done at that age.[143] Possibly to document her mother's oeuvre, she also continued copying her works. She likely received technical help from Edma Morisot Pontillon, an aunt who by then was living in Julie's building and making her own pastel copies of paintings by Morisot.

Julie and Ernest began photographing Morisot's works, leading to the publication of two catalogues raisonnés, the first in 1933 and a more comprehensive edition in 1961.[144] Without seeking attention for herself, she oversaw the publication of two monographs on her mother, one by her brother-in-law Louis Rouart.[145] Valéry wrote two essays about Morisot, the second published in the catalogue for the important centennial exhibition at the Musée de l'Orangerie. Julie's youngest son, Denis, edited the book of Morisot's correspondence.[146] Between 1905 and 1920 Julie and her husband donated six Morisot paintings to French museums but saved her most unfinished canvases to prevent them from being reworked,[147] as she had seen happen with incomplete works by her uncle.[148] In 1930 they donated a large Manet painting that her parents had acquired in 1884 to the Louvre—one her mother hoped someday would hang there.[149] Whenever traveling, she took with her Manet's smallest portrait of her mother, *Portrait of Berthe Morisot Reclining*, packed in a specially made valise. She teasingly called it her "Manet de Poche."[150]

Julie painted still lifes and landscapes but focused on portraits of her cousins, her three sons (Clément, Julien, and Denis), and her four grandchildren. She painted until the very end of her life, but exhibited only once, in 1955, at age seventy-six. The installation, in her late husband's studio,

included ninety-seven paintings from 1892 to 1955, and her watercolor copies of works by her uncle.[151]

At seventeen, Julie bought a watercolor by Paul Cézanne,[152] and years later she traded a portrait of Suzanne Manet by her uncle[153] for a large water lily canvas by Monet.[154] Except for these two paintings, her collection primarily comprised works she inherited from her parents and some first owned by her father-in-law, Henri Rouart, bought by her husband in 1912 and 1913 at the auctions of his estate.[155] Julie and Ernest's sons lived on the first, second, and third floors, respectively, of the rue Villejust. Valéry, Jeannie, and Paule lived together on the fourth floor. Julie and Ernest were on the top floor. Impressionist paintings were everywhere, prompting one family member to later recall, "In those years it was not the Musée du Jeu de Paume but this building, Julie Manet's home, that was the true museum of Impressionism."[156]

BILL SCOTT

Ernest Rouart (1874–1942)

Ernest Rouart is best remembered as the sole student of Edgar Degas and the husband of Julie Manet, the niece of Édouard Manet. The fourth of five children, Rouart trained to take over the successful engineering firm founded by his father, Henri Rouart. However, impressed by his father's painting and perhaps more importantly by his vast art collection, Ernest decided that he too wanted to paint (fig. 18.1).

Ernest echoed Henri in his support of other artists. In 1868 Henri began showing his paintings at the Paris Salon, and while serving in the Franco-Prussian War (1870–71) he became reacquainted with Degas, who had been a child-hood friend. Soon thereafter Henri ceased showing at the Salon. In 1874 he took part in the first Impressionist exhibition. As one of the wealthiest members of the group, Henri went on to finance several of their shows, including the 1882 exhibition, which, ironically, was the only one of the eight in which he did not participate.

Henri encouraged Ernest and asked Degas to be his son's mentor. Degas agreed and commenced to teach him the materials and techniques used by the Old Masters. In 1897, with Degas's guidance, Ernest painted a copy of Andrea Mantegna's *Triumph of the Virtues* on a canvas the same size as the original.[157] A family member observed that Ernest thereafter "had for Degas the affection of a son as well as the reverence of a disciple."[158]

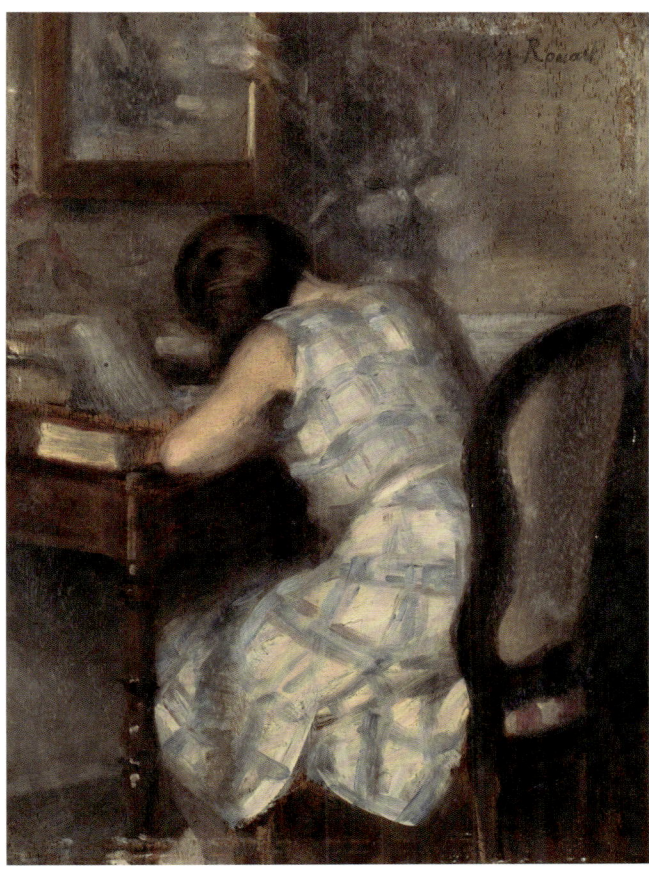

Fig. 71. Ernest Rouart, *Young Girl at Work*, before 1931. Oil on wood, 22.3 × 16 cm. Musée d'Orsay, Paris. Don Ernest Rouart, 1931

Working in oil, pastel, watercolor, drawing, and print-making, Ernest depicted family members, friends, professional models, and groups of figures in domestic interiors, on city streets, and at the beach. Like his father, he never had a solo exhibition, but he was included in group shows, beginning in 1899 at the Société Nationale des Beaux-Arts. A few months earlier, Degas had introduced him to Julie Manet, the twenty-year-old daughter of Berthe Morisot and Eugène Manet. They were soon engaged, and on May 31, 1900, they married in a double wedding with Julie's cousin Jeannie Gobillard and poet Paul Valéry. The two couples remained lifelong friends, living in different apartments in the five-story Paris building on the rue de Villejust constructed by Julie's parents in 1883. Ernest oversaw the printing of Morisot's eight drypoints in 1904–5 and a few years later began having her work photographed, possibly in tandem with dealer Ambroise Vollard, who was organizing the first (never-realized) catalogue raisonné.[159]

In January 1912 Henri Rouart died. Ernest and his four siblings organized three auctions to sell their father's collection of some nine hundred works, including multiple paintings by Degas, Manet, Eugène Delacroix, Honoré Daumier, and more than fifty by Jean-Baptiste-Camille Corot. Although there is no known personal interaction between Henri and Morisot, he owned three works by her as well as an early landscape by her sister Edma Morisot Pontillon, made when both sisters were studying with Corot.[160] Ernest bought many works at the auctions,[161] including Corot's *Gardens of the Villa d'Este at Tivoli* (Musée du Louvre, Paris).[162]

While serving in World War I, Ernest contracted an incurable lung disease that weakened him for the rest of his life. He continued to paint in the studio in his late father's house on the rue de Lisbonne. Fearing the two-mile commute was too stressful for her ailing husband, Julie had a studio built for him behind their home in 1927 in what had been the garden where she played as a child and where her mother and father had painted her. With a twenty-one-foot-high ceiling and a huge south-facing window, it paralleled the first-floor salon that had been Morisot's studio.

Julie and Ernest had three sons, all of whom posed for their father, both as themselves or dressed as mythological characters. In 1931 Clément, their second son, married Victoria Rapin, the younger sister of Juliette, who several months earlier had married Clément's first cousin, painter Augustin Rouart. Thereafter, Victoria, Juliette, and their sister Espérance frequently posed for Ernest.[163] The year of Clément's marriage, Ernest donated one of his paintings of his daughter-in-law to the Musée du Luxembourg (fig. 71). It may have been an homage to Clément because hanging on the wall behind Victoria is a painting by Morisot that the artist herself had rolled up and hidden. It remained undiscovered until twenty years after her death. As a child Clément found it while playing and he remembered excitedly running with it to give to his mother.[164]

Ernest devoted the last decade of his life to organizing exhibitions at the Musée l'Orangerie in Paris in honor of the centennials of the births of Manet in 1932, Degas in 1934, and Morisot in 1941. After Ernest's death in February 1942, his family mounted a memorial exhibition of his paintings at the Galerie Berri-Raspail in June.

BILL SCOTT

Manet Oil Paintings Featuring Select Family Members

Family Member	Number of Depictions	Title
Suzanne Leenhoff Manet	21	*Portrait of Madame Manet* (RW 117)
		Madame Manet (RW 116) (fig. 31)
		Fishing (RW 36) (cat. no. 6)
		Portrait of Madame Manet at Bellevue (RW 345)
		Woman with a Cat (RW 337) (fig. 27)
		Madame Manet in the Conservatory (RW 290) (fig. 30)
		Madame Manet at the Piano (RW 131) (cat. no. 9, figs. 29, 47)
		Madame Manet au Balcon (RW 202)
		Interior at Arcachon (RW 170) (cat. no. 10)
		Reading (RW 136) (cat. no. 11)
		Surprised Nymph (RW 40) (fig. 1)
		Study for Moses Saved from the Waters (No RW) (cat. no. 4)
		Surprised Nymph Study I (RW 38)
		Study for Surprised Nymph/Moses Saved from the Waters (RW 39) (cat. no. 5)
		On the Beach (RW 188)
		The Swallows (RW 190)
		Interior (RW 217)
		Music in the Tuileries* (RW 51) (fig. 4)
		The Croquet Party* (RW 173) (cat. no. 12)
		Women at the Races* (RW 95)
		Madame Édouard Manet on a Blue Sofa (RW 3 in vol. 2) (fig. 28)[165]
Léon-Édouard Koëlla, better known as Léon Leenhoff	18	*Spanish Cavaliers* (RW 26) (cat. no. 2)
		The Balcony (RW 134) (fig. 6)
		View of the 1867 Exposition Universelle (RW 123)
		Boy with a Sword (RW 37) (fig. 34)
		Boy Blowing Bubbles (RW 129) (cat. no. 7)
		Young Boy Pealing a Pear (RW 130) (cat. no. 8)
		Luncheon in the Studio (RW 135) (fig. 7)
		The Velocipede (RW 171)
		Eva Gonzales Painting in Manet's Studio (RW 153)
		Oloron-Sainte-Marie (RW 163)
		Fishing (RW 36) (cat. no. 6)
		Interior at Arcachon (RW 170) (cat. no. 10)
		Reading (RW 136) (cat. no. 11)
		The Croquet Party (RW 173) (cat. no. 12)
		Study for Moses Saved from the Waters* (cat. no. 4)
		Music in the Tuileries* (RW 51) (fig. 4)
		The Fifer* (RW 113)[166]
		The Old Musician* (RW 52)

Family Member	Number of Depictions	Title
Berthe Morisot	11	*Berthe Morisot Reclining* (RW 209)
		Woman in Rose Shoes (Berthe Morisot) (RW 177)
		Berthe Morisot with a Bouquet of Violets (RW 179)
		Berthe Morisot with a Fan (RW 181)
		Portrait of Berthe Morisot with a Fan (RW 229)
		Portrait of Berthe Morisot in Mourning (RW 228)
		Veiled Young Woman (RW 178)
		Berthe Morisot in Profile (RW 139)
		Berthe Morisot (RW 138) (cat. no. 13)
		The Balcony (RW 134) (fig. 6)
		Repose (RW 158) (fig. 8)
Eugénie-Desirée Fournier Manet	5	*Madame Auguste Manet* (RW 62) (cat. no. 1, fig. 12)
		Madame Manet Mère in the Bellevue Garden (RW 346)
		Monsieur and Madame Auguste Manet (RW 30) (cat. no. 3)
		Music in the Tuileries* (RW 51) (fig. 4)
		The Croquet Party* (RW 173) (cat. no. 12)
Eugène Manet	3	*Music in the Tuileries* (RW 51) (fig. 4)
		Le Déjeuner sur l'herbe* (RW 67) (fig. 84)[167]
		On the Beach (RW 188)
Gustave Manet	3	*Music in the Tuileries* (RW 51) (fig. 4)
		Le Déjeuner sur l'herbe (RW 67) (fig. 84)
		Young Man in the Costume of a Majo (RW 70) (fig. 67)
Leenhoff Brothers (Rudolf and Ferdinand)	3	*Le Déjeuner sur l'herbe* (RW 67) (fig. 84)
		Argenteuil (RW 221)
		Boating (RW 223)
Julie Manet	2	*Julie Manet at Fifteen Months* (RW 298)
		Julie Manet on a Watering Can (RW 399)
Jules Dejouy	1	*Monsieur Jules Dejouy* (RW 294) (cat. no. 15)
Auguste Manet	1	*Monsieur and Madame Auguste Manet* (RW 30) (cat. no. 3)
Edma Morisot	1	*In the Garden* (RW 155)

*   Any title marked with an asterix likely includes the sitter but is not confirmed.

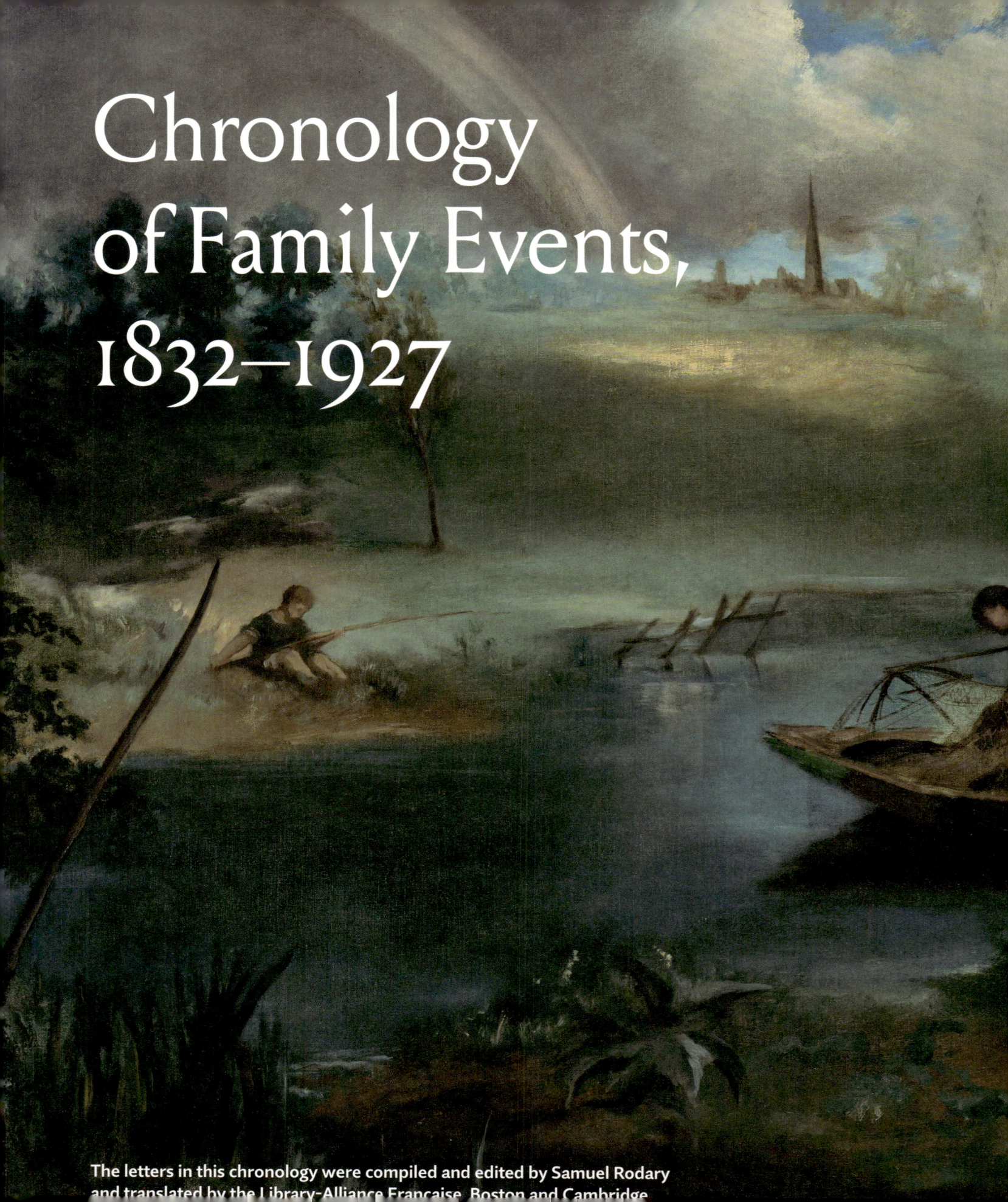

Chronology
of Family Events,
1832–1927

The letters in this chronology were compiled and edited by Samuel Rodary
and translated by the Library-Alliance Francaise, Boston and Cambridge

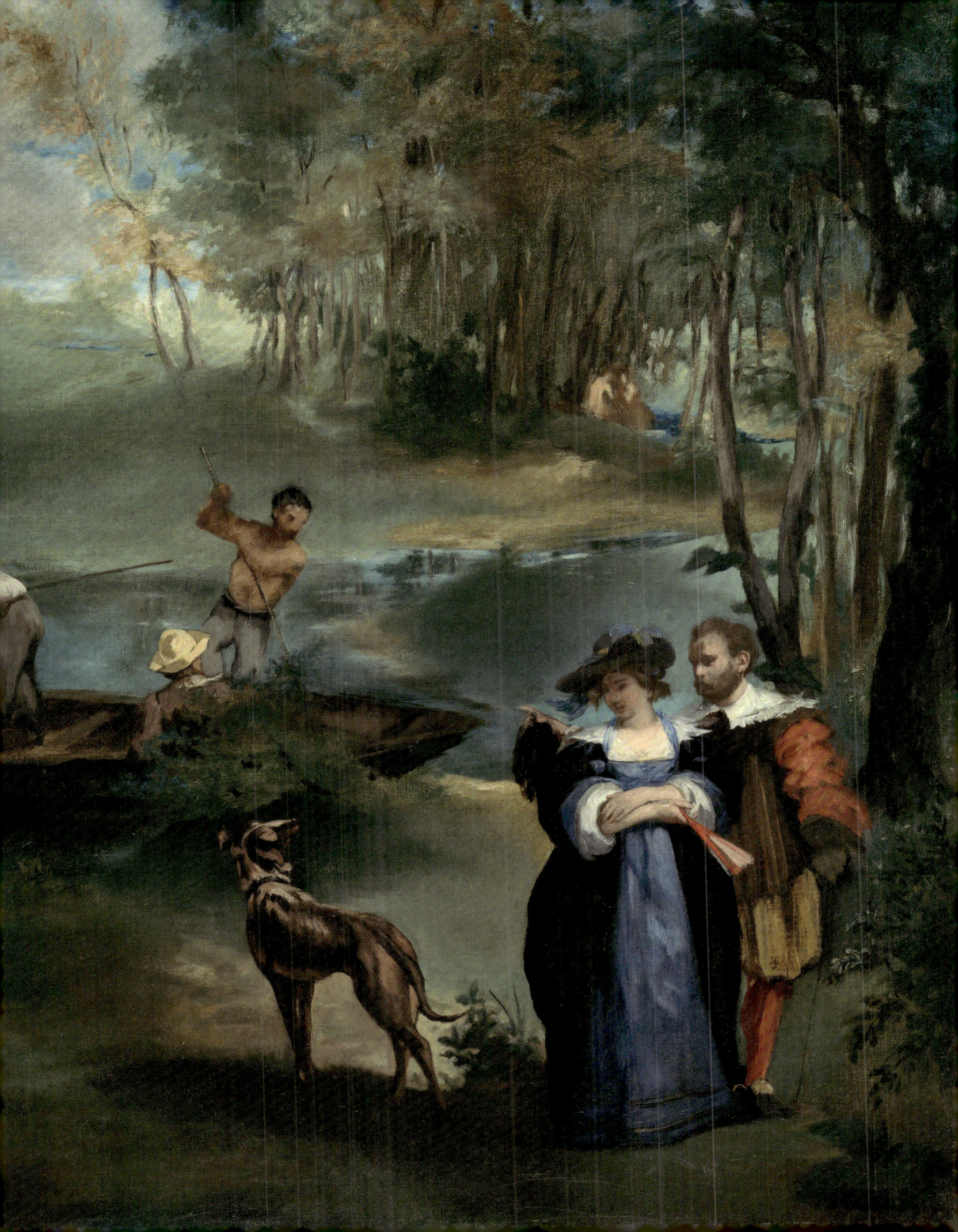

1832	JANUARY 23: Édouard Manet is born in Paris at 5, rue des Petits-Augustins (now rue Bonaparte) to Auguste and Eugénie Manet.
	JANUARY 25: Auguste is named a chevalier of the Legion of Honor, the highest order of merit in France.[1]
1833	NOVEMBER 21: The artist's younger brother Eugène Manet is born.
1835	MARCH 16: The artist's youngest brother Gustave Manet is born.
1841	Auguste is appointed a judge of the Court of First Instance, a trial court for the Department of Seine.[2]
1844	Manet enrolls at the private secondary school Collège Rollin. His maternal uncle, Edmond Fournier, takes him to the Louvre and encourages his artistic interests.[3]
1847	LATE JULY: Manet fails the entrance exam for the French naval academy.[4]
1848	DECEMBER 9: Manet sets sail on the *Havre et Guadeloupe* from Normandy to Rio de Janeiro, Brazil, in a failed attempt to qualify for the navy.[5]
1849	MARCH 11: Édouard Manet, *Havre et Guadeloupe*, Rio de Janeiro Harbor, to Eugène Manet[6]

My dear brother,

I have no hope of being accepted this year, as we are even more disturbed aboard a ship than on land, and this stupid measure that was just adopted makes it almost inaccessible to enroll in the school.

From what Mother tells me in her letter, mathematics put you off. Do not be discouraged! Beginnings have the same effect on everyone. I charge you to say many good things on my behalf to my friends at the Collège Rollin and to give them good handshakes from me.

I hope to find Edmond [Fournier] at Saint-Cyr on my return. Is our dear cousin getting on very well? Did he have all the pleasures he hoped to have this winter? His father had given him permission to go to the Bal de l'Opéra this year. I thought of him during the Mardi Gras celebrations. Our carnival was not very cheerful. Did you read in Mother's letter, the strange custom in the country of throwing water balloons? That's how the three days go.

Jules [Dejouy] wrote to me, as you must know. He told me that he left the rue Guénégaud. He was so well there, I thought. I hope, despite Louis Napoleon, to still find him working at the court on my return.

Your devoted brother,
Édouard Manet

Dear Father,

So you still had feelings in Paris. Try to keep a good republic for us for our return, because I fear that L. Napoleon is not very republican.

A friend of Mr. R., Mr. Guillemot, chargé d'affaires in Montevideo, just arrived in Rio. He's returning to France. Perhaps he will embark on our ship. Paul, if you remember, wanted me to give him a letter of recommendation.

I learned with sorrow about Grandma's illness. She is finally better now. I hope it will last.

The letters of Eugène and Edmond made me very happy. In my spare time, I read and reread your letters.

Farewell, dear Papa, embrace Mama and everyone, for me. I am closing my letter and will hand it over. I was on chores all day and didn't have any time.

Your respectful son,
Édouard Manet

BY JUNE: Eugénie and Auguste hire Suzanne Leenhoff as piano teacher for the younger Manet brothers, Eugène and Gustave. It is unclear exactly when she started working for the family.[8]

JUNE 13: Édouard returns from Rio and likely meets Suzanne in the following weeks.[9]

1850   Manet starts studying with the innovative history painter Thomas Couture and registers as a copyist at the Louvre for the first time.[10]

1852   JANUARY 29: Léon-Édouard Koëlla, known as Léon Leenhoff, is born to Suzanne Leenhoff. It is unclear who fathered Léon, who would have been conceived in April or early May 1851.[11]

JULY 19: Manet travels to Holland, where he visits the Rijksmuseum. This is his first trip to another European country beyond France.[12]

1853   SEPTEMBER 17: Édouard travels to Venice with Eugène.

OCTOBER 7: The brothers arrive in Florence and Édouard paints copies in the Uffizi. They travel to Rome approximately ten days later.[13]

1855   The Manet family moves from 5, rue des Petits-Augustins to 69, rue de Clichy.[14]

I am so unhappy and so sad, my dear Édouard, that I fear not to have sufficiently expressed to you how grateful I am for your visit yesterday.

In almost all the letters, my poor Edmond was talking about you and asking us about your work and your success. Unfortunately, it was impossible for me to answer his questions because of the separation that exists between me and all of you.

This separation, you know, cannot be healed. So, your visit yesterday increasingly proves the nobility of your heart and of your feelings. Keep these feelings, my dear Édouard, and rest assured that you will always find in me a tender and good friend.

Athénaïs and I embrace you with great affection.

Yours,
Fournier

You cannot believe how, in Pontcelles, everyone was moved and touched by your visit. Your praise is in every mouth.

NOVEMBER 4: Léon is baptized at the Dutch Reformed Church in Batignolles, a neighborhood in Paris, with Suzanne's grandmother as godmother and Édouard as godfather.[16]

1856   **FEBRUARY:** Manet leaves Couture's studio and moves into a studio at 4, rue Lavoisier shared with animal painter Albert de Balleroy.[17]

1857   **OCTOBER 21:** Édouard and Eugène travel to Florence for the marriage of their friend Émile Ollivier to Blandine Liszt.[18]

DECEMBER 18: Paralyzed, Auguste ceases to report to his chambers. He is diagnosed with "cerebral congestion," a euphemism for tertiary syphilis.[19]

1858   Manet moves to a studio at 52, rue de la Victoire after the tragic suicide of his young studio assistant.[20]

1859   **FEBRUARY 26:** Auguste's official retirement begins.[21]

1860   **SUMMER:** Édouard possibly moves in with Suzanne and Léon on the rue de l'Hôtel de Ville (now rue des Batignolles). Establishes his studio on the rue de Douai.[22]

1861   Manet moves his studio to 81, rue Guyot.

1862   **SEPTEMBER 22:** Auguste dies. He is buried at the Montmartre cemetery in the Manet family crypt. An obituary in the *Gazette des tribunaux* attributes his death to overwork.[23]

1863

Dear Madame,

I am very grateful for your gracious invitation. As for the feelings I may have for your son, you know that I express them poorly, and what you say about it is far too graceful, for it seems very difficult not to love his character just as much as his talents.

I ask you, madame, to accept the assurance of my highest regard.

Charles Baudelaire

AUGUST: The Manet brothers sell some of the family property in Gennevilliers and divide the proceeds.[25]

SEPTEMBER 17: A Parisian notary draws up a marriage contract for Édouard and Suzanne; his mother and his brothers, and her brother, sister, and brother-in-law, are witnesses.[26]

OCTOBER 28: Manet and Suzanne marry in Zaltbommel in the Netherlands and spend a month in Holland. Léon is not present at the marriage; his uncles Eugène Manet and Ferdinand Leenhoff take him to a boarding school for boys, Marc-Dastès, in Batignolles.[27]

1864

NOVEMBER: Manet, Suzanne, and Léon (when home from school) move to 34, Boulevard des Batignolles.[28]

1865

AUGUST: Manet travels to Spain.

SEPTEMBER 5: Suzanne Manet, château de Vassé, to Charles Baudelaire[29]

Dear Sir,

In my husband's absence, your letter to Édouard arrived here in the countryside, at the residence of one of his uncles. The urgency of your mail dictated to me the obligation to break the seal.

Forgive me, sir, for having thus intruded into your private troubles. Please allow me to thank you from the bottom of my heart for thinking of the sensitivity of my poor Édouard, and of the worries he has for his own future!

Édouard left Paris eight days ago, intending to extend his stay in Spain, to pick me up in Maine[30] and stay there for a while. I am letting you know, sir, that you will be able find another friend who will promptly be able to see the people you mention on your behalf. Perhaps that will be easier for you, since my dear husband is a very poor businessman, even though his friendship for you is vital! The Lejosnes did return to Paris, and we saw the *commandant* before your departure. I have not yet heard from Édouard, and this silence seems long.

My mother-in-law asks me to thank you for your good wishes and sends you her best in return. Please accept, sir, the assurance of my own highest regard.

Suzanne Manet

SEPTEMBER 13: Édouard joins his family–certainly Suzanne, and likely his mother and Léon as well–on vacation at the château de Vassé, in the Sarthe.[31]

1866   FALL: Édouard, Suzanne, and Léon move in with Eugénie at 49, rue de Saint-Pétersbourg.[32]

1867   MAY 24: With financial support from his mother, Édouard mounts a solo exhibition of fifty paintings at the Pont de l'Alma, outside the grounds of the Exposition Universelle.[33]

SUMMER: Manet and his family start an annual tradition of vacationing in Boulogne-sur-Mer.[34]

1868   AROUND JULY: Artist Henri Fantin-Latour introduces painters and sisters Berthe and Edma Morisot to Édouard at the Louvre.

1870   MARCH 2: Eugénie Manet to Henri Fantin-Latour[35]

Dear Sir,

Since, with the greatest happiness, Édouard renounces this ugly café, having no hope of meeting you there, please be kind enough to come and dine with us tomorrow Thursday. You know the attachment he has for you. Do not deprive him of the pleasure of seeing you, a pleasure that is very much shared by Suzanne and me. Help us keep him away from this place that is so dangerous for his lively and generous nature.

I hope this letter will be happier than the last one, the address of which I had so badly written.

Please receive, sir, my most gracious compliments.

Eugénie Manet

AUGUST 8: Manet and his brothers are drafted into the national guard after France's declaration of war on Prussia. He is assigned to be part of the surveillance of the fortifications of Paris near the port of Saint Ouen.

SEPTEMBER 4: Following the military defeat and fall of Napoleon III, the Third Republic is proclaimed. Confronted by a Prussian invasion, Manet sends his family to Oloron-Sainte-Marie, in the Pyrenees. Many of his letters to them are dispatched by balloon.[36]

OCTOBER 30: Édouard Manet, Paris, to Suzanne Manet[37]

My dear Suzanne,

I am writing to you tonight before going to bed. Truly, fate pursues us, because the rumor is circulating this evening, and is almost officially confirmed at this hour, that the Prussians have just taken back Le Bourget, [where] we have been fighting since last night. Details are lacking. I really do not know to what I should attribute all these setbacks. Still no news from you, which is for me very cruel, I assure you, and when will this all end? We are doing well despite everything.

We become terribly selfish here, no one sees each other, all relationships are interrupted, it is boring and sad. What a beautiful day it will be when it is all over. I would like to know if you are doing well. I hope you work at your piano. It would be quite unfortunate to neglect it for so long. I can always repeat the same thing to you. I would like to see this war over and everything back in order. The house is horribly sad. I leave at 7:00 in the morning and only come home for lunch and dinner, and I go to bed at 10:30. I will not close my letter until tomorrow, after having read *Officiel*.

The news is confirmed, what generals we have. It's pouring rain this morning, we're on call, luckily, we have everything we need [to] cover ourselves well. Batignolles is in desolation. The Batignolles brigade was indeed in Le Bourget. They were almost all taken prisoner.

Farewell, my dear Suzanne, I embrace you as I love you.

Your husband,
Édouard M.

Kiss Léon for me and advise him to work and be extremely kind to you.

My dear Suzanne,

Please answer me in the following order with a yes or a no.

4. Are you doing well?

5. Have you received my letters?

6. Do you need money?

I hope to hear from you through this newly invented process.
Follow the instructions.

Édouard

1871

JANUARY 1: Édouard Manet, Paris, to Suzanne Manet[39]

My dear Suzanne,

Are you doing well? I keep thinking about you. I think this is the first time since I met you that I can't kiss you on the first day of the year. Still no news from you, it's very cruel, and we may still have a month to go. Do you have everything you need there?

I look forward to the day when I can see you again. Embrace Léon for me.
My kindest regards and wishes for the good health of all.

Your husband who loves you,
Édouard

FEBRUARY 12: Édouard leaves Paris to join his family at Oloron-Saint-Marie and then continues on to Bordeaux.[40]

MARCH 1: The Paris Commune is declared, and the city is cut off from the rest of France. Manet and his family stay in Arcachon, near Bordeaux, for a month.[41]

1872

Léon volunteers for military service and requests a replacement birth certificate (the original burned in the Commune). He discovers his father's name is listed as Koëlla and his mother is listed as Suzanne Leenhoff. His uncle Ferdinand Leenhoff helps him make this request. It is unclear how much Léon knew about his birth before this point in time.[42]

JANUARY: The art dealer Paul Durand-Ruel purchases twenty-four of Manet's paintings for 35,000 francs (about 170,000 in today's dollars), a financial windfall for the artist and his immediate family.[43]

JUNE: Édouard visits the Frans Hals Museum, recently opened in Haarlem, and the Rijksmuseum in Amsterdam with Suzanne and her brother Ferdinand.[44]

1874

SUMMER: The Manet and Morisot families spend part of the summer together at Fécamp in Normandy, though Édouard does not join them.[45]

DECEMBER 22: Eugène Manet and Berthe Morisot marry in Paris.[46]

1875

OCTOBER: Édouard and Suzanne visit Venice with artist James Tissot.[47]

1876

JULY: Édouard develops symptoms of late-stage syphilis.[48]

1878

JUNE: Édouard, Suzanne, and Eugénie move from 49 to 39, rue de Saint-Pétersbourg.[49]

Édouard Manet to Henri Fantin-Latour[50]

Monday night

My dear Fantin, when I came back just now, I was scolded by these ladies who had instructed me to invite you for dinner on Thursday at 7:00. The guests are my sister-in-law and one of her sisters, Father Hurel, and Degas, none of whom scare you, I believe. Please write to me that you accept.

Édouard Manet

NOVEMBER 14: Julie Manet is born to Berthe Morisot and Eugène Manet.[51]

1879

APRIL 1: Édouard establishes his final studio, at 77, rue d'Amsterdam.[52]

Édouard Manet to Claude Monet[53]

My dear Monet,

I have also just gone through terrible emotions because my wife is still lying down in bed without being able to move at all. However, she is now out of danger, and you know better than anyone what it's like to be forced to give constant care to someone ill. I don't go out, I don't see anyone, and I can't help you as I wish. I took three of your studies to the studio and I have already tried to sell them. I even asked Mademoiselle Lemonnier to talk to Charpentier about it, but no success.

Get back to work if you can. This is the only distraction that the great sorrow you have can allow you. Poor Mrs. Monet will not be able to see the great success that certainly awaits you one day. As for Jean, write to my brother. Perhaps he could get him into some college in the city.

My best regards to the Hoschedé family and to you,
Édouard Manet

1880   JUNE–NOVEMBER: Édouard's health deteriorates, and he develops paralysis in his left leg. Doctors prescribe hydrotherapy and rest in the country. Manet rents a small house in Bellevue. Suzanne and Eugénie join him and Léon visits on the weekends. Bored, he keeps up an active correspondence and sends a range of illustrated letters to friends.[54]

1881   DECEMBER 19: Édouard Manet, Paris, to Berthe Morisot[55]

My dear Berthe, as I prefer not to send you anything than to send you an ugly present, I stick to simple wishes for the moment. I will certainly find a way to catch up during the year. Are you taking a small trip to Italy? I would have liked to see you in Venice and bring back some very personal paintings. I have seen your house lately, but it is so covered with scaffolding that it is impossible to judge its appearance. People were working on it.

The year is not ending very well for me in terms of health. However, Paturin seems to believe in a diagnosis that could give hope, so I conscientiously follow his prescription.

Pastié has not yet sent me my portrait, but I have written to him. Today I have had the visit of the brave Fantin, who came to compliment me, and then Faure, all radiant because he is included in the New Year's Day promotion, and he even commissioned his portrait from me. Suzanne is starting to be able to use her arm and to regain her health. Mummy only thinks about her little girl [Julie Manet]. Yesterday, she received a visit from Angèle, not understanding that it was all about the gifts.

We send you all our best regards, Eugène and Bibi [Julie],
Édouard Manet

DECEMBER 30: Édouard's lifelong friend Antonin Proust becomes Minister of Culture for a short time and supports naming the artist a chevalier of the Legion of Honor.[56]

1882   SEPTEMBER 30: Édouard draws up a will, designating Suzanne as his sole heir and Léon as residual legatee. He names his cousin Jules Dejouy executor and charges his friend Théodore Duret with the responsibility of either offering the works in his studio for sale or destroying them.[57]

1883   APRIL 20: Due to infection, Manet's left leg is amputated in the living room of his home. Gustave is at his bedside during the procedure; Suzanne and Léon wait in the dining room.[58]

APRIL 30: Édouard dies at age fifty-one.[59]

MAY 3: Édouard is buried at Passy Cemetery in Paris. Eugène, Gustave, and Jules Dejouy lead the funeral procession. Antonin Proust, Émile Zola, Théodore Duret, Henri Fantin-Latour, Philippe Burty, Alfred Stevens, and Claude Monet are his pallbearers. Ferdinand Leenhoff sculpts the bust for Manet's gravesite.[60]

JULY: Eugénie suffers a stroke and becomes paralyzed.[61]

1884   JANUARY 6–28: Suzanne, Léon, Gustave, Eugène, Berthe, and Jules Dejouy help organize a retrospective exhibition of 179 of Manet's works at the École des Beaux-Arts.[62]

FEBRUARY 4–5: Théodore Duret organizes a studio sale at the Hôtel Drouot, Paris, with the help of Édouard's family.[63]

DECEMBER 18: Gustave Manet dies at the age of forty-nine in Menton, Alpes-Maritimes, France.[64]

1885   JANUARY 8: Eugénie dies in Paris without knowing that her youngest son had died only a month earlier.[65]

1892   APRIL 13: Eugène Manet dies.[66]

1895   MARCH 2: Berthe Morisot dies.[67]

JULY 20: Léon marries Marie Eugénie Mathilde Fanfillon.[68]

1900   With a civil act Suzanne officially recognizes Léon as her son.[69]

1906   MARCH 8: Suzanne Manet dies at the age of seventy-six. At her funeral, Léon is still referred to as her youngest brother on engraved cards.[70]

1927   SEPTEMBER 3: Léon Leenhoff dies at the age of seventy-five. His wife predeceased him, and he has no children. Julie Manet and her husband do not allow him nor his wife to be buried in the Manet family plot.[71]

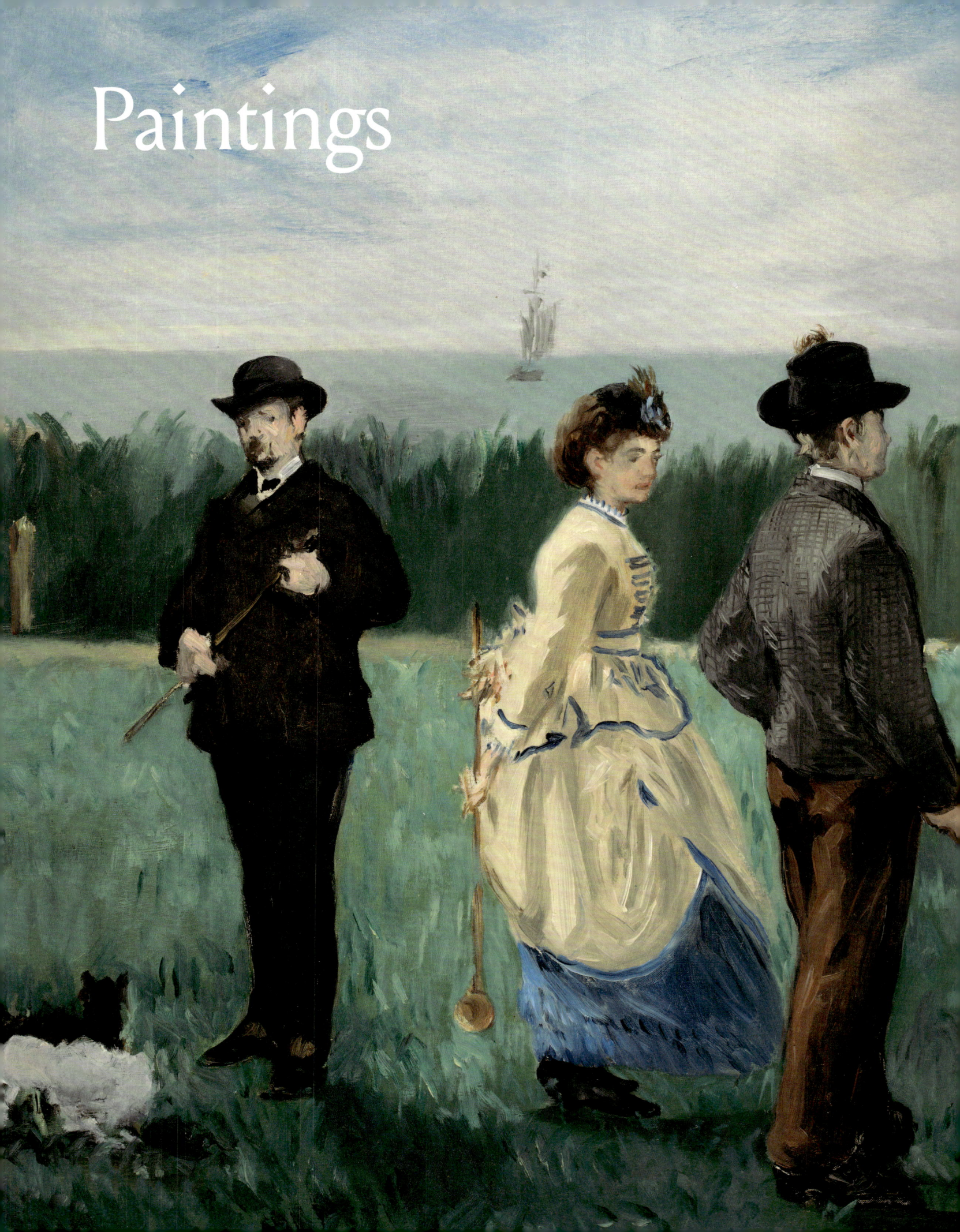

Paintings

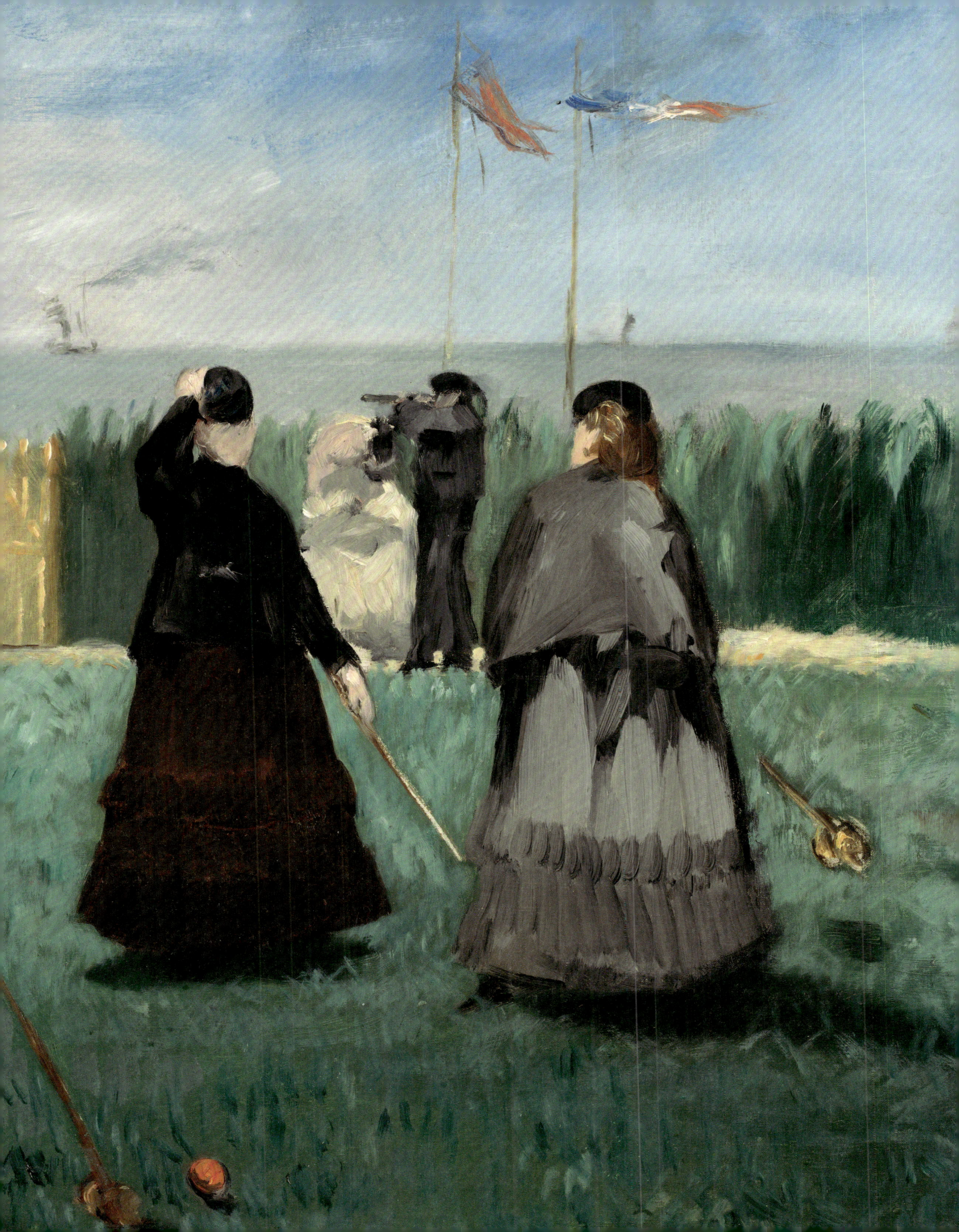

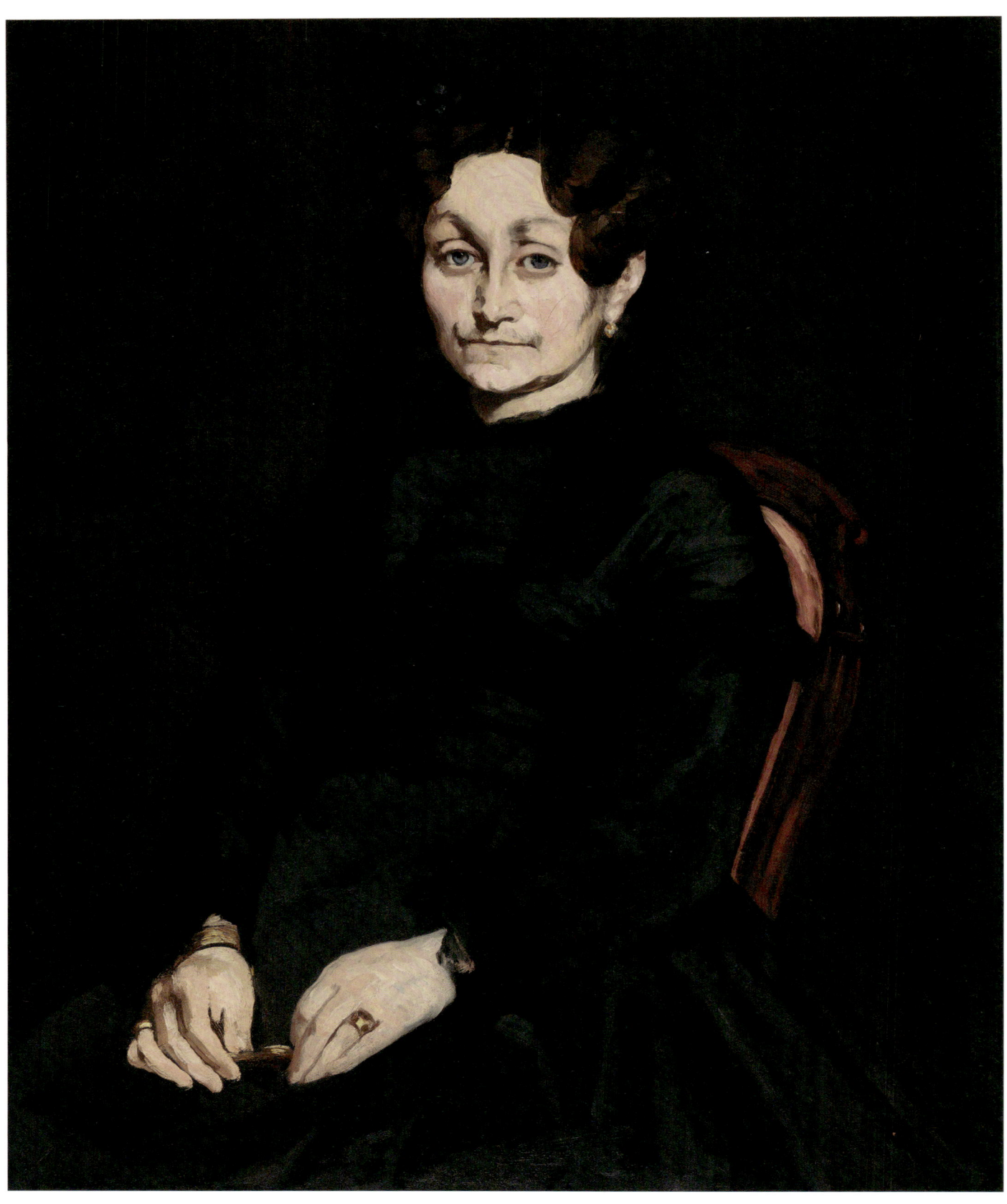

Madame Auguste Manet, about 1866
Oil on canvas, 98 × 80 cm
Isabella Stewart Gardner Museum, Boston

Madame Auguste Manet, about 1866

I

This portrait of Eugénie-Désirée Fournier Manet (1811–1885), the artist's mother, has long held court in the Isabella Stewart Gardner Museum. It entered the collection in 1910 and did not leave the galleries for more than a century.[1] Excluded from major Manet exhibitions and their catalogues, the painting has been understudied from a scholarly and technical perspective. It has also not been conserved since 1976 and is in a remarkable state of preservation. In 2022, it received a transformative cleaning that revealed a virtuosity long obscured by a badly discolored and inappropriately shiny varnish (fig. 72).[2]

Eugénie appears in the widow's black mourning dress she donned after her husband's—the artist's father's—death. The type of clothing and jewelry she is wearing, based on social conventions for widows at the time, suggests that this could have been painted at the earliest (or Manet could have started painting it) in the fall of 1863, one year after her husband's death.[3]

The brushwork throughout most of the painting is beautifully bold. It shows confidence and dynamism that speaks to a certain speed of working that was not always typical of Manet. We know from the testimony of some of his subjects that there were often many long sittings.[4] Nonetheless, he was occasionally capable of producing work in one session. His close friend Antonin Proust, whom Manet painted in 1880, reported that after many false starts and "using up seven or eight canvases, the portrait came all together at once. Only the hands and parts of the background needed to be finished."[5] Looking at much of the surface of the portrait of his mother, there is evidence of similar speed and confidence in the final execution. A thick impasto in passages around the hair indicates Manet was handling a large amount of paint on the brush in an effort to capture the texture of his mother's hair. The artist left ample evidence of his brushwork in the swirls and swathes of black-on-black in the dress and by allowing furrows to form in places like the hands, where he likely used a stiff hog-hair brush to impart extra texture to the paint surface.

The bold brushwork, however, belies evidence of significant revisions Manet made to the composition, namely the repainting of the sitter's face and the position of the hands. In the lower portion of the painting, the dramatic brushwork of the earlier position of the hands, dress sleeves, and skirt is visible through the thin, finished layers of the black dress. The x-radiograph more clearly shows the considerable shifts in this area of the composition (fig. 73).[6] Most notable of these changes is the repositioning of the hands, which initially were placed somewhat higher on the canvas, and with the proper left hand lightly grasping the fingers of the right hand. In the final, the hands are placed slightly apart and hold an object, which is probably a *lorgnon*—a pair of handheld eyeglasses.[7]

Though less evident in the X-ray, Madame Manet's face also underwent considerable reworking, revealed by the removal of the dark veil of yellowed varnish. Remarkably, Manet did not entirely cover the earlier version of the face. In portions of the forehead, most notably along the right side, brush marks of the pale-yellow paint that made up the first version of the face are still visible through the cooler, pink pigments that define the final version (fig. 74).

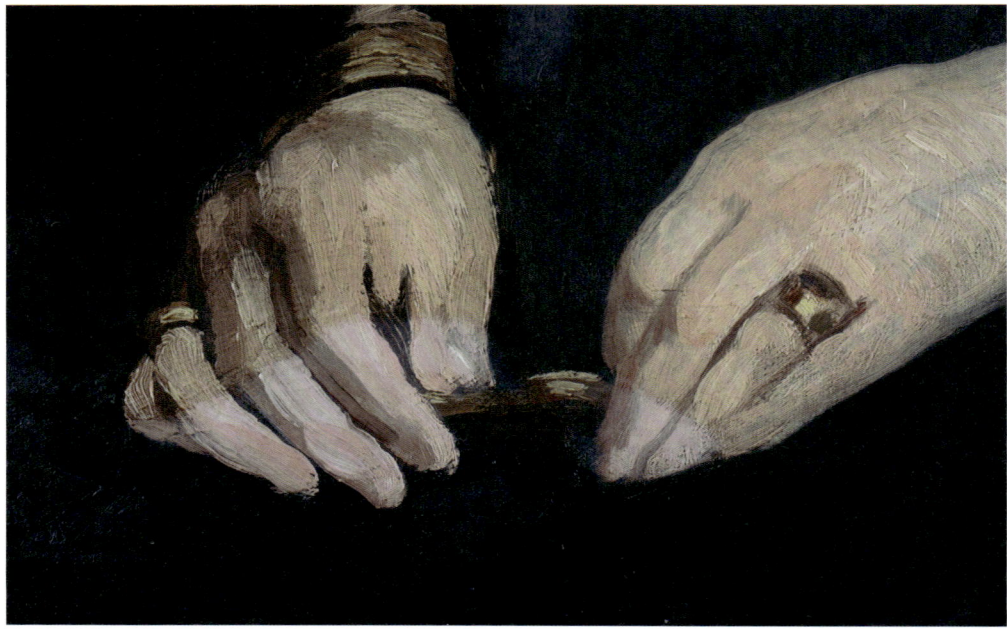

Fig. 72. Detail of *Madame Auguste Manet* (cat. no. 1), showing the hands during 2022 cleaning

Further evidence of revisions can be seen in the brown shadow between the nose and the proper right eye, an area that was not entirely repainted when the artist revised the face. Of note here are the horizontal scratch marks lying beneath the bright pink highlight of the nose that Manet made in the earlier version. This suggests that he was not satisfied with this area of the painting and distressed it with a sharp instrument in preparation for repainting. The changes were made after the earlier paint layers had sufficiently dried and hardened, but beyond that the timeline is unclear. Given that the earlier applications of paint in the face retain their rich brushwork (i.e., not worked wet over wet), it is plausible to assume that many months or perhaps even a year or two may have elapsed before Manet reworked the image. This comes as no surprise, as Manet was known to work on canvases for months and could revisit them over years.[8]

Traditionally, the painting has been dated to around 1863. However, in *Manet by Himself* (1991), Juliet Wilson-Bareau applied a date range of 1863 to 1866. The start date of 1863, based on Eugénie's mourning dress, is appropriate. Madame Manet's black dress and jewelry identify a start date but not an end date; she wore widow's black for the rest of her life.[9] However, archival evidence suggests the painting was finished—and maybe started—in 1866.

In a 1907 issue of the obscure publication *Le Journal des curieux,* an author named André Chatté quoted Émile Zola's 1867 biography of Manet. Zola writes that in 1866 the paint was "just dry" on four works: "*Le fumeur, la Joueuse de guitare,* un *Portrait de Mme M . . .,* [and] *Une jeune dame en 1866.*"[10] From titles and descriptions, three of the paintings are identifiable, but the title *Portrait de Mme M . . .* is ambiguous.[11] By 1866 there were two Madame Manets in the artist's life: his mother *and* his wife. *Mme M . . .* could have been Suzanne Manet in the painting now called *Reading* (cat. no. 11). Chatté suggests otherwise. After quoting Zola's praise that the portrait of Mme M . . . is one of the artist's best works, the writer states:

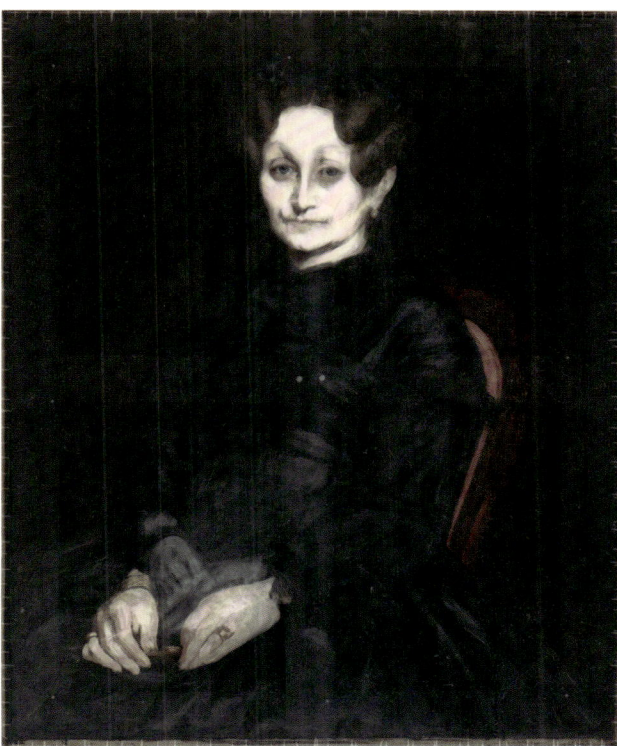

Fig. 73. X-ray of *Madame Auguste Manet* (cat. no. 1) overlaid with the visible light image, showing the repositioning of the hands

> The portrait of Madame Manet mère shows her seated in a natural, familiar pose, holding her lorgnette [handheld eyeglasses] in both hands; the background of the painting is black, and she is completely dressed in black. . . . Her hair is arranged in the fashion of the 1830s, which she has kept all her life. . . . The pleats adorning her sleeves, the ribbon of her belt, and the buckle are visible, although everything is black. The figure is energetic, with an expressive gaze that follows you wherever you go. . . . [Her] features reveal . . . a firm and authoritative character.[12]

Clearly, Chatté knew, or thought he knew, that *Mme M* . . . referenced by Zola as a work completed in 1866 was, in fact, the portrait of the artist's mother rather than an image of Suzanne.

Apart from his writing at a relatively early date, why should one take Chatté's word for this identification? Perhaps because Chatté (who has no other known bylines in the French press) may be Léon Leenhoff writing under a pseudonym.[13] In the same issue, there is a reprint of a selection of notes about Manet's life that Léon later provided to the scholar Adolphe Tabarant.[14] There are also reproductions of archives that are explicitly noted as being supplied by Léon. Finally, the end of the description of *Mme M* . . . reads like part of a sales pitch: "A great European museum has already lined up to try to acquire this remarkable work."[15] Léon, whose mother had died the year before, was now responsible for the disposition of Manet's works that had remained in his and Suzanne's possession. Among them was *Madame Auguste Manet,* which he sold to a London dealer in 1909 for 90,000 francs.[16] It was in Léon's financial interest to attract attention to a painting that had been in the family for decades and, therefore, barely exhibited; in fact, it had been shown publicly only in Manet's self-funded 1867 solo show.[17]

Finally, Chatté—probably Leenhoff—provides another clue about the painting. He specifically references two Old Master painters related to the work: Frans Hals and Francisco Goya.[18] The Louvre had some works by Hals, and Manet had already traveled to the Netherlands in 1852.[19] However, in the fall of 1863, after marrying Suzanne, Manet spent a full month in the Netherlands, likely immersed in Dutch art, including Hals's paintings of older women in black. Two years later, in 1865, he traveled to Spain, where he saw many more works by Spanish masters, such as Goya and Velázquez, than he had access to in Paris. At the Prado, he was enchanted by Velázquez and, though his letters say he was less taken by Francisco Goya, the latter artist had a well-documented effect on Manet's work after the trip.[20]

Madame Auguste Manet combines details that feel Dutch and Spanish. The restrained palette is reminiscent of Velázquez. The pose and depiction of a powerful older woman in black recall Dutch portraits like Hals's *Maritge Claesdr. Vooght* (fig. 75). The black lace head covering almost resembles a *mantilla*, harkening to Goya's *Majas on a Balcony* (fig. 76), which Manet openly admired and directly informed *The Balcony* (1868–69, see fig. 6). Muting the colors of his mother's face to shift from rosy pink to cooler pale white suggests a change—perhaps—from a Hals-like image of flushed cheeks to a more restrained skin tone.

Therefore, an educated estimate places this painting as possibly being started in years following Manet's extended 1863 wedding trip to the Netherlands and likely completed (and perhaps started) after his excursion to the Iberian peninsula from August to September 1865. That trip was immediately followed by a vacation with his family—including his mother—in the French countryside.[21] By October 1865 Manet was back in Paris, hard at work on a series of paintings, likely including *Madame Auguste Manet*, that would be finished by 1866. Here we assign the completion date to the painting.

DIANA SEAVE GREENWALD AND GIANFRANCO POCOBENE

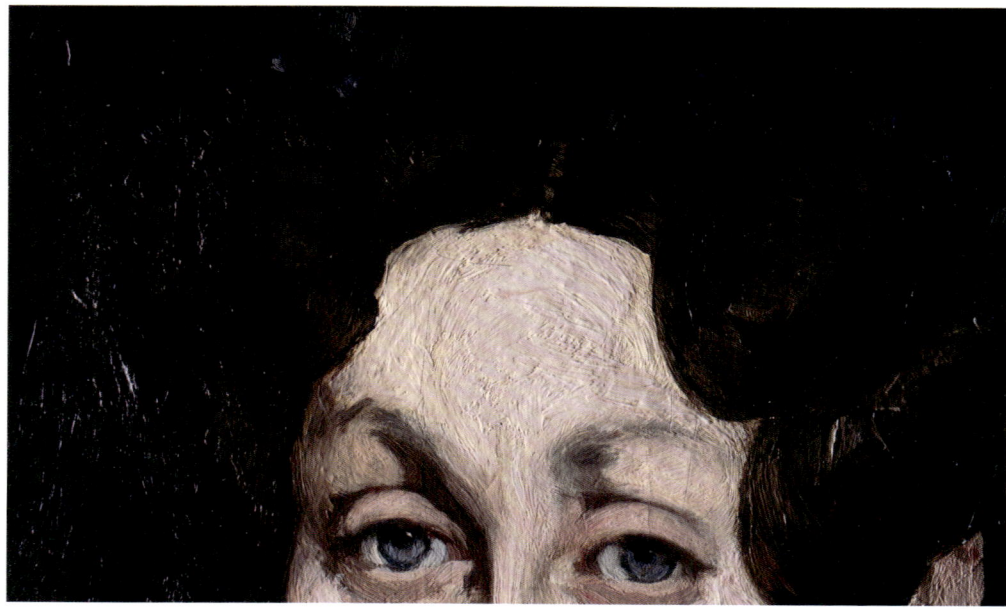

Fig. 74. Detail of *Madame Auguste Manet* (cat. no. 1) in raking light, showing the forehead

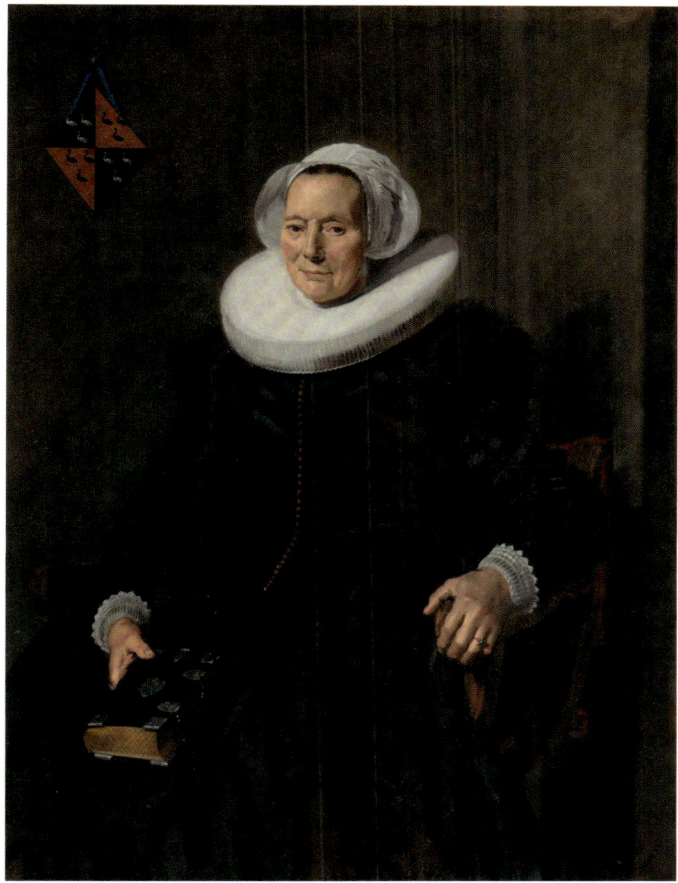

Fig. 75. Frans Hals, *Maritge Claesdr. Vooght (1577–1644)*, 1639. Oil on canvas, 126.4 × 93.2 cm. Rijksmuseum, Amsterdam

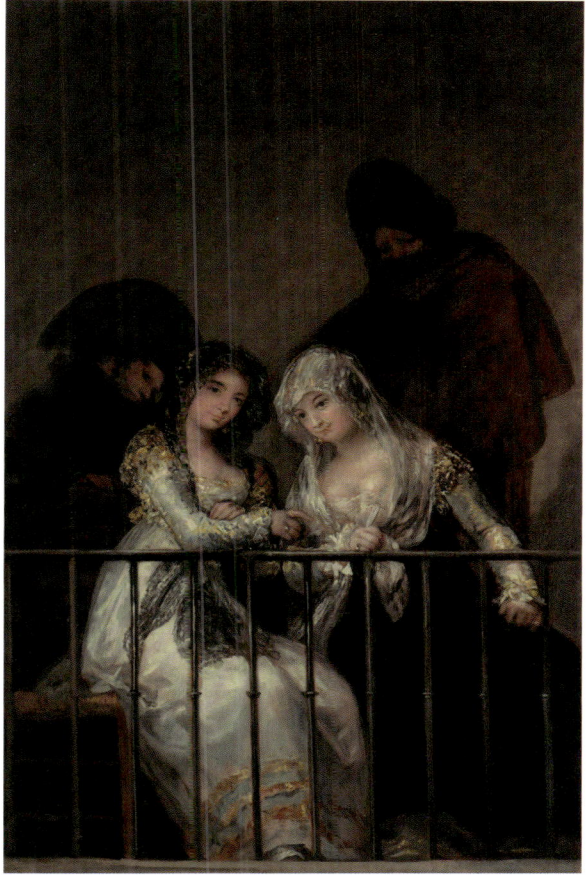

Fig. 76. Attributed to Francisco de Goya, *Majas on a Balcony*, about 1800–1810. Oil on canvas, 194.9 × 125.7cm. The Metropolitan Museum of Art, New York. H. O. Havemeyer Collection, Bequest of Mrs. H. O. Havemeyer, 1929

PROVENANCE

Collection of the sitter, Eugenie Manet, Paris; exhibited in Paris at the Avenue de l'Alma, 1867; presumably bequeathed to Suzanne Manet or Léon Leenhoff in 1895, certainly in Leenhoff's collection by 1902; purchased by a Mr. Thompson, London, at the "Fair Women" exhibition of the International Society of Sculptors, Painters and Gravers from Léon Leenhoff for 90,000 francs in 1909; purchased by the art dealer Wallis & Son (The French Gallery), London, by April 1909; purchased by Isabella Stewart Gardner from Wallis & Son, London, for 5,000 pounds on May 2, 1910, through the American art historian Bernard Berenson.

INVENTORY NUMBERS

P3s4; RW 1975 1, 62

SELECT LITERATURE

Avenue de l'Alma 1867, 11, no. 14; Duret 1902, no. 124 (as 1869–70); Chatté 1907, 5–7, no. 1; Pennell 1909, 313; Carter 1925, 233–34; Moreau-Nélaton, vol. 1, no. 89 (as 1866); Flament 1928, 243 (as 1866); Tabarant 1931, 109, no. 68; Jamot and Wildenstein 1932, no. 134 (as 1866); Tabarant 1947, 79 (as date uncertain); Orienti 1970, 126, no. 63 (as 1863); Hendy 1974, 150–52, pl. 37 (as after Manet's visit to Madrid in 1865); Rouart and Wildenstein 1975, vol. 1, 70–71, no. 62 (as 1862); Locke 1991, 250, fig. 27 (as about 1863); Mena 2003, 153, 155, ill. (as 1853); Cars, Guégan, and Pludermacher 2023, 33.

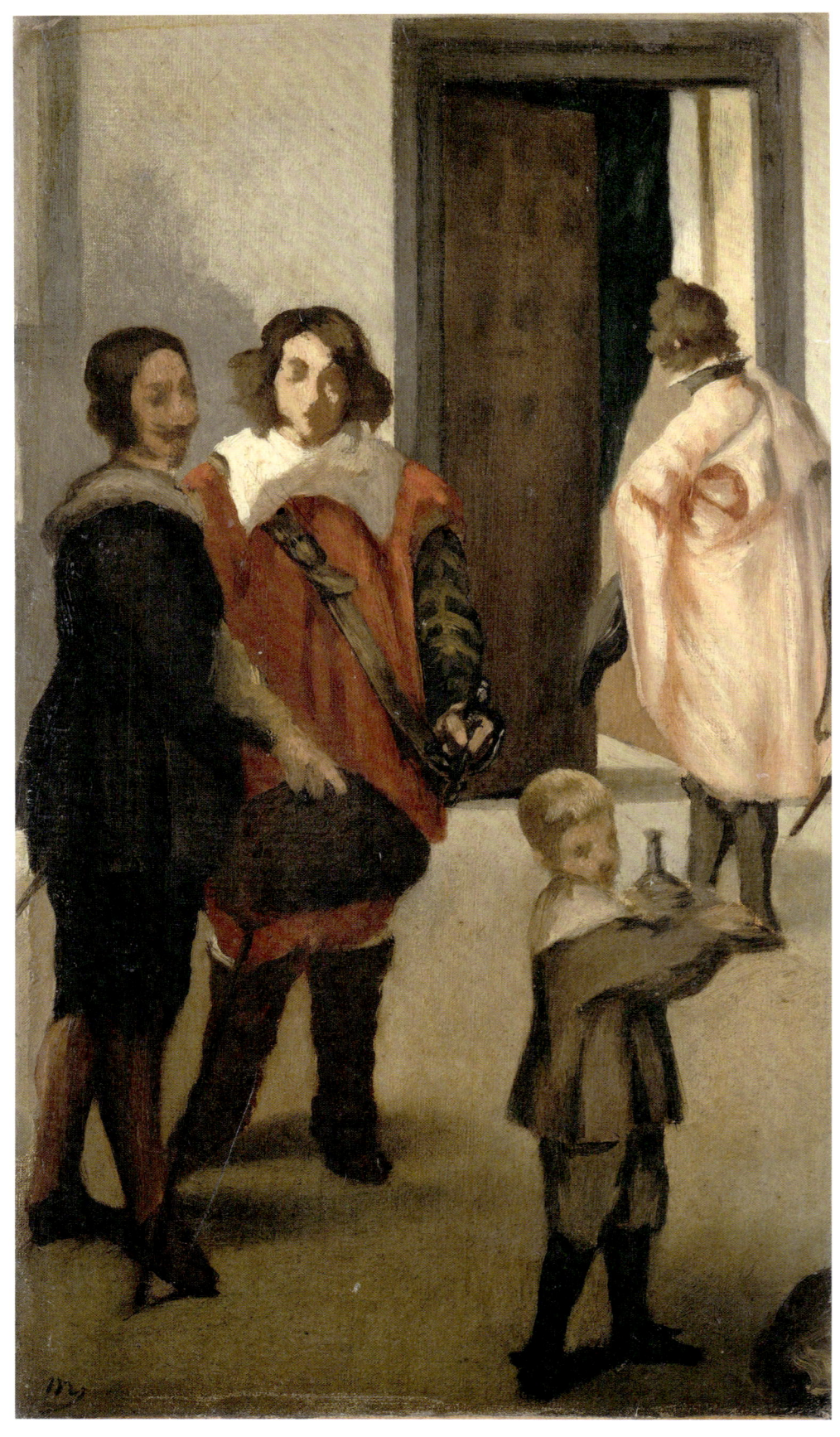

Spanish Cavaliers (Cavaliers espagnols), 1859–60
Oil on canvas, 45 × 26 cm
Musée des Beaux-Arts, Lyon

2 *Spanish Cavaliers (Cavaliers espagnols)*, 1859–60

Together with another painting called *Spanish Studio Scene*, *Spanish Cavaliers* may have been part of a larger scene, realized probably around 1859, when Manet was a registered copyist at the Louvre. He was working from paintings in the museum's collection to foster his own evolving practice.[22] Jacques-Émile Blanche, who at one time owned *Spanish Studio Scene* (fig. 77), recalled seeing the "elaborate sketch:" as part of a bigger canvas. As he wrote in 1940, "The Velázquez in his studio, with two Cavalier-visitors, [was] the original scheme of a bigger canvas I saw at Manet's studio when I was a boy. This canvas remained unfinished—so far as I can remember: perhaps destroyed."[23] Whether the two canvases originally formed part of a larger whole, and why Manet might have severed them, is still to be determined. Manet initialed *Spanish Cavaliers* with an "M" in the lower left, probably added before he sold the painting to Paul Chéramy, the Manet family lawyer and a collector of nineteenth-century art who was particularly interested in copies after art historical precedents.[24]

Manet borrowed the figures that populate the *Spanish Studio Scene* from *The Gathering of Gentlemen*, a painting he saw in the Louvre and then thought to be by Diego Velázquez but now recognized as a work by the artist's pupil and son-in-law, Juan Bautista Martinez del Mazo. He copied the painting and called it *The Little Cavaliers* (see fig. 35), signed "Manet d'après Velázquez." The same painting is seen on the easel of the *Spanish Studio*, where Velázquez, palette in hand, turns to two other figures in the studio that resemble those in the very scene he is painting. The open doorway at right in *Spanish Cavaliers* recalls Velázquez's *Las Meninas*, which Manet would have known through an etching of the composition by Francisco Goya, accessible in the Bibliothèque Nationale de France, before seeing it firsthand at the Prado in the fall of 1865.

While certain elements in *Spanish Cavaliers* were adapted from earlier paintings, either based on firsthand inspection or through printed reproductions, others were the product of studio invention. Manet likely posed Léon Leenhoff, then around seven years old, as the boy carrying a tray in the foreground. This is the first of many appearances Léon makes in Manet's paintings of the late 1850s to the 1870s. The pose itself may come from another Spanish source: Francisco de Zurbarán's *Circumcision of Christ* (fig. 78), which hung in the Louvre during the reign of Louis Philippe (1830–48). Manet was perhaps inspired by the young boy striding forward in the foreground carrying a tray, facing the viewer.[25] He later depicted Léon in this pose in watercolor and in etching (fig. 79). It is the first instance in which Manet translated a painted version of Léon across media.[26]

KATHRYN KREMNITZER

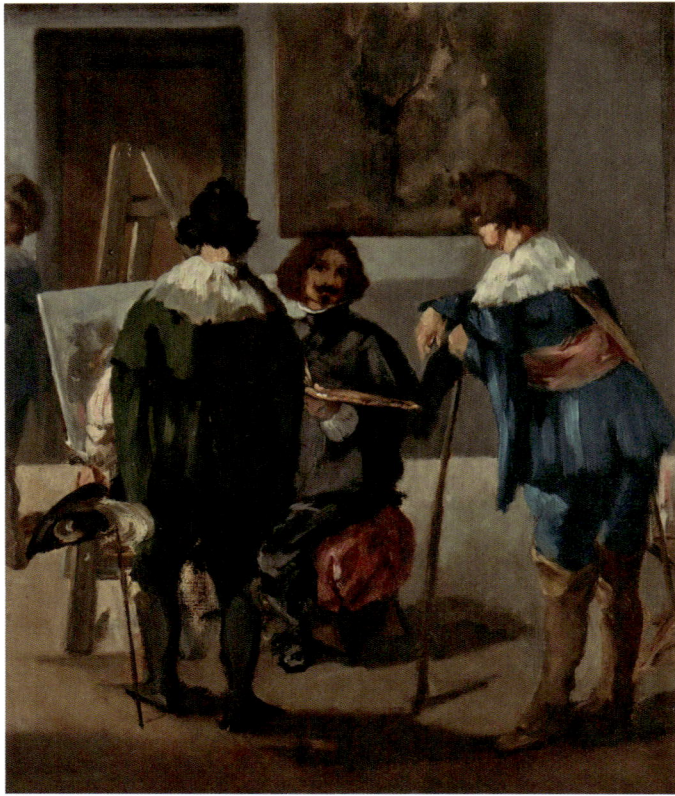

Fig. 77. Édouard Manet, *Spanish Studio Scene*, about 1860–62. Oil on canvas, 46 × 38 cm. Private collection

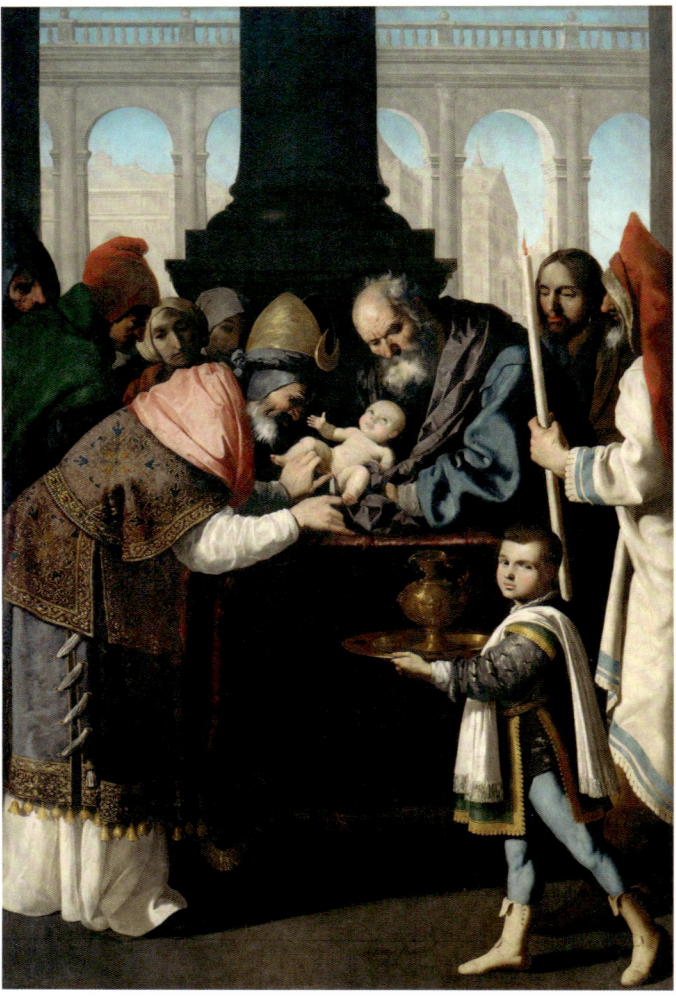

Fig. 78. Francisco de Zurbarán, *The Circumcision of Christ*, 1638–39. Oil on canvas, 263 × 175 cm. Musée de Peinture et de Sculpture, Grenoble

PROVENANCE

Purchased by Paul Chéramy, Paris, from the artist;[27] Chéramy sale, Galerie Charpentier, Paris, lot 219, May 5–7, 1908; purchased by Durand-Ruel, Paris, at the above sale; Raymond Tripier; bequeathed to the Musée des Beaux-Arts, Lyon, 1917.

INVENTORY NUMBERS

B.1153b; RW 1975 1, 26

SELECT LITERATURE

Duret 1902, no. 28; Salon d'Automne 1905, no. 6, 191; Moreau-Nélaton 1925–26,[28] cat. no. 9; Tabarant 1931, 37; Jamot and Wildenstein 1932, 10; Tabarant 1947, 31; Marseilles 1961, cat. no. 7; Orienti 1967, 25; Rouart and Wildenstein 1975, vol. 1, 44, no. 26; Farwell 1981, 58; Cachin et al. 1983, no. 2, 46–48, ill.; Rudd 1994, 747–49; Pickvance 1996, no. 11; Augé et al. 1999, no. 46; Mauner and Loyrette, 2000, 16, 34, 66, 170, pl. 13; Meller 2002, 72, 75, 82, fig. 20; Tinterow and Lacambre 2003, no. 130.

Fig. 79. Édouard Manet, *Boy Carrying a Tray*, 1862. Etching and aquatint, second state, image: 22.2 × 14.5; sheet 46.7 × 29.8 cm. The Art Institute of Chicago (fig. 38)

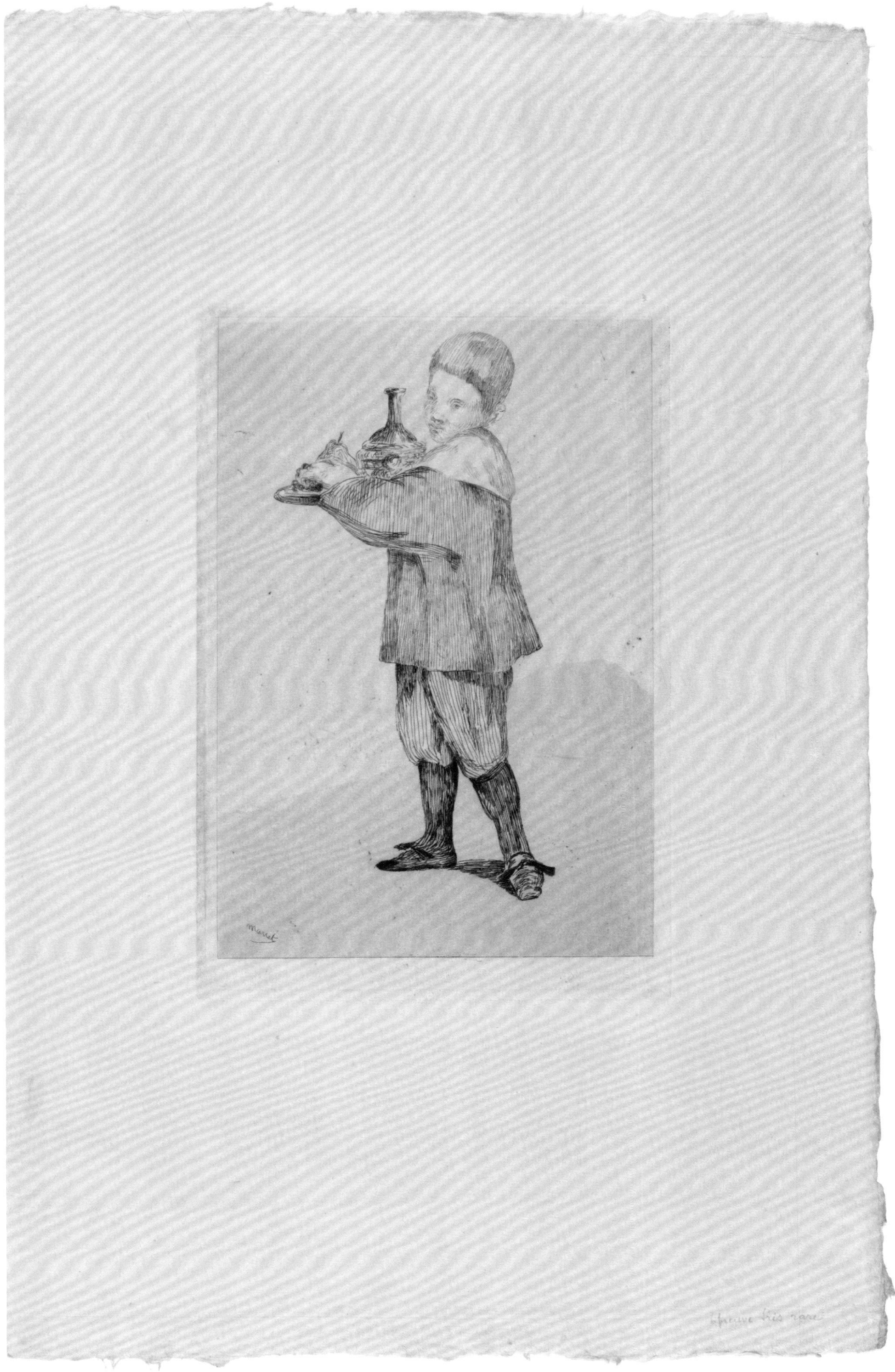

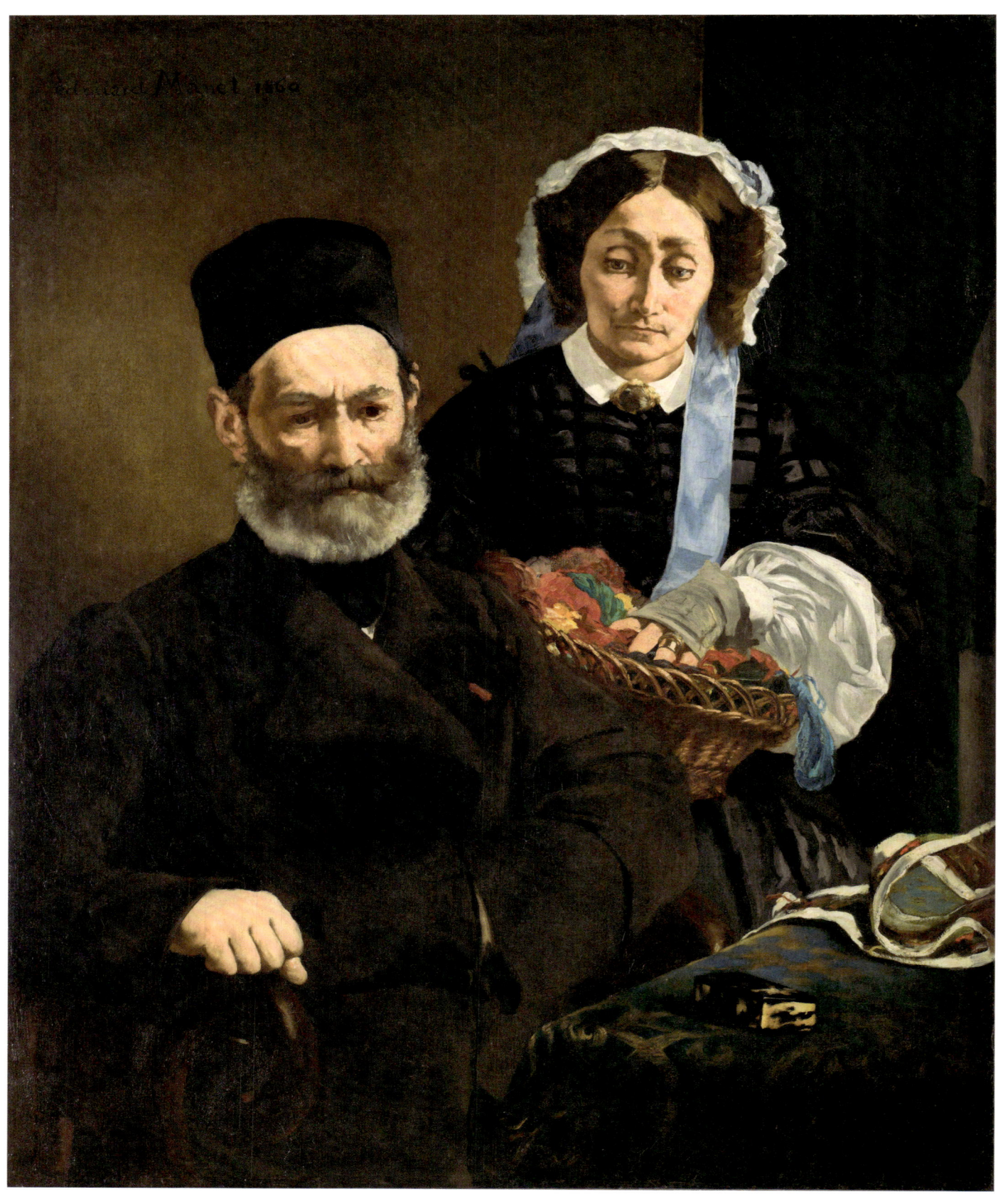

Monsieur and Madame Auguste Manet, 1860
Oil on canvas, 110 × 90 cm
Musée d'Orsay, Paris

3 *Monsieur and Madame Auguste Manet*, 1860

At Manet's debut at the Salon in 1861, he exhibited two vastly different works. One was *The Spanish Singer* (1860; Metropolitan Museum of Art, New York), one of Manet's distinctly Spanish works, which earned him an honorable mention. The other was a double portrait of Manet's parents. In contrast to the animated, quasi-ethnographic *Spanish Singer*, this double portrait is—as Carol Armstrong has aptly called it—a "native-tongued" portrait of a more somber nature.[29]

Auguste Manet is seated on the left and Eugénie-Désirée Fournier Manet is standing behind him. Due to his late-stage syphilis, Manet's father was nearly paralyzed at the time Manet painted this portrait. Drawings and etchings show that Manet struggled with how his debilitated father should appear. In particular, he experimented with different ways of rendering his father's gaze. In a preparatory sketch and a contemporaneous etching, Auguste faces forward. Even the underpainting, revealed by X-radiograph, shows a more forward-looking gaze. In these other images, however, Auguste "fails to engage the viewer."[30] Manet instead makes his father and mother both look down. The new handling of his father's gaze looks like a depiction of contemplative reservedness rather than of disability.

This double portrait captures the spousal togetherness demanded by his father's condition. In 1858, a letter requesting a temporary extension of professional leave for Auguste was in fact written by Eugénie and to "which [Auguste] could only affix a trembling signature."[31] This collaborative letter written by two hands captures the sentiment visually represented in this painting, which fittingly features only two of the subjects' hands, as if visually representing their partnership. Even though Eugénie's left hand is obscured by fabrics and a fingerless glove, her wedding band is visible. The ring—like the overall composition—is a symbol of the marital unity expressed by that earlier dual-author letter.

Despite his parents' similar postures, there are subtle differences between the two figures that indicate their differing levels of ability. Again, the hands are revealing: Auguste's hand is clenched in a fist, while Eugénie's is open, plunged into a basket of fabrics. This sensuous detail—of a hand feeling around amid the eye-catching, colorful fabrics—introduces a tension between his paralysis and her ability to both move freely and perform nimble fabric work, including stitching the red thread of the *Legion d'honneur* visible on his lapel. Just one year after the 1858 letter that Auguste could only feebly sign, Eugénie sent another letter—now entirely in her own hand—requesting his resignation.[32]

Manet seems to call attention to Auguste's immobile clenched fist in the double portrait, which stands out prominently as a rare pocket of light against his father's dark garb. Manet made a drawing of another older, bearded man in which the hand again emerges as a prominent focus (*Chrysippos*, fig. 80). Only tentatively dated to around 1862—the year of his father's death—it could also date to the period in which Manet was working on the double portrait. In this red-chalk sketch of a Roman copy of a Greek statue at the Louvre, Manet draws attention to the details of the hand by using pencil on only this one feature. In ancient Greece, the gesturing hand referred to the act of debate and argumentation.[33] By contrast, his father—who had once been an accomplished judge, presumably deft with his words and legal arguments—could, cruelly, barely speak toward the end of his life.

The statue's other hand, wrapped in the toga, also resembles Auguste's other hand, tucked into his jacket, in the double portrait. Made sometime around Manet's father's death, whether before or after the double portrait, the artist could have drawn connections between the last years of his father's life and this depiction of an aged, wizened Greek philosopher.[34] Manet's representation of his father's immobile fist—and the mobile hand of his father's statue surrogate—might also deal with the anxieties of an able-bodied working artist, reflecting on the future effects of disease or aging (fig. 81). This is a poignant harbinger considering he would also suffer from tertiary syphilis and deal with paralysis, though in his leg rather than his hand.

In the double portrait, his father's condition became a compositional precondition; if Auguste could not hold the gaze of the viewer, neither could Eugénie for fear of calling attention to Auguste's inattentiveness. Following her husband's death, however, Eugénie's

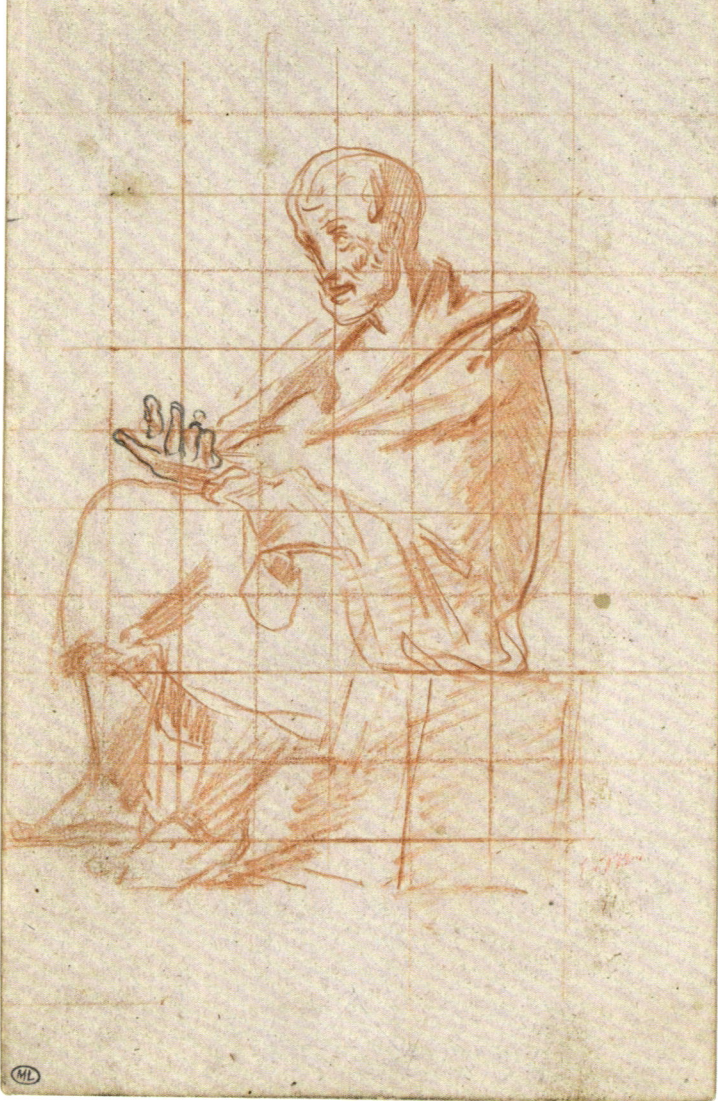

Fig. 80. Édouard Manet, *Chrysippos*, about 1862. Red chalk and graphite on paper, 22.8 cm × 14.2 cm. Musée du Louvre, Paris

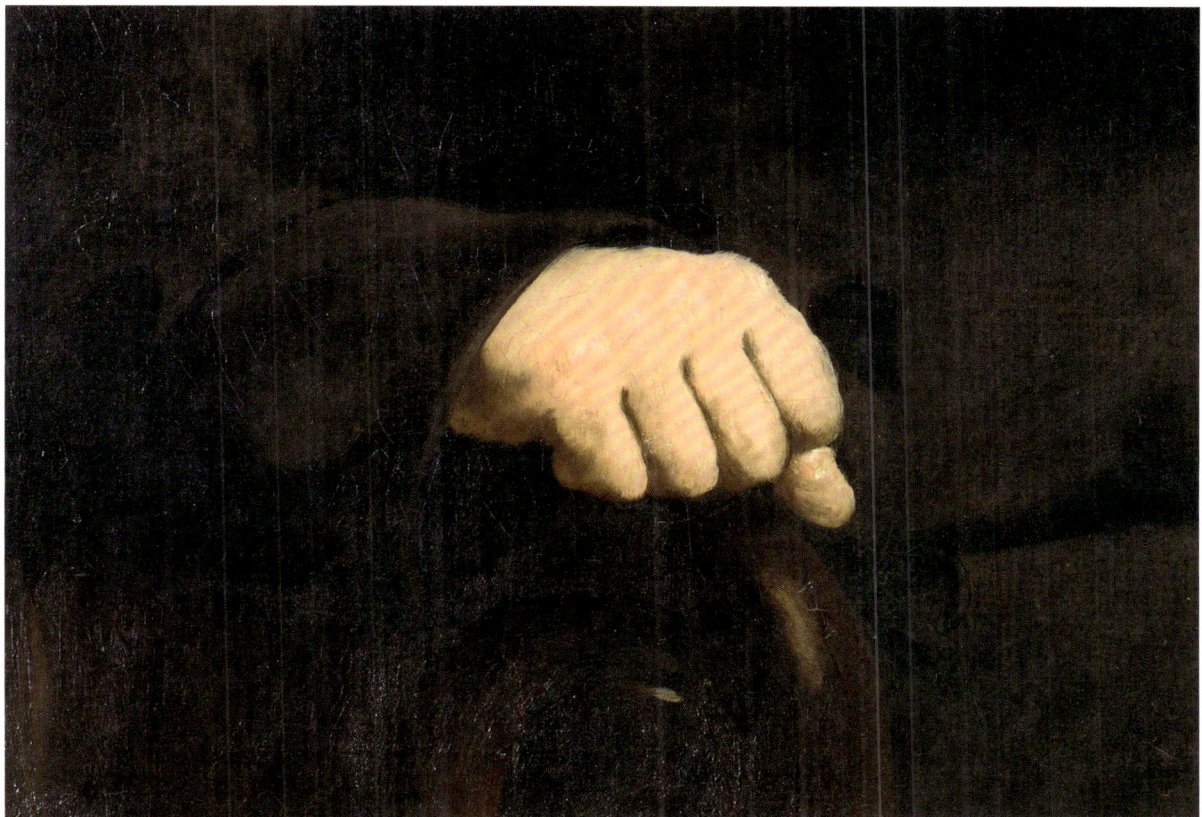

Fig. 81. Detail of *Monsieur and Madame Auguste Manet* (cat. 3)

gaze pierces the audience directly in her individual portrait (cat. no. 1). Her light face and hands contrast with the dark background. Again, the hands carry weight: her wedding ring remains visible. The prominence of the ring and Eugénie's mourning clothing also make this later image a double portrait of sorts—an homage to their marriage, a sequel to the period of illness captured in the enduring portrait made of his parents alive together.

ALEX ZIVKOVIC

PROVENANCE

Collection of Eugène Manet, Paris; bequeathed to Julie Manet Rouart and Ernest Rouart, Paris; acquired by the Musée du Jeu de Paume, Paris, through the descendants of Julie Manet Rouart and Ernest Rouart, Mrs. Jeannette Veil-Picard, and an anonymous donor, 1977; transferred to the Musée du Louvre, Paris, 1977; transferred to the Musée d'Orsay, Paris, 1986.

INVENTORY NUMBERS

RF 1977 12; RW 1975 1, 30

SELECT LITERATURE

Jamot and Wildenstein 1932, no. 37; Tabarant 1947, no. 37; Orienti 1970, no. 28; Rouart and Wildenstein 1975, vol. 1, no. 30; Cachin et al. 1983, no. 3; Locke 1991, 249–52; Fried 1996, 62–65, 108–9, fig. 40.

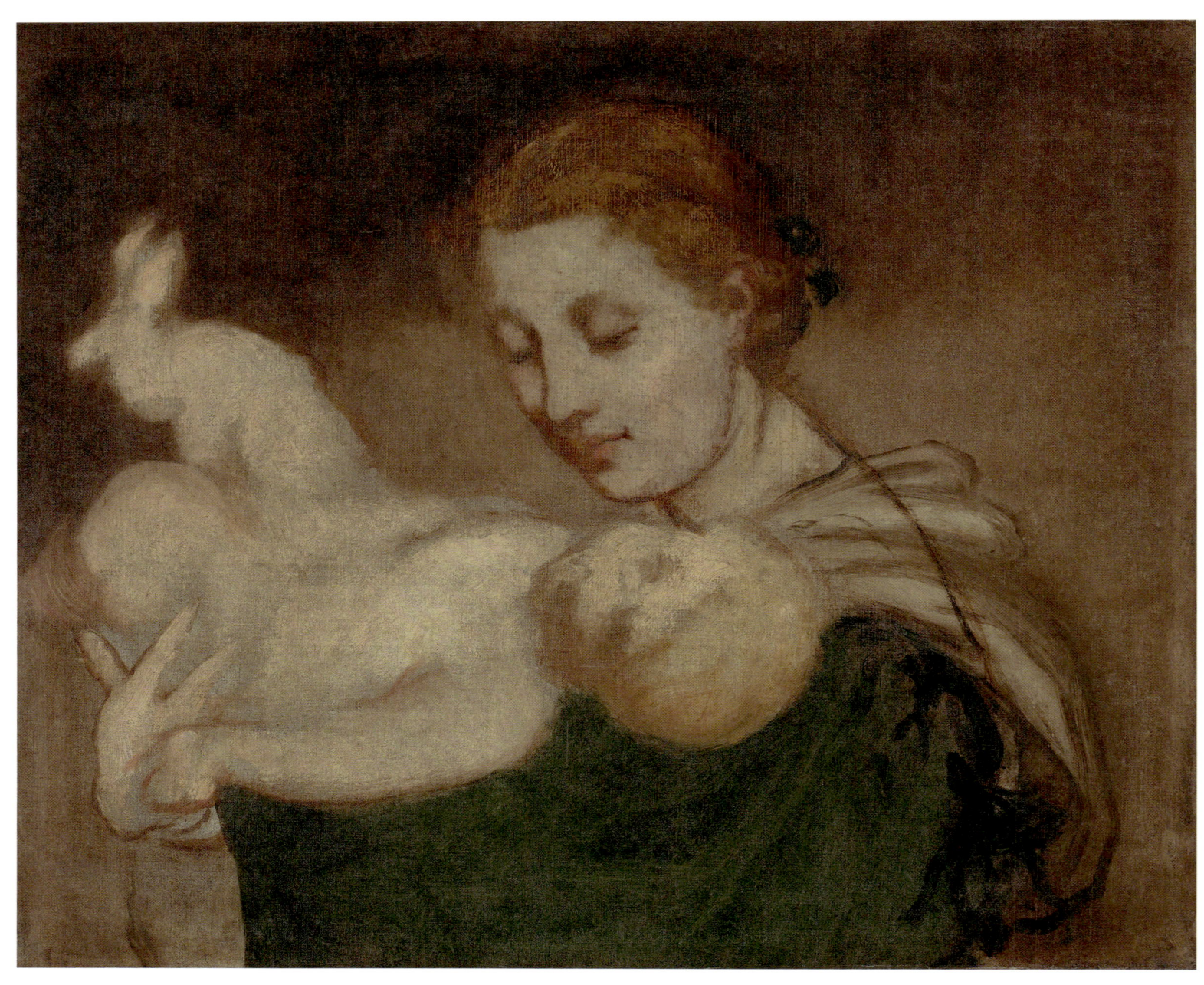

Study for *Moses Saved from the Waters*
(*Étude pour Moïse sauvé des eaux*), 1852–61
Oil on canvas, 50.8 × 61 cm
Private collection

4 Study for *Moses Saved from the Waters* (Étude pour *Moïse sauvé des eaux*), 1852–61

This little-known and recently resurfaced work is likely related to a series of pieces that Édouard Manet created starting around 1858. Antonin Proust, who published his *souvenirs* of his friend in the periodical *La Revue blanche* in 1897, recalled how the canvas *Surprised Nymph* (see fig. 1) was cut from a larger composition called *Moses Saved from the Waters*.[35] *Surprised Nymph,* which generally has a date range of 1859 to 1861, helps guide the dating for this linked work. However, the style of this sketch closely resembles that of Thomas Couture, Manet's teacher from 1850 to 1856. In particular, the lightly applied brown background resembles the mix of paints, called "sauce," that Couture recommended his students use.[36] This resemblance to his teacher's approach sets the quite early beginning of the date range applied to this work, which will need to be studied at greater length to be narrowed further. This catalogue entry is simply a starting point.

Throughout a series of sketches Manet engaged with the subject of the discovery of Moses, which had been painted by a range of artists whom he admired.[37] These efforts include an oil sketch now in Oslo (cat. no. 5) and a drawing attributed to Manet in the Museum Boijmans Van Beuningen collection in Rotterdam (fig. 20). The latter of these two is dated to 1858. The drawing seems to be a sort of *modello* for another effort to depict this famous biblical subject.[38] Several interpretations of this subject were directly available to Manet when he was visiting or copying at the Louvre, including paintings by Veronese (now on deposit in the Musée de Beaux Arts in Lyon), Nicolas Poussin, and others. However, in this sketch, Manet does not seem to engage with any of those, but with another version of the subject created by the studio of Veronese that now hangs in the Walker Art Gallery (fig. 82).

Though not certain, the Walker painting—one of several of this subject attributed to Veronese and his workshop—was possibly part of the famed art collection largely assembled by Philippe II, duc d'Orléans.[39] The collection, which was housed in the Palais Royale, Paris, was the subject of a well-known series of engravings. By Manet's lifetime, the collection had already been sold by Christie's in London at the behest of an heir who had a significant gambling problem.[40] Many of the artworks—like the Walker canvas—remained in Britain. However, the engravings, which had been printed since the late eighteenth or early nineteenth century, remained fully accessible and were conserved in volumes in the collection of the Bibliothèque Nationale.[41] The engraving after Veronese's *Finding of Moses* from this series of prints is clearly a source for this oil study (see fig. 21). The reversal of the pose from the original painting, the positioning of the head of the woman holding the baby Moses, and even the way the fabric drapes around the woman's shoulders are all echoed in Manet's work. The pose of the female figure holding a baby also resembles a woman in Manet's *The Gypsies* (about 1861). Manet cut this ambitious canvas into pieces, but its elements are at least partially recorded in an etching, called *Les Gitanos*.[42]

The living model for Manet's attempt at creating his own *Moses Saved from the Waters* is clearly Suzanne Leenhoff (fig. 83). As described and analyzed at length elsewhere in this volume, Suzanne entered the orbit of the Manet family as a piano teacher and, in 1863, became the artist's wife. Suzanne gave birth to her son Léon in January 1852.

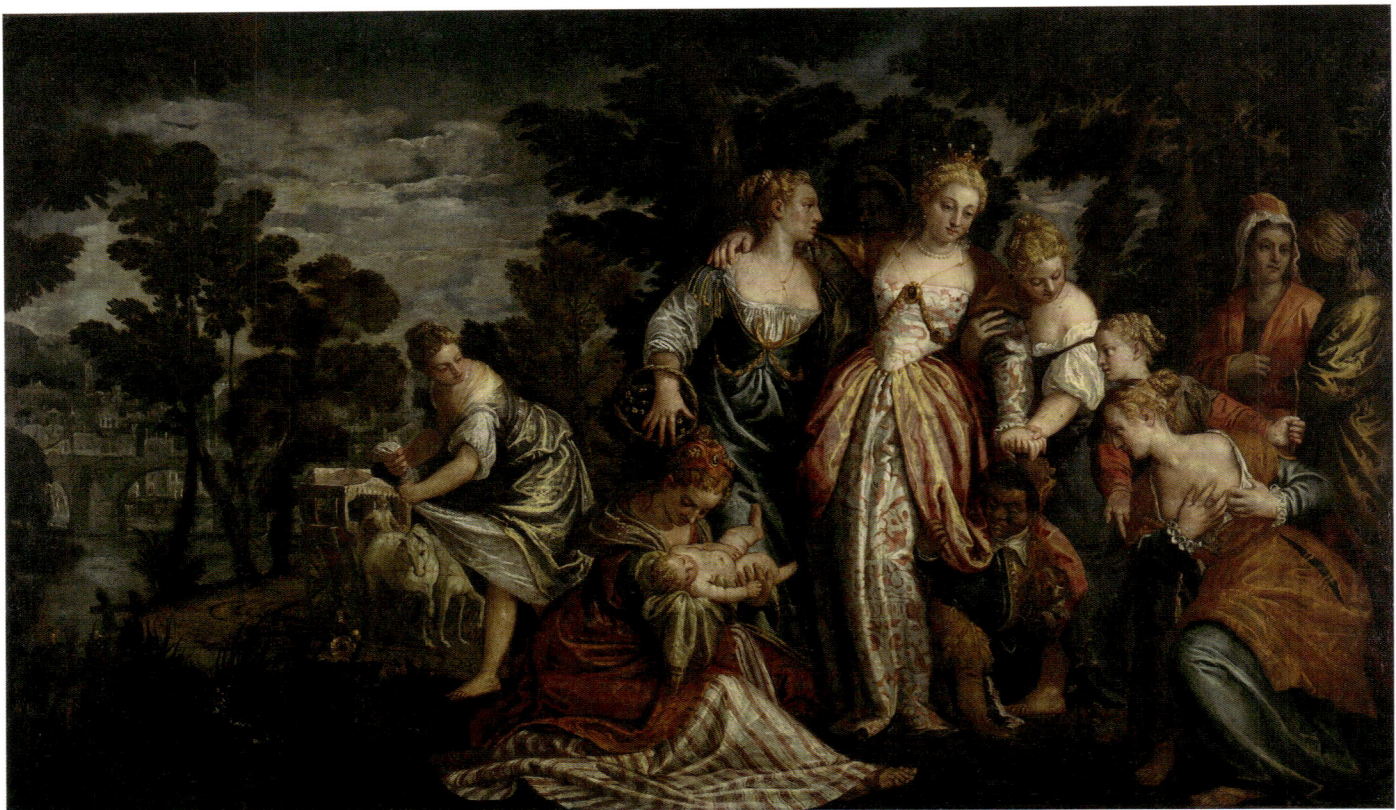

Fig. 82. Workshop of Paolo Veronese, *The Finding of Moses*, about 1580. Oil on canvas, 153 × 255 cm. Walker Art Gallery, Liverpool

Juliet Wilson-Bareau has carefully documented that Suzanne modeled frequently for Manet between the late 1850s and their marriage. In this piece, Suzanne looks particularly young. Furthermore, though the baby is faceless, Manet could have had access to Léon as an infant model after his birth. The baby has blonde hair and the suggestions of facial features that recall Manet's earliest confirmed depiction of Léon, *Spanish Cavaliers* (cat. no. 2). Considered together, these details suggest that this work is among the artist's earliest depictions of his future wife—and is possibly his first depiction of her son as early as the year of his birth in 1852.

DIANA SEAVE GREENWALD

PROVENANCE

Listed and illustrated in the sale of works belonging to René De Gas (wrongly attributed to Edgar Degas and called *Etude de maternité* (*Maternity Study*), Drouot, Paris, lot 80, 1927; purchased by M. Augry, possibly the director of Galerie George Petit or more likely the dealer Georges Aubry, Paris, at the above sale; private collection, Spain; sold at Tajan, Paris, lot 5, November 23, 2022; private collection.[43]

INVENTORY NUMBERS

No Rouart-Wildenstein number, though officially recognized by the Wildenstein Institute in 2002 as part of Manet's oeuvre.

SELECT LITERATURE

Hôtel Drouot 1927; Tajan 2022.[44]

Fig. 83. Detail of Study for *Moses Saved from the Waters* (Étude pour *Moïse sauvé des eaux*) (cat. 4)

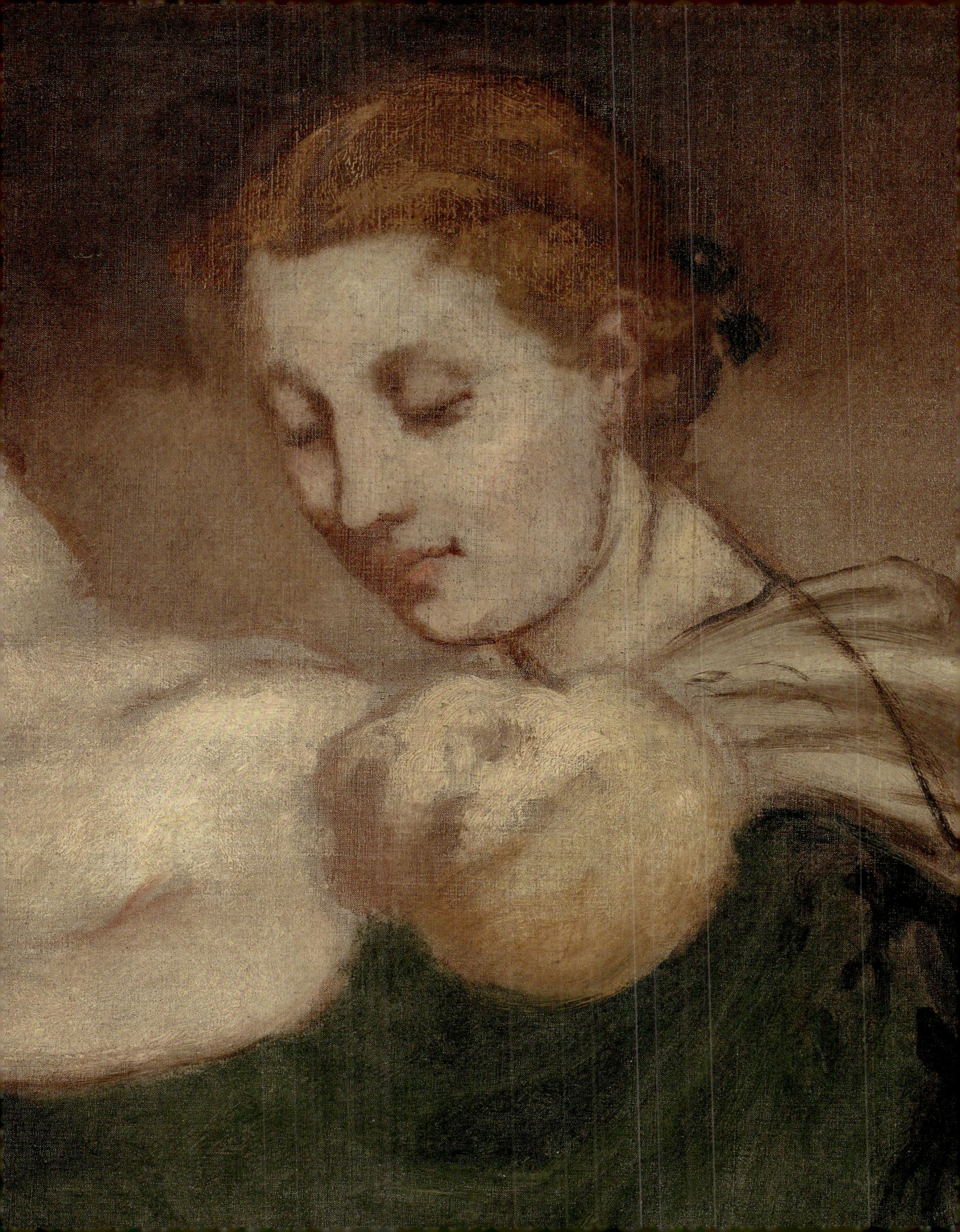

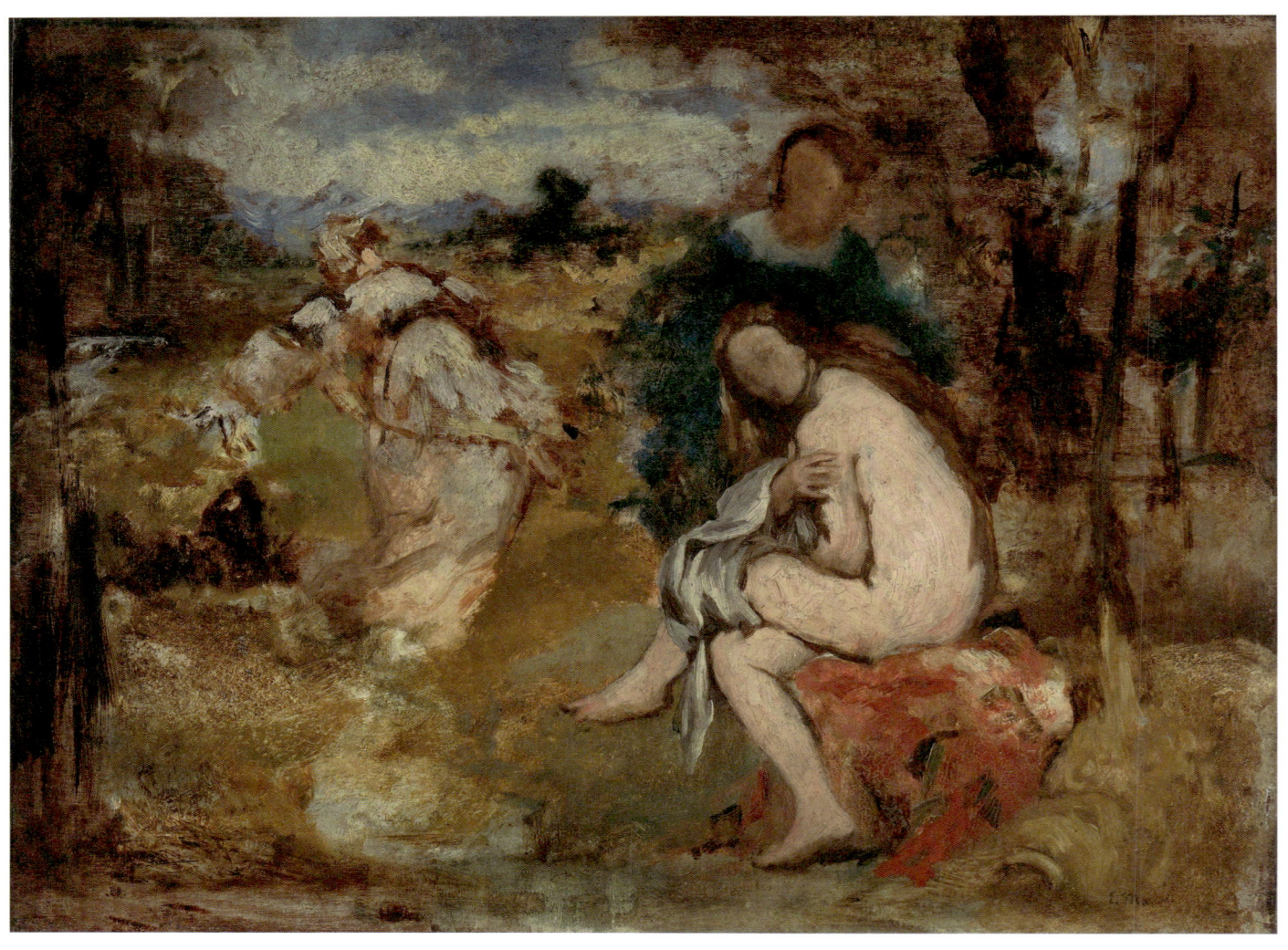

Study for *Surprised Nymph/Moses Saved from the Waters* (Étude pour
La Nymphe surpris/Moïse sauvé des eaux), about 1858–61
Oil on board, 35.5 × 46 cm
Nasjonalmuseet, Oslo

5 Study for *Surprised Nymph/Moses Saved from the Waters* (Étude pour *La Nymphe surpris/Moïse sauvé des eaux*), about 1858–61

This modest study is a key to some of Manet's greatest works: *Surprised Nymph* (see fig. 1), *Le Déjeuner sur l'herbe* (see fig. 84), and *Olympia* (see fig. 54). Others have described how the x-radiograph of this work reveals that Manet painted this scene over a reclining nude posing in a way similar to *Olympia*—possibly the artist's first step on his path toward that iconoclastic canvas.[45] This entry focuses on its connections to *Le Déjeuner sur l'herbe*.

Its title has long been in flux, primarily because of the recollection of the artist's friend Antonin Proust. He wrote: "Manet started in rue Lavoisier [his studio from 1856–59], a large painting, *Moses Saved from the Waters*, which he never finished, and from which there remains only one figure cut out from the canvas, which he titled *Surprised Nymph*." The oil sketch relates to *Surprised Nymph,* which prominently features a nude Suzanne Leenhoff, but more interestingly, is likely the most complete surviving guide to the Moses canvases that Proust saw and Manet later destroyed. In this sense, it may be more accurate to call it *Study for Moses Saved from the Waters* than *Study for Surprised Nymph,* which was a fragment of a larger canvas rather than the goal of this preparatory work. Considering the scale of the fragmentary nymph, the original painting must have been monumental—similar in size to *Le Déjeuner sur l'herbe*.

Since the 1980s scholars—notably Françoise Cachin and Juliet Wilson-Bareau—have linked this oil study to the *Le Déjeuner sur l'herbe*.[46] However, this connection has remained somewhat obscure in scholarship about Manet's work in general and in the rich literature on that painting in particular.[47] One of the clearest ways to see the links between this study and the *Le Déjeuner sur l'herbe* is to consider both paintings alongside a shared Old Master source: Titian's *Concert champêtre*, which in the 1800s was attributed to Giorgione (fig. 85).[48]

Looking at the *Concert champêtre* alongside *Le Déjeuner sur l'herbe,* one can see similarities in layout and content. And looking at *Concert champêtre* alongside this study for *Moses Saved from the Waters* is also instructive. The structure of the two paintings is similar. The placement of the trees and the blue mountains visible in the background is reminiscent of the Titian. Suzanne's body position and orientation are closer to the Renaissance model than in *Le Déjeuner sur l'herbe*, where the nude figure—posed by Victorine Meurent—is flipped.[49] Manet also places a tall, twisting figure on the left side of the composition. However, rather than a nude pouring a pitcher of water as in *Concert champêtre*, a clothed servant points toward a basket holding the baby Moses. When both Manet works are considered alongside the Titian, it seems as if the destroyed *Moses Saved from the Waters* may have been a first draft for *Le Déjeuner sur l'herbe,* an early attempt to engage with Old Master models of a nude that the artist ultimately felt was unsuccessful.[50]

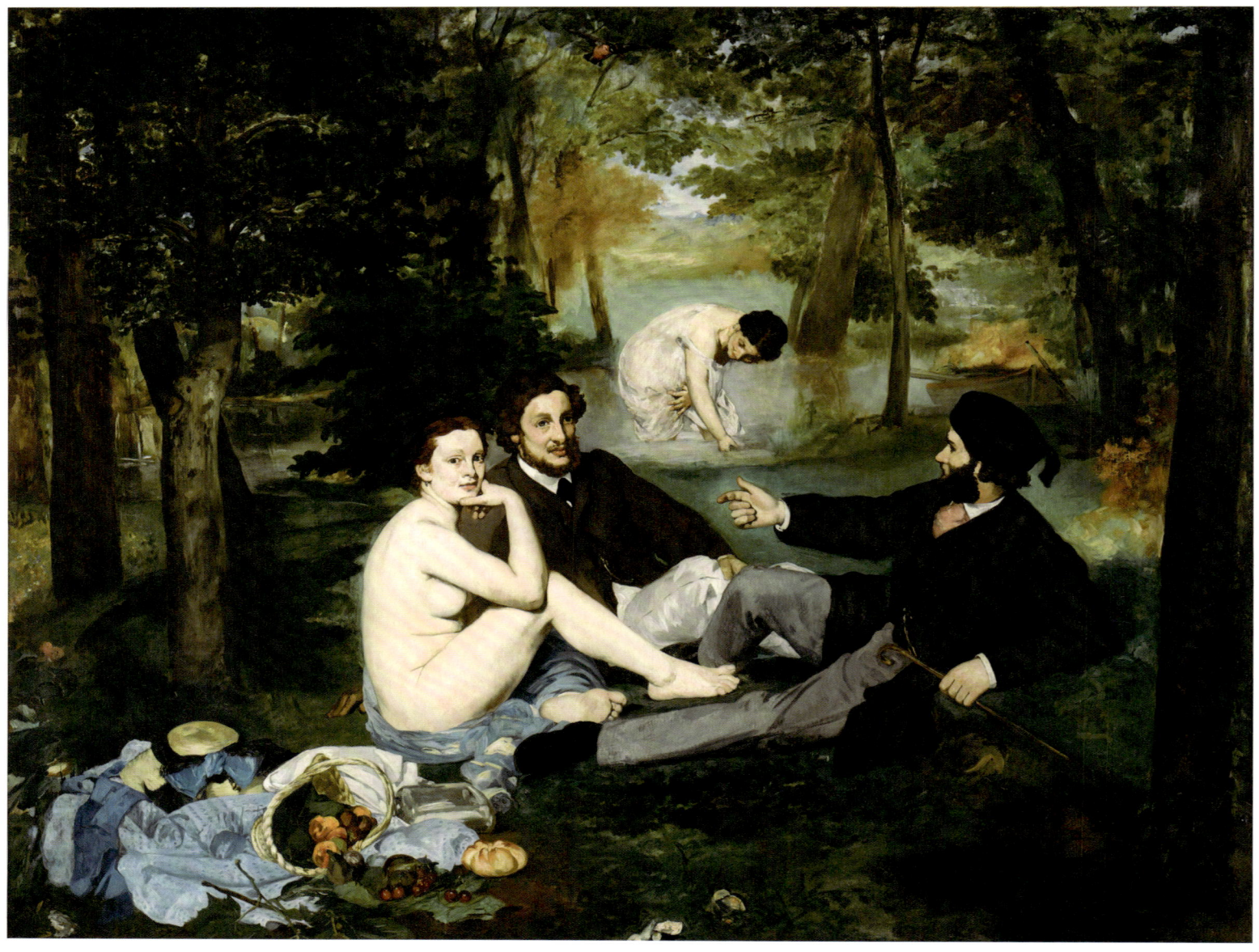

Fig. 84. Édouard Manet, *Le Déjeuner sur l'herbe*, 1863. Oil on canvas, 207 × 265 cm. Musée d'Orsay, Paris

Proust's recollections, though not always reliable, reinforce this interpretation:

On the eve of making *Déjeuner sur l'herbe* and *Olympia*, we were on a Sunday at Argenteuil, stretched out on the shore . . . Women were bathing. Manet fixed his eye on the women's flesh coming out of the water. It seems, [Manet] said to me . . . Well, I'm going to do them a nude. When we were in the studio, I copied Giorgione's women . . . with musicians . . . I want to do that again [with] the transparency of the atmosphere and with characters like the ones we see there.[51]

Some have argued that Proust misremembered and that the painting linked to *Concert Champêtre* was, in fact, *Surprised Nymph*.[52] However, both *Le Déjeuner sur l'herbe* and *Surprised Nymph* are linked to this shared Old Master source. That Manet says he wants to

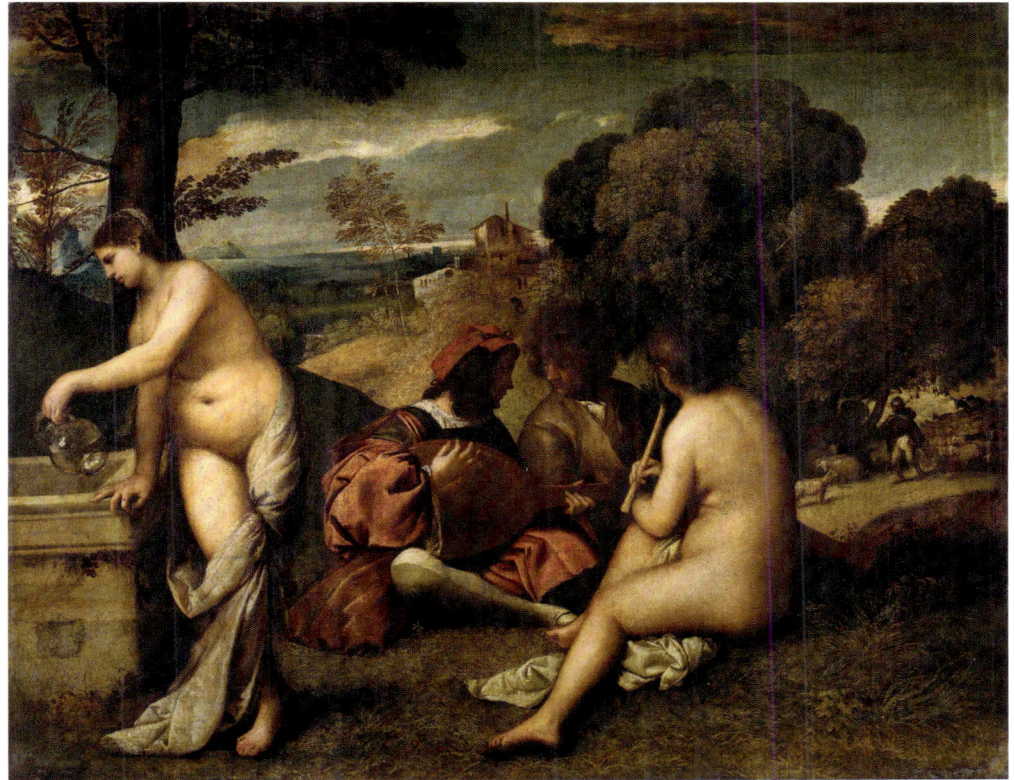

Fig. 85. Titian, *Concert champêtre*, 1509. Oil on canvas, 105 × 137 cm. Musée du Louvre, Paris

do "Giorgione's women . . . *again* [added for emphasis]" is telling. While he could be referring to a lost copy of the work made as a student in Couture's studio, it is possible that he is referring to an earlier attempt to engage with this subject when he was in his first studio on the rue Lavoisier: namely the destroyed *Finding of Moses* recorded by this modest oil sketch. This small, early-stage image of Suzanne was a critical step in Manet's artistic development.

DIANA SEAVE GREENWALD

PROVENANCE

Recorded in Léon Leenhoff's 1884 inventory of the artist's studio and photographed by Fernand Lochard (no. 261); purchased by Léon Leenhoff at the artist's estate sale, Drouot, Paris, February 1884; purchased by Alexandre Berthier, prince de Wagram, before his death in World War I; purchased by art dealer Georges Bernheim from Berthier's estate; purchased by the Nasjonalmuseet, Oslo, in 1918.

INVENTORY NUMBERS

NG.M.01182; RW 1975 1, 39; Lochard no. 261

SELECT LITERATURE

Krauss 1967, 622–27; Cachin et al. 1983, 86–87; Wilson-Bareau 1986, 26–41; Locke 2001, 79–84.

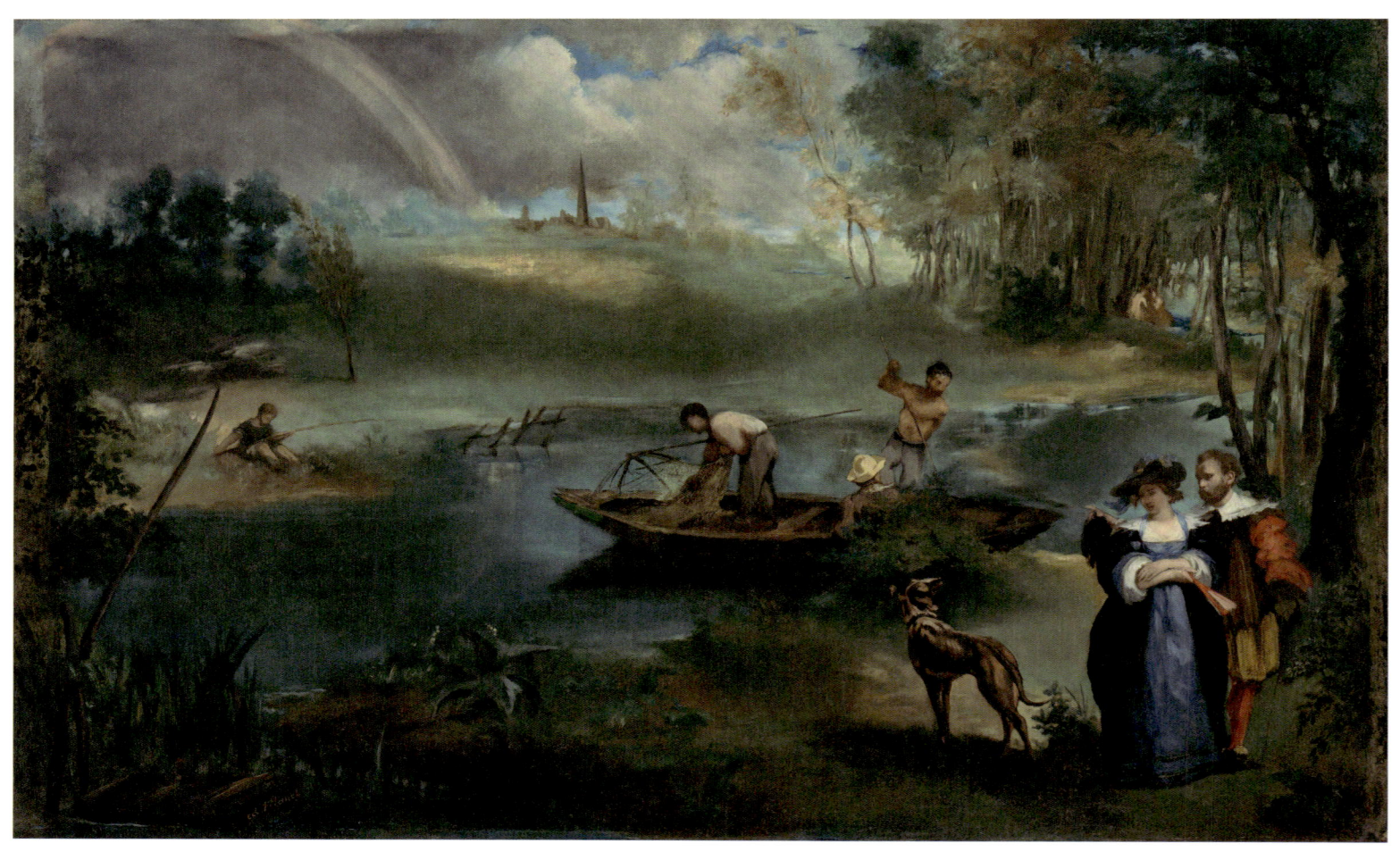

Fishing (La Pêche), about 1862–63
Oil on canvas, 76.8 × 123.2 cm
Metropolitan Museum of Art, New York. Purchase,
Mr. and Mrs. Richard J. Bernhard Gift, 1957

6 *Fishing (La Pêche)*, about 1862–63

Although aspects of *Fishing* remain enigmatic, there is little doubt that Manet's family figures prominently. In the lower right, Édouard Manet poses with Suzanne Leenhoff; they are dressed in seventeenth-century costume. The couple, who would marry in October of 1863, stands on a riverbank that stretches across the picture's foreground. Three fishermen work their craft from a boat near the picture's center. Across the river, a blonde boy—recognizable as Suzanne's son, Léon Leenhoff—holds a fishing rod over the water. If the relationship between the boy and the couple remains ambiguous, the viewer can nevertheless detect a subtle gesture linking them; Manet holds a hat behind Suzanne's shoulder and points in the direction of Léon.

According to records in Manet's studio at the time of his death, the painting was entitled *Paysage–Saint-Ouen*, or simply *Saint-Ouen*, which would place it among works and studies based on landscapes in Gennevilliers (where the Manet family owned considerable property) and Saint-Ouen, a commune that borders Gennevilliers to the south.[53] Like *Le Déjeuner sur l'herbe* (see fig. 84), *Fishing* connects to Manet's family both in the artist's use of familial models and its setting, where the family spent holidays and summers. The painting, still called *Paysage–Saint-Ouen*, stayed in the family until after the artist's death.[54]

The composition of *Fishing* and the appearance of the landscape combine elements of the quotidian—here, the swarthy fishermen—with allusions to landscape paintings by Peter Paul Rubens, including several in the Louvre. Manet's painting borrows elements from one painting in particular, Rubens's *Landscape with Rainbow* (1635; Hermitage, St. Petersburg), which he might have known through an engraving that reverses Rubens's painted composition (fig. 86).[55] In the engraving, a couple enters the landscape from the lower right, with the man nudging the woman forward. Ahead of them, a dog turns its head to look back even as its body is oriented on the diagonal, like the bridge in the middle ground, and a rainbow arcs toward the print's center from the upper left. In *Fishing*, Manet and Suzanne face frontally but stand in the same spot as the couple in the print; in fact, their dress and poses derive from a couple in another engraving after Rubens, *The Park of the Castle of Steen*.[56] The costumed Manet and Suzanne strike poses reminiscent of Rubens and his second wife and muse, Helena Fourment (fig. 87). Manet also situates the dog to duplicate the one in *Landscape with Rainbow*: same body type, same leg and tail position, identical turn of the muzzle to look back at the couple. Not only has Manet painted the rainbow in the same part of the composition, but he also included a pair of slender tree trunks that cross each other in the upper right, just like Rubens.

Could Manet be alluding to the Dutch artistic tradition of juxtaposing a couple with a fisherman to suggest that fishing was "a metaphor for amorous pursuit" (i.e., "fishing for someone"), whether overt or hidden?[57] As Charles S. Moffett notes, *Fishing* is the only extant side-by-side painting in which Édouard Manet and Suzanne Leenhoff appear together.[58] Their relationship prior to their 1863 marriage was a secret. The very existence of Suzanne Leenhoff was news to Charles Baudelaire when Manet announced his imminent wedding, and the parentage of Léon remained a family secret.[59] An iconographic tradition that associated fishing with erotic diversion or courtship, especially one that

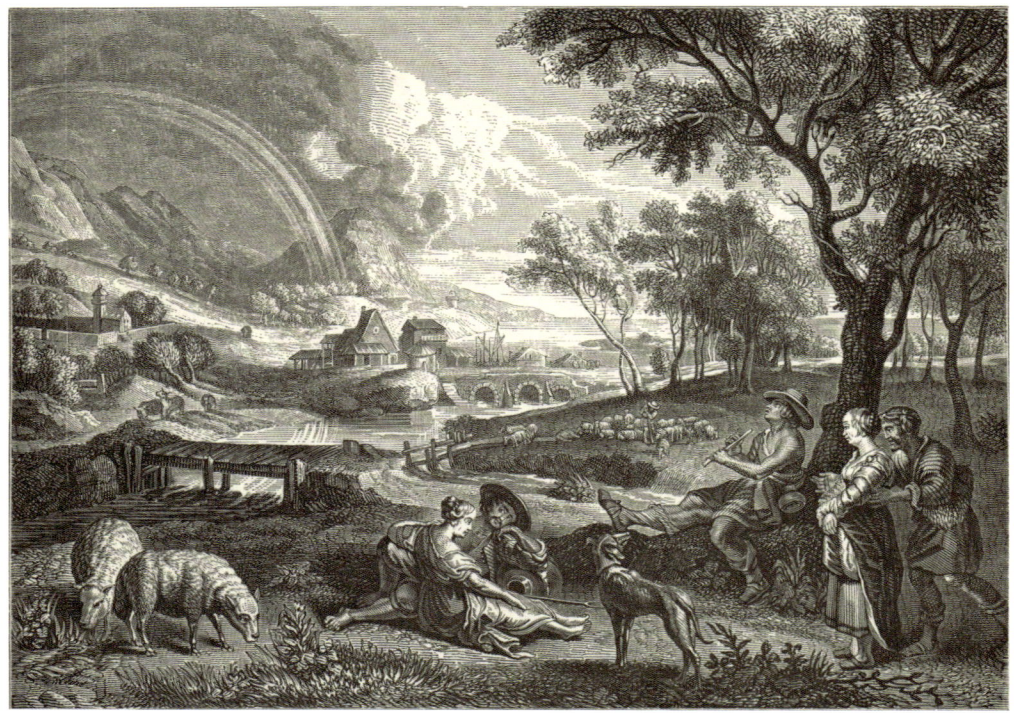

Fig. 86. Louis Marvy and Auguste Trichon after Peter Paul Rubens, *Landscape with Rainbow*, 19th century. Wood engraving, 12.4 × 17 cm.

could be adapted for stories of seduction as well as love hidden, could account for Manet's placement of fishermen in a work that already referred to seventeenth-century art. The painting deploys early modern Flemish and Dutch iconography to create an allusive but private fantasy around the artist's close family members.

NANCY LOCKE

PROVENANCE

Collection of the artist; likely given to Eugénie Manet and then by exchange or after her death through inheritance to the artist's widow, Suzanne Manet; purchased by Gaston-Alexandre Camentron, Paris, 1897; purchased by Durand-Ruel, Paris, for 5,500 francs, April 1, 1897; transferred to the Société Artistique George V, Paris, June 20, 1950; purchased by Sam Salz, New York, about 1956–57; purchased by the Metropolitan Museum of Art, New York, 1957, through Mr. and Mrs. Richard J. Bernhard.

INVENTORY NUMBERS

57.10; RW 1975 1, 39; Lochard no. 320

SELECT LITERATURE

Duret 1902, 100–101, 201, no. 33; Moreau-Nélaton 1926, vol. 1, 29–30, fig. 16; Jamot 1927, 38–40, 42; Tabarant 1931, 60–61, no. 35; Jamot and Wildenstein 1932, vol. 1, 57, 117, no. 30; vol. 2, fig. 13; Bazin 1932, 153–55, figs. 17–22; Tabarant 1947, 34–36, 61–62, 524, 534, no. 29, fig. 29; Sandblad 1954, 41–44; Sterling and Salinger 1967, 25–27; Fried 1969, 28–29, 33–34, 50, 52, 69 n. 35, 69 n. 36d, 71 n. 69; Reff 1970, 456–57; Rouart and Wildenstein 1975, vol. 1, no. 36; Farwell 1975, 224–27, 229; Mauner 1975, 21–22, 24–27, 149, figs. 11, 16, 17; Cachin et al. 1983, 70–73; Locke 2001, 65–66, 71–72, 74, 78–79, 81–83, 121, 145, 192 n. 114, 194 n. 155, 194 n. 157; Dombrowski 2013, 83.

Fig. 87. Detail of *Fishing (La Pêche)* (cat. 6)

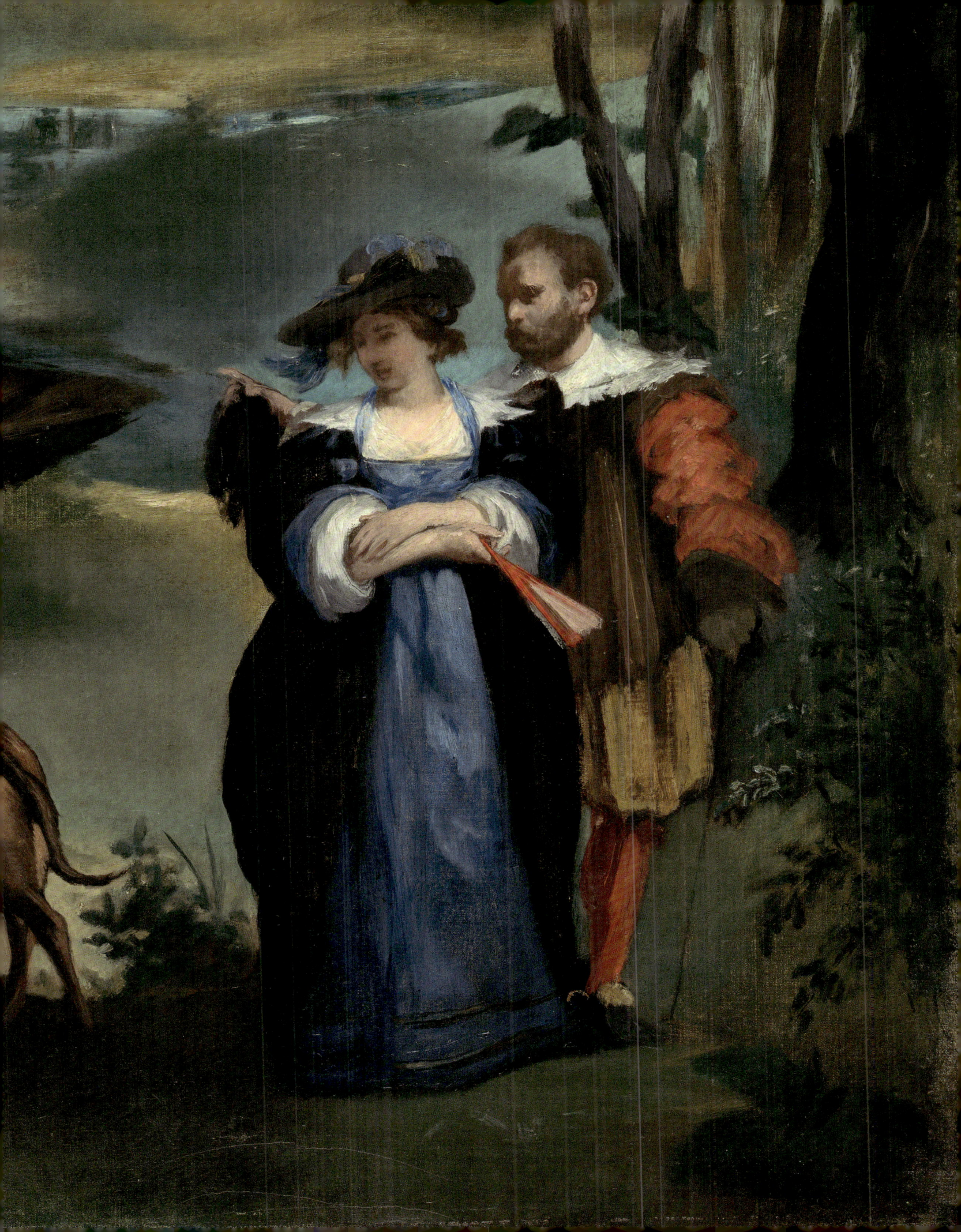

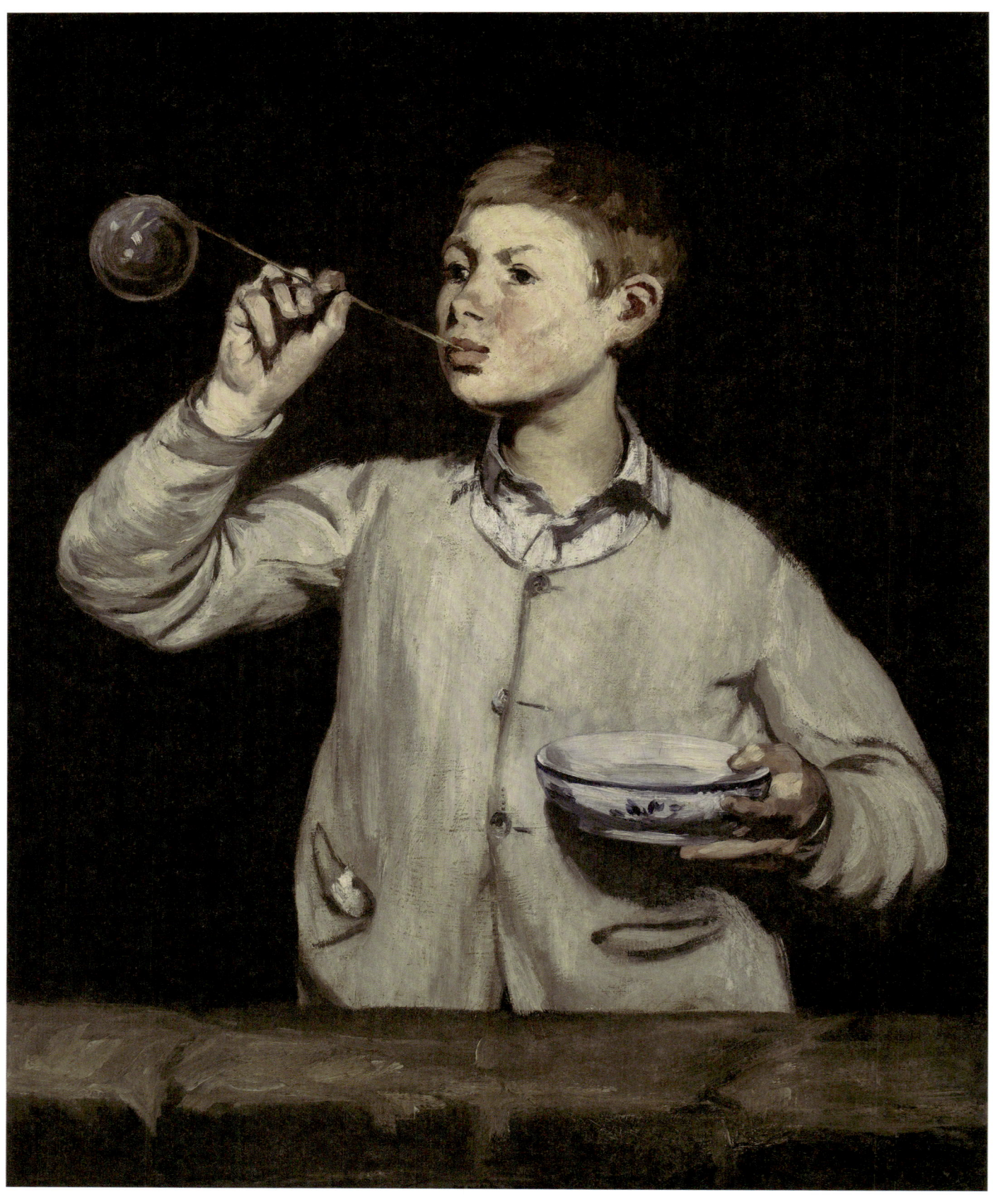

Boy Blowing Bubbles (Les bulles de savon), 1867
Oil on canvas, 100.5 × 81.4 cm
Museum Calouste Gulbenkian, Lisbon

7   *Boy Blowing Bubbles (Les bulles de savon)*, 1867

This work featuring Léon Leenhoff (1852–1927), the son of Manet's wife, Suzanne, is typically cited as referencing a subject painted by eighteenth-century French painter Jean Baptiste Chardin (1699–1779): a young boy blowing a soap bubble (fig. 88).[60] Manet's painting is also the basis for a print that appears in several states in which the artist plays with the reversal of the figure in print form (fig. 89).[61]

Chardin's painting participates in the artistic tradition of allegories for *vanitas*, the sense that worldly pleasures—like beautiful soap bubbles—are ultimately fleeting. Artists often represented this concept in the form of *vanitas* still lifes of food and wine that are ultimately consumed or rot.[62] Extending this symbolism, artists also engaged with the linked concept of *homo bulla* (man is a bubble), which made clear that human life, like the soap bubble, is beautiful but fragile.

Manet may have looked to a range of seventeenth-century Dutch artists, including Jan Steen (1626–1679) and Frans van Mieris the Elder (1635–1681), who painted *vanitas* themes and bubble motifs in particular. The blue-and-white bowl that Léon holds in his right hand is reminiscent of Delftware and could be a reference to these Dutch sources as well as to Léon's heritage on his mother's side. In Chardin's work, which was itself indebted to Dutch sources, the moral message related to soap bubble paintings shifted. Rather than emphasizing the shortness of life, Chardin celebrates childhood as a joyful yet transient time.[63] This message of the transience of boyhood aligns with transitions in Léon's life that occurred around the time this painting was likely completed.

Léon was one of Manet's most frequent models, and depictions of him fall into roughly three periods: 1859–62, then 1867–69, and finally the early 1870s.[64] The division between the first and second period corresponds to Léon's departure for boarding school.[65] Manet's preferred model was suddenly less available to be painted. Léon reappeared in 1867–69, when he returned home and started working as a clerk for financial firms. He left for school at age eleven—very much a boy—and came home as a young man of fifteen.

In *Blowing Bubbles,* Léon appears very youthful—much younger than in *Young Boy Peeling a Pear* (1868, cat. no. 8), which is another painting that includes still life and deals with themes of passing time; it is also the next known depiction of him. Although Léon recalled that he posed for this painting in the fall of 1867, when he was fifteen years old, this youthful look and Manet's use of the stone ledge—a hallmark of his early 1860s oeuvre—suggest that the painting could be earlier than that, or at least that Manet started working on it prior to 1867.[66] More technical information, which is currently unavailable, could reveal the extent to which the canvas was worked and reworked.

Although Manet may have seen prints like Pierre Filloeul's (1696–1754) *Soap Bubbles* (1739) after Chardin, which would have allowed him to engage with this subject at an earlier time, there is an important detail that reinforces the 1867 date. One of Chardin's iconic canvases—now in the collection of the National Gallery of Art, Washington—was sold as part of the Laurent Laperlier collection at the Parisian auction house Hôtel Drouot in April 1867.[67] This would have presented an opportunity for Manet to see Chardin's work and take inspiration from it. While Léon's paternity is ambiguous, he clearly played a filial role to his *parrain* (godfather), as he called the artist.[68] One can see Manet's canvas through the

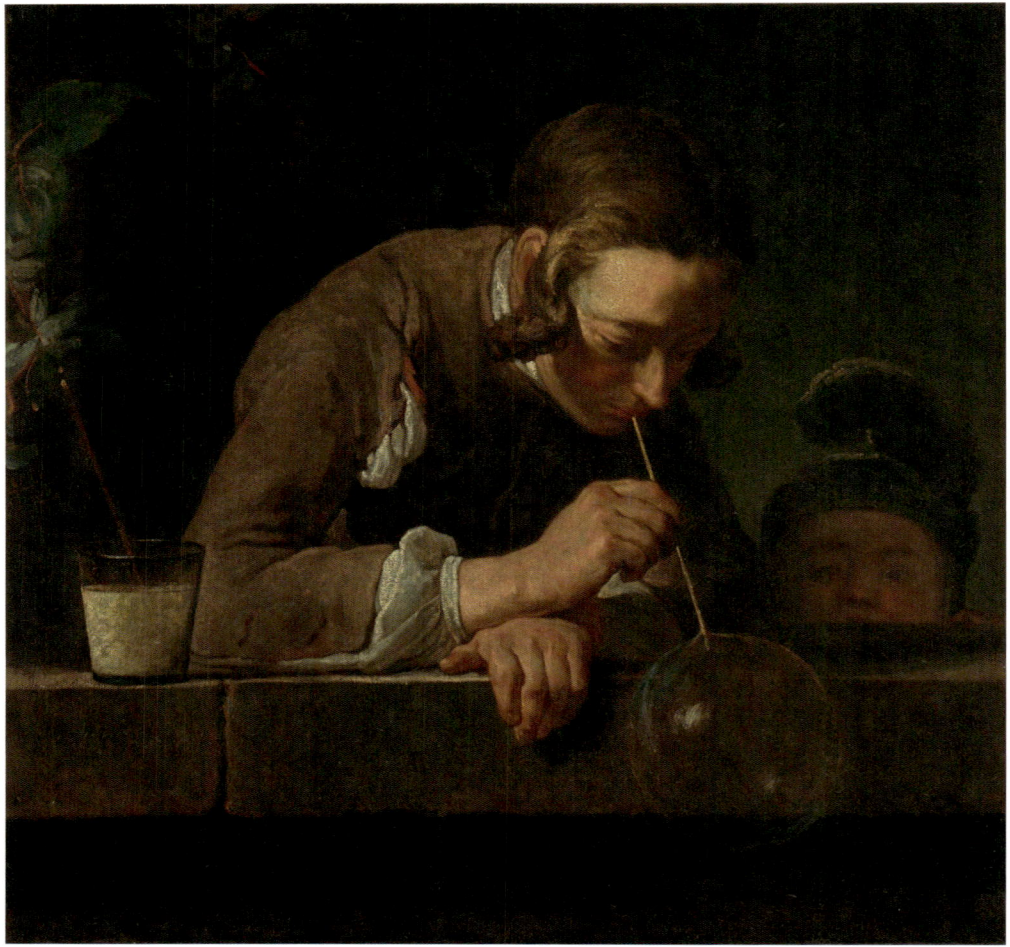

Fig. 88. Jean Baptiste Chardin, *Soap Bubbles*, about 1733–34. Oil on canvas, 61 × 63.2 cm. The Metropolitan Museum of Art, New York. Wentworth Fund, 1949

lens of a parent's sentimentality. The picture is a nostalgic portrayal of his faithful model—this sort-of-son whose childhood Manet immortalized several times before but which was now coming to a close.[69]

ADRIENNE CHAPARRO

PROVENANCE

Purchased from the artist by Albert and Henri Hecht, Paris, 1872 for 500 francs; bequeathed to Emmanuel Pontremoli, Paris, 1916; purchased by Georges Bernheim, Paris, from Emmanuel Pontremoli for 150,000 francs, 1916; transferred to his gallery Bernheim-Jeune, 1918; with Durand-Ruel, Paris, New York, 1919; purchased by Adolf Lewisohn, New York, 1919; purchased by Calouste Gulbenkian, Lisbon, through André Weil, New York, November 1943.

INVENTORY NUMBERS

2361; RW 1975 1, 129

SELECT LITERATURE

Rouart and Wildenstein, 1975, vol. 1, no. 129; Cachin et al. 1983, 268–70, no. 102; Stevens et al., 2012, 84–5, 179, no. 9; Locke 2001, 118–28, 153, fig. 57; Cars, Guégan, and Pludermacher 2023, 26, 29, no. 19.

Fig. 89. Édouard Manet, *The Boy with Soap Bubbles* (detail), 1868–69. Etching, 40.7 × 27.5 cm. The Miriam and Ira D. Wallach Division of Art, Prints and Photographs: Print Collection, The New York Public Library

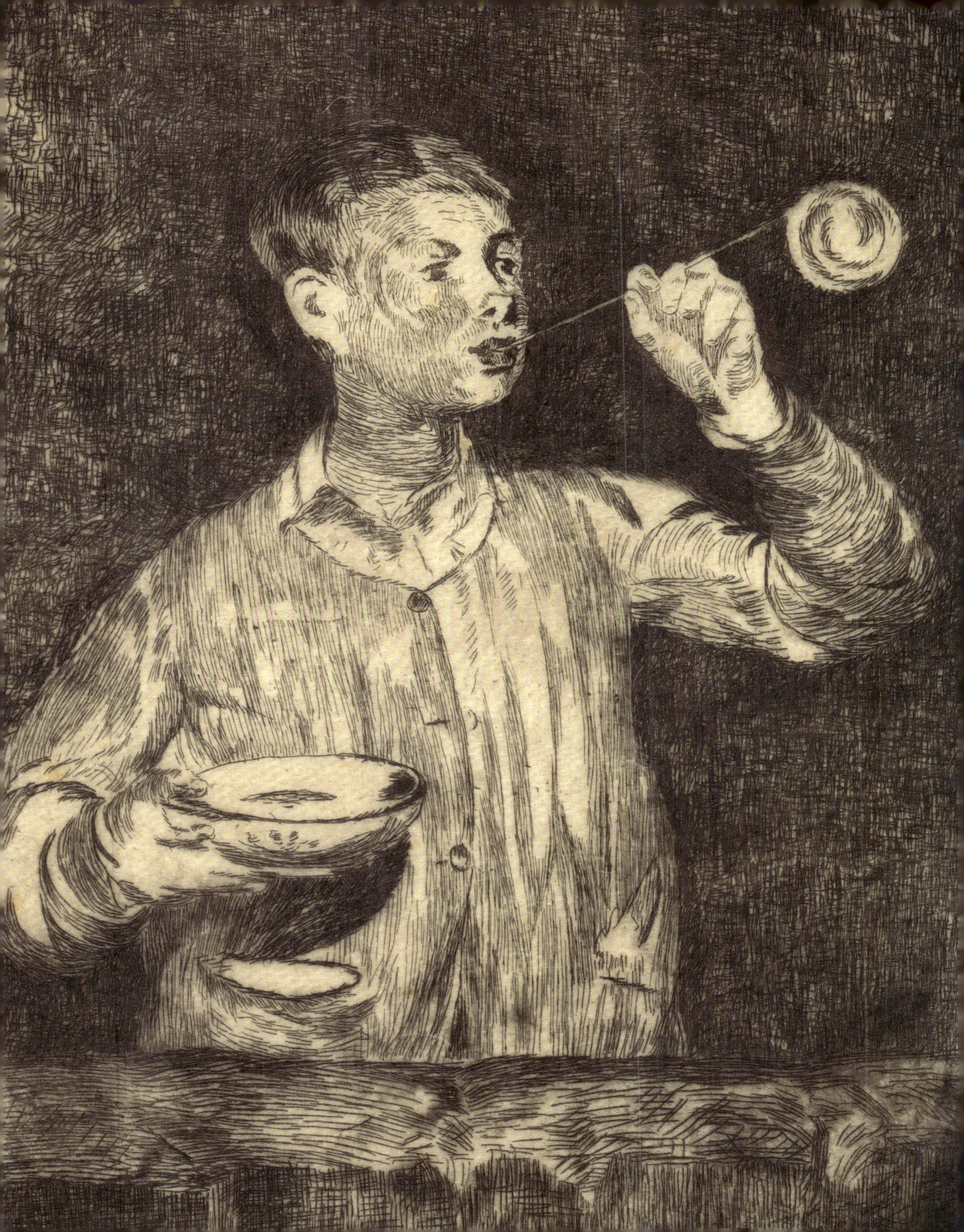

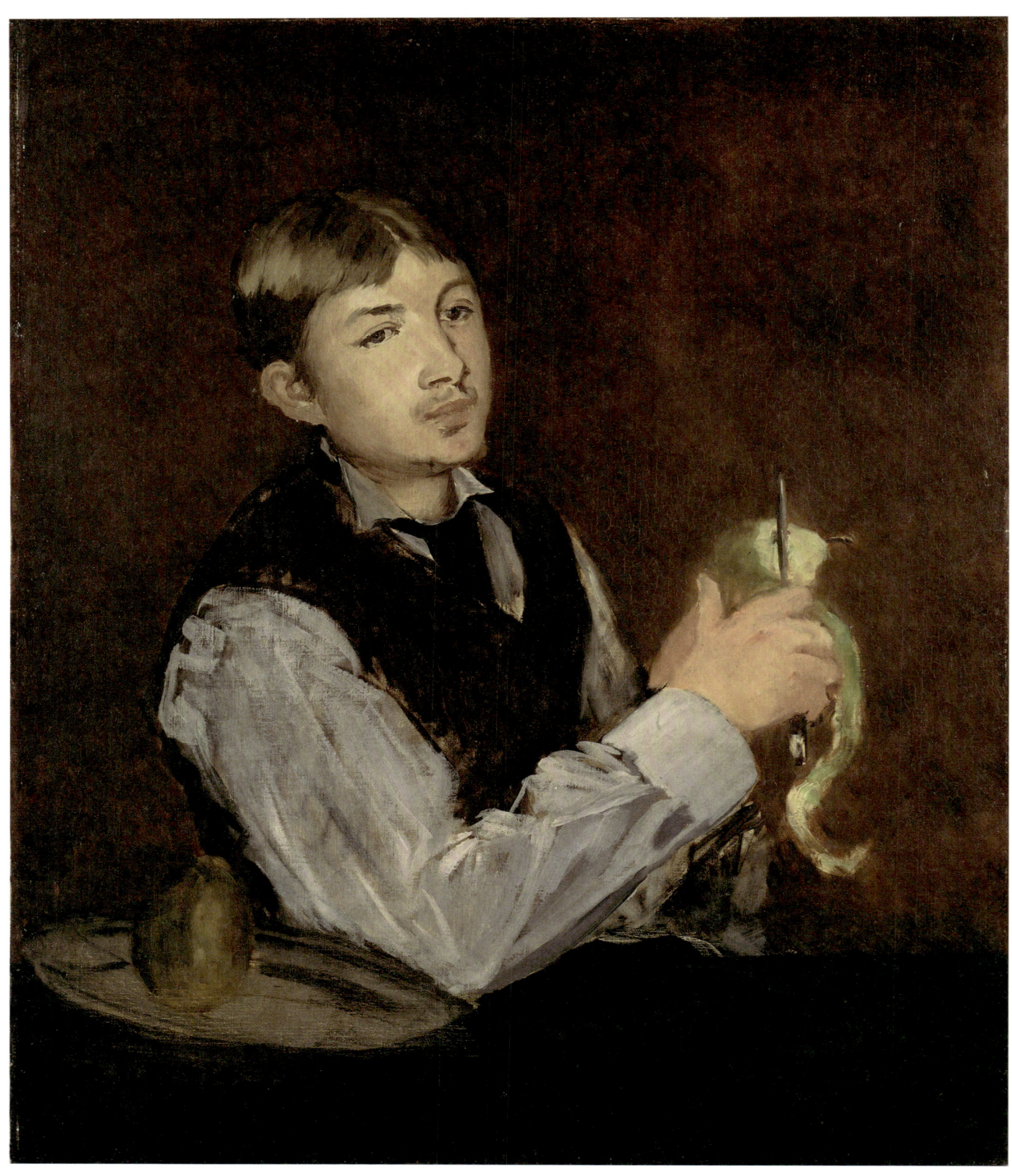

Young Boy Peeling a Pear (L'Éplucheur), about 1868
Oil on canvas, 85 × 71 cm
Nationalmuseum, Stockholm

8   *Young Boy Peeling a Pear (L'Éplucheur),* about 1868

In 1868, Édouard Manet painted Léon Leenhoff peeling a pear in a simple composition. There is very little else in the scene. Accompanying the boy and pear is a barely defined tabletop and a plate with another pear in the foreground. The subject of a person in the act of peeling produce appears infrequently in the history of painting—although notable examples include Caravaggio's *Boy Peeling Fruit* (1592–93; Cumberland Art Gallery, Presence Chamber, Hampton Court Palace) and Jean Baptiste Chardin's *The Kitchen Maid* (1738; National Gallery of Art, Washington). Manet studied other works by both artists, but neither composition obviously relates to this painting. Instead, Manet almost certainly drew upon a tradition of allegorical sense paintings, specifically Spanish painter Jusepe de Ribera's *The Sense of Smell* (fig. 90), about 1615, a copy of which existed in a private collection in Paris during Manet's lifetime.[70] There are a number of convincing visual parallels that support this connection—from the overall composition of a half-turned subject down to the extra objects in the foreground or even the gray color of the sleeve. Unlike Ribera's allegory of smell, which features a fragrant, cut onion and garlic resting on the table, Manet's choice of a pear does not obviously privilege scent. In fact, other senses might jump out like the tactile act of peeling a fruit or the sound of cutting a crisp, crunchy pear.

The peeled skin of the pear unspools from Léon's hand, a prominent example of a new motif emergent in Manet's work around this time. Between 1866 and 1869, Manet regularly featured peeled fruits in paintings across different genres including in portraits (*Portrait of Astruc,* 1866, Kunsthalle Bremen); allegorical scenes (*Young Lady in 1866,* 1866, Metropolitan Museum of Art); and still lifes (*Salmon,* 1868–69, Shelburne Museum). A peeled lemon also appears in *Luncheon in the Studio* (1868, see fig. 7), a painting that similarly featured Léon. With the peel motif, Manet was drawing on another art historical tradition: Dutch still-life painting. Exotic citrus fruits were status symbols of wealth in the Netherlands in the seventeenth century. Widespread production of still life was part of what Svetlana Alpers calls a new interest in description in the Dutch Renaissance. The half-peeled fruit allowed artists to represent fruits and other objects in ways that revealed inner anatomy and otherwise hidden textures. By contrast, all of Manet's contemporaneous peeled fruits are far less detailed than any Dutch precedents and the pear in Léon's hands is the sketchiest of his efforts. While the forms of the fruit in his hands and on the table are both distinctly pear-like, the color and flesh inside are indistinct and muted. In particular, the thick, sensuous brushstrokes that compose the peel give only a vague outline of its shape and texture. If the Dutch peels were meant to be "a feast for the attentive eye" in a culture that enjoyed celebrating and studying material goods, then Manet's peels are a feast for a new, modernist painting culture dedicated to a self-reflexive painterly surface and an interest in fleeting temporality.[71]

The two themes interrelate. Manet's thickest brushstrokes appear in zones of movement and transition: in the peel (capturing the act of falling), the bent movement of Léon's right sleeve (capturing the act of peeling) and the faint mustache on his upper lip (capturing the act of aging). With this portrait of a boy turning into a young man—Léon was around sixteen at the time—Manet thematizes the passing of time with a multitude of suspended

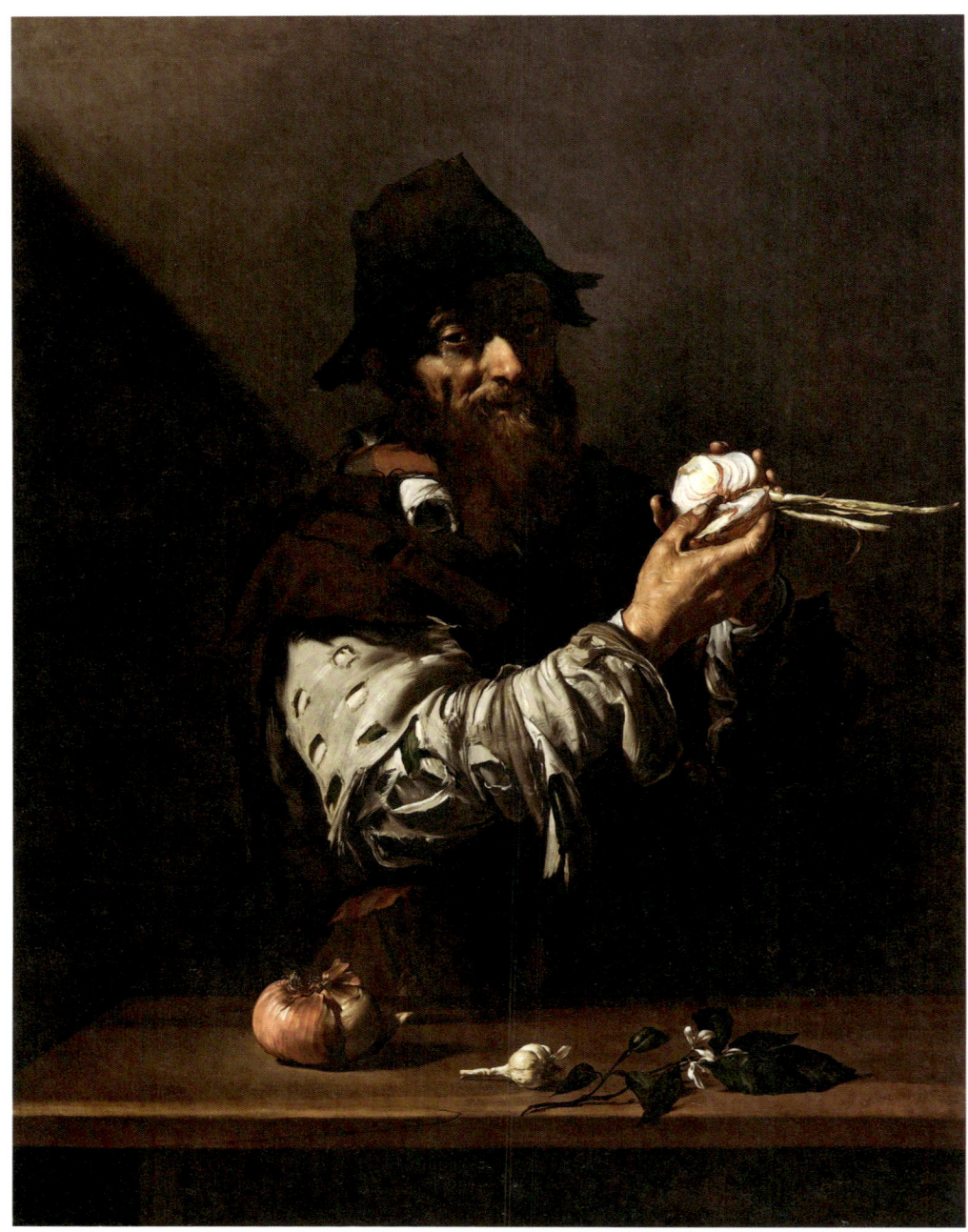

Fig. 90. Jusepe de Ribera, *The Sense of Smell*, about 1615. Oil on canvas, 114.8 × 88.3. Abelló Collection, Madrid

actions. Compared to the *Boy Blowing Bubbles* (cat. no. 7) from perhaps a year prior or even *Luncheon in the Studio* of the same year, in this painting, Léon appears significantly older. In *Boy Blowing Bubbles*, the blown bubble's precarious nature is understood as an obvious symbol for the fleetingness of sensory experiences and—especially when paired with a young subject—it might also suggest the fleetingness of boyhood. So too does *Boy Peeling a Pear* convey fleetingness in both senses. It is a picture of an action caught in a moment in time, but it is also a portrait of a young man in a particular moment in his life.

With his diverse set of art historical references, Manet's work embodies both halves of his friend Charles Baudelaire's famous notion that "modernity is the transient, the fleeting, the contingent; it is one half of art, the other being the eternal and the immovable."[72] As in many of his paintings, Manet here is grappling with modern art's place in history: drawing on historical predecessors while using his new, distinctive vocabulary. Putting Léon at the center of this painting thematizes this concern balancing the aesthetic demands of both the eternal and the contingent: Manet uses the young man as both a model for an ahistorical allegorical treatment but also as a specific modern subject in a portrait. To most viewers, he is just a boy peeling a pear, but to Manet, he is always also Léon Leenhoff, captured in paint during his last vestiges of boyhood.

ALEX ZIVKOVIC

PROVENANCE

Purchased by Jean-Baptiste Faure from the artist, 1882; given by Jean-Baptiste Faure to Anders Zorn, Mora; bequeathed by him to the Nationalmuseum, Stockholm, 1896.

INVENTORY NUMBERS

NW 1498; RW 1975 1, 130

SELECT LITERATURE

Rouart and Wildenstein 1975, vol. 1, no. 130; Mauner and Loyrette 2000, 34–35, 72–73, 168, no. 10; Gunnarson and Brummer 2002, 68, ill., 97, no. 137; Locke 2001, 124, ill., 25.

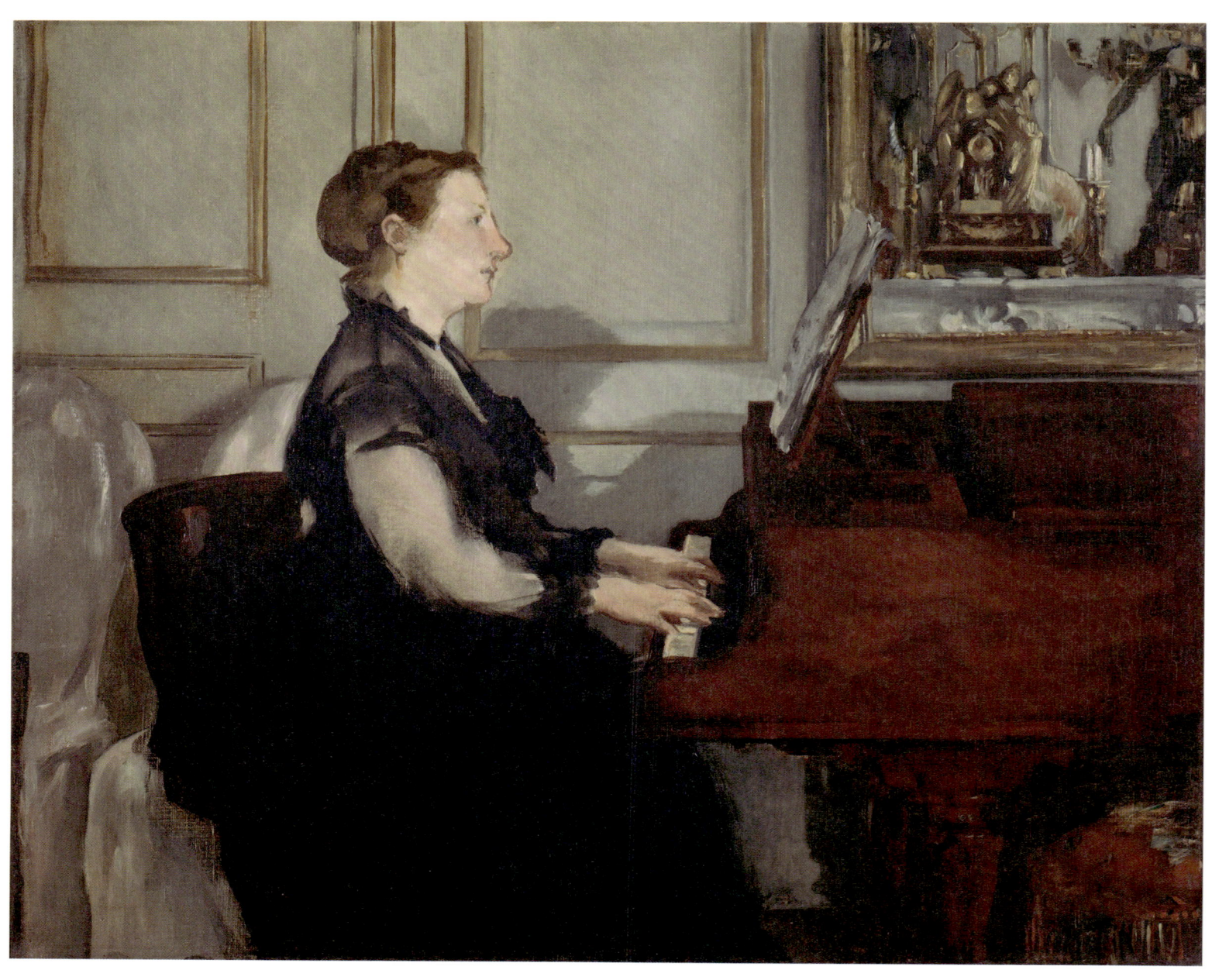

Madame Manet at the Piano (Madame Manet au piano), 1868
Oil on canvas, 38.5 × 46.5 cm
Musée d'Orsay, Paris

9   *Madame Manet at the Piano (Madame Manet au piano)*, 1868

My dear Manet,

You are close, I believe, to Whistler. What a fine painting: at the Piano, no. 1561!
Oh I would very much like to have it, to put in the middle of my old masters.

Would you be kind enough to find out whether the painting stil belongs to Whistler
and how much he will sell it for.

If the price is not frightening for an artist like me, I shall try to acquire this painting
which I would place very well alongside my van der Meer of Delft.

All good wishes,

W. Burger[73]

In the spring of 1867, the art critic Théophile Thoré-Burger wrote to Édouard Manet asking for help. An art collector well known for his study and holdings of seventeenth-century Dutch art, Thoré-Burger wanted to add a contemporary work to his collection: *At the Piano* (1858–59, Taft Museum, Cincinnati) (fig. 91) by American expatriate artist James McNeill Whistler (1834–1903).[74] Though completed years earlier, Whistler exhibited the work at the 1867 Salon, where Thoré-Burger spotted it and asked Manet—a friend of Whistler's since 1861—to help him acquire it.[75] Although he previously lived and trained in Paris for a number of years, Whistler had since settled in London, and the collector relied on Manet for an introduction. The acquisition was not successful, though surviving correspondence proves that Manet not only saw Whistler's painting but was involved in negotiations around its sale.[76]

Madame Manet at the Piano, which Manet completed just one year later, bears a striking resemblance to Whistler's *At the Piano*. Both works feature a woman in profile wearing black, playing the piano in a gilded, white paneled interior. Whistler's larger painting includes a young girl listening to music, whereas Manet's has a cropped focus on the performer alone, his wife Suzanne. He also added a personal detail: the clock on the mantle was a wedding gift to his mother from the king of Sweden.[77]

Madame Manet at the Piano responds to several contemporary paintings. It has, rightly, been interpreted as an artistic rebuttal to Edgar Degas's double portrait of Manet listening to his wife playing the piano (see fig. 45), which Degas gave to the couple around 1867. Unhappy with the painting, Manet brutally cut his wife's profile from the canvas. This subsequent portrait of Suzanne was presumably an attempt to create his own, more flattering, depiction of her.[78] However, it also provides evidence of another ongoing artistic dialogue with Whistler—a dialogue that seems to have centered around Suzanne. Manet's *Reading* (about 1868–73)—a beautiful image of his wife clothed in white—may have been inspired by Whistler's landmark *Symphony in White, No. 1: The White Girl* (1861–62, National Gallery of Art, Washington).[79]

In Whistler's painting of a woman at the piano, Thoré-Burger saw aesthetic resonances with his collection of Dutch paintings. His letter indicates he wanted to buy and install Whistler's piece among his "old masters," specifically "my van der Meer of Delft"— now better known as Johannes Vermeer. Thoré-Burger owned three Vermeer paintings of women playing keyboard instruments: *A Young Woman Standing at a Virginal* (1670–72,

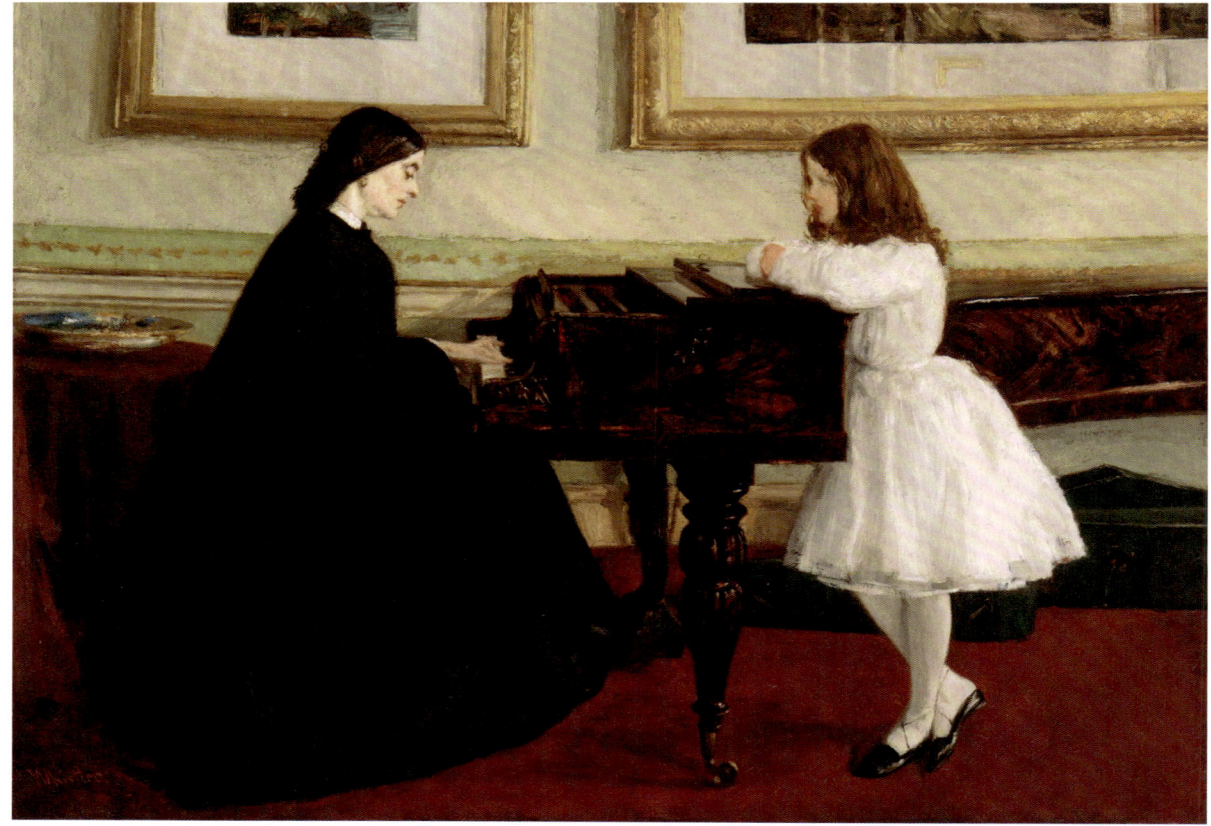

Fig. 91. James McNeill Whistler, *At the Piano*, 1858–59. Oil on canvas, 67.3 × 93.3 cm. Taft Museum of Art, Cincinnati. Bequest of Louise Taft Semple

National Gallery London), *A Young Woman Seated at a Virginal* (1670–72, National Gallery London), and *The Concert* (1663–66) (fig. 92), which would later become Isabella Stewart Gardner's first major art purchase.[80] Whistler's painting would be at home among these works since he could have been inspired directly by *The Concert*. The painting was offered for sale in London in 1860 and was likely held in that city from the 1830s until Thoré-Bürger acquired it around 1867. Whistler lived and worked in the British capital when he painted *At the Piano* in 1858–59.[81] He may well have seen the Vermeer.

Returning to *Madame Manet at the Piano*, was Manet aware of his friend's Dutch inspiration? Did he also see the Vermeer piano scenes—including *The Concert*—when they were added to Thoré-Bürger's collection and before painting *Madame Manet at the Piano*?[82] In and around this failed acquisition of a Whistler painting, there are possibly a series of closer connections between this portrait of Suzanne Manet and the collection of Isabella Stewart Gardner than one might expect.

DIANA SEAVE GREENWALD

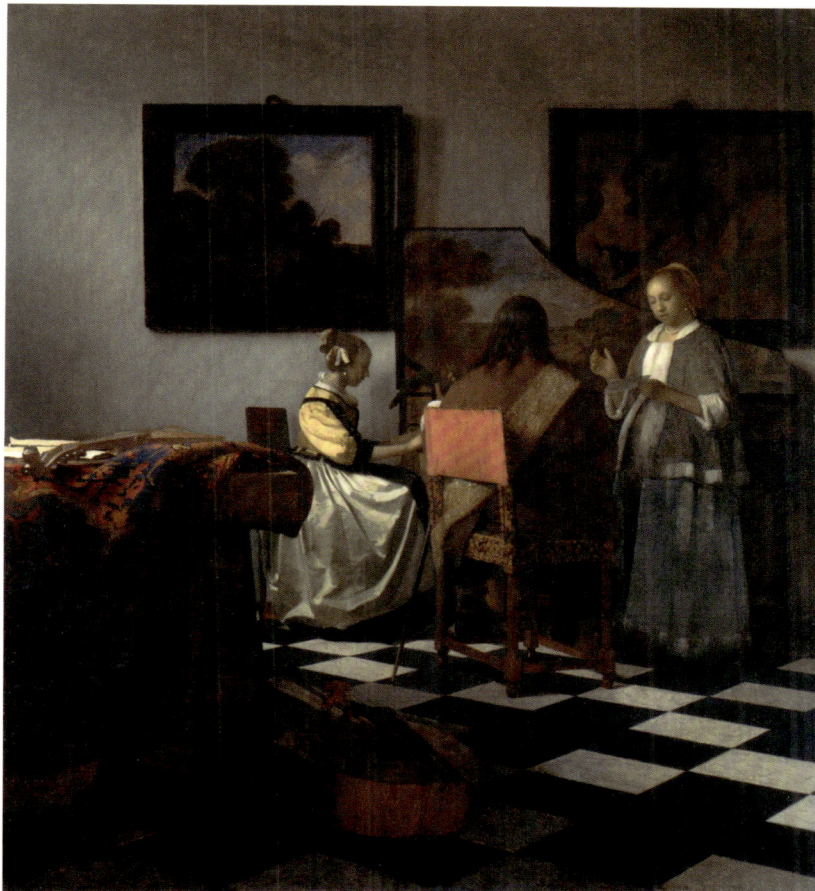

Fig. 92. Johannes Vermeer, *The Concert*, 1663–66. Oil on canvas, 72.5 × 64.7 cm Isabella Stewart Gardner Museum, Boston

PROVENANCE

Collection of the sitter, Suzanne Manet, Paris, until 1894; purchased by Maurice Joyant, director of the Galerie Boussod et Valadon from Suzanne Manet for 5,000 francs, 1894; purchased by Count Isaac de Camondo, Paris, 1895; accepted by the French state as part of the bequest of Camondo to the Musée du Louvre, Paris, 1911; transferred to Galerie du Jeu de Paume, Paris, 1947; transferred to the Musée d'Orsay, Paris, 1986.

INVENTORY NUMBERS

RF 1994; RW 1975 1, 131

SELECT LITERATURE

Jamot and Wildenstein 1932, no. 142; Tabarant 1947, no. 142; Orienti 1970, no. 122; Rouart and Wildenstein 1975, vol. 1, no. 131; Cachin et al. 1983, no. 107; Stevens et al. 2012, no. 7; Singletary 2017, 74–82, plate 16; Cars, Guégan, and Pludermacher, 12-23, plate 12.

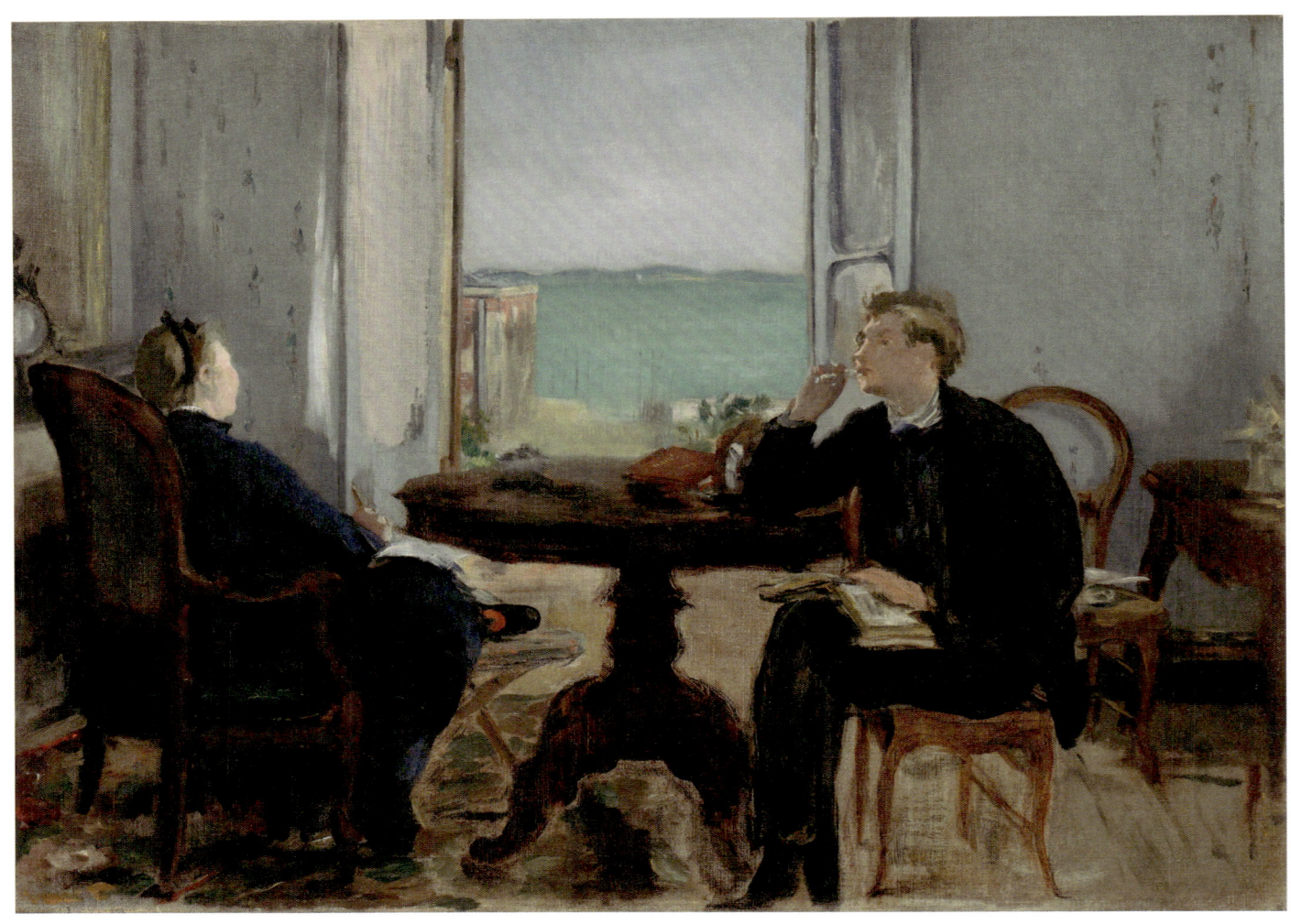

Interior at Arcachon (Intérieur à Arcachon), 1871
Oil on canvas, 39.2 × 54 cm
Clark Art Institute, Williamstown

10 *Interior at Arcachon (Intérieur à Arcachon)*, 1871

This painting dates to a distinct moment in Édouard Manet's life. The Franco-Prussian War broke out in the summer of 1870, and by September it was clear Paris was under threat. With Napoleon III's loss at Sedan on September 2 and the declaration of a new government days later, France was in chaos. Concerned for his family's safety, Manet sent his mother Eugénie, his wife Suzanne, and Suzanne's eighteen-year-old son Léon to Oloron-Sainte-Marie in the Pyrenees in the country's southwest while he stayed behind to help defend the capital.[83] They stayed there for months until Manet joined them in mid-February 1871, and the whole family then moved to the seaside town of Arcachon—outside of Bordeaux—for March. Manet keenly felt his family's absence and sent them a series of moving letters.[84] This painting and a beautiful linked drawing are related to their moment of reunification (fig. 93). Both works serve as touching double portraits of Suzanne and Léon. In these images, Léon finally seems to be the subject of a portrait rather than serving as a studio model. As Charles Moffett wrote about the two pieces, they should not be considered a preparatory drawing and a finished painting but rather part of a linked process of refinement and reworking of the subject across media.[85]

The drawing records an earlier stage of Manet's decision-making about how to pose Léon. A light pencil outline along the right-hand sill of the window suggests that the artist initially considered showing him standing with his face largely turned away from the viewer, book in hand. However, Manet abandoned this idea. Rather than show him three-quarters turned away from the viewer—a view somewhat similar to another painting from this period *Oloron-Sainte-Marie* (about 1871, Emil Bührle Collection, Kunsthaus Zurich), he shows him three-quarters turned toward the viewer. We get a complete view of Léon's face, and the great quantity of working and reworking of his face and body in graphite, ink, and watercolor shows that Manet spent considerable time and effort creating the drawing. The shadowy suggestion of sideburns and heavy ink outline of Leon's ears and chin make him look older than his nineteen years. An air of seriousness also comes from the pose: book open on his crossed legs, distant gaze, and perhaps the suggestion of a pen or cigarette grasped in his hand, which is held just in front of his mouth.[86] He looks deep in thought, possibly pausing to consider something he just read.

Manet is trying to capture his likeness as the man whom the artist had asked to care for Suzanne and Eugénie during the family's separation. As he wrote to his wife, "I hope that Léon is well-behaved and that he is treating you with care and consideration. Remind him that I sent him with you [and Eugénie] to stand in for me and protect the two of you. I hope he has proven himself worthy of my confidence."[87] Considering these significant changes and details not included in the painting—like the boat visible through the window—the drawing is, possibly, the more finished of the two works. Regardless of the order of completion, there is an air of serenity and calm across both images. Suzanne and Léon seem happy in each other's company, and Manet's presence—implied by his recording of the scene—is part of this domestic comfort.

DIANA SEAVE GREENWALD

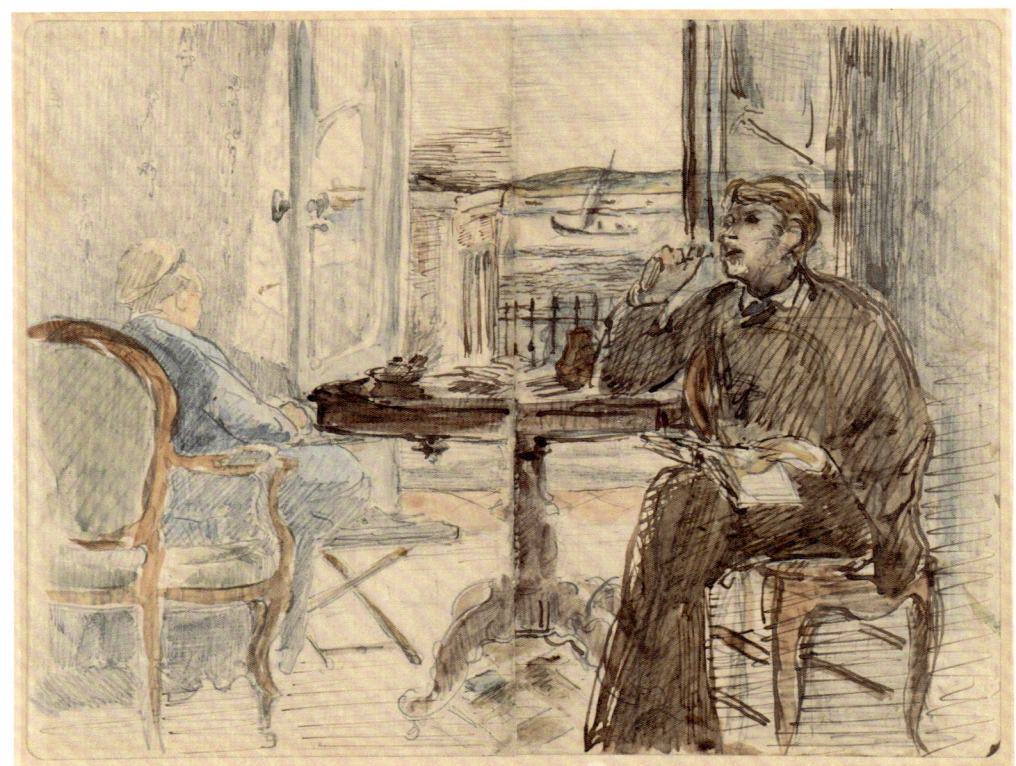

Fig. 93. Édouard Manet, *Study for "Interior at Arcachon,"* 1871. Watercolor, brown ink, and graphite on off-white wove squared paper, 18.5 × 23.7 cm. Harvard Art Museums/Fogg Museum. Bequest of William G. Russell Allen

PROVENANCE

Recorded in Léon Leenhoff's 1884 inventory of the artist's studio and photographed by Fernand Lochard (no. 160 bis); possibly with Durand-Ruel, Paris, New York; purchased by Mr. and Mrs. H. O. Havemeyer, New York, presumably from Durand-Ruel, 1902–7; bequeathed to their daughter Electra Havemeyer Webb, New York, 1929; consigned to Knoedler & Co., New York, April 1, 1943; Knoedler, New York; purchased by Robert Sterling Clark, New York, April 12, 1943, as *Intérieur de la famille Manet à Arcachon*; Sterling and Francine Clark Art Institute, 1955.[88]

INVENTORY NUMBERS

1955.553; RW 1975 1, 170; Lochard no. 160 bis

SELECT LITERATURE

Lochard 1883b, 160 bis, ill.; Moreau-Nélaton 1926, vol. 1, 129, 135, fig. 150; vol. 2, 114; Tabarant 1931, 217, 580, no. 165; Jedlicka 1941, 114, 243; Tabarant 1947, 189, 538, 608, no. 179; Rouart and Wildenstein 1975, vol. 1, no. 170; Wollheim 1987, 150–51, fig. 113; Kern et al. 1996, 66–67; Locke 2001, 127–28; Lobstein 2002, 73; Soubiran 2004, 41–42; Lees, 2012, 474–76, fig. 150.

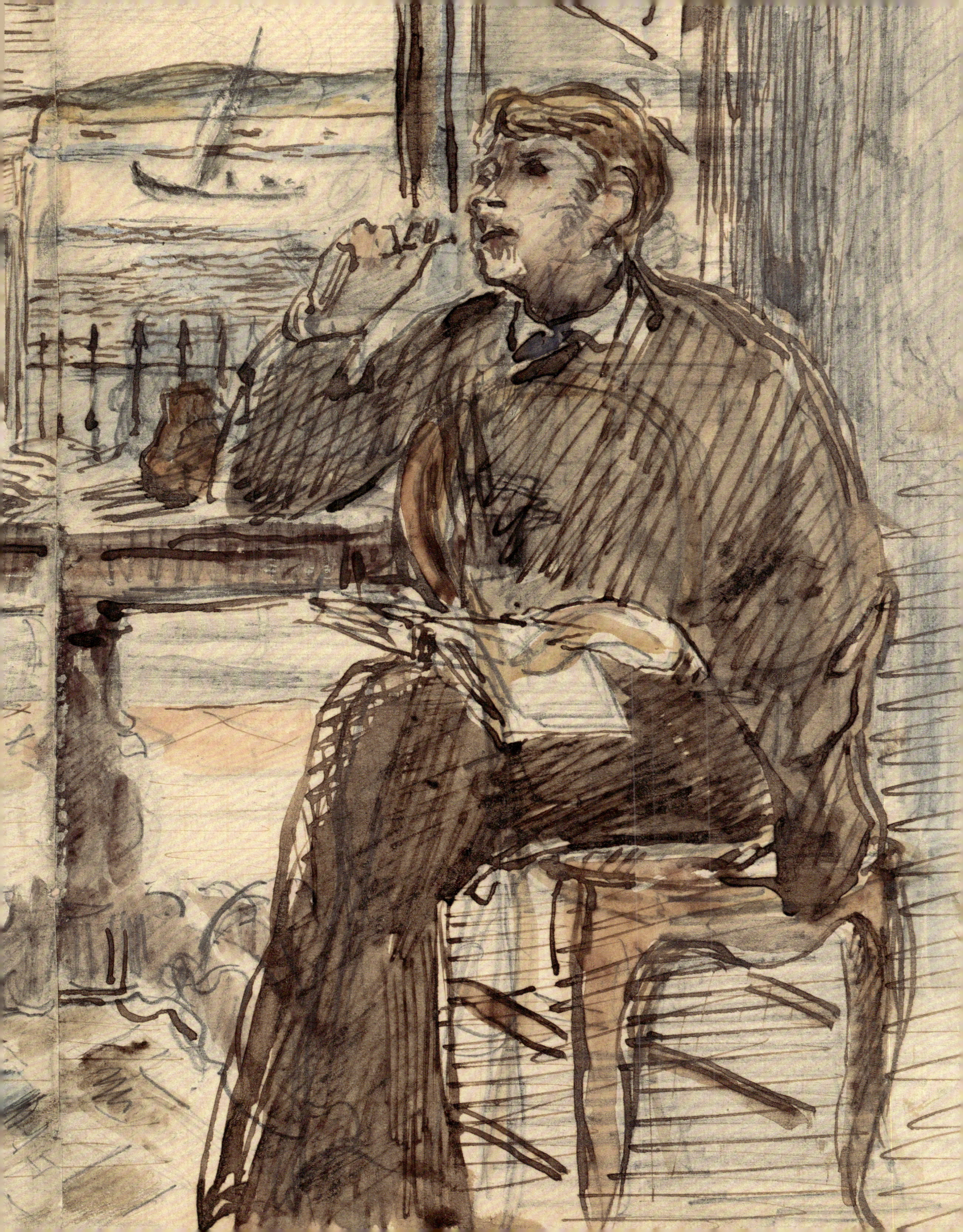

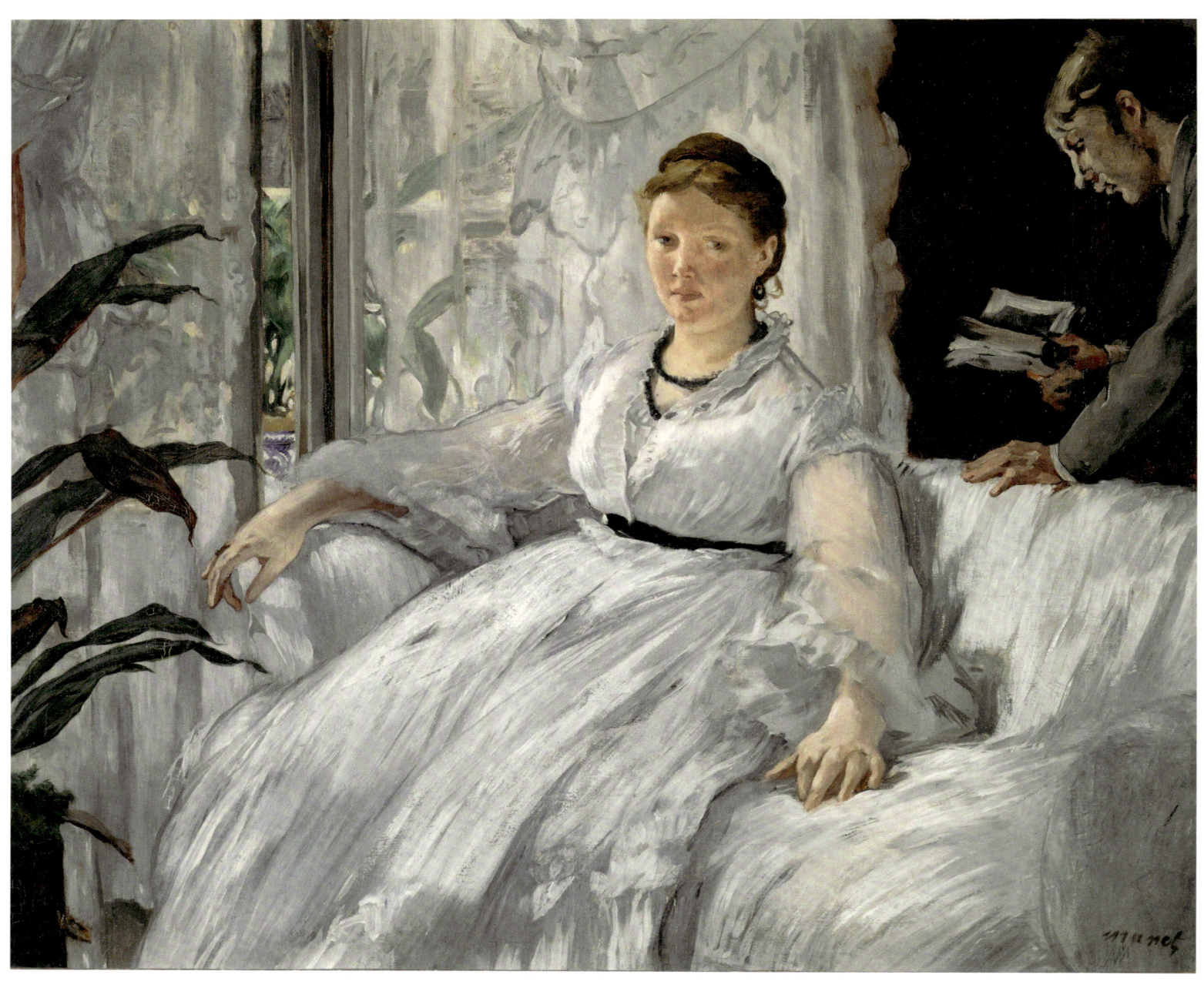

Reading (La Lecture), about 1868–73
Oil on canvas, 61 × 73.2 cm
Musée d'Orsay, Paris

II *Reading (La Lecture)*, about 1868–73

Suzanne Leenhoff was Manet's most frequent model. The artist painted her very early—before their marriage—casting her in mythological or biblical scenes, such as *Surprised Nymph* (see fig. 1 and cat. nos. 4 and 5). He also hid her among the crowd in *Music in the Tuileries* (see fig. 4). After their marriage in 1863, they settled with the painter's mother at 49, rue de Saint-Pétersbourg.[89] From then on, the way Suzanne is portrayed changes: she officially becomes the spouse in the bourgeois universe of the family apartment.

In *Reading*, Suzanne sits on the sofa of this Parisian living room. The same sofa covered with a white sheet appears in *Madame Manet at the Piano* (see cat. no. 9), and in Degas's portrait of the Manet couple in the late 1860s (see fig. 45). Dressed in a white dress that echoes the color of the sofa, Suzanne poses with her body at an angle to the picture plane, but turns her gaze toward the viewer. She is placed in front of a half-open window, which shines through white semi-transparent curtains. Beyond the window, there is a wrought iron balcony with a green plant. Another plant in its pot occupies the left side of the composition. Léon Leenhoff, placed in the top right corner of the painting, is reading with one hand resting on the sofa and the other holding a book. From the pot to the face of the young man, a perfect diagonal is formed that crosses the composition from one corner to another. The scene is bathed in light that softens Suzanne's face and makes the painting one of the most touching portraits Manet ever made of his wife. Suzanne, who was not noted for her physical beauty, is flattered and transformed in an image that testifies to her husband's deep love for her.

Technical examinations of the canvas show that Manet modified the painting extensively, likely several years after it was first completed (fig. 94).[90] The appearance of the figures in the painting already hints at this revision: Suzanne looks young and must have been painted in the late 1860s, but Léon is obviously older and must have been added in the mid-1870s. The treatment of his face does not have the contouring that Suzanne's does; instead, it is rougher and corresponds to the later style of the painter (fig. 95). Scientific analysis confirms Léon's late addition.

The painting, however, underwent more change than simply adding Léon. In an early version, the sofa was dark in color. Suzanne herself may have been dressed in a dark-colored garment. The position of her left arm seems to have been changed: it was initially in her lap but was moved away from her body in the repainting. The green plant and the details appearing behind the curtain were also added or modified in a second phase. The result of these alterations was, as one journalist wrote at the solo exhibition that the Galerie de la Vie Moderne devoted to Manet in 1880, "a symphony in white major."[91]

Some historians have compared the work to the *Symphony in White, No. 1: The White Girl* (1861–62, National Gallery of Art, Washington) exhibited by James McNeill Whistler at the Salon des Refusés of 1863.[92] But the late date of Manet's reworking of the painting and—above all—the use of white recalls the work of the artist's close friend, colleague, and later sister-in-law, Berthe Morisot. She created several "symphonies in white," from *The Artist's Sister at a Window* (1869, National Gallery of Art, Washington) to the *Woman at Her Toilette* (1870–80, Art Institute of Chicago). Was it Manet who influenced Morisot, or the

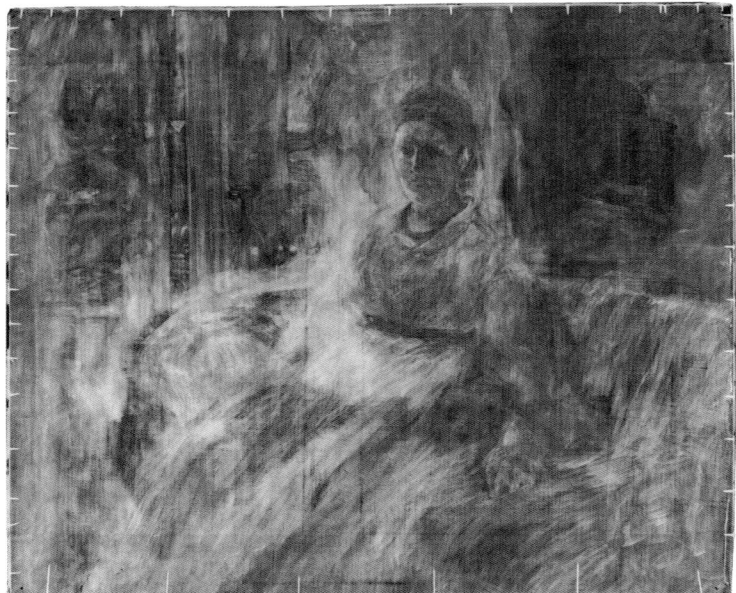

Fig. 94. X-ray of *Reading* (cat. no. 11)

other way around? Regardless, with *Reading*, Manet paints his wife in an artistic dialogue with Morisot, an artist who modeled for him, whom he mentored, and whose work is stylistically connected to his own.

Ultimately, *Reading* evokes a classic interior scene found in Dutch painting of the seventeenth century, but Manet's painterly touch anchors it firmly in modernity. The white sofa and Suzanne's dress are painted with wide broad strokes quickly applied that have been compared to the gestural or action painting associated with Abstract Expressionism.[93] It is interesting to note that these modern, gestural touches were only added later when Manet returned to this work and transformed *Reading* into a modern symphony.

SAMUEL RODARY

PROVENANCE

Collection of the sitter Suzanne Manet, Paris; purchased by Winaretta Singer, an American heiress who later became princesse de Polignac from Suzanne Manet in about 1890; accepted by the French State as a bequest of princesse de Polignac to the Musée du Louvre, Paris, 1944; transferred to Galerie du Jeu de Paume, Paris, 1947; transferred to the Musée d'Orsay, Paris, 1986.

INVENTORY NUMBERS

RF 1944 17 ; RW 1975 1, 136

SELECT LITERATURE

Jamot and Wildenstein 1932, no. 167; Tabarant 1947, no. 143; Orienti 1970, no. 123; Rouart and Wildenstein, vol. 1, 1975, no. 136; Cachin et al. 1983, no. 97.

Fig. 95. Detail of *Reading (La Lecture)* (cat. 11)

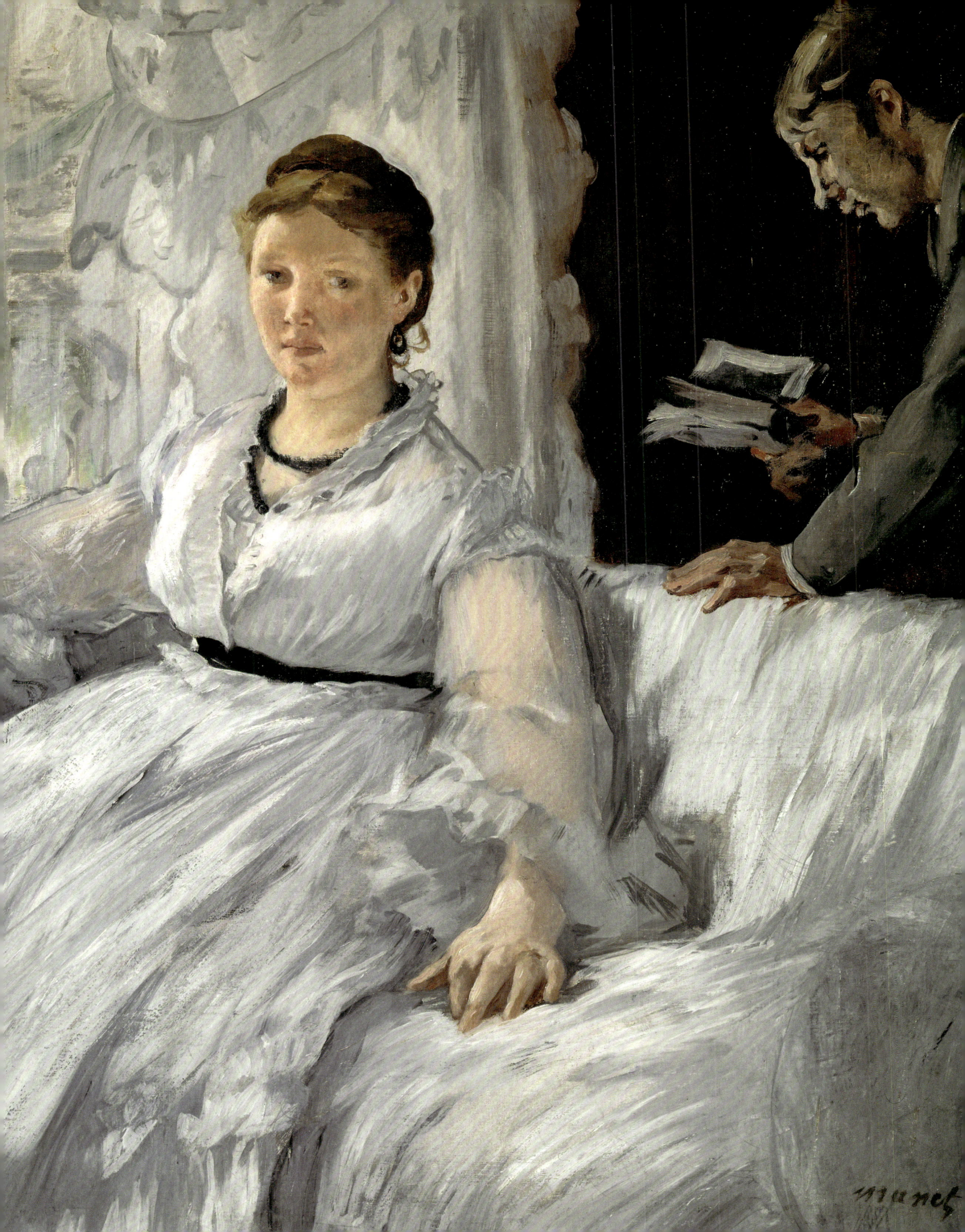

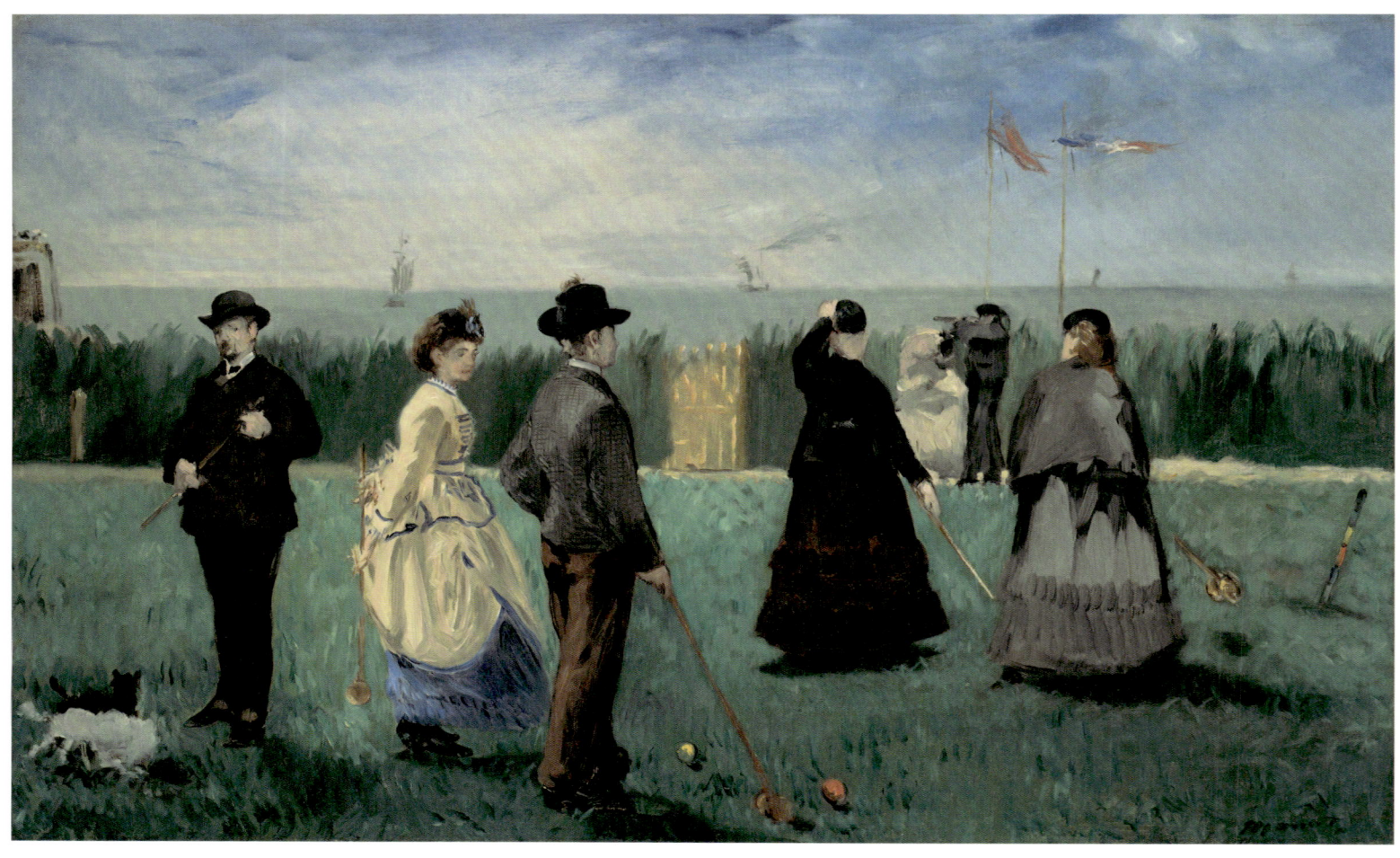

The Croquet Party (La partie de croquet), 1871
Oil on canvas, 45.7 × 73 cm
Signed lower right: Manet
The Nelson-Atkins Museum of Art, Kansas City
Gift of Henry W. and Marion H. Bloch

12 *The Croquet Party (La partie de croquet)*, 1871

In the summer of 1871, following the siege of Paris and the Commune, Édouard Manet sought respite in Boulogne-sur-Mer, a seaside resort on the north coast of France.[94] There, he painted this vibrant *plein air* scene depicting family and friends playing the fashionable English game of croquet on the lawn of the local beach club and casino.[95] At first glance, the painting presents a casual vision of a French bourgeois holiday, with sunlit skies, sailboats, and well-dressed individuals. However, it is a more calculated composition,[96] reflecting Manet's awareness of the postwar impact on Parisian art sales and patronage.

Situated halfway between London and Paris, Boulogne-sur-Mer was an international seaport convenient for English travelers, to whom it catered."[97] Recognizing the atrophied art market in postwar Paris, Manet seized the opportunity to engage an English audience.[98] He enlisted his family and friends as models, blurring boundaries between individuals and representative types. Here, they play well-heeled seaside tourists.

From left, we observe Manet's childhood friend, Paul Roudier, with a walking stick in a black suit and bowler hat.[99] Jeanne Gonzalès (1852–1924), the younger sister of Manet's pupil, Eva, impresses with her fashionable yellow and blue dress and a feathered bird on her hat. Léon Leenhoff, Manet's stepson, biological son, or half-brother, turns his back to the others, emanating detached stylishness with his bespoke black-and-gray checked jacket, brown trousers, and a black fedora with brown ostrich feather (fig. 96).[100] Adjacent to Léon, a faceless figure, possibly the Gonzalès matriarch, Marie-Céline Ragut (1829–1880), or the artist's mother, Eugénie Manet (1812–1885), wears a black jacket and tiered chocolate skirt, gesturing with her mallet toward Suzanne Manet (1829–1906), who appears poised to "croquet" (or send) her opponent's ball away from the wicket. She wears an elegant charcoal gray shawl with matching skirt.

During the 1860s croquet became popular as an outdoor summer game in Europe and North America. It was synonymous with wealthy elites, a segment of society Manet aimed to attract as patrons.[101] Manet, during his 1868 visit to London, likely encountered this craze firsthand or saw numerous press images of croquet. One image, created by English artist James Leech (1817–1864) and published in a London newspaper in 1861, resembles the composition of Manet's *Croquet Party*, albeit in reverse (fig. 97).[102] Both compositions center a dandy contemplating his next move on (or off) the course, alongside a female player in a voluminous skirt. And both feature silky pups observing the game. While Leech included a single dog, Manet adds another canine; a black and brown dog appears next to a white dog at lower left.[103] Although the animals in Manet's painting are undoubtedly dogs, their pairing, diminutive scale, and mirrored position of raised tails and back legs may allude to Normandy's red flag with two yellow lions,[104] playfully called "les p'tits chats [the little cats]." This reference, possibly flying to the left of the French tricolore flag in the background, contributes to the layered symbolism in Manet's composition.[105]

Cats appeared in many of Manet's works, and one appears in another composition with Léon as a dandyish figure (*Luncheon in the Studio*, see fig. 7). By connecting Léon with the black and brown cat-like dog, whose dual-tone scruffy coat mirrors the texture of the boy's cross-hatched jacket, Manet evokes the association of cats with dandies made by

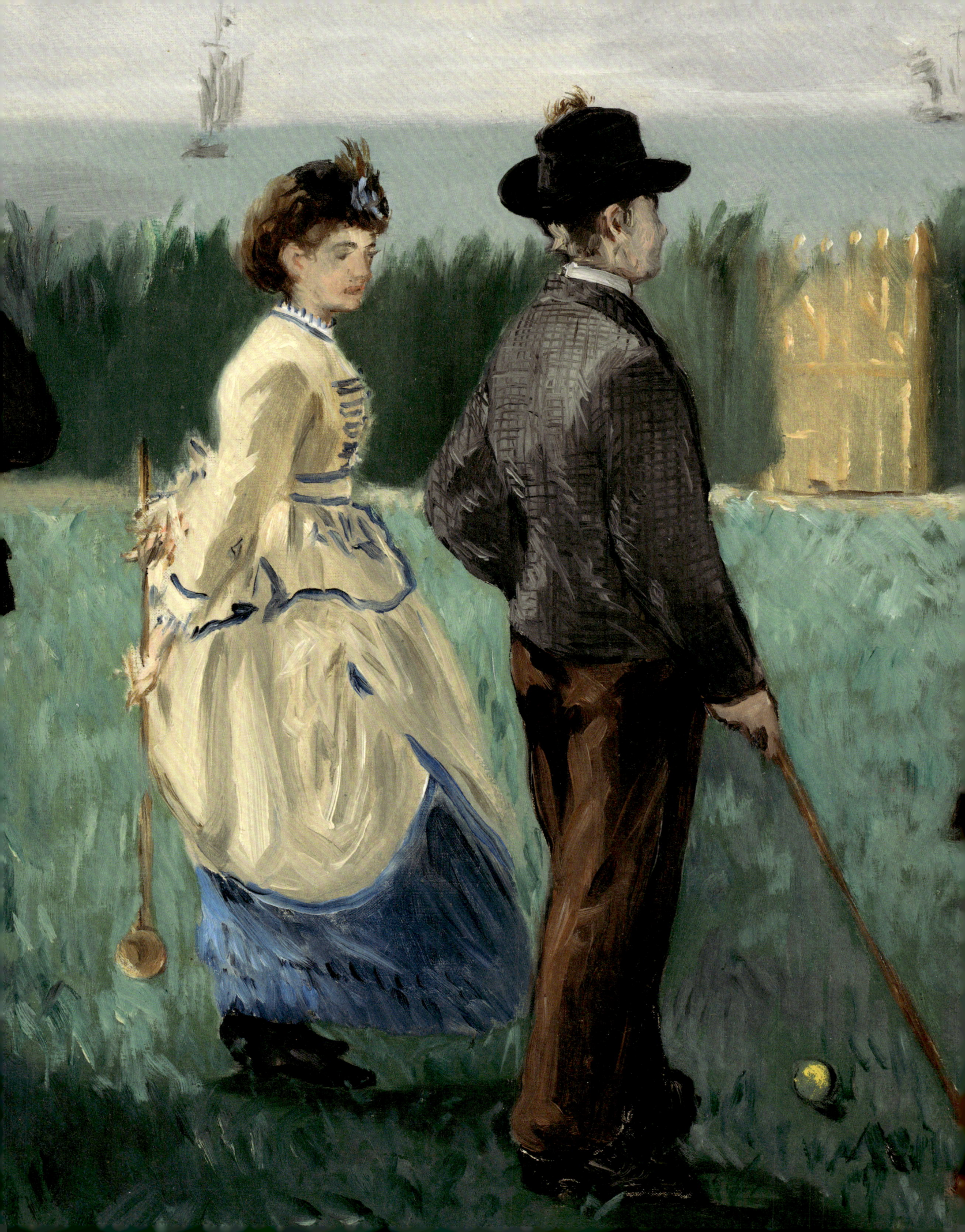

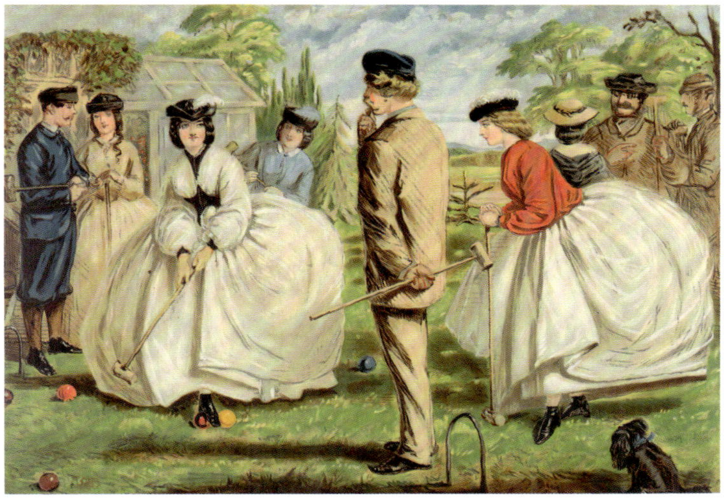

Fig. 97. John Leech, *A Nice Game for Two or More*, 1861. Lithograph

writers like Champfleury and Charles Baudelaire.[106] This connection signifies independence, individuality, and an aesthetic sensibility challenging conventional standards, much like the nature of the complicated relationships within the Manet-Leenhoff family. The English were particularly fascinated with canine companions, which might have motivated Manet to incorporate dogs to appeal to an intended British audience.[107]

Despite his intentions, the painting never went to England. Instead, Manet's friend, Gustave Caillebotte (1848–1894), bought it for just 600 francs.[108] Nevertheless, Manet's masterful portrayal of Léon as a cat-like dandy, aloof on the sun-soaked shores of Normandy, reveal the artist's attention to detail and the complexity and depth of his artistic vision.

AIMEE MARCEREAU DEGALAN

PROVENANCE

Purchased by Gustave Caillebotte, Paris, from the artist, 1879; given to his brother, Martial Caillebotte, Paris, 1894; bequeathed to his wife, Marie Caillebotte, Paris or Pornic, France, 1910; bequeathed to her daughter, Geneviève Chardeau (née Caillebotte), Paris, 1931; deposited with Galerie Lorenceau, Paris, by a member of the Chardeau family, 1973; possibly with Galerie Schmit, Paris; purchased by Juan Guillermo de Beistegui, Paris, possibly from Galerie Schmit after January 1973; purchased by Marion (née Helzberg) and Henry Bloch, Shawnee Mission, from de Beistegui, through Margo Pollins Schab, New York, 1986; given to the Nelson-Atkins Museum of Art, Kansas City, by Henry and Marion Bloch, 2015.[109]

INVENTORY NUMBER

2015.13.11; RW 1975 1, 173

SELECT LITERATURE

Godet 1872, n.p., ill.; Leenhoff 1883, folio 16; Duret 1902, no. 169, 102, 243–44; Meier-Graefe 1912, 219–20, ill.; Duret 1919, no. 169, 137, 259, as *La partie de croquet*; Moreau-Nélaton 1926, vol. 1, 134–35, 153; vol. 2, 3–4, 111; Tabarant 1931, no. 194, 243–44; De Leiris 1969, 35 n. 48, 71 n. 20, 119–20; Rouart and Wildenstein 1975, no. 173, 5–6, 27, 154–55, ill.; Wilson-Bareau 1991, 197, 311, ill.; Locke 2001, 126, 128, 222, ill.; Wilson-Bareau and Degener 2003, 72–73, 96 n. 78, 96 n. 79, 96 n. 80, 97 n. 82, 135, ill.; Brettell and Pissarro 2007, 2, 11, 15, 30–33, 153, 155, ill.; Rubin 2010, 290–92, 294, ill.; Locke 2014, ill.

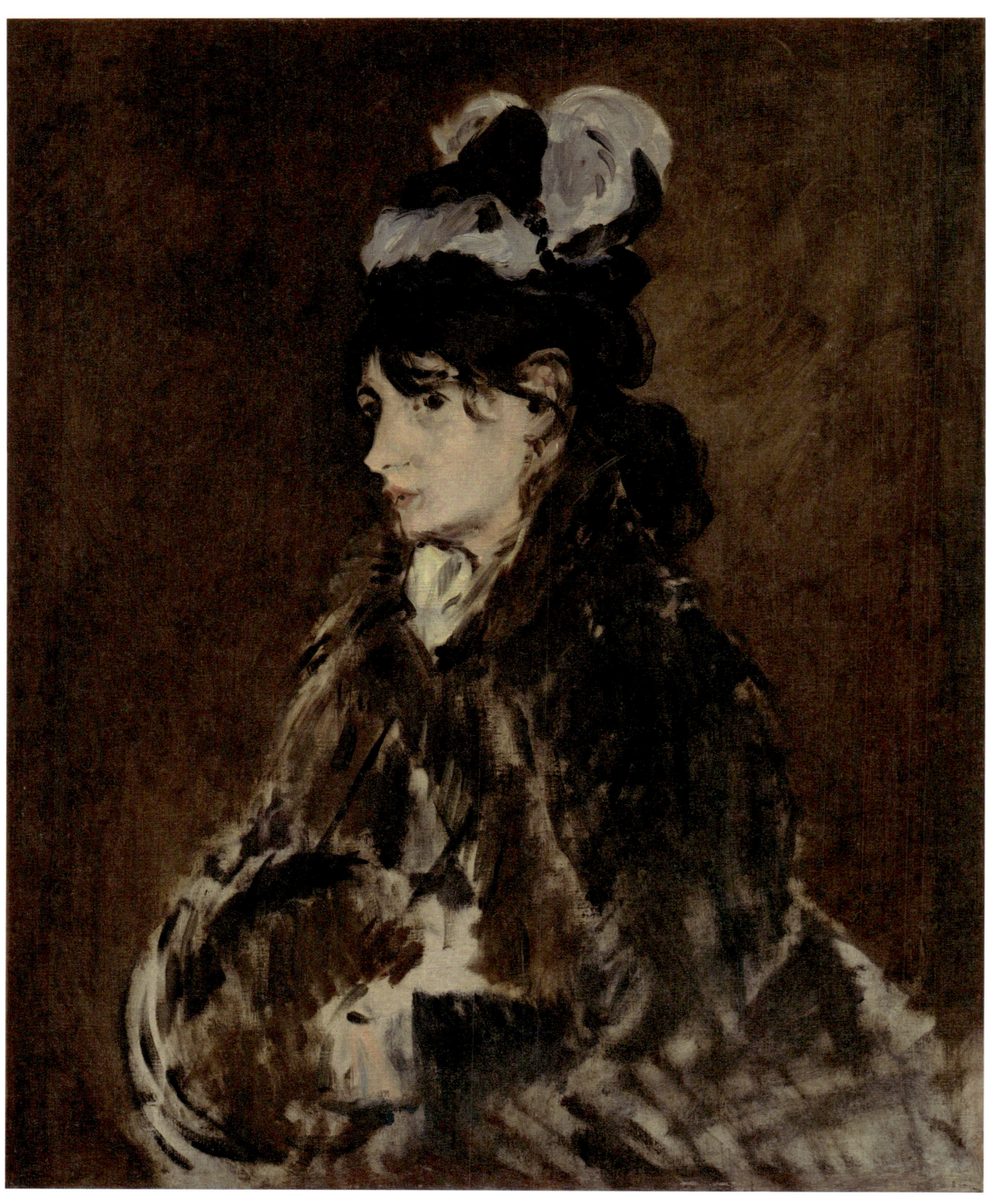

Berthe Morisot, 1869–73
Oil on canvas, 74 × 60 cm
Cleveland Museum of Art. Bequest of Leonard C. Hanna, Jr.

Berthe Morisot, 1869–73

Édouard Manet and Berthe Morisot met at the Louvre in the summer of 1868. Within weeks Morisot was posing for the pivotal seated figure in Manet's large canvas, *The Balcony* (see fig. 6).[110] Two years later she posed alone for a second large painting, *Repose* (see fig. 8). Both works were exhibited at the Paris Salon, where Morisot's own works were also displayed. Whether Morisot saw Manet's independent exhibition in 1867 is unknown, but she would have seen his paintings previously at the Salon as well as the two depictions of him by their mutual friend Henri Fantin-Latour,[111] who introduced them.

Morisot's sister, Edma, was also an artist—the two women painted together for almost a decade—but she abandoned painting after she married in 1869 (fig. 98). In 1867, their mother wrote to Edma that Manet was thinking of acquiring a painting of hers he saw at a gallery.[112] But it was Morisot who would become a muse for Manet, as he was for her during the next six years until she married his younger brother Eugène. This portrait is likely the first of eight smaller canvases for which she posed. Unlike *The Balcony* and *Repose*, he never exhibited any of these but sold two[113] and gave two others to Morisot.[114] After Manet's death, Morisot acquired a third[115] and Edgar Degas owned another.[116] This, the largest of the eight, remained in Manet's studio and at his estate sale was acquired by his widow, Suzanne. Morisot's daughter, Julie Manet, first saw the portrait in 1899, when she was invited to visit collector Auguste Pellerin. Julie wrote of seeing this "sketch" of her late mother "in profile in a violet hat and fur coat, which is so lifelike. I would dearly love to have this one."[117]

In 1869, without Edma, Morisot was at a critical point in her life as an artist. She was stepping away from the shadow of their teacher, Jean-Baptiste-Camille Corot, whose atmospheric landscapes were an obvious influence on both sisters' paintings.[118] When she met Manet, Morisot was copying a canvas by Peter Paul Rubens, whom both admired. One can imagine how inspiring it was for her to see Manet's earlier paintings, including *Fishing* (cat. no. 6), in which he references Rubens. Being in his studio, watching him paint, and seeing both finished and unfinished canvases was pivotal as Morisot developed her own artistic vision.

Morisot observed that Manet once reworked a canvas twenty-five times[119] to achieve an image that to him appeared effortless. Her aspiration was parallel, but conversely it was her "principle never to try to rectify a blunder."[120] For much of her career, she abandoned unsuccessful starts rather than rework a canvas. She lamented how Manet "talked to me about finishing my work" and added, "I do not see what I can do."[121] The speed at which this portrait of her appears to have been painted, with its sketchy brushwork and unfinished appearance, echoes Morisot's own ambition and may have been Manet's nonverbal way to acknowledge her painting desires and to show her how he would achieve them.

Concurrent to posing for Manet, Morisot started her own series of paintings of Edma. Unlike Manet, who painted her in his studio, Morisot generally painted her sister outdoors. After showing the first of these to Manet, she told Edma, "I have been told without knowing it I produced masterpieces."[122] Morisot gave Manet the painting he most admired, *The Harbor at Lorient*, portraying Edma seated on a low wall by that city's harbor (fig. 99).

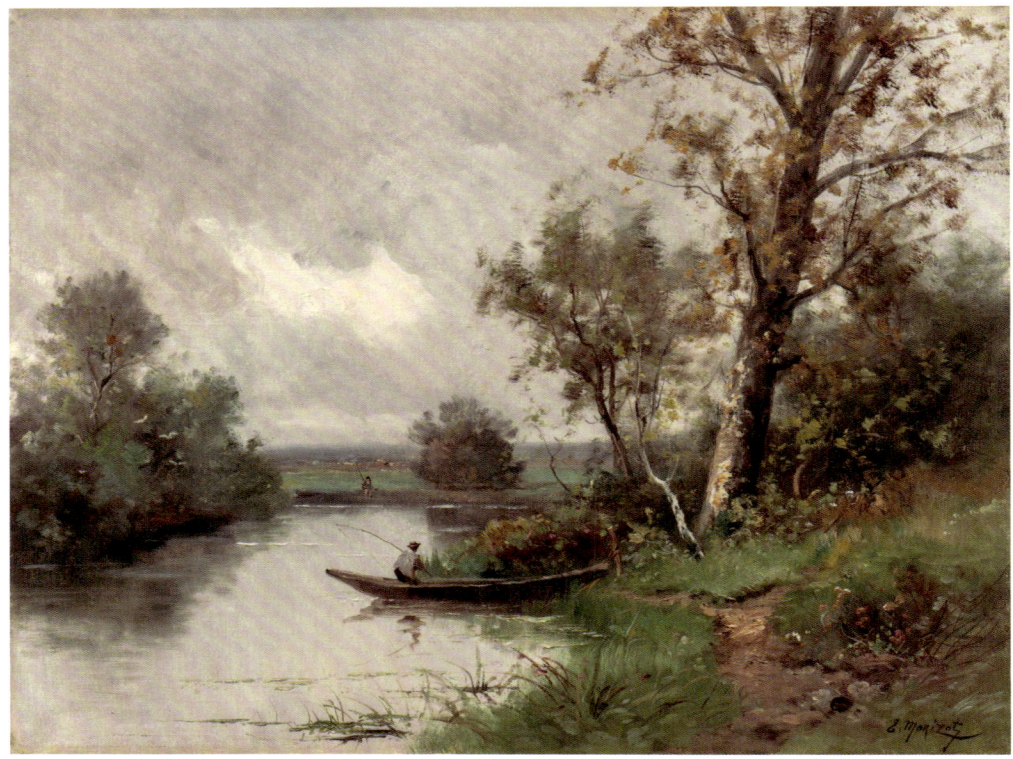

Fig. 98. Edma Morisot, *Fishing*, about 1863. Oil on canvas, 50 × 65 cm. Private collection

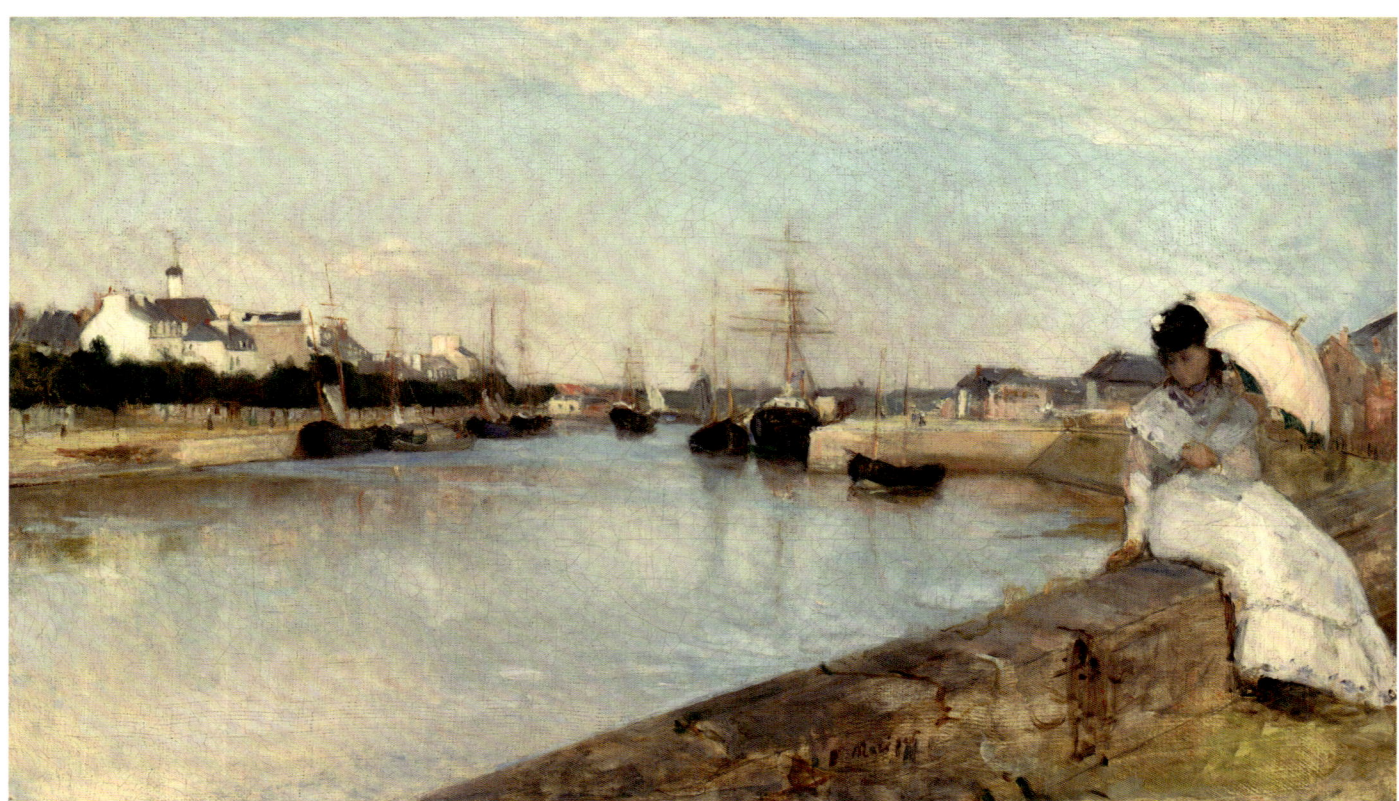

Fig. 99. Berthe Morisot, *The Harbor at Lorient*, 1869. Oil on canvas, 43.5 × 73 cm. National Gallery of Art, Washington. Ailsa Mellon Bruce Collection

Several months after receiving this gift, Manet painted Edma sitting outside on the ground in her parents' garden, *In the Garden* (1870, Shelburne Museum, Shelburne).[123]

Even though Manet once annoyingly reworked one of Morisot's canvases, she continued to show him her new paintings.[124] Four years later she gave him a more recent portrait of Edma, *Cache-cache*, the French term for the game hide-and-seek.[125] Manet declined invitations from Degas, Pissarro, and possibly Morisot to join the Impressionists but was unsuccessful in discouraging Morisot from participating.[126] Morisot exhibited *Cache-cache* in the first Impressionist exhibition, where it was listed as lent by Édouard Manet. Her paintings continued to evolve and change, yet Manet remained an endless source of inspiration. As Morisot wrote to Edma, "I shall never forget the days of my friendship with him, when I sat for him and when the charm of his mind kept me alert during those long hours.[127]

BILL SCOTT

PROVENANCE

Recorded in Léon Leenhoff's 1884 inventory of the artist's studio and photographed by Fernand Lochard (no. 73); purchased by Suzanne Manet at the artist's estate sale, Drouot, Paris, February 1884; August Pellerin, Paris, 1910; Jules Strauss, Paris, 1912; Galerie Georges Petit, Paris, December 1932, lot 48; purchased by Turner, London, at the above sale; Jacques Balsan, Paris, 1935; consigned by Mrs. Jacques Balsan to Knoedler & Co., New York; purchased by Leonard C. Hanna, Jr., Cleveland, from Knoedler & Co., November 1947; bequeathed to the Cleveland Museum of Art by Leonard C. Hanna, Jr., 1958.

INVENTORY NUMBERS

1958.34; RW 1975 1, 138; Lochard no. 73

SELECT LITERATURE

Moreau-Nélaton 1926, vol. 1, 109, fig. 119; Janot and Wildenstein 1932, vol. 2, 65, fig. 152; Duret 1937, pl. 42; Tabarant 1947, 144, 157–58; Hanson 1966, 121, 123, no. 105; Rouart and Wildenstein 1975, vol. 1, no. 138; Monneret 1978, vol. 2, 19; Stevens et al. 2012, 101, no. 19.

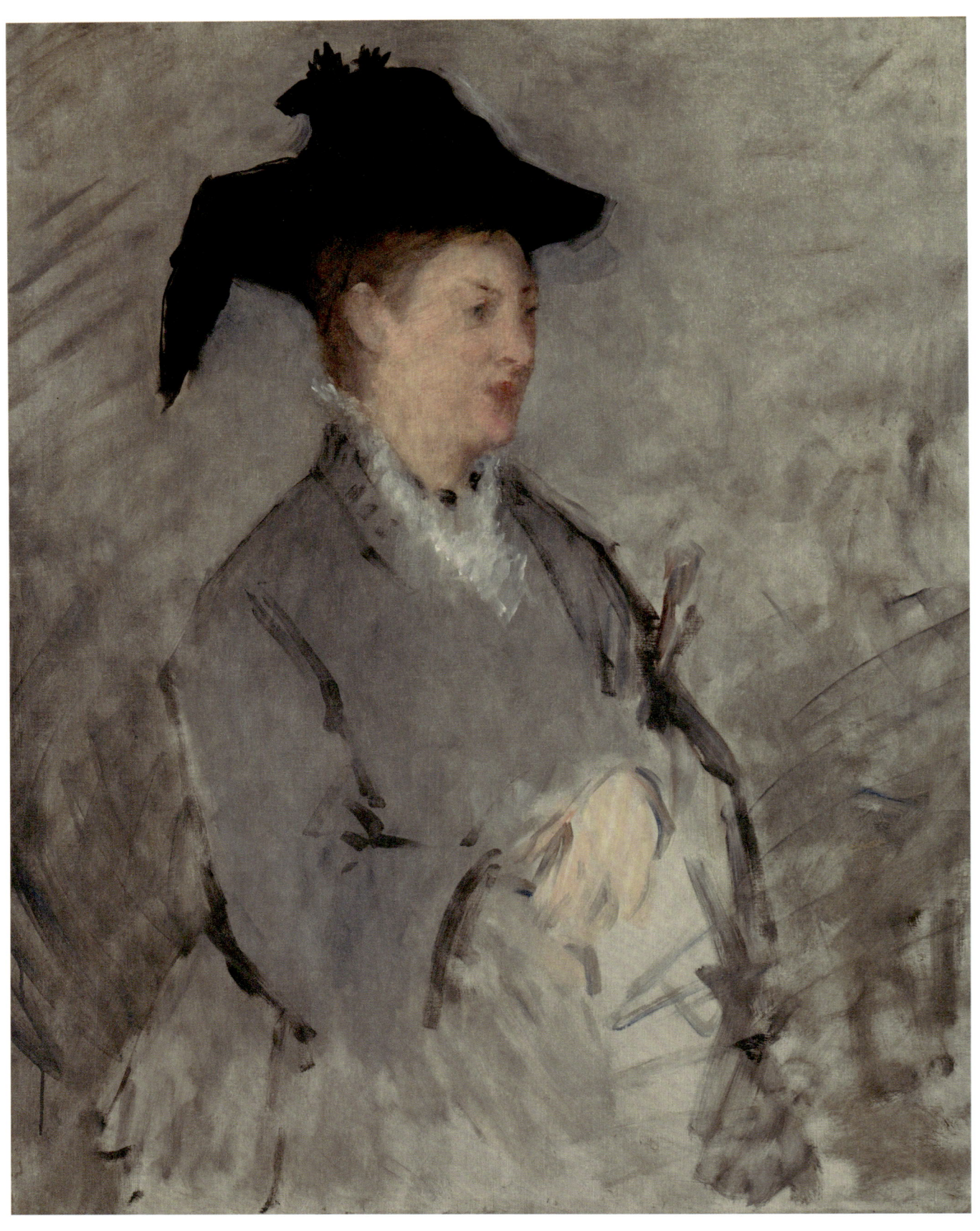

Madame Édouard Manet (Suzanne Leenhoff), about 1873
Oil on canvas, 100.3 × 78.4 cm
Metropolitan Museum of Art, New York. Bequest of
Miss Adelaide Milton de Groot (1876–1967), 1967

14 *Madame Édouard Manet (Suzanne Leenhoff), about 1873*

Of all the portraits Manet made of his wife, the painting at the Metropolitan Museum of Art is the clearest representation of Suzanne as a social creature. She is depicted in three-quarter profile, wearing a light gray dress with a white collar and an elaborately shaped black hat. The handle of an umbrella protrudes from under her left arm. Suzanne, whom Manet often represented in an intimate or family setting, here seems ready to call on a friend.

Duret, Tabarant, and Rouart and Wildenstein date the work about 1866.[128] Research on nineteenth-century clothing, however, suggests that the painting must have been executed about 1873. Suzanne appears to be wearing the same dress in two later works: her portrait at the Norton Simon Museum (see fig. 30), dated 1874–76, and *Madame Manet in the Conservatory* (Oslo, Nasjonalmuseet, see fig. 31), painted about 1879. The hat in this painting seems to be the same one placed on the bench next to Suzanne in the greenhouse.[129]

The work is obviously unfinished, which makes it possible to see the painter's creative process. Manet built Suzanne's dress with long lines of black paint; the gray of the garment is likewise set down quickly and enhanced with a few touches of blue. The hands and the collar seem to have been painted with the same speed. Areas of pentimenti are still visible: on the hat, whose silhouette originally had fallen lower, and on the handle of the umbrella, which is angled in two different directions and not yet securely wedged under the arm. The model's face, especially, has obviously been scraped and then retouched, perhaps repeatedly. The painter ultimately left the work unfinished. Was he dissatisfied with this rendering of his wife's visage? We know that Manet was particularly sensitive to the way Suzanne was depicted: the fate of Degas's portrait of her—which Manet slashed—testifies to this, as does the fact that Manet himself repeatedly painted Suzanne with her back turned, or hidden by a hat, as if to evade the challenges of painting his lifelong partner's likeness.

Left uncompleted by Manet, the portrait was evidently "finished" by another hand. After the painter's death, Léon Leenhoff had all the works that remained in the studio photographed, and a comparison of the painting in its current state with the period photograph[130] shows that the portrait was retouched after the death of the painter (fig. 100). The face and surrounding areas, in particular, have been redone. This practice of "finishing" a work to make it more fit for sale is unfortunately not an isolated case, and several members of the family were involved.[131]

In notes accompanying the photographs already cited, Léon provided details on each work that helped him prepare for the retrospective exhibition of 1884. And it seems that from this period on, the practice of retouching unfinished works continued. Describing *Autumn* (Musée des Beaux-Arts, Nancy), Léon writes: "The hand that holds the sleeve was finished by the painter from [the picture framer] Kiewert for the Exhibition of the School of Fine Arts." Was *Autumn* an isolated case? Preparing for the 1884 exhibition, Léon sent many works to framers, including Kiewert and Nivard. It is not known how many paintings were then "retouched."

When her brother-in-law Jules Vibert died in 1889, Suzanne welcomed her newly widowed sister, Marthe, and Marthe's son, Édouard, into her home. A sickly boy, Édouard Vibert

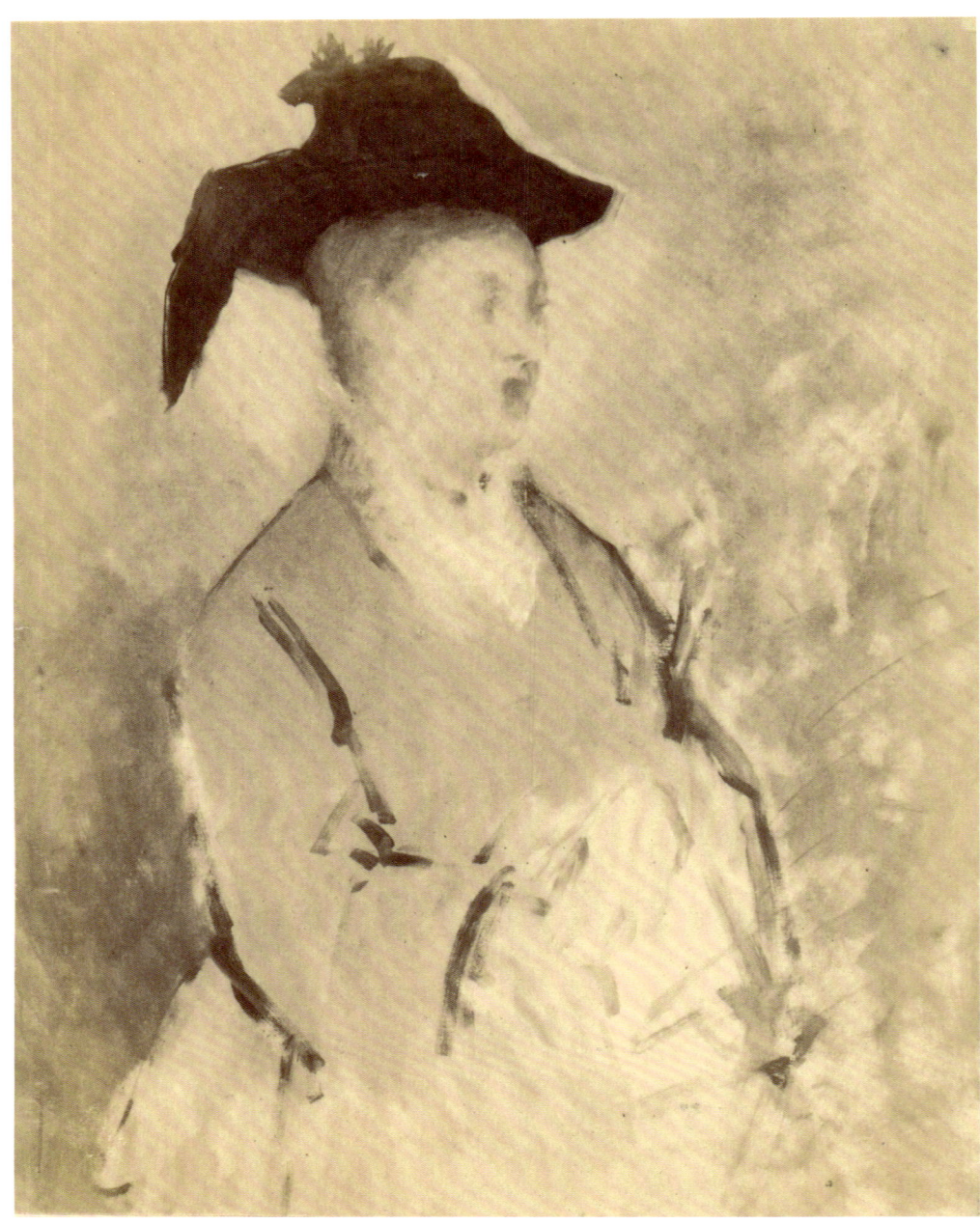

Fig. 100. Fernand Lochard, *Madame Manet*, in Album of photographs of the work of Édouard Manet, about 1883, 59r. The Morgan Library & Museum, New York (MA3950). Purchased as the gift of Mrs. Charles Engelhard and children in memory of Mr. Charles Engelhard, 1974

devoted himself to two passions: music and painting. We know he made a large enough number of copies of Manet's works[132] for Jacques Damourette—a friend of the Manets—to describe "the fake Manet paintings made by Édouard Vibert."[133] It is possible that Vibert was responsible for "finishing" some of Manet's paintings.

Frustrated at seeing some of her uncle's paintings finished by another hand, Julie Manet noted that "[Suzanne's] own brother repainted several of [Manet's] canvases."[134] As Bill Scott suggested, this brother may be Rudolf, himself a painter, whom Suzanne or Léon could have solicited for such tasks.[135] Finally, dealers and collectors also often engaged in retouching Manet's work, unimpeded and possibly helped by Suzanne. Julie, saddened by what happened to paintings once they were in the hands of industrialist Auguste Pellerin— and disturbed by the complicity of the Bernheim Gallery, which sold him the paintings— complained to Suzanne. However, the widow replied, "That's what always happens to the sketches."[136]

Friends of the deceased painter were not fooled by these alterations. Monet burned unfinished paintings so they would not suffer the same fate as the Manets.[137] And Renoir, to whom Julie Manet recounted that Pellerin had paintings by Manet "which are not known at all," suggested that she give a sharp reply to the collector: *Even Manet never saw them.*[138] This painting is, therefore, both a testament to Manet's work and to the fate suffered by some of his paintings after his death.

SAMUEL RODARY

PROVENANCE

Recorded in Léon Leenhoff's 1884 inventory of the artist's studio and photographed by Fernand Lochard (no. 117); collection of the sitter, Suzanne Manet, Paris; purchased by Ambroise Vollard, Paris, from Suzanne Manet for 60 francs in 1894; purchased by Mme Louise Aline Ménard-Dorian for 250 francs in 1895; purchased by Durand-Ruel at the Ménard-Dorian sale at Galerie Georges Petit, Paris, lot 12, for 155,000 francs on December 2, 1929; Durand-Ruel, Paris, New York; New York stock no. 5141; purchased by Adelaide Milton de Groot, New York, from Durand-Ruel for 11,500 dollars, 1935; on loan to the Metropolitan Museum of Art, New York, 1936; bequeathed to the Metropolitan Museum of Art by de Groot, 1967.

INVENTORY NUMBERS

67.187.81; RW 1975 1, 117; Lochard no. 117

SELECT LITERATURE

Lochard 1883a, no. 117, ill.; Duret 1907, 219, no. 106; Moreau-Nélaton 1926, vol. 1, 109, fig. 118; Tabarant 1947, 129–30, 536, no. 124, fig. 124; Stuckey 1983, 161; Moffett 1985, 38–39; Van Kempen and van de Beek 2014, 243 no. 10, 313 no. 8, ill.; Baum, Bayer, and Wagstaff 2016, 299, pl. 77; Finckh 2017, 272, ill.; Pullins 2019, 63, 67–70, 72–74, 79 no. 47, fig. 25.

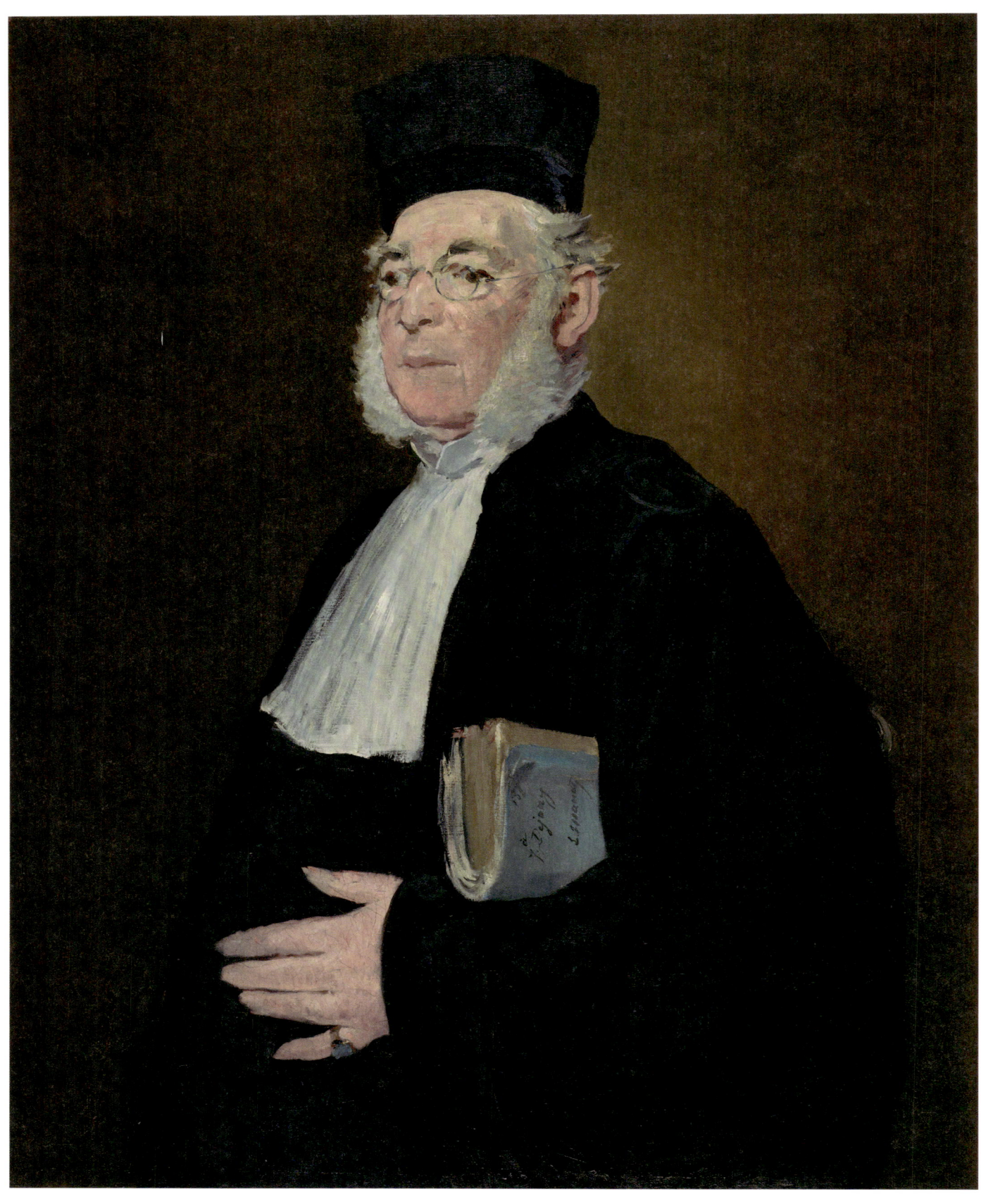

Monsieur Jules Dejouy, 1879
Oil on canvas, 81.7 × 67 cm
Inscribed, signed, and dated: To J. Dejouy/E. Manet/1879
Amgueddfa Cymru–National Museum Wales

15 *Monsieur Jules Dejouy, 1879*

Upon seeing *Monsieur Jules Dejouy* at the Musée de l'Orangerie in Paris in 1932, a Dutch critic grouped it together with *Boy Blowing Bubbles* (cat. no. 7) and exclaimed that in these paintings, "the blood seems to pulsate under the living skin."[139] When the portrait was exhibited in Berlin in 1928, critics called it "splendid; Manet at his best" and "a warmer Daumier," recalling Honoré Daumier's caricatures of barristers that preceded Manet's portrait of his cousin, a lawyer for the Paris appeals court.[140] A Cologne critic referred to "the immortal image of Judge Dejouy: the pinnacle of cultivated culture, a creation in which [there is] spirit and dignity, charming mastery and kindness."[141] These remarks recall the portrait's active exhibition history in the first half of the twentieth century, before its owners withheld it from exhibition for almost sixty years. As a result, it has faded from scholarly attention. That changed when the work entered the collection of Amgueddfa Cymru–Museum Wales in 2020 and went on public display in 2023.

With Manet's characteristic panache, the painter evoked the keen intelligence and professional demeanor of his cousin (fig. 101). Dejouy poses in his lawyerly garb: black robe, white bands in front, and black toque; he holds a sheaf of papers against his body, and Manet has replicated the dull cerulean of the paper covers on ministerial circulars of the time.[142] Sandwiched between the blue and white briefs is a bound volume, and one can even see the ends of red ribbon bookmarks within it. The bespectacled lawyer looks toward the picture's left, allowing Manet to silhouette the flyaway hair above his ears and the fullness of his gray mutton chops. Layers of pink tinged with blue and flecks of red model the face, but when it comes to the area around the eyes, Manet thins the paint considerably around Dejouy's bushy eyebrows and the lines tracing his wire-rimmed glasses. The canvas's reserve shows through here; Manet almost uses the yellow of the primed canvas as a color to complement the pink flesh and blue lines of the glasses' frames.[143] All these details contribute to the effect noted by critic Karl Scheffler in 1925: "It is dazzlingly painted."[144]

Dejouy's pose—standing with papers under his arm—gives him a purposeful air. Manet, who could be playful with his signatures, inscribed the blue cover: "To J. Dejouy / E. Manet" along with the year 1879 (the last digit barely visible). The blue of the paper cover finds an echo in the blue of the stone on a pinkie ring. Close examination of the ring reveals that the blue brushstrokes are curved, not squared off like the facets of a gemstone; this could be an Egyptian scarab, which were often incorporated into nineteenth-century rings. Apart from the detail of the ring, Manet has left the contours of Dejouy's hand fairly open (fig. 102). Fingernails are unarticulated even as Manet brushes in the black of the robe around the fingers, then occasionally reinforces a pink flesh tone near a finger's edge over and against the black. In some places, like the fold between thumb and forefinger, a stroke of pink actually goes gray where it comes into contact with the black, suggesting wet-on-wet painting.

Antonin Proust recounted the story of Manet meeting Méry Laurent—actress, courtesan, and hostess of an artistic salon—and showing her an earlier no longer extant portrait of Dejouy. "You can almost hear him bellowing, can't you?" Manet said to Laurent. "Forgive the expression, but lawyers—their job is to bellow. Ours is to reproduce them. Ah! It's hard

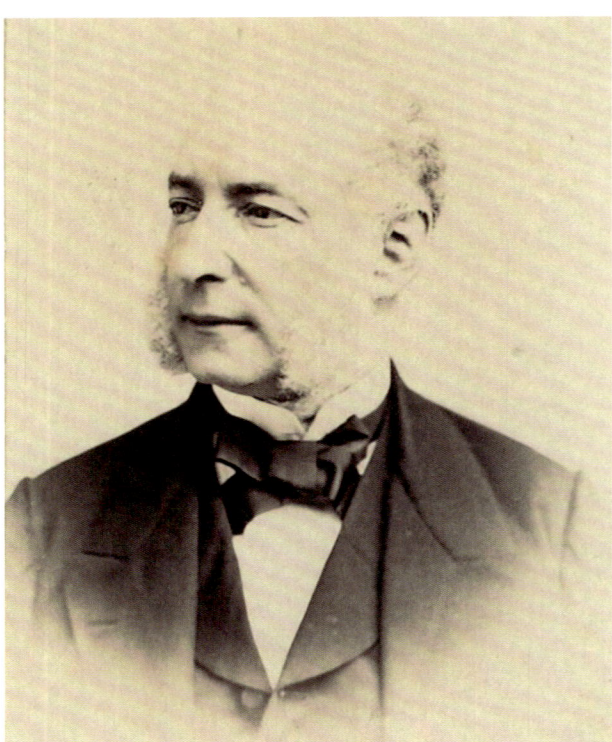

Fig. 101. Bureau, *Jules Dejouy*, from *Album of Cartes-de-visite Portraits Belonging to Édouard Manet*, 1870s. Carte-de-visite, 9.2 × 5.6 cm. Bibliothèque Nationale de France, Paris

to make a painting interesting when it features just one person. We must not merely paint portraits. There is the ground which must be supple, living, because the ground lives. If the ground is opaque, the picture dies."[145] In the 1879 portrait, Manet varies the way he handles the background, which is anything but opaque: it is darker on the left side of the work—the better to bring out the white of the beard and the bands—and lighter (and greener) to the right of the head, to complement the pink of the face, and to allow light to trace the oval epaulet on the robe. Dejouy does not bellow; he instead projects both a lively mind and a certain equanimity, qualities that no doubt served him well over his fifty-five-year career in the Paris courts.

NANCY LOCKE

PROVENANCE

Collection of the sitter, Jules Dejouy, Paris, recorded by Léon Leonhoff and photographed by Fernand Lochard (no. 328); bequeathed to Émile Maugras, Paris; Erich Goeritz, Berlin and London; by family descent, London; accepted in lieu of inheritance tax March 31, 2020, and allocated to Amgueddfa Cymru–Museum Wales.

INVENTORY NUMBERS

NMW A 24961; RW 1975 1, 294; Lochard no. 328

SELECT LITERATURE

Lochard 1883a, no. 328, ill.; Proust 1897, 179–80; Duret 1902, 258–59; Scheffler 1925, 72–73; Moreau-Nélaton 1926, vol. 2, 67; Friedrich 1928, 7; Westheim 1928, 7; Witthaus 1930, 2; Musée de l'Orangerie 1932, 57–58; *Algemeen Handelsblad* 1932, 9; Amsterdam 1938, 100; Niehaus 1938, 7; *De Tijd* 1938; Jedlicka 1941, 287–88, 377; Tabarant 1947, 360; Hamilton 1954, 227; Orienti 1970, 111, no. 277.

Fig. 102. Detail of *Monsieur Jules Dejouy* (cat. 15)

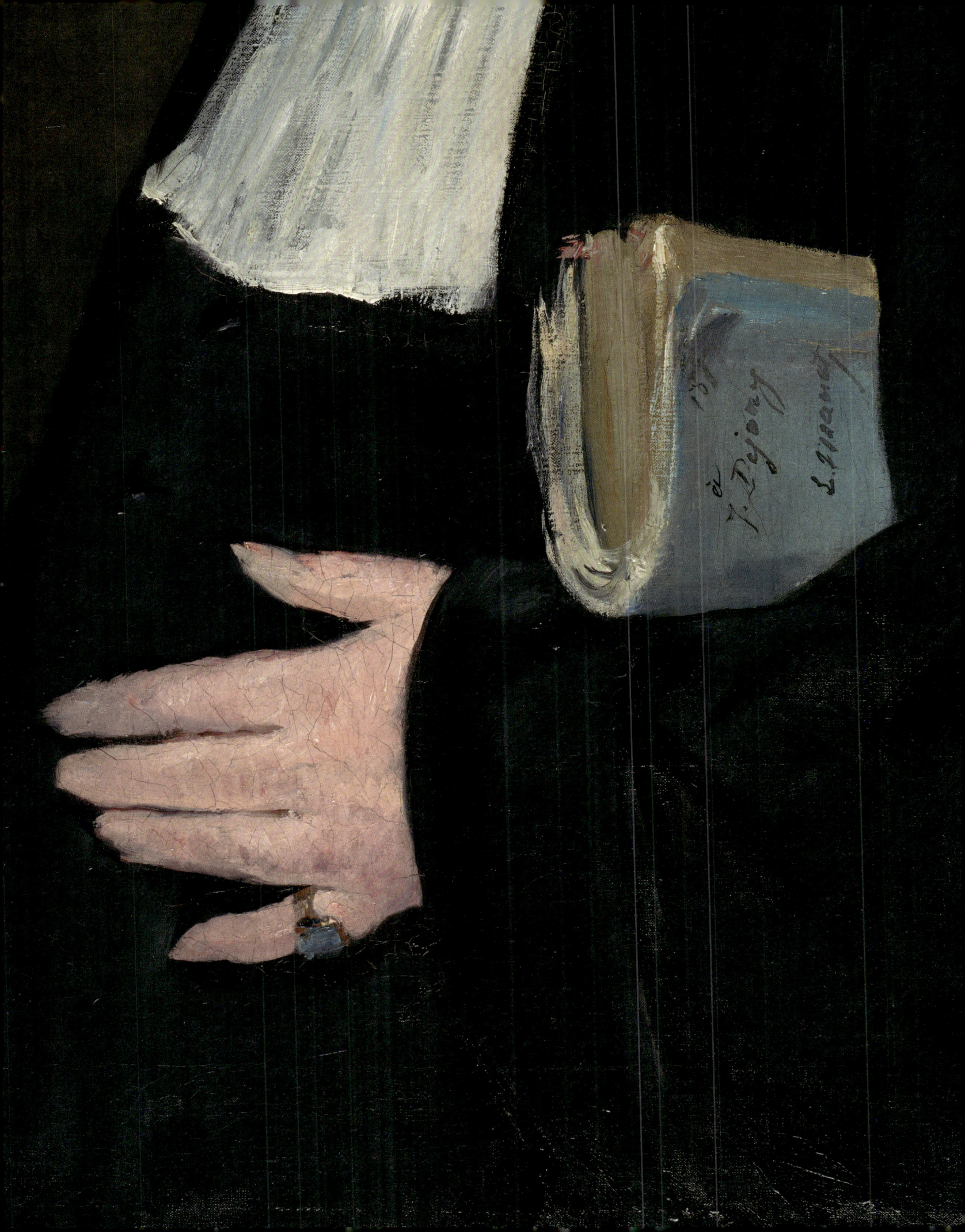

Notes

ÉDOUARD MANET: A FAMILY STORY

1. Locke 2001 is a notable exception.
2. See, for example, Fried 1996; Clark 1999; and Armstrong 2002.
3. Charles Baudelaire to Étienne Carjat, October 6, 1863, in Baudelaire 1947–53, vol. 4, 193–94.
4. See edited letter by Rodary in the Chronology, 124, in this volume.
5. These counts are approximate because, in some instances, it is impossible to definitively identify the model. See 116–17, in this catalogue, for more detail.
6. Brombert 1997, 3.
7. See Greenwald, 102, in this volume.
8. See Locke, 103, in this volume.
9. See ibid., 103–4.
10. Brombert 1997, 11.
11. Ibid., 14.
12. Ibid., 14–15.
13. Ibid., 15.
14. Wilson-Bareau 1991, 18–23; see Locke, 111–13, in this volume, for more information about Jules Dejouy.
15. Ibid., 18.
16. Ibid., 18.
17. Ibid., 21–23.
18. Ibid., 19.
19. Brombert 1997, 31–32, 38–40.
20. See Rodary, 104, in this volume.
21. See family tree, 100–101, in this volume; and Rodary, 104–5, in this volume. One of her brothers, also named Rudolf, did not survive to maturity.
22. Coppens 2022, 1218; and Rodary, 104, in this volume.
23. Rodary, 104, in this volume.
24. Brombert 1997, 40.
25. Mauner 2003, 126; and Coppens 2022, 1218. Rodary, 104, in this volume disagrees with this suggestion.
26. Locke 2001, 47; and Brombert 1997, 64. The timing of the trip to the Netherlands the summer after Léon's birth suggests both a personal *and* artistic agenda. Locke has posited that Manet traveled to assure Suzanne's father of her well-being. Rodary, 104, in this volume suggests that Suzanne

and baby Léon may have also traveled to the Netherlands with Manet.
27. Meller 2002; Tinterow and Lacambre 2003, 388; and Wilson-Bareau, 41, in this volume.
28. Brombert 1997, 51.
29. Leenhoff 1900–1910, 73.
30. Quoted in Wilson-Bareau 1991, 26.
31. See Wilson-Bareau, 41–49, in this volume.
32. For summary of critical response, see Hamilton 1954, 26; and Cachin et al. 1983, 50.
33. Greenwald, 102, in this volume.
34. It was first exhibited in St. Petersburg in 1861. Contemporaneous photography shows that it once included an image of a satyr, explaining its title in that exhibition: *Nymph and Satyr*. See Corradini 1983 for the most comprehensive study of the painting's history and complex technical attributes.
35. This is despite the fact that it has not left the Museo Nacional del Bellas Artes in Buenos Aires, Argentina, in decades.
36. See Rodary, 105; and Beeny, 51–63, for a survey of post-marriage portraits, in this volume.
37. The studies of this oil sketch and its sources are manifold. See, for instance, Krauss 1967, 622–27; Farwell 1975, 225–29; Corradini 1983; Wilson-Bareau 1986, 30; and Beeny 2018, 66–81. The print after Giulio Romano's *Toilette of Bathsheba* (1530, Loggia di Davide, Palazzo del Te, Mantua) is J. Corneille le Jeune after Giuliano Romano, *The Toilette of Bathsheba*, etching and engraving, before 1695. The eighteenth-century nude painting is Francois Boucher, (French, 1703–1770) *Diane sortant du bain (Diana Leaving Her Bath)*, 1742. Oil on canvas, 56 × 73 cm. Musée du Louvre, Département des Peintures, Paris (2712).
38. Thompson 1993, xxvii–xxviii.
39. Locke 2001, 78–79.
40. For identifications of creatives, see Brombert 1997, 102; and Dolan 2013.
41. Cachin et al. 1983, 122.
42. See Locke, 89; and Greenwald and Pocobene, 133, in this volume.
43. Locke 2001, 75–77.
44. See Locke, 155, in this volume.
45. Ibid., 155.

46. Cachin and Moffett, 1983, 70–72; and Locke, 155, in this volume.
47. Locke 2001, 114–15, 118–19; and Kremnitzer, 65, in this volume.
48. See Kremnitzer, 65–72, in this volume.
49. Dating Manet paintings is challenging—he worked and reworked canvases over long periods. Many technical studies—for example, Wilson-Bareau 1986; and Groom and Westerby 2017—find these changes significant.
50. See Chaparro, 159, in this volume.
51. Ibid., 159.
52. See Zivkovic, 163, in this volume.
53. Mauner 2003 first made this argument. This theory has recently been repeated, though in a less persuasive way and without citing Mauner, by the Dutch journalist Thera Coppens (Coppens 2022). The birth certificate was actually a replacement acquired after the original burned during the Commune; see Greenwald, 105, in this volume.
54. Mauner 2003.
55. Ibid.
56. See Pludermacher, 83, in this volume.
57. Brombert 1997, 97–98, summarizes this point of view, including citations of Manet's friend the painter Giuseppe de Nittis. On Suzanne, see Rodary, 104–5, in this volume. For another take on this issue of Manet's relationship with Suzanne—and on the wives of artists more generally—see Steinberg 2023, 1–25.
58. Locke 2001, 115–17.
59. See ibid., 118, for more about this argument in relation to Cézanne in particular; and Anne M. Wagner, "Why Monet Gave Up Figure Painting," *Art Bulletin* 76, no. 4 (1994): 613–29.
60. From 1804 to 1923 adoption of non-natural children was extremely limited by the Napoleonic Code; see Gutton 1993; and Fuchs 2008.
61. Quoted in Wilson-Bareau 1991, 34.
62. Quoted in Mathieu, 23. Mathieu notes the original source: "Eugénie Manet's words were related by her son Gustave in a letter to Jules Dejouy, June 28, 1883, Paris, Musée Marmottan Monet, inv. D4–1986.2013.625."

63. Locke 2001, 56–62.
64. Ibid., 47.
65. Quoted in Wilson-Bareau 1991, 191.
66. See Mauner 2003, 129–30; and Pluder-macher, 80, in this volume, about how someone may have "whispered in his ear" about Suzanne's maternity around the time he got his replacement birth certificate.
67. Tabarant 1947, 483.
68. Édouard Manet to Eva Gonzalès, Paris, September 10, 1870, reproduced in Wilson-Bareau 1991, 57.
69. Édouard Manet to Suzanne Manet, Paris, Sunday, September 11, 1870, reproduced in ibid., 57; and Édouard Manet to Suzanne and Eugénie Manet, Paris, October 5, 1870, reproduced in ibid., 60.
70. Édouard Manet to Suzanne Manet, Paris, October 23, 1870, reproduced in ibid., 61.
71. Ibid., November 23, 1870, reproduced in ibid., 63.
72. See Rodary, 175, in this volume.
73. See Greenwald, 171, in this volume.
74. See Scott, 109, in this volume.
75. Rouart 1987, 40.
76. See Scott, 109, in this volume.
77. Rouart 1987, 45.
78. Ibid., 46.
79. See Locke 2001, 155–56, for a summary of this yearning.
80. Quoted in Brombert 1997, 235.
81. See Scott, 109–10, in this volume.
82. Ibid., 110.
83. See Beeny, 51, 58, in this volume. In an 1872 letter to Edma, Berthe writes that Manet "left today with his fat Suzanne for Holland, and in such a bad humor that I do not know how they will get there"; see Rouart 1987, 89.
84. See Scott, 185, in this volume; and Cleveland Museum provenance: https://www.clevelandart.org/art/1958.34.
85. See Beeny, 54, 58, in this volume.
86. Manet's foot became gangrenous and had to be amputated. It could not save him from an infection that had already spread; see Brombert 1997, 451–53; and Chaparro, 111, in this volume.
87. Théodore Duret, *Histoire de Édouard Manet et son oeuvre* (Paris: Benheim-Jeune, 1902), 201–12.
88. See Kremnitzer, 71–72, in this volume.
89. See Scott, 110, in this volume.
90. Léon Leenhoff to Eugène Manet, May 12, 1883, Musée Marmottan Monet, Paris, quoted in Mathieu 2022, 22.
91. Eugénie Manet to Jules Dejouy, July 10, 1883, Paris, Musée Marmottan Monet, quoted in ibid. 23.
92. Suzanne Manet, "Carnet des comptes: autograph notes, 1892–1900," Morgan Library & Museum, New York, notebook 2, MA 3950.
93. See Tabrant 1947, 524–27, for an early accusation about selling copies. A receipt on Léon's business stationary (Tabarant archive, Morgan Library & Museum, MA 3950) lists prices for paintings that were no longer in the family's possession, suggesting he was selling copies. See Rodary, 105, 187–89; Scott, 114n148; and Beeny, 57, 60–61, in this volume.
94. See Mathieu 2022, 259; and Beeny, 57, in this volume.
95. The Manet archive belonging to Adolphe Tabarant has been at the Morgan Library & Museum since 1974 and is now being catalogued at an item level. The archive belonging to Étienne Moreau-Nelaton was given to the French State, and the Manet materials are held at the Bibliothèque Nationale. Both collections contain materials from Léon Leenhoff.

SUZANNE LEENHOFF: MANET'S EARLY INSPIRATION

1. Proust 1897, 129–33.
2. He is recorded as going in July 1852 to Amsterdam, where he signed into the Rijksmuseum. See Chu 1972, 105. For his trips to Italy, see Meller 2002. For possible trips to Cassel, Dresden, Prague, Vienna, and Munich, see Bazire 1884, 10.
3. Cachin et al. 1983, 506.
4. See Rodary, 104–5, in this volume.
5. See Scott, 107n71, in this volume.
6. Another version of this drawing is squared for transfer.
7. Wilson-Bareau 1986, 32–34.
8. Meller 2002, 68n5.
9. Proust 1897, 168.
10. Meller 2002, 89; and Greenwald, 151, in this volume.
11. The studies of this painting and its sources are manifold. They include Krauss 1967; Corradini 1983; Wilson-Bareau 1986, 27–38; Farwell 1975; and Beeny 2018.
12. Corradini 1983.
13. Cachin et al. 1983, 86.
14. Wivel, Fineson, and Wilson-Bareau 1989, 160–71.
15. Lesage 1784, iii–iv.
16. Wilson-Bareau 1986, 87n19.

SUZANNE: THE PRIVATE PORTRAITS

1. I wish to thank Diana Greenwald, Isabella Lores-Chavez, Bridget Alsdorf, and Abraham Frank for their close reading and thoughtful feedback. I am also enormously grateful to Sal Robinson for her insights into the Tabarant archive, to Scott Allan for generously sharing his research files, and to Juliet Wilson-Bareau for her peerless body of scholarship. Unless otherwise noted, translations are my own.
2. On Suzanne's biography and relationship with Manet, see Juliet Wilson-Bareau's essay in this volume. See also Cachin et al. 1983, 70–74, 83–86, 258–60, 286–87, 329–32, 344–45, 365–66, 437–38; Wilson-Bareau 1991, 11–13; Coppens 2014; Van Kempen and Van de Beek 2014, footnotes; Pullins 2019, 63–79; and Locke 2001, 56–7.
3. Although Édouard Manet was long thought to have fathered Léon, some circumstantial evidence suggests Auguste Manet may have been the boy's father; see Curtiss 1981; and Locke 2001, 47–48, 116–18. More recently, Thera Coppens, Ton van Kempen, and Nicoline van de Beek have suggested a Swiss musician Gustave-Adolphe Koella was in fact the father. See note 2, above. For more on this question see Greenwald, 23–27, in this volume. After Suzanne's death, Léon reported to Manet's biographer Étienne Moreau-Nelaton that she and Manet had begun living together in 1860; see Greenwald, 16, in this volume.
4. Baudelaire to Étienne Carjat, October 6, 1863; Baudelaire 1947–53, vol. 4, 193–94. As David Pullins has pointed out, if this was true, the couple must have been unusually secretive, given Baudelaire's apparent surprise upon learning of Manet's engagement three years later; Pullins 2019, 63.
5. Quoted in Wilson-Bareau 1991, 13.
6. It is possible that the two women did not live together during the last two years of Eugénie's life, as the latter died at the home of Berthe and Eugène on the rue Villejuste; see Locke, 104, in this volume. In the Manet-Leenhoff marriage contract, Eugénie gave Édouard and Suzanne a wedding present of 10,000 francs, reserving the right to retract it if her son predeceased her, leaving no heirs; see Locke 2001, 60. As discussed below, Eugénie disinherited Suzanne. Of course, if Manet's father, Auguste, was the natural father of Suzanne's son, Eugénie had every reason to harbor complicated feelings toward her daughter-in-law. Her correspondence demonstrates a suspicion toward both Suzanne and the whole "monde Leenhoff" that may point in this direction; see Greenwald, 24–27, 31, in this volume.
7. For detailed information on Suzanne's finances during this period, see Mathieu 2021, 23–24, 30.
8. Eugénie and Berthe believed that Paul Durand-Ruel should be entrusted with the sale. See Eugénie Manet to Suzanne Manet,

May 12 and 13, 1883, Morgan Library & Museum, New York, MA 3950. On the sale, see Bodelson 1968, 341–44.

9. Georges Jeanniot, quoted in Moreau-Nélaton 1926, vol. 2, 107.

10. Suzanne Manet, *Carnet de comptes, 1892–1900.*

11. *On the Beach* and *The Swallows* went to Henri Rouart and Albert Hecht, respectively, in 1873.

12. Lot 14, *procès-verbaux*, no. 148, sold to "Lemailleur" listed in Bodelson 1968, 344.

13. See Cachin et al. 1983, 258–60, no. 97.

14. Manet may have added Léon in preparation for the picture's exhibition at the Vie Moderne gallery in May 1880; see Wilson-Bareau 2011, 822. The resulting picture closes the scandalous age gap between the two "siblings," who were in fact mother and son: Suzanne remains thirty-five, while Léon, barely a teenager when the picture began, appears in his twenties. On the reworking of the painting, see February 24, 2012, technical report by Bruno Mottin of the C2RMF; my thanks to Samuel Rodary for sharing this document.

15. Ernest Duez to Winaretta Singer, 1885; Musée d'Orsay archives; cited in Cachin et al. 1983, 260.

16. For a detailed account of the financial arrangements summarized here, see Mathieu 2021, 22–25, 42.

17. Suzanne Manet to Berthe Morisot-Manet, March 23 [1894]: "I am happy to think that Julie will have a fine fortune. I do wish her well, I love her so much. . . . Above all, do nothing for me that could be costly for Julie. I am old, I could perhaps obtain (after the distribution) a rent that would be provided to me for 5 years, and not necessarily, for I may be dead in 5 years." Suzanne Manet to Berthe Morisot, March 30, 1894, Musée Marmottan Monet: "I make no secret of my feelings, but I wish I could have stayed there all my life. I fear the move, I fear everything that is fatigue. I am used to this place, and where I go, I shall take my grief with me." Both letters translated in Mathieu 2022, 42.

18. Per funeral announcements, 94, rue Saint-Dominique was her final address.

19. "1894 . . . /10 mars ik met de kat—100/ payé.; Suzanne Manet, *Carnet de comptes 1892–1900*, Morgan Library & Museum, New York, MA 3950.2:2, fol. 40v.

20. See Allan, Beeny, and Groom 2019, 295, no. 35, entry by Scott Allan.

21. Two of his letters from that summer are illustrated with likenesses of Suzanne's cat, Zizi, evidently based on the same pencil

sketch as the creature pictured in *Woman with a Cat*, see Manet to Isabelle Lemonnier and Manet to Henri Charles Guérard, summer 1880, in Rouart and Wildenstein 1975, vol. 2, no. 573 and no. 599, respectively. For the sketchbook drawing see Rouart and Wildenstein 1975, vol. 2, no., 640. On the relationship between these works on paper, see Allan, Beeny, and Groom 2019, nos. 30 and 34, 293–95; and Beeny 2019a, 1005, 1010, and 1011. Manet retained his sketchbooks and may well have returned to the cat years later for the portrait of Suzanne.

22. She sold her portrait with a cat to Vollard two weeks before writing her first plea for Berthe's help.

23. Vollard 1937, 74. Vollard misremembered this initial visit as having taken place at Asnières. The later Camondo collection picture was *Suzanne Manet at the Piano* (see below).

24. See Rabinow 2006, 143.

25. See Ives, Stein, and Steiner 1997, 88.

26. Degas also owned an early nude drawing surely posed for by Suzanne and purchased, via Durand-Ruel, at the 1884 studio sale; see ibid., 90. A fragment from an abandoned painting of the *Finding of Moses* (Private collection), likely posed for by Suzanne, is first documented in the collection of Degas's brother, René. It originally may have belonged to the painter himself and was, indeed, mistakenly attributed to Degas in the catalogue of René's sale. My thanks to Kathryn Kremnitzer and Diana Greenwald for sharing this information.

27. "10 Avril 1894/reçu pour pastel/ Chez Portier 1200 fr"; Suzanne Manet, *Carnet de comptes 1892–1900*, fol. 40r.

28. Cachin et al. 1983, 365–66.

29. Compare, for example, the prices realized by pastel portrait heads at the 1884 sale, averaging about 400 francs; see Bodelson 1968, 342. On Degas's acquisition, see Ives, Stein, and Steiner 1997, 89.

30. On Manet's interest in eighteenth-century art, see Beeny 2019b.

31. Alexandre, "Essai sur Monsieur Degas," *Les Arts*, no. 166 (1918): 8; cited in Isolde Pludermacher, "Masculin-féminin," in Cars, Guégan, and Pludermacher 2023, 153.

32. See Ann Dumas et al. 1997, 45, 195n22; Allan, Beeny, and Groom 2019, 295; and Isolde Pludermacher, "L'énigme d'une relation," in Cars, Guégan, and Pludermacher 2023, 17.

33. See Vollard 1924, 85–86; Lemoisne 1946–49, vol. 2, 64; and Boggs et al. 1988, 140–42. See also Isolde Pludermacher, "L'énigme d'une relation," in Cars, Guégan, and Pludermacher 2023, 17; and Wolohojian and Dunn 2023, 65.

34. Degas later described this still life to Vollard as a picture of plums. It was in fact a still life of walnuts; see Stephan Wolohojian, "Degas après Manet" in Cars, Guégan, and Pludermacher, 2023, 180nn18–19, 181.

35. On the myth of Degas's misanthropy in later years, see ibid., 178.

36. Vollard's account of these transactions in his memoir (1937, 71–76) is not entirely accurate; Degas bought the first fragment from Alphonse Portier and the rest from Vollard. See John Leighton and Juliet Wilson-Bareau, "The Maximilian Paintings: Provenance and Exhibition History," in Juliet Wilson-Bareau, ed., *Manet's "The Execution of Maximilian": Painting, Politics and Censorship*, exh. cat. (London: National Gallery, 1992), 112–13. Scrambled accounts of the *Maximilian* story resulted in various misunderstandings regarding Suzanne's role. For example, a writer for the *Mercure de France* reported in 1917, "Degas avait une grande amitié pour Manet; c'est ainsi qu'il racheta à sa veuve les études d'atelier de Manet et les brula pour qu'elles ne fissent aucun tort à sa mémoire"; see Pludermacher, "L'énigme d'une relation" in Cars, Guégan, and Pludermacher 2023, 17.

37. See Stuckey 1983, 177.

38. Julie Manet, *Journal*, February 7, 1899, in Manet 1979, 213.

39. Suzanne Manet, *Carnet de comptes, 1892–1900*, fol. 40v: "1894 . . . buste nue 500f/moi chapeau noir/manteau gris 60/ Faure . . . 200/Vollard doit 760/Avril [crossed out]/ Mai/Juin/payable" (1894 . . . nude bust 500f/ me black hat/gray coat 60/Faure . . . 200/ Vollard owes 760 April [crossed out]/ May/June/payable.)"

40. See Cachin et al. 1983, 286–87.

41. Suzanne Manet, *Carnet de comptes, 1892–1900*, fol. 38v: "23 Novembre 1894/verkocht à Joyant en Manzi/voor vyf duizend fr/Portret—[illegible]."

42. See Rouart 1950, 22. Arthur O'Shaughnessy inscribed a copy of his 1874 *Music and Moonlight: Poems and Songs*, "À Madame Édouard Manet—souvenir d'une soirée de Chopin"; Morgan Library & Museum, New York, PML 128812.

43. Suzanne Manet and Eléonore-Palmyre Meurice played excerpts from Tannhauser for the dying poet in his final year; see Champfleury (Jules-François-Félix Fleury-Husson) to Auguste Poulet-Malassis, August 15, 1866, in Baudelaire 1887, 95n1.

44. Eléonore-Palmyre (Madame Paul) Meurice to Baudelaire, January 5, 1865; see Champion 1973, 262–64. Of course, Manet might have requested Haydn from Madame Meurice precisely because his work was not in Suzanne's repertoire. Pierre Prins

also describes Haydn as one of Manet's favorite composers.

45. More detailed information on Suzanne's musical career appears in Coppens 2014; and in the footnotes to Van Kempen and Van de Beek 2014.

46. Baudelaire to Étienne Carjat, October 6, 1863; see note 5, above.

47. Once in October 1847 and once in January 1848; see Van Kempen and Van de Beek 2014, 44n19.

48. Moreau-Nélaton 1926, vol. 1, 95. On the totemic significance of this object, see Locke 2001, 46.

49. The specific reference may have been to a painting by Gabriel Metsu (Petit Palais, Paris) reproduced in Charles Blanc's *Histoire des peintres;* see Cachin et al. 1983, 286–87; and Stevens et al. 2012, no. 7, 178.

50. Philippe Burty inscribed a copy of his 1877 *Maitres et petits maitres: A la grande pianiste & l'excellente amie Madame E. Manet,* Morgan Library & Museum, New York, PML 128791 Eléonore-Palmyre Meurice to Baudelaire, about February 15, 1865: "Madame Manet, a joué comme un ange; M. Bosch a gratté sa guitare, comme un bijou; Chérubin-Astruc a chanté; la commandante Thérèse a chanté aussi"; see Champion 1973, 265–67. Marie-Joséphine Morisot wrote to Berthe Morisot on, July 14, 1871: "une chaleur suffocante, les gens parqués dans l'unique salon, les boissons chaudes et pourtant Pagans a chanté, Mad. Éd. a joué et M. Degas était présent"; see Rouart 1950, 65–66. On Suzanne's domestic performances, see also Samuel Rodary, "Manet and Astruc, Astruc and Manet: Correspondance/Correspondence," in Hansen 2021, 116.

51. Bibliothèque Jacques Doucet, E IV 11, Ex. no. 48/195. Théodore de Banville also inscribed a copy of his 1875 *Poésies; les exiles; les princesses* with a poem in praise of Suzanne's playing: "La musique aux charmantes voix/S'éveille et chant sous vos doigts,/Parlant des vieux qu'elle devine;/Et mes vers, oiseaux las d'errer,/Volent vers vous, pour s'enivrer,/Aux sons de la lyre divine"; Morgan Library & Museum, New York, PML 128784.

52. Higonnet 1990, 84: " Her nose appears long, her face extremely full, her arms and hands chubby. This manner of portrayal is more consistent with the way Suzanne is described by the mother of the slender Berthe Morisot, who once went so far as to write that Manet was 'at home making a portrait of his wife and laboring to make of that monster something slender and interesting!'" See also Locke 2001, 61. Further remarks about Suzanne's weight appear in

Marie-Joséphine Morisot to Berthe Morisot, July 24, 1871 ("Sa femme se remet un peu, mais il a dû éprouver un gros choc à la vue de cet épanouissement campagnard"); and Berthe Morisot to Edma Pontillon, about 1872: "J'ai vu hier l'ami Manet; il est parti aujourd'hui avec la grosse Suzanne pour la Hollande et de si mauvaise humeur que je ne sais comment ils arriveront"; Rouart 1950, 73.

53. De Nittis 1895, 188–89.

54. "payé de l'argent du portrait au piano/ Novembre 1896"; Suzanne Manet, *Carnet de comptes, 1892–1900,* fol. 37v.

55. See Allan, Beeny, and Groom 2019, 277.

56. On this work and the trio to which it belongs, see Pullins 2019, 63–79. Still in Manet's studio at the time of his death, this picture was signed by Suzanne and belonged to George Moore by 1899, when he lent it to an exhibition. How Moore acquired it remains uncertain.

57. According to Tabarant 1947, 341.

58. "6000/reçu zes duizend franken/voor portrait au/ banc vert/16 Aout 1895/vendu à Mr Joyant/rue Forest 9/le portrait au banc/ vert"; Suzanne Manet, *Carnet de comptes, 1892–1900,* fol. 37r.

59. Listed in a journalist's description of the studio; see Jean de Paris 1876.

60. See Allan, Beeny, and Groom 2019, 275–77.

61. Tabarant 1947, 340. Tabarant here confuses the location of Manet's studio at the time; see Wilson-Bareau 2010; and Wilson-Bareau 2012. On the Guillemets, see also Stevens and Nichols 2012, 192.

62. On this date, see Allan, Beeny, and Groom 2019, 277, no. 5.

63. See "Paris Studios: M. Manet's," *Architect* 18 (December 1, 1877): 298; reprinted in Wilson-Bareau et al. 2008, 80–81.

64. De Nittis 1985, 188–89.

65. Ibid.

66. On their correspondence, see Rodary 2019; on their relationship, see Chavanne et al. 2005.

67. On this copy, see Jaskierny and Roberts 2016. On Vibert, son of Suzanne's sister, Marthe and the genre painter Jules Vibert, see Tabarant 1947, 35–36. *Editor's note:* In conjunction with publishing the image of this painting, the owner requests that the following provenance information be presented: Mme Suzanne Manet's Estate, 1906, by descent to Léon Leenhoff; Théodore Duret, 1910; Otto Gerstenberg, Berlin (sold at Drouot, July 3,1912, for 25,000 francs); Max Silberberg, Breslau; Paul Graupe Auction, Berlin, March 23, 1935, lot no. 25; Leopold Ullstein, Berlin, 1935; H. J. P. Bomford, Aldbourne, England, 1938 until November 1964, when sold at Christie's,

November 27, lot number 29 (sold after the sale for 11,000 pounds); Private collection, Newbury, England, until November 2014; currently in a Private collection, England. There is disagreement among early Manet sources about the authenticity of this work. Duret and Meier-Graefe state it is a first version for the painting of the same subject in Oslo (fig 4.5); Tabarant and all sources published since, state that it is a copy made by Édouard Vibert or another hand that is not Manet's.

68. Cachin et al. 1983, 70–72.

69. On this work, see Locke 2001, 10, 71–74. Manet's art historical reference points are multiple; see Locke, 155–56, and Wilson-Bareau, 49, in the present volume. See also Cachin et al. 1983, 70–71; and Fried 1996, 25, 82–89.

70. See Locke 2001, 71.

71. See Reff 1962, 185. As Locke has pointed out, the reasons Auguste may have opposed the union were likely complex.

72. This work might be one of two items in the June 18, 1883, inventory of Eugénie's apartment taken following Édouard's death: "Paysage, rivière avec barque par Manet" or "Esquisse de M. Manet et sa femme"; see Jamot and Wildenstein 1932, vol. 1, 106, 108.

73. "vendu Février 1897/6 milles cinq cents francs/le vieux musicien à Camentron/ pour Durand Ruel le/vieux musicien avec la femme/au chapeau de Bellevue/—/ St Ouen vendu/3 mille cinq cents fr."; Suzanne Manet, *Carnet de comptes, 1892–1900,* fol. 36v. Another painting said to be of Suzanne (New York, Metropolitan Museum of Art, 1997.391.4, New York, RW I 345) appears on the same page, listed as "la femme au chapeau de Bellevue." The pert profile more closely resembles that of Madame Guillemet, who visited the Manets at Bellevue in 1880; see Allan, Beeny, and Groom 2019, 297. Suzanne surely would not have described a portrait of herself in such impersonal terms.

74. This copy later became the subject of a lawsuit; see Tabarant 1947, 35–36.

75. On these letters, see, most recently, Rodary 2014.

76. Édouard Manet to Suzanne Manet, September 10, 1870; ibid., 22–23.

77. Ibid., September 15, 1870; ibid., 33–35.

78. Ibid., October 23, 1870; and November 19, 1870; ibid., 58–60, 73–74.

79. Ibid., November 23 [postmarked 22], 1870; ibid., 75–76. The painter's advice to his wife, "Prends de l'exercice, promène-toi," has sometimes been read as a suggestion to watch her figure but seems better

understood in context as a reminder to look after herself and take pleasures where she may. The letter continues, "travaille ton piano et surtout ne t'inquiète pas, je ne cours aucun danger."

80. Ibid., November 24, 1870; ibid., 77.

81. Ibid., December 22, 1870; ibid., 85–86.

82. Ibid., December 25, 1870; ibid., 87–88.

LÉON LEENHOFF: MODEL ACROSS MEDIA

1. This study considers prints realized during Manet's lifetime; posthumous states and editions are excluded. For a larger discussion of Manet's work across media in the 1860s, see Kremnitzer 2020.

2. See Greenwald, 23–27, in this volume.

3. See Locke 2001, 119, for this count of paintings. However, there are possibly some works that are currently unlocated but photographed in the Lochard album—such as *Léon and Eva Gonzalès in the Loge*—that are not included in this count. On Léon's presence in the *Races at Longchamp* project, *Music in the Tuileries*, and *Reading*, see Wilson-Bareau 2017, with the assistance of Kathryn Kremnitzer and Genevieve Westerby, "Manet, Cat. 12, The Races at Longchamp: Curatorial Entry," in Manet Paintings and Works on Paper at the Art Institute of Chicago (Art Institute of Chicago, 2017), para 26.

4. The painting is now recognized as a work by Velázquez's pupil and son-in-law, Juan Bautista Martinez del Mazo.

5. See *Registre des cartes d'artistes*, no. 149, 125, Archives des Musées Nationaux, https://www.siv.archives-nationales.culture.gouv.fr/siv/media/FRAN_IR_054378/c1i5fz1k6jso--1b1zneczk9k7d/FRAN_0374_0473_L; on Manet's copying at the Louvre, see Tinterow and Lacambre 2003, Manet/Velázquez, 205–9, 388.

6. The etching was realized across five states. On the various states and editions and the preparatory watercolor frontispiece design, see Wilson 1977, cat. no. 10; Wilson 1978, cat. no. 23; Cachin et al. 1983, cat. no. 37; and Harris 1990, cat. no. 5. It may have been among those shown at Alfred Cadart's storefront on the rue Richelieu in 1862, as noted by Charles Baudelaire in his first article devoted to the etching revival, published in *La Revue anecdotique* on April 15, 1862. Cadart published the third state of the etching in *8 Gravures à l'eauforte par Édouard Manet* in 1862 (no. 2) and in 1863 it was one of fourteen published by the artist in an edition made for friends on the occasion of his marriage to

Suzanne on October 28, 1863 (no. 12). On the frontispiece cover design, see Cachin et al. 1983, cat. no. 37; and Harris 1990, cat. no. 5.

7. As "*Les Petits cavaliers* d'après Vélasquez," no. 674. See Wilson 1978, cat. no. 23; Cachin et al. 1983, cat. nos. 9, 37; and Harris 1990, cat. no. 5.

8. Cachin et al. 1983, cat. no. 37.

9. Work to clarify the relationship between these two canvases is ongoing, with the recent reappearance of *Spanish Studio Scene* at Sotheby's, London. See Kremnitzer, 139, in this volume, for more information about *Spanish Cavaliers* and its relationship to *Spanish Studio Scene*.

10. The watercolor study (RW D 346) was likely first owned by Berthe Morisot.

11. Thanks to conservators and curators at the Phillips, we were able to study the watercolor under magnification, but unfortunately not out of the frame. This object-based close looking was carried out in July 2018.

12. The drawing (RW D 45.6) measures 25.5 by 18 cm. It is unlocated.

13. The New York Public Library impression is *bon à tirer*, with instructions to pull twenty-five prints on the same paper.

14. "Après la mort de Manet, j'ai eu l'idée de faire photograph er tout ce qui restait dans l'atelier. Je me suis adresse à Lochard, photographe connu des artistes. Je ne voulais pas faire trop de frais ayant encore a payer les cadres. Il fut convenu entre nous que pour un certain nombre, le prix serait de tant. Les factures sont dans l'inventaire. J'ai donc établi un registre numérote de 1 à 327 et sur les toiles le numéros correspondant à celle collé. Il figure au-dessus des photographies. Ces numéros se retrouvent entre eux c'est ce qui fait que tous les renseignements correspondent ensemble." On the hiring of Lochard, see Leenhoff 1900–1910, fols. 73–74. On the Lochard photographs, see Kremnitzer 2023.

15. Lochard 1883a; and Lochard 1883b.

16. École Nationale des Beaux-Arts 1884, 66, no. 160, as *L'énfant a l'épée (gauche). Les petits Cavaliers, d'après Velázquez. L'enfant a l'epée (droite)*; Lochard 1883a, no. 201, vol. 2, fol. 77; and Lochard 1883b, no. 428, fol. 26, as *l'enfant a l'épée/Les petits cavaliers/L'enfant a l'epée*.

17. École Nationale des Beaux-Arts 1884, 65, no. 159, as *Le buveur d'absinthe. Les Gitanos. Enfant portant un plateau*. Illustrated in Lochard 1883a, no. 430, vol. 1, fol. 73; Lochard 1883b, no. 428, fol. 26; Lochard 1883a, no. 430, vol. 2, fol. 21; Lochard 1883a,

no. 201, vol. 2, fol. 77 Lochard 1883a, no. 216, vol. 2, fol. 35.

18. Léon first annotated the page in penci but later wrote over some notes in ink.

19. See Léon Leenhoff, *Ensemble de notes et de documents sur le peintre*, about 1900–1910, Bibliothèque Nationale de France Paris, Département des Estampes et de la Photographie, RESERVE 8-YB3-2401. https://gallica.bnf.fr/ark:/12148/btv1b10548955r; and Étienne Moreau-Nélaton, *Catalogue général [manuscrit de l'œuvre d'Édouard Manet]: peintures et pastels*, about 1925–26, Bibliothèque Nationale de France, Paris, Département des Estampes et de la Photographie, 4-Z-89. https://gallica.bnf.fr/ark:/12148/btv1b52501604r.

20. Proust 1913, 120: "Je ne veux pas, m'avait-il répondu, pénétrer dans les musées par morceaux. Je veux y arriver tout entier ou pas."

CUT PAINTINGS, ILLEGITIMATE CHILDREN, AND TWO EXCEPTIONAL ARTISTS: EDGAR DEGAS AND THE MANET FAMILY

1. On the Manet-Degas relationship, see Des Cars, Guégan, and Pludermacher 2023, and more particularly (in connection with this essay), the chapters: "L'énigme d'une relation," "Deux fils de famille," and "Masculin Féminin."

2. For the Manet family's reaction, see Greenwald, 15, in this volume. Degas's father was a great art lover and seems to have accepted his son's choice fairly easily.

3. Barrias and Lamothe, and a brief stint at the École des Beaux-Arts, for Degas; Thomas Couture for Manet.

4. For Manet's various workshops, see Des Cars, Guégan, and Pludermacher 2023, 252.

5. Loyrette 1991, 20. In the *Almanach du commerce*, from at least 1857 and until 1876, "De Gas banq." is listed at 28, rue de la Victoire.

6. *Manet/Degas*, Musée d'Orsay, Paris, March 28 – July 23, 2023 and Metropolitan Museum of Art, New York, September 24, 2023–January 7, 2024.

7. Alexis 1879, 2–3.

8. Reff 2020, vol. 1, 45.

9. Ibid., vol. 2, 270. Marcel Guérin, "Le Portrait du Chanteur Pagans et de M. de Gas père, par Degas," *Bulletin des musées de France*, March 1933, 34. Suzanne also performed at the De Nittis home, where Degas was also a regular guest.

10. This painting, much larger than the one by Degas, was later covered by Bazille. It became *Ruth and Boaz* as revealed by an X-ray made by the C2RMF. It showed a

woman in profile playing the piano, and a man in the background lying on a white sofa. Thanks to Paul Perrin for pointing out this comparison. See Paul Perrin, "Une jeune fille joue du piano et un jeune homme l'ecoute" in *Frédéric Bazille, La jeunesse de l'Impressionisme* (2016–17), 74–77, and "Hidden Paintings in the work of Frédéric Bazille," https://www.nga.gov /features/bazille-hidden-compositions.html.

11. Although Degas only painted one portrait of Manet, he also made drawings and prints of him, whereas Manet never represented Degas. See Cars, Guégan, and Pludermacher 2023, 12–17.

12. Moreau-Nélaton 1926, vol. 2, 40.

13. Renoir, who saw the painting at Degas's home with Julie Manet (see note 17), according to Vollard (1938, 187–88), reports Manet judging that, "he would be better alone." Manet cut some of his own paintings (e.g., *The Gitanos, Episode d'une course de taureaux*) to improve their composition. However, to cut another artist's work without consent is quite a different matter.

14. Galerie Georges Petit 1924, 23.

15. Vollard 1924, 85.

16. Vollard 1938, 187. See also Jeanniot 1933, 301.

17. Degas, in the presence of Renoir, Mallarmé, and Bartholomé, related this version of the facts to Julie Manet, when she discovered the painting in his salon in 1895. See entry from November 20, 1895, in Julie Manet 1985, 72. Degas gave an identical account to Ambroise Vollard. "Manet thought that Mrs. Manet was hurt." Vollard 1924, 85–87.

18. Blanche 1912, 162. The use of the word *faiblesse* (weakness) may suggest that Suzanne requested Manet do this because she was not satisfied with the way Degas represented her.

19. Blanche 1924, 45. The mention of Berthe Morisot as being a member of the Manet family suggests that this discussion took place after her marriage to Eugène Manet (December 22, 1874). However, in a spring 1869 letter, Morisot's mother evokes a "replastering" between Manet and Degas, which is perhaps a reconciliation following the episode of the cut painting. The letter is incorrectly dated in Rouart 1950, 69. New dating proposed by Rodary in Cars, Guégan, and Pludermacher 2023, 236.

20. Vollard 1938, 187.

21. It is interesting to note that when Manet represents Suzanne in profile, she disappears behind a hat or a veil (*On the Beach*, Musée d'Orsay, Paris; *Mme Manet at Bellevue*, Metropolitan Museum of Art, New York). X-rays reveal traces of a portrait of

Suzanne in profile beneath Manet's *Self-Portrait with a Palette*; see Cachin et al. 1983, 405–6. In the rare instances in which Léon is depicted in profile—as in *Reading*—he strongly resembles his mother.

22. Paintings by Fantin-Latour and Bazille show Manet surrounded by a group of artists in a studio. See Henri Fantin-Latour, *Studio in the Batignolles (Homage to Manet)*, 1870, and Frédéric Bazille, *Bazille's Studio*, 1870, both Musée d'Orsay, Paris.

23. "Madame Édouard Manet never appeared in the studio; this studio was decidedly an annex of the Café de Bade;—there, Édouard was no longer the son of M and Mme Manet: it was the lair of the terrible painter"; Blanche 1912, 161.

24. See exhibition history: https://www.musee -orsay.fr/fr/oeuvres/madame-manet-au -piano-245#artwork-history.

25. Blanche 1912, 162; Galerie Georges Petit 1924, 23; and Moreau Nélaton 1926, vol. 2, 40.

26. Moore 1891, 321. Blanche 1912, 162 agrees: "It was the life itself; it was the man."

27. See Beeny, 51, in this volume for contemporaneous commentary about Suzanne's calming nature.

28. Moreau Nélaton 1926, vol. 2, 40.

29. Boggs 1962, 22–25; and Rodary, 104, in this volume.

30. Moreau Nélaton 1926, vol. 2, 40.

31. I thank Sefy Hendler for suggesting this comparison. On the subject of Manet's possible boredom, Proust recounts in his *Souvenirs* that Manet "had little taste for music." See Proust 1913, 11.

32. The attitude of the man leaning against the door in *Interior*, hands in pockets, evokes how Degas shows Manet in a wash drawing (Musée d'Orsay, RF41651), a gesture also in *Portrait in a Workshop (Henri Michel Lévy)*. Duranty 1876, 35, probably references Degas: "hands that we hide in our pockets can be eloquent."

33. Tabarant 1947, 481.

34. Léon also appears as an elegant young man in *View of the Exposition Universelle* (Oslo).

35. Tabarant 1947, 481; and Greenwald, 27, in this volume.

36. A letter from Degas (November 11, 1872) during his stay in New Orleans mentions Augustine Malot; see Pludermacher 2021 and Reff 2020, 159.

37. "Acte de naissance de Paul Achille." 1874, Naissances, 17, V4E 4748, number 1536, Archives de Paris, 10.

38. The Civil Code originally stated that in the absence of maternal recognition, the filiation of a natural child to his or her mother was not legally established. Just mentioning

the mother's name on the birth certificate was not sufficient to establish filiation. This provision was not always followed but was further affirmed by the Court of Cassation in 1872. For more information, see Nizard 1977, 91–122. According to Gabrielle Houbre, whom I thank, maternal recognition could happen later but generally before the child reached majority. Unmarried mothers sometimes legally recognized a child when they married, as could have been the case here. Recognition also took place because of issues of inheritance or custody.

39. The death declaration of Paul Legrand was made at the city hall of the seventeenth arrondisement: "Paul Legrand, 8 months old, born in Paris, died rue Guyot, no. 8, yesterday morning [March 22] at eleven o'clock. Son of (no other information) the witnesses: Claude Marie Bombois, 53, police officer, rue Lacondamine no. 13, and Pierre Redon, 35, coachman, rue de la Roquette, no. 1." *Acte de décès de Paul Achille*: 1875, Décès, 17, V4E 4770, no. 1033, Archives de Paris, 18.

40. See "Gazette des tribunaux," *Le Figaro*, September 25, 1875, 3, and "Chronique de tribunaux,' *Le Gaulois*, September 26, 1875, 3.

41. "Gazette de palais," Le XIXe siecle, September 26, 1875. The mention made of Manet's celebrity ignores the fact that it could have been his brother Gustave, a lawyer who sometimes attended court.

42. Undated letter (before September 1874), Morgan Library & Museum, New York, MA 3950 (61).

43. A letter from Degas to Suzanne dating from 1898–99 attests to the role she played in Degas's meeting with Pierre Romanelli; see Reff 2020, vol. 2, 270.

44. This quote appears in Blanche 1912, 160. Two letters confirm Degas's participation; Léon's organization of this banquet was not universally appreciated by Manet's family and friends, including Pissarro, as it happened soon after Gustave Manet's death; Morgan Library & Museum, New York, Tabarant archives, MA 3950.3. These letters are not yet catalogued at the item level, but are being progressively cataloged by the Morgan.

45. *The Ham* and a lithograph of *Polichinelle*.

46. The traces of this old framing (folding and tacks) are still visible on the canvas. We do not know whether this was the state of the canvas when Degas recovered it from Manet, or Degas did it himself.

47. Vollard 1938, 187.

48. J. Manet 1985, 72 (November 20, 1895). In the same passage, Julie Manet notes that

Degas was "very occupied with arranging a lamp that he had just bought that would give a sparkling light." This was certainly related to his preparations for the photograph.

49. Between the date of this photograph, which corresponds to Julie Manet's account, and the date of the death of Suzanne Manet (1906).

50. Galerie Georges Petit 1924, 23.

51. Vollard 1924, 85–86. *Rétablir* has a very particular meaning in French. It specifically means restoring something to its original state or to restore to good condition; it can also mean to bring something into existence again or even to give back to someone something of which they have been stripped. For example you use *rétablir* when talking about restoring one's honor.

52. We know it was in his studio because of the red stamp at the bottom of the added section of canvas. The painting may have been kept in Degas's studio longer than it hung in his living room. Blanche (1912, 162) refers to the painting, which he specifically says he knows about through a photograph.

53. A curious anecdote is peddled by a journalist upon Degas's death: "Degas had a great friendship with Manet; thus, he bought Manet's studio studies from his widow and burned them so that they would do no harm to his memory," *Mercure de France 1917*, October 16, 1917, 759.

54. Degas's handwritten notes on his collection about a drawing in brush and India ink purchased through Durand-Ruel at the Manet sale of 1884. They are specifically, "Inventaire autograph de Degas mentionnant des oeuvres de Manet figurant dans sa collection. Ensemble de dix feuillets manuscrits, 20 × 15.8 cm (le Feuillet)." In English: "Autograph inventory by Degas mentioning works by Manet appearing in his collection. Set of ten handwritten sheets, 20 × 15.8 cm (sheet)." These notes were acquired in 2024 by the Musée d'Orsay after the *Manet/Degas* exhibition.

55. It is also not mentioned in the Met catalogue of Degas's collection. Dumas et al. 1997. It should be noted that the folios Degas devoted to Manet do not deal with all the works in his collection (for example, neither *The Gypsy* nor the *Portrait de Berthe Morisot in Mourning* appear).

56. *Maternity Study*, Estate sale René De Gas, 1927, lot no. 80.

57. Degas's handwritten notes on his collection indicate that *Mrs. Manet with a Cat* was acquired in 1895, while Arsène Alexandre remembers Degas trying to buy the pastel *Mrs. Manet on a Blue Sofa* "circa 1894."

58. Handwritten notes by Degas on the works in his collection. See note 54.

59. Ibid.

60. Ibid.

61. The pastel is visible in the background of a photograph showing *Élie and Louise Halévy in Degas's Salon,* dated "probably Fall 1895" in Daniel 1999, 132–33, fig. 60, cat. no. 27.

62. In the same way, in the *Portrait of Mrs. Manet, Mother,* Manet paints the widow seated in the place of his father (in *Portrait of the Parents,* she is standing behind her seated husband).

63. Interestingly, Degas does not buy it directly from Suzanne but through an intermediary, Portier, to whom he gives one of his works. Note that it is also from Portier that Degas acquires the fragment of the sergeant arming his rifle belonging to the second version of *The Execution of Maximilian.*

64. Alexandre 1918, no. 166, 22.

65. It's curious to note that one of the pages of an album of *cartes de visites* belonging to Manet there are side-by-side portraits of Suzanne and a young man referred to in the penciled caption as "Degas" without it being possible to identify his features with certainty (the order of the photos might also have been rearranged).

66. Degas's personal notes on his collection; see note 57 for more information. This theory about Léon cutting the canvas is also supported by Julie Manet's diary, which says he first cut it. See Roberts 2017, 52.

67. In Degas's letters confirming his participation in the banquet at Père Lathuille's, he addressed Léon "My dear Leenhoff." Morgan Library & Museum, New York, Tabarant Archive, MA 3950.3. These letters are not yet catalogued at the item level.

68. Vollard 1938, 126.

MADAME AUGUSTE MANET AND THE PAINTING OF MODERN LIFE

1. Zola 2003, 280–81, folio 31.
2. Bernard Berenson to Isabella Stewart Gardner, April 1, 1909 (ARC.008327), in Berenson and Gardner 1987, 440.
3. Staffe 1891, 300.
4. Lutz 2016, 217.
5. Chatté 1907, 7.
6. Stéphane 1932, 174–76.
7. Matthieu 2022, 15.
8. Berenson and Gardner 1987, 440.
9. Baudelaire 1968, 260; and Baudelaire 1981, 118.
10. Ibid.; and ibid., 119.
11. Ibid.; and ibid., 118.

12. Chatté 1907, 5, notes that she rarely accepted invitations.

13. Baudelaire 1968, 260; and Baudelaire 1981, 118.

14. Manet 2010, no. 14 (*Portrait de Mme M . . .*). No dimensions are given. Zola 1867, 37, considers the *Portrait of Mme M . . .* alongside three canvases "à peine sèches: le *Fumeur,* la *Joueuse de guitare,* un *Portrait de Mme M . . . , une Jeune dame en 1866.* Le *Portrait de Mme M . . .* est une des meilleures pages de l'artiste; je devrais répéter ce que j'ai déjà dit: simplicité & justesse extrêmes, aspect clair & fin." The painting exhibited might well be one of several portraits of Suzanne Manet, since Zola may not have described *Madame Auguste Manet* as having a "light and fine appearance."

15. Pennell 1909.

16. Imperial International Exhibition 1909, 20–22, describes an exhibition of paintings in the context of the exhibition of domestic architecture. See also *Cambridge Independent Press* 1909, 7.

17. Coverage in the French press was brief: *Journal des débats* 1909, 1, mentions the painting by name; *Figaro* 1909, 3, refers to it as "un superbe portrait de Mme Manet mère."

18. Mew 1909, 433; *Times* 1909, 14.

19. Binyon 1909, 299.

20. *Manchester Courier* 1909, 10.

21. *Athenaeum* 1909, 263.

22. Rinder 1909, 118.

23. Fry 1909, 14.

24. Pennell 1909, 313.

25. Haskell 1951, 443.

26. Joseph Pennell to Isabella Stewart Gardner from 14 Buckingham Street, Stand, W.C., London, October 28, 1906, Isabella Stewart Gardner Museum, Boston.

27. Bernard Berenson to Isabella Stewart Gardner, March 30, 1909 (ARC.008326), in Berenson and Gardner 1987, 439.

28. *Boston Journal* 1910, 13.

29. Clay 1983, 24–25.

BIOGRAPHIES OF THE MANET FAMILY

1. Brombert 1997, 3.
2. Ibid., 3, 5; and Locke 2001, 45.
3. See Locke, 103–4, in this volume.
4. Brombert 1997, 6.
5. Locke 2001, 45.
6. Ibid., 45.
7. Ibid., 47–48.
8. See Brombert 1997, 8–13.
9. Proust 1913, 5.
10. This loophole allowed candidates an eased path to success on the competitive *concours;* see Brombert 1997, 14–15.

11. Wilson-Bareau 1991, 18.

12. Brombert 1997, 31–32, 38–40.

13. Brombert 1997, 40; and Rodary, 104–5, in this volume.

14. See Greenwald, 15–16, in this volume.

15. Locke 2001, 47.

16. Ibid., 48.

17. "Permettez-moi, en vous renvoyant la démission de M Manet. Rectifiée selon votre désir, de vous supplier de respecter la faiblesse de ce pauvre homme si mal-heureux! Si vous avez entendu, M le Minis-tre, le sanglot qui s'est échappé de sa poitrine, vu l'expression de douleur qui s'est peinte sur sa figure, lorsque avec tous les ménagements possibles, j'ai rempli la mission dont vous m'avez chargée. Vous en eussiez été touché aux larmes!" This information is quoted from the judicial *dossier* assigned to Auguste Manet, and studied by Locke in preparation for her book. The dossier is in the *dossiers de remplacement*, Archives Nationales, BB6II 276, Tribunal de première instance. The letter is summarized and cited in Locke 2001, 48nn41–42. Transcription from Locke, email, February 21, 2023.

18. Locke 2001, 48, 189n54.

19. Naissances, V3E N918, Archives de Paris, https://archives.paris.fr/. She was born February 11, 1811, in Paris. This corrects information in Locke 2001, 45, which was based on a secondary source.

20. "Bretigny-sur-Orge. Naissances, mariages, décès: registre d'état civil (1824–1832)," 4E/347, Archives Départementales, Essonne, https://archives.essonne.fr /ark:/28047/59lqhrp1gmkj/.

21. Mariages, V3E/M 392, Archives de Paris, https://archives.paris.fr/.

22. Décès, 1830 (Tours), Archives d'Indre-et -Loire, Décès, 1830–6NUM8/261/128, no. 552, https://archives.touraine.fr /ark:/37621/nfk2c89thpvj.

23. "Inventaire après décès de Mme Fournier, 12 mars 1851," Archives nationales, MC/ET/ XCVI/782. Thanks to Emmanuel Clause for making this document available.

24. Proust 1913, 3–4. According to the "Inven-taire après décès de Mme Fournier," he was still on active duty in Algeria in March 1851.

25. Flament 1928, 94–95.

26. Proust 1913, 3; and edited letter by Rodary in the Chronology, 122, in this volume.

27. "Inventaire après décès de Mme Fournier."

28. Leenhoff 1910, 12.

29. "Contrat de mariage d'Édouard Manet," Archives nationales, DMC/2022/1691. The full contract is reproduced in Rouart and Wildenstein 1975, vol. 1, 12.

30. Brombert 1996, 83–84, 135–36.

31. Chatté 1907, 5–6.

32. Wilson-Bareau and Degener 2003, 61–62.

33. Higonnet 1990, 170.

34. Ibid., 171; Décès, 1885, Archives de Paris, V4E 7322, p. 16.

35. Répertoires annuels d'inhumation, 1885, Archives de Paris, 1889 MTM_ RA18851889_01.

36. Suzanne "went to Paris in 1847 to pursue her musical studies at the Conservatoire, but [said], she never had a better teacher than her father." Ferdinand Leenhoff to Jacques Hartog, May 29, 1889, quoted in Van Kempen and Van De Beek 2014, 39.

37. First reported by Anton van Anrooy in *Impromptu* (1941); recent discoveries show it could be true. See Brussee, Lelie, and Scholcz 2011, 5–6.

38. Suzanne's father remained alone in Zaltbommel.

39. See Scott, 107n71, in this volume. One brother, Carolus Antonius, was not an artist. He served in the military and died prematurely.

40. "Suzanne Leenhoff, ineligible." Candidates and students: general file, lists established for admission and examinations 1817–1920. Candidates to piano classes (women), AN / A7/37/325/ page 226/ 10-11-1847 and AN / A7/37/325/ page 251/ 1-9-1848, French National Archives: National Conservatory of Music of Paris.

41. Suzanne probably first taught the painter's two younger brothers, and did not meet her future husband until his return from Rio in June 1849. Thera Coppens's hypothe-sis (Coppens 2022, 1216–23) that Suzanne met the Manets through Liszt's companion, Marie d'Agoult, seems unlikely. Manet met Émile Ollivier in Venice in 1853 and met d'Agoult at the marriage of Liszt and d'Agoult's daughter, Blandine, to Ollivier, in 1857.

42. Reconstituted vital record certificates, Archives de Paris, 5Mi1 734, f. 33.

43. The couple formalized this union after Auguste Manet's death in September 1862. Even a friend as close as Baudelaire was surprised by Suzanne's existence and Manet's impending marriage. See Green-wald, 14, 16, 22, in this volume.

44. In 1865 Manet congratulated Zacharie Astruc and his wife on having a child, add-ing: "We would like it to happen to us as well." See Hansen 2021, 132.

45. Mairet 1907, 287–89.

46. Ibid. Degas shows one of these reveries in fig. 45.

47. Proust 1913, 129.

48. Letter from Berthe Morisot to Edma Morisot Pontillon, no date, but presumably about 1883, Private Collection. See "Léon versus Julie" in Mathieu 2021, 23–24.

49. Suzanne Manet to Berthe Morisot, May 26, 1892, Musée Marmottan-Monet, Paris.

50. Jeanniot 1907, 844–60.

51. For the bequest from Morisot, see Beeny, 58, in this volume.

52. Proust to Suzanne, April 27, 1900: "Mr. Faure must have paid you once again, through his notary, the part of the annuity he granted you." Morgan Library & Museum, New York, MA 3950.

53. See Greenwald, 23–27, in this volume.

54. Locke 2001, 62.

55. Tabarant 1947, 17; and Mauner 2001, 123.

56. Tabarant 1947, 483.

57. Locke 2001, 119 and Kremnitzer, 65, in this volume.

58. Tabarant 1947, 481.

59. Duret 1902, 199; and Tabarant 1947, 481.

60. Eugenie Manet's will describes the "very tender, devoted care that he gave my poor Édouard during his two cruel months of suffering"; quoted in Mathieu 2022, 23. Léon describes Manet's final days in grue-some detail in a letter in the Tabarant Archive: Léon Leenhoff to "Chers Enfants," April 12, 1920, Vernon, France, Morgan Library & Museum, New York, 12041920, MA 3950.

61. Quoted in Wilson-Bareau 1991, 191.

62. See Rodary, 104, in this volume.

63. Tabarant 1947, 483.

64. Duret 1902, 205.

65. Leenhoff 1883. See catalogue notes for Fernand Lochard, Three albums of photo-graphs of the work of Édouard Manet, about 1883, Morgan Library & Museum, New York, MA 3950.1:1–3.

66. See Greenwald 24–27, 31, in this volume.

67. Suzanne Manet, "Carnet de Comptes: Autograph Notes, 1892–1900," Morgan Library & Museum, New York, notebook 2, MA 3950; and Tabarant 1947, 485–86.

68. In this volume, see Greenwald, 31; Beeny, 57, 60–61; and Mathieu 2022, 259–62.

69. See Scott, 114n148, in this volume.

70. Tabarant 1947, 483.

71. Suzanne's brother Ferdinand, a sculptor, learned engraving from his father-in-law, Alphonse François. Her brother Rudolf was a painter who posed for Manet. Her sister Martha married artist Jules Vibert; their son, Édouard Vibert, was also a painter who copied paintings by Manet as Suzanne sold them. Her sister Mathilde married sculptor Joseph Mezzara, whose parents, Thomas François Gaspard Mezzara and Marie Angélique Foulon, were painters.

72. *On the Beach (Sur la plage)*, 1873. Oil on canvas, 59 × 73 cm. Musée d'Orsay, Paris.

73. Drawings and pastels of the Longchamp racetrack may date to 1865, when Manet painted there. Two of these pastels were in the 1961 Berthe Morisot exhibition (Musée Jacquemart-André, Paris, numbers 178 and 179), both titled *Les courses* (whereabouts unknown). This was the first time Eugène's works appeared publicly.

74. Rouart 1959, 25–26.

75. Ibid., 81.

76. After her parents' deaths, Julie catalogued their artworks. She could not definitively attribute a number of colored pencil drawings to her mother or father. My thanks to Clément Rouart for showing them to me.

77. Monneret 1979, 24. Gustave was the first Manet brother to meet Monet and witnessed his 1870 marriage to Camille-Léonie Doncieux.

78. Rouart 1959, 113.

79. *Berthe Morisot et sa fille*, 1882. Oil on canvas, 73 × 60 cm. Whereabouts unknown.

80. Rouart 1959, 89.

81. Ibid., 100.

82. Ibid., 109.

83. Ibid., 105.

84. Ibid., 110.

85. See Mathieu 2022, 128–29.

86. Rouart 1959, 133.

87. Mathieu 2023, 74. See Eugène Manet, Journal 1885–1886, voyage en Holland Sept-Oct 1885, Notes et souvenirs de Gorey, Répertoire Général de mon Journal, 2021.1.3808, JM32, Musée Marmottan Monet, Paris. Thank you to Marianne Mathieu and Françoise Rouart for these references.

88. Patry 2018, 207.

89. Rouart 1959, 171.

90. "My grandmother has lived little in this property . . . as there was a part of the roof that needed to be redone, she had to rent it the first year to . . . pay for this work. She thought of settling there, at least in the summer with her husband who was in delicate health, after the departure of the tenants, but in 1892 my grandfather . . . died." Morisot's grandson Clément Rouart to the author, April 19, 1973.

91. Ives, Stein, and Steiner 1997, 111–12; and Amornpichetkul 1990, 62.

92. Cachin et al. 1983, 510; and Clairet, Montalant, and Rouart 1997.

93. Rouart 1959, 89.

94. Renard 1939, 71.

95. *The Lady with Fans*, 1873. Oil on canvas, 113 × 166.5 cm. Musée d'Orsay, Paris.

96. Rouart 1959, 122.

97. *Study for "Music in the Tuileries,"* 1862. Chinese ink wash on double sheet, 18 × 22.5 cm. Whereabouts unknown. See Rouart and Wildenstein 1975, vol. 1, 122.

98. *Berthe Morisot with a Bouquet of Violets*, 1872. Oil on canvas, 55.5 × 40.5 cm. Musée d'Orsay, Paris.

99. *Jeune femme en toilette de bal*, 1879. Oil on canvas, 71.5 × 54 cm. Musée d'Orsay, Paris.

100. Rouart 1959, 187.

101. Samuel Rodary, email to author, May 3, 2023.

102. Locke 2001, 56; Brombert 1997, 293; and Nord 1989, 450.

103. Locke 2001, 56; and Brombert 1997, 287–90, 293.

104. Nord 1989, 450.

105. Rouart 1987, 140. Obituaries in *La Justice*, December 25, 1884, and *Le Radical*, December 27, 1884, list his occupation as *"inspecteur général des services administratifs."* Gustave seems to have held many administrative titles throughout his career.

106. Cachin et al. 1983, 192. The 1983 catalogue entry for the work in Cachin, 1983, written by Charles Moffett, refers to a letter from Édouard Manet's grandnephew Denis Rouart, May 9, 1961, in which he informed the Metropolitan Museum of Art "that it is absolutely certain" it was Gustave Manet who posed, and that Berthe Morisot would also always say as such.

107. Locke 2001, 55. Among the conflicting accounts, Nancy Locke is preferential to Proust, and references Adolphe Tabarant, who claimed it was Gustave, and Étienne Moreau-Nélaton, who said it was Eugène.

108. Stevens 2012, 72; Rouart 1987, 30–31; and Leenhoff documents, Tabarant Archives, J. Pierpont Morgan Library, New York, transcribed in De Medeiros 2006, 142–43.

109. Rouart 1987, 141.

110. Monneret 1979, 24. See Scott in this volume, 107–8.

111. Brombert 1997, 287.

112. Léon Leenhoff, December 4, 1920, Morgan Library & Museum, New York, transcribed in De Medeiros 2006, 72: "Ma mère et moi nous étions dans la salle à manger où Gustave venait nous donner à chaque instant les nouvelles de l'opération."

113. Brombert 1997, 452–53.

114. Rouart 1987, 118–20.

115. De Medeiros 2006, 61; and Morris 2018, 4. Gustave's exact ailment is not currently known, but his move to Menton suggests he might have had tuberculosis. Menton had become a popular destination for tuberculosis patients.

116. Rouart 1987, 133, and Locke 2001, 54.

117. Rouart 1987, 140–41.

118. Jules Dejouy was born on March 7, 1815. Naissances, N 1810–1819, Archives municipales de Gennevilliers, https://archives.ville-gennevilliers.fr/.

119. Mariages, M 1810–1819, Archives municipales de Gennevilliers, at https://archives.ville-gennevilliers.fr/.

120. Mariages, V3E/M 272, Archives de Paris, https://archives.paris.fr/.

121. Roy 1849, 4, and DQ8 02628, Archives de Paris, https://archives.paris.fr/.

122. Prestation de serment des avocats, Archives de Paris, D7U9 7.

123. *Almanach 1850*, 357, 892, 895. The *Cours d'appel* were called "Cours royales" during monarchies and "Cours impériales" during periods of empire.

124. Branlard 2010, 67.

125. *Le Droit 1894*, 246; and Leymarie 1893, 69.

126. Cour d'appel de Paris, Arrêts civils, D1U9, Archives de Paris.

127. Leymarie 1893, 69.

128. Ibid., 68.

129. Zola 2003, 404–13.

130. Ibid., 404–5, folio 249.

131. Ibid., 394–95; see also Lethbridge 2010, 231–40.

132. Zola 2003, 408–9.

133. The case is summarized in *Annuaire encyclopédique 1872*, 1967–68. For Dejouy's appeals, see Guillemet contre Préfet de la Seine 1865, 184–86; Guillemet contre Ville de Paris 1868, 134–35, D1U9 218, Archives de Paris.

134. Barreau de Strasbourg 1931, 7.

135. Rouart 1950, 171.

136. Décès, V4E 8032, no. 165, Archives de Paris, https://archives.paris.fr/.

137. *Le Droit 1894*, 246.

138. Huisman 1963, 26; Rodary, 2023.

139. Patry, Wilhelm, and Patin 2002, 344.

140. I am grateful to the artist's son Clément Rouart and his wife, Victoria, who, in the early 1970s, showed me copies of works by other artists made by Julie Manet when she was young.

141. The journal, J. Manet 1979, was first published thirteen years after Julie's death. The most recent English-language edition is Roberts 2017.

142. Roberts 2017, 126.

143. Amornpichetkul 1990, 368.

144. Ambroise Vollard planned to publish the first catalogue raisonné but abandoned the project in 1931; see Rabinow 2006, 288. The first catalogue raisonné was Angoulvent 1933 followed by Bataille and Wildenstein 1961.

145. Forreau 1925; and Rouart 1941.

146. Valéry, 1941. Rouart 1950. The first English-language edition, Rouart 1957, was translated by Betty W. Hubbard.

147. Conservations with Clément Rouart 1975 and 1980.

148. Roberts 2017, 163.

149. Édouard Manet, *La Dame aux éventails*, 1873. Oil on canvas, 113 × 166.5 cm. Musée d'Orsay, Paris. See Rouart 1959, 122.

150. Édouard Manet, *Portrait de Berthe Morisot étendue*, 1973. Oil on canvas, 26 × 34 cm. Musée Marmottan Monet, Paris. Thanks to Françoise Rouart for reminding me of this.

151. I am grateful to Clément Rouart who, in 1973, first told me about this exhibition he organized. Françoise Rouart told me about two other solo exhibitions he organized of paintings by Ernest Rouart and another of paintings by his friend Jean Simian, both in 1955. The pamphlet for Julie's exhibition includes an essay by Louis Rouart: *Exposition Julie Manet (Madame Ernest Rouart), Peintures & Aquarelles*, May 20 to June 3, 1955, Atelier E. Rouart, 40, rue Paul Valéry, Paris-XVI.

152. Roberts 2017, 78.

153. Édouard Manet, *Madame Édouard Manet*, 1873. Pastel, 61 × 49 cm. Toledo Museum of Art, Ohio.

154. Claude Monet, *Water Lilies*, 1914–17. Oil on canvas, 130 × 153 cm. Musée Marmottan Monet, Paris.

155. See Mathieu 2022, 255–83.

156. Conversation with François Valéry, 1998.

157. Ernest Rouart's copy is 160.5 × 192.6 cm and Mantegna's original is 160 × 192 cm. In 1975 Rouart's copy was donated to the Musée du Louvre by his son Clément. In 1986 the painting was assigned to the Musée d'Orsay (RF 1975 8). In the Louvre, Rouart also made a small copy of Mantegna's *Virgin of Victory*, 1897. Oil on wood, 27 × 21.6 cm. Private collection.

158. Rouart-Valéry 1960, 60.

159. Rabinow 2006, 288

160. Edma Morisot, *In the Forest*, about 1864–67. Oil on canvas, 65 × 92 cm. Whereabouts unknown (sold, Maître Frédéric Lefranc, Eurl Auxerre Enchéres, February 7, 2021, location unknown). Henri Rouart may have acquired Edma's painting after the marriage of Ernest and Julie, when he and Edma would have frequently see each other when visiting them.

161. See Dormoy 1932, 257–59.

162. In 1943, a year after the artist's death, Ernest Rouart's family donated this Corot to the Louvre in his memory. I am grateful to the artist's granddaughter Françoise Rouart for sharing these details and other family information with me.

163. I am grateful to the artist's granddaughter Françoise Rouart for sharing these details with me.

164. Clément Rouart to author, summer 1975. The Morisot painting is *Jeune femme remettantant son patin*, 1879. Oil on canvas, 46 × 55 cm. Private collection.

165. Given its size and importance, we have decided to include *Madame Édouard Manet on a Blue Sofa* in this list even though it is a pastel.

166. *The Fifer*, in particular, has been described as a blend of models, of which Léon is one.

167. Gustave Manet is noted as the model in Rouart and Wildenstein 1975, but there are differing accounts, one being that Edouard's younger brothers served as the model and the figure in the painting is a composite of both.

CHRONOLOGY OF FAMILY EVENTS, 1832–1927

1. Tabarant 1931, 9; and Brombert 1997, 4, 458n1.
2. Brombert 1997, 5, 458n1.
3. Brombert 1997, 7; and Proust 1913, 5.
4. Morreau-Nélaton 1926, vol. 1, 7; and Brombert 1997, 15.
5. Meier-Graefe 1912, 11–12; and Cachin et al. 1983, 504.
6. Manet 1928, 61–65.
7. Ibid., 66–67.
8. Leenhoff 1900–1910, 71–72.
9. Ibid., 71; and Locke 2001, 47.
10. Reff 1964, 556; and Cachin et al. 1983, 504.
11. Tabarant 1947, 480–85; and Brombert 1996, 136–37, 466n28.
12. Rijksmuseum register cited in Verbeek 1958, 64; and Chu 1972, 10.
13. Ollivier 1961, 168.
14. Rouart 1987, ix.
15. Morgan Library & Museum, New York, MA 3950 (40).
16. Brombert 1997, 51.
17. Proust 1913, 31; and Cars, Guégan, and Pludermacher 2023, 229n15.
18. Cars, Guégan, and Pludermacher 2023, 229n18.
19. Locke 2001, 48, 189nn41–42.
20. Proust 1897, 168; Baudelaire 1975, 328–31; Cachin et al. 1983, 506; and Cars, Guégan, and Pludermacher 2023, 252.
21. Locke 2001, 48, 189n43.
22. Moreau-Nelaton 1926, vol. 1, 30; and Cachin et al. 1983, 506.
23. Locke 2001, 48, 189n54.
24. Baudelaire 1973, vol. 2, 296.
25. Locke 2001, 78, 194n156.
26. Brombert 1996, 135, 137–38, 466n27, transcribed in Rouart and Wildenstein 1975, vol. 1, 12–13.
27. Leenhoff 1900–1910, 72; Tabarant 1947, 80; Cachin et al. 1983, 508; Brombert 1997, 136; and Locke 2001, 55, 118–19, 123, 190n70.
28. Tabarant 1931, 128; and Cachin et al. 1983, 508.
29. Osenat 2018.
30. A traditional province of France, now covered by the Sarthe and Mayenne Departments.
31. Manet to Baudelaire, September 24, 1865, Pichois 1973, p. 236. "Lettres d'Édouard Manet sur son voyage en Espagne," *Arts* (March 16, 1945); and Duret 1902, 35–36.
32. Stevens et al. 2012, 168.
33. Onet to Bazille, May 20, 1867; see Rouart and Wildenstein 1975, vol. 1, 423. Zola to Valabregue, May 29, 1867; see Cars, Guégan, and Pludermacher 2023, 234.
34. Proust 1897, 175 quoted in Cachin et al. 1983, 510. On these regular trips, see Brombert 1997, 204, 271.
35. Eugénie Manet to Henri Fantin-Latour, March 2, 1870, Dossier VII, 1997-A-660, Fondation Custodia, Paris.
36. Moreau-Nelaton 1926, vol. 1, 121; Wilson 1978, no. 107; and Cachin et al. 1983, 512.
37. Morgan Library & Museum, New York, MA 3408 (12).
38. Ibid. (14).
39. Ibid. (22).
40. Moreau-Nelaton 1926, vol. 1, 128; and Cachin et al. 1983, 512.
41. Tabarant 1947, 187; Wilson 1978, no. 107; and Stevens et al. 2012, 171.
42. Locke 2001, 61–2 as found in Cuno and Kaak 2004, 34n31.
43. Leenhoff 1900–1910, 130–31. Historical currency conversion from https://www.historicalstatistics.org/Currencyconverter.html.
44. Verbeek 1958, 64; and Stevens et al. 2012, 172.
45. Rouart 1987, 93.
46. Ibid., 95.
47. Cachin et al. 1983, 514.
48. Bazire 1884, 103; Cachin 1983, 515; and Brombert 1996, 398.
49. Tabarant 1947, 319; Cachin et al. 1983, 515; and Stevens et al. 2012, 174. It is unclear where Léon was living at the time but likely in an apartment below one of Manet's studios.
50. Édouard Manet to Henri Fantin-Latour, Paris, June 1878, Dossier VII, 1997-A-644, Fondation Custodia, Paris.
51. Rouart 1987, x.
52. Tabarant 1947, 326; and Wilson-Bareau 2012.
53. Aguttes 2021.
54. Proust 1913, 129; Cachin et al. 1983, 516; and Wilson-Bareau 1995, 242.
55. Manet, Paris, to Berthe Morisot, December 19, 1881, Private collection. Transcribed at Aristophil sale (Aguttes), April 1, 2019.
56. Bazire 1884, 108; Proust 1887, 313; Duret 1902, 152–53; Cachin et al. 1983, 517; and Stevens et al. 2012, 175.
57. Rouart and Wildenstein 1975, vol. 1, 25; and Cachin et al. 1983, 517.

58. Bazire 1884, 121; Cachin et al. 1983, 517; De Medieros 2006, 72; and Stevens et al. 2012, 175.

59. Cachin et al. 1983, 517.

60. "The pallbearers [were] Antonin Proust, Émile Zola, Philippe Burty, Alfred Stevens, Duret, Claude Monet," Le Figaro, May 4, 1883; Cachin et al. 1983, 517; and Brombert 1997, 127.

61. Higonnet 1990, 171.

62. Bataille 1983, 129; Rouart 1987, x; and Stevens et al. 2012, 175.

63. Duret 1902, 201–12; Stevens et al. 2012, 175; and Reff 2020, vol. 1, 234, 236, 357, 359.

64. "Gustave Manet" (genealogical entry), Geneanet.org, https://gw.geneanet.org/pierfit?lang=en&n=manet&oc=0&p=gustave.

65. Locke 2001, 54.

66. See Scott, 108, in this volume.

67. Rouart 1987, 212.

68. "Carolus Antonius Leenhoff" (genealogical entry), Geneanet.org, https://gw.geneanet.org/titeufs6?lang=en&n=leenhoff&oc=0&p=carolus+antonius.

69. See Rodary, 104, in this volume.

70. Tabarant 1947, 17, 482; and Locke 2001, 62, 191n97.

71. See Greenwald, 106, in this volume.

PAINTINGS

1. Its first loan since Gardner's acquisition was in 2023; Cars, Guégan, and Pludermacher 2023, 3.

2. Swicklick 1993.

3. See Locke, 89, in this volume.

4. Rouart 1987, 25.

5. Proust 1913, 101.

6. The authors wish to thank Rhona MacBeth, Eijk and Rose-Marie van Otterloo Conservator and Head of Paintings Conservation, Museum of Fine Arts, Boston, for undertaking the x-radiograph of the painting.

7. Lobstein 2012, 43, suggests it could be a "picture of the deceased," but Chatté's description (see later in the essay) says otherwise. As Locke pointed out in a gathering at the Gardner in November 2022, the fact that Auguste was paralyzed by the time he could have sat for a carte de visite makes it less likely he had his picture taken.

8. For an introduction to Manet's working methods, see Wilson-Bareau 1986, i–98.

9. See Locke, 89, in this volume.

10. Chatté, 6. Translated by D. Greenwald.

11. They are Le Fumeur (Minneapolis Institute of Art), The Guitar Player (Hill-Stead Museum, Farmington, Conn.), and Young Lady in 1866 (Metropolitan Museum of Art, New York).

12. Chatté 1907, 7. Translated by D. Greenwald.

13. Isolde Pludermacher first suggested this possibility at a meeting in Paris in October 2022.

14. See "Notes sur la vie de Manet," Tabarant archive, Morgan Library & Museum, New York, MA 3950.

15. Chatté 1907, 7.

16. See provenance in this entry.

17. As number 14, Portrait de Madame M . . .

18. Chatté 1907, 7.

19. See Chu 1972, 112n1.

20. Wilson-Bareau 2003, 229–34.

21. Cachin et al. 1983, 509.

22. On Manet as a copyist, see Wilson-Bareau, 41, and Kremnitzer in this volume, 66. His request to copy the painting then known as Réunion de portraits (Gathering of Portraits) is missing. See Registre des cartes d'artistes, no. 149, 125, Archives des Musees Nationaux, https://www.siv.archives-nationales.culture.gouv.fr/siv/media/FRAN_IR_054378/c1i5fz1k6jso--1b1zneczk9k7d/FRAN_0374_0473_L; and Tinterow and Lacambre 2003, 205–9, 388.

23. Jacques-Emile Blanche, April 17, [1940], in curatorial file for Monk in Prayer (Museum of Fine Arts, Boston); see Tinterow and Lacambre 2003, 485n5. Beatrice Farwell (1981, 58–59) was the first art historian to suggest that Spanish Cavaliers and Spanish Studio were fragments of a larger work.

24. Chéramy also owned Manet's copy after Delacroix's The Barque of Dante (1854–58, Musée de Beaux-Arts, Lyon).

25. Nancy Locke points to this comparison in Locke 2001, 119.

26. See Kreminitzer, 65–72, in this volume.

27. Paul Chéramy, the Manet family lawyer whose address appears in Manet's notebook, purchased the painting directly from the artist; see Tinterow and Lacambre 2003, 485 n 1. Sold in the Chéramy sale, Paris, May 5–7, 1908, no. 219.

28. Étienne Moreau-Nélaton, "Catalogue général, manuscrit de l'oeuvre d'Édouard Manet: peinture et pastels," 1925–26, Bibliothèque Nationale de France, Paris, Département des Estampes et de la Photographie. Paris, 4-Z-89. https://gallica.bnf.fr/ark:/12148/btv1b52501604r.

29. Armstrong 2002, 17.

30. Locke 1991, 252.

31. Ibid., 249.

32. Ibid.

33. De Leiris 1964, 402.

34. The statue is damaged and missing its head. Previously, two different heads—including one of Aristotle—had been attached to the torso, but today the statue is shown without a replacement head. For an illustration of how it likely looked in Manet's time, see de Clarac 1832–34, pl. 327.

35. Proust 1897, 168; and Greenwald, 151, in this volume.

36. Couture 1867, 32.

37. The sketches are discussed in Wilson-Bareau, 41–44, in this volume.

38. Ibid.

39. Willis 2014, 48.

40. Penny 2008, 466.

41. Manet had been issued a carte de travail for the Cabinet d'Estampes (the print collection) on November 28, 1858. The discovery of this carte de travail was first published by Reff 1964, 552–59. Then called the Bibliothèque Impériale.

42. Juliet Wilson-Bareau first indicated this link in an email, October 2023. For comprehensive information about The Gypsies, see Groom and Westerby 2017, cat. no. 14.

43. Reconstructing the provenance for this painting remains a work in progress; through exhibition and study we hope to learn more about its path after the René De Gas sale and before its 2022 sale.

44. There is almost no literature about this painting apart from its appearance in the 1927 and 2022 sale catalogues. This is the first time this painting has been publicly exhibited and studied in the context of Manet's life and work.

45. Wilson-Bareau 1986, 42–43.

46. Cachin et al. 1983, 86–87; and ibid., 26–41.

47. See Tucker 1998; Fried 1996, particularly 293–97; Locke 2001 for a Freudian approach; and Armstrong, 2002, 150–55, as part of a chapter on Victorine's representation and the mutability of personhood.

48. For an example of the earlier attribution, see Haskell 1971. For later attribution, see Holberton 1993.

49. Wilson-Bareau 1986, 37–40 attributes this reversal to Manet's use of print sources, including prints after the Concert champêtre.

50. Wilson-Bareau 1986, 39, states, the sketch is a "direct predecessor" to the Le Déjeuner sur l'herbe.

51. Proust 1897, 171; translated by D. Greenwald.

52. Cachin et al. 1983, 166.

53. Tabarant 1947, 34.

54. It seems to first be called Fishing in Duret's 1902 publication; it is unclear if Duret or someone else—possibly Paul Durand-Ruel or Gaston-Alexandre Camentron—applied the title.

55. Another Rubens painting, sometimes called Pastoral Landscape with Rainbow (Musée des Beaux-Arts, Valenciennes), was in the Musée du Louvre until 1957.

56. Reff 1970, 457, points out that Manet could have seen engravings of both Rubens landscapes in Blanc 1864.

57. Nevitt 1997, 167.

58. Cachin et al. 1983, 72.

59. Baudelaire 1947–53, vol. 4, 194.

60. For information about Léon, see Greenwald, 105–6, in this volume.

61. Cachin et al. 1983, 271.

62. Calouste Gulbenkian Museum 2022; and Tate 2023.

63. Coue and Mödersheim 2002–3.

64. Locke 2001, 114–15, 118–19.

65. Locke 2001, 55, 118–19, 123, and Brombert 1997, 89 and 136. His uncles Eugène Manet and Ferdinand Leenhoff took him to Marc-Dastès, a school located in the Batignolles. Léon recalls Édouard taking him out every Thursday and Sunday.

66. Tabarant 1931 in De Medeiros 2002, 177.

67. *Chronique des Arts 1867*: 122.

68. Locke 2001, 62; and Stevens 2012, 74.

69. In contrast, Cachin et al. 1983, 268–70, describes Manet's treatment as "revers[ing] the emphasis, giving the subject an unprecedented immediacy, and removing all trace of sentimentality."

70. Mauner 2000, 54–55.

71. Alpers 1983, 91.

72. Baudelaire 1863, 403.

73. Étienne Joseph Théophile Thoré (Théophile Thoré-Bürger) to Édouard Manet, Paris, [April/May 15, 1867], MS Whistler B212 in MacDonald 2003-10.

74. For an introduction to Thoré-Burger as an art collector see Jowell 2003.

75. For the friendship between Manet and Whistler see Singletary, 2017, 74-99.

76. Whistler acknowledges that Manet forwarded Thoré-Burger's letter in James Abbott MacNeil Whistler, London, to Henri Fantin-Latour, Paris, [May/June 1867], Library of Congress, Manuscript Division, Pennell-Whistler Collection, PWC 1/33/27 in MacDonald 2003-10.

77. The most comprehensive consideration of the relationship between the paintings is Singletary 2017, 74-80; the connection between the two canvases also appears in Stevens et al. 2012, 178. The clock is mentioned in Stevens et al. 2012, 178, and Cachin 1983, 287.

78. See Beeny, 58, and Pludermacher, 75–77, in this volume.

79. See Rodary, 175, in this volume; Singletary 2017, 80–83.

80. Nielsen 2017, 11–12.

81. Sandberg 1964, 500–503, suggests this connection; for Thoré-Burger's acquisition of *The Concert* see Jowell 2003, 91.

Gardner and Whistler were also friends. On this friendship see Chong 2003, 196–201.

82. Some scholars have linked this painting to other Dutch sources, specifically a work by Gabriel Metsu; see Cachin 1983, 286–87, and Stevens et al. 2012, 178.

83. Moreau-Nélaton 1926, vol. 1, 121; and Édouard Manet to Eva Gonzalès, September 10, 1870, Paris, reproduced in Rodary 2014, 24–25.

84. See Greenwald, 27–28, in this volume.

85. Charles S. Moffett, "128. Interior at Arcachon," in Cachin and Moffett 1983, 332.

86. Leenhoff 1883, Register no. 160. In his notes in the register, Léon states he is holding as a cigarette.

87. Édouard Manet to Suzanne Manet, November 23, 1870, Paris, reproduced in Rodary 2014, 75.75. Translated by D. Greenwald.

88. The archival record surrounding this painting is complicated. Manet never exhibited the work during his lifetime, and its first appearance in the archive is in the register of works that Léon Leenhoff created after Manet died and the corresponding Lochard photographs. In the register, it appears as 160, but in the Lochard photographs, it appears under a linked but atypical number, 160 bis. (The "bis" distinction in French is used either to mean "encore" in a musical setting or for addresses that are distinct from a main street address, i.e., 160a rather than 160.) The bis could refer to the fact that a copy of the painting was made or that Léon, who specifically noted the existence of the watercolor in his register, knew that the drawing was a more complete stage of the work than the painting (Leenhoff 1883, 160).

89. They moved in together in 1866.

90. I would like to thank Bruno Mottin for letting me consult his report on *La Lecture*, which he studied in 2012 at the Centre de Recherche et de Restauration des Musées de France (File F 3778).

91. Javel 1880, 1–2.

92. Cachin et al. 1983, 259.

93. "Bertrand Lavier: 'The Reading' by Édouard Manet," Musée d'Orsay, June 4, 2021, Youtube video, https://www.youtube.com/watch?v=DjFvcLpQTik.

94. Tabarant 1935, 35.

95. Léon Leenhoff noted that Manet's idea for this picture came from croquet games in the beach club garden at Boulogne-sur-Mer. See Leenhoff 1883, folio 16.

96. *The Croquet Party* was based on at least ten watercolor and pencil studies, probably made in 1871, suggesting it was carefully composed in the studio rather than en plein air. See Simon Kelly in Marcereau DeGalan 2021, n18. There are no underdrawings in the composition, but rather passages of wet-into-wet, as well as wet-into-dry brushwork. He likely allowed portions of the canvas to dry before adding elements. For technical information see Diana M. Jaskierny in ibid.

97. A popular guidebook noted, "The managing director [of the beach club] converses freely in both the French and English languages." The guidebook included ads from local purveyors selling English books and renting equipment for English games, including croquet. See Merridew 1874, 70–71.

98. Manet's interest in London as a venue for his work began in the 1860s; see Spencer 1991, 228nn7–8, 231n36. In June 1871 the Paris-based dealer Paul Durand-Ruel, who moved to London during the Franco-Prussian War, bought several artworks from Manet's friends, and exhibited work by Manet. However, he had to wait until 1872 for Durand-Ruel to purchase more than twenty-six paintings (not including *Croquet Party*). See Zarobell 2015, 78, 82, 85–86.

99. Proust 1913, 37: "dans le cercle des amis de Manet, au premier rang desquels était Paul Roudier qui l'accompagnait partout, aux jeudis de son père et de sa mère et aux vendredis du café Guerbois."

100. See Greenwald, 23–27, in this volume.

101. Heath 1874, 9.

102. This print first appeared in *Punch, or the London Charivari*, August 17, 1861, as an etching. Thomas Agnew and Sons Ltd., English, printed and sold it as a mounted chromolithograph in 1865.

103. A black and white animal recalls Manet's etchings of black and white rooftop cats for the cover of Champfleury's *Les Chats*. See Champfleury 1869, 35; and Rubin 2010, 292.

104. In heraldry, these are referred to as leopards.

105. Including flags and the seaside setting with well-dressed individuals echoes Claude Monet's *Garden at Sainte-Adresse* (1867; Metropolitan Museum of Art) that Manet saw in Fréderic Bazille's studio four or five years earlier.

106. See Collins 1978, 112, for the connection between Léon in Manet's *Luncheon in the Studio*, 1868, and the cat in that painting.

107. Paint extends beneath the croquet balls, wicket, and dogs, confirming these elements were added later in the painting process. See Jaskierny, "Édouard Manet, *The Croquet Party*, 1871," technical entry.

French painter James Tissot (1836–1902), whom Manet befriended in England, included numerous dogs in his work from the mid-1860s and 1870s including *Croquet* (about 1876, The Art Gallery of Hamilton, Ontario). Manet recognized the popularity of dogs and painted several "portraits" of them in the mid-1870s. See *Tama, The Japanese Dog* (about 1875, National Gallery of Art, Washington).

108. See Distel et al. 1994, 42–43.
109. There are further explanatory notes on the provenance in Ivey 2021.
110. The author would like to thank Marianne Mathieu, Françoise Rouart, and Charles Stuckey.
111. See Henri Fantin-Latour's *Homage to Delacroix*, 1864, oil on canvas, 160 × 250 cm, Musée d'Orsay, Paris, exhibited in 1864 Salon, and *Édouard Manet*, 1867, oil on canvas, 117.5 × 90 cm, Art Institute of Chicago, exhibited in 1867 Salon.
112. Rouart 1959, 21.
113. *Berthe Morisot with a Fan,* 1872, oil on canvas, 60 × 45 cm, and *Berthe Morisot with a Bouquet of Violets,* 1872, oil on canvas, 55 × 38 cm, both in the Musée d'Orsay.
114. *Portrait of Berthe Morisot Reclining,* 1873, oil on canvas, 26 × 34 cm, Musée Marmottan Monet, Paris, and *Portrait of Berthe Morisot,* 1874, oil on canvas, 61 × 50 cm, Musée d'Orsay.
115. *Berthe Morisot with a Bouquet of Violets,* 1872, oil on canvas, 55 × 38 cm, Musée d'Orsay.
116. *Portrait of Berthe Morisot in Mourning,* 1874, oil on canvas, 61 × 50 cm, private collection. Degas acquired the painting in 1897.
117. Roberts 2017, 160.
118. For information on Edma Morisot's paintings, see Meissner 2021.
119. Rouart 1959, 39.
120. Ibid., 44.
121. Ibid., 39.
122. Ibid., 39.
123. *In the Garden,* 1870, oil on canvas, 43 × 55 cm, Shelburne Museum. The painting also shows Edma's brother, Tiburce, and her infant daughter, Jeanne Pontillon.
124. Rouart 1959, 40.
125. *Cache-cache,* 1873, oil on canvas, 45 × 55 cm, private collection.
126. Rouart 1959, 108.
127. Ibid., 116.
128. Duret 1902, no. 106; Tabarant 1947, 129–130; Rouart and Wildenstein 1975, 1, no. 117.
129. See Asher Ethan Miller in Baum, Bayer, and Wagstaff 2016, 299.
130. Fernand Lochard, photographs of the works of Édouard Manet, The Morgan Library & Museum, New York, MA 3950, vol. 3, f. 59.
131. See Greenwald, 31, in this volume.
132. See, in particular, Tabarant 1947, 357, 524.
133. Catalogue *L'omnibus de Corinthe*, Librairie Pierre Saunier, Paris, 20, rue de Savoie, lot 131.
134. Quoted in Mathieu, 2022, 259.
135. Bill Scott, private e-mail, February 27, 2023.
136. Julie Manet, *Journal,* February 7, 1899.
137. Martha de Fels 1929 cited in Stuckey 1983, 159–177, 239–241.
138. Julie Manet, *Journal,* April 22, 1899.
139. *Algemeen Handelsblad* 1932; Paris 1932, 57–58.
140. Friedrich 1928, 7; and Westheim 1928, 7.
141. Witthaus 1930, 2.
142. According to museum conservator Adam Webster (personal communication, May 9, 2023), cerulean pigment was used for the blue cover, although cobalt blue can be found in the work as a whole.
143. Jedlicka 1941, 287, discusses the color of the primed canvas.
144. Scheffler 1925, 72.
145. Proust 1897, 179–80.

Bibliography

Aguttes 2021
"Lot 145," in *Les collections Aristophil. De Cranach à Picasso*. Aguttes, Neuilly-sur-Seine (September 23, 2021). https://www.aguttes.com /en/lot/117506/15859146-manet-Édouard -18321883las-e-masearch=&.

Allan, Beeny, and Groom 2019
Allan, Scott, et al., eds. *Manet and Modern Beauty: The Artist's Last Years*. Exh. cat. Getty Center. Los Angeles, 2019.

Alexandre 1918
Alexandre, A. "Essai sur Monsieur Degas." *Les Arts* 166 (1918): 2–24.

Alexis 1879
Alexis, Paul. "Manet." *Le Voltaire*, July 25, 1879.

Algemeen Handelsblad 1932
"Twee Tentoonstellingen van Beteekenis." *Algemeen Handelsblad*, July 1, 1932.

Almanach 1850
Almanach national: annuaire de la République française pour 1848–1849–1850. Paris, 1850.

Alpers 1983
Alpers, Svetlana. *The Art of Describing: Dutch Art in the Seventeenth Century*. Chicago, 1983.

Amornpichetkul 1990
Amornpichetkul, Chittima. "Berthe Morisot: A Study of Her Development from 1864 to 1886." Ph.D. diss. Brown University, Providence, 1990.

Angoulvent 1933
Angoulvent, Monique. *Berthe Morisot*. Paris, 1933.

Annuaire encyclopédique 1872
Annuaire encyclopédique: politique, économie sociale, statistique, administration, sciences, littérature, beaux-arts, agriculture, commerce, industrie. Paris, 1872.

Architect 1877
"Paris Studios: M. Manet's." *Architect* 18 (December 1, 1877).

Armstrong 2002
Armstrong, Carol M. *Manet Manette*. London, 2002.

Athenaeum 1909
"'Fair Women' at the New Gallery," *The Athenaeum* 4244 (February 27, 1909): 263.

Augé et al. 1999
Augé, Jean-Louis, et al. *Velázquez et la France: la découverte de la Velázquez par les peintres française*. Exh. cat. Musée Goya. Castres, 1999.

Avenue de l'Alma 1867
Catalogue des tableaux de M. Édouard Manet exposés Avenue de l'Alma en 1867. Exh. cat. Avenue De l'Alma. Paris, 1867.

Barreau de Strasbourg 1931
Ordre des Avocats du Barreau de Strasbourg. *Textes relatifs à l'exercice de la profession d'avocat*. Strasbourg, 1931.

Bataille 1983
Bataille, Georges. *Manet*. Geneva, 1983.

Bataille and Wildenstein 1961
Bataille, Marie-Louise, and Georges Wildenstein. *Berthe Morisot: catalogue des peintures, pastels et aquarelles*. Paris: Les Beaux-Arts, 1961.

Baudelaire 1862
Baudelaire, Charles. "L'eau-forte est à la mode." *La Revue anecdotique* (April 15, 1862): 169–171.

Baudelaire 1863
Baudelaire, Charles. "The Painter of Modern Life." In *Selected Writings on Art and Literature*. Translated by P. E. Charvet. Paris, 1863. Reprint, London, 1972.

Baudelaire 1887
Baudelaire, Charles. *Oeuvres posthumes et correspondances inédites*. Paris, 1887.

Baudelaire 1947–53
Baudelaire, Charles. Correspondance générale, 6 vols. Edited by Jacques Crépet. Paris, 1947–53.

Baudelaire 1981
Baudelaire, Charles. *Art in Paris, 1845–1862: Salons and Other Exhibitions*. Translated and edited by Jonathan Mayne. Oxford, 1981.

Baum, Bayer, and Wagstaff 2016
Baum, Kelly, Andrea Bayer, and Sheena Wagstaff, eds. *Unfinished: Thoughts Left Visible*. Exh. cat. Metropolitan Museum of Art. New York, 2016.

Bazin 1932
Bazin, Germain. "Manet et la tradition." *L'Amour de l'art* 13 (May 1932): 153–55.

Bazire 1884
Bazire, Edmond. *Manet*. Paris, 1884.

Beeny 2018
Beeny, Emily A. "Manet's Boucher." *Metropolitan Museum Journal* 53, no. 1 (2018): 66–81.

Beeny 2019a
Beeny, Emily A. "Evidence of Tracing in Manet's Late Watercolors." *Burlington Magazine* 161, no. 1401 (2019): 1002–11.

Beeny 2019b
Beeny, Emily A. "Manet and the Eighteenth Century." In Allan, Beeny, and Groom 2019: 89–112.

Berenson and Gardner 1987
Berenson, Bernard. *The Letters of Bernard Berenson and Isabella Stewart Gardner, 1887–1924*. Edited by Rollin van N. Hadley. Boston, 1987.

Binyon 1909
Binyon, Lawrence. "Fair Women at the New Gallery." *Saturday Review* (March 6, 1909): 299–300.

Blanc 1864
Blanc, Charles. *Histoire des peintres de toutes les écoles. École flamande*. Paris, 1864.

Blanche 1912
Blanche, Jacques-Émile. *Essais et portraits*. Paris, 1912.

Blanche 1924
Blanche, Jacques-Émile. *Manet*. Paris, 1924.

Bocher 1876
Bocher, Emannuel. *Les gravures françaises du XVIIIe siècle; ou, Catalogue raisonné des estampes, eaux-fortes pièces en couleur, au bistre et au lavis, de 1700 a 1800*. Vol. 3, *Jean-Baptiste Siméon Chardin*. Paris, 1876.

Bodelson 1968
Bodelson, Maret. "Early Impressionist Sales 1874–94 in the Light of Some Unpublished 'Procès-Verbaux.'" *Burlington Magazine* 110, no. 783 (1968): 330–49.

Boggs 1962
Boggs, Jean Sutherland. *Portraits by Degas*. Berkeley, 1962.

Boggs et al. 1988
Boggs, Jean Sutherland, et al., eds. *Degas, 1834–1917*. Exh. cat. Metropolitan Museum of Art. New York, 1988.

Boston Journal 1910
"200 Visit Museum of Mrs J. L. Gardner," *Boston Journal* (March 30, 1910): 13.

Branlard 2010
Branlard, Jean-Paul. *L'essentiel de l'organisation judiciaire en France*, 3rd ed. Paris, 2010.

Brettell and Pissarro 2007
Brettell, Richard R., and Joachim Pissarro, eds. *Manet to Matisse: Impressionist Masters from the Marion and Henry Bloch Collection.* Exh. cat. Nelson-Atkins Museum of Art, Kansas City, MO. Seattle, 2007.

Brombert 1997
Brombert, Beth Archer. *Édouard Manet: Rebel in a Frock Coat.* Chicago, 1997.

Brussee, Lelie, and Scholcz 2011
Brussee, Albert, Christo Lelie, and Peter Scholcz. "Franz Liszt in the Netherlands." *Journal of the Franz Liszt Kring* (2011): 3–19.

Cachin et al. 1983
Cachin, Françoise, et al. *Manet, 1832–1883.* Exh. cat. Metropolitan Museum of Art. New York, 1983.

Calouste Gulbenkian Museum 2022
"Boy Blowing Bubbles." Calouste Gulbenkian Museum, updated June 15, 2022. https://gulbenkian.pt/museu/en/works_museu/boy-blowing-bubbles/.

Cambridge Independent Press 1909
"The White City. A Visit to the Great Imperial International Exhibition: Some Striking Improvements." *Cambridge Independent Press*, July 9, 1909.

Cars, Guégan, and Pludermacher 2023
Cars, Laurence des, Stéphane Guégan, and Isolde Pludermacher, eds. *Manet/Degas.* Exh. cat. Musée d'Orsay. Paris, 2023.

Carter 1925
Carter. Morris. *Isabella Stewart Gardner and Fenway Court.* 1925. Reprint, Boston, 1972.

Champfleury 1869
Champfleury. *Les chats: histoire—moeurs—observations—anecdotes*, 3rd ed. Paris, 1869.

Champion 1973
Champion, Honoré. "Paul Meurice and Madame Paul Meurice." *Études Baudelairiennes* 4–5 (1973): 260–71.

Chatté 1907
Chatté, André [pseud.]. "Notes sur Manet." *Le Journal des curieux* (1907): 5–14.

Chavanne et al. 2005
Chavanne, Blandine, et al., eds. *Méry Laurent: Manet, Mallarmé et les autres.* Exh. cat. Musée des Beaux-Arts, Nancy. Versailles: Art Lys, 2005.

Chong 2003
Chong, Alan, et. al, eds. *Eye of the Beholder: Masterpieces from the Isabella Stewart Gardner Museum.* Boston, 2003.

Chronique des arts 1867
"Vente Laperlier." *Chronique des arts* 181 (April 21, 1867): 122.

Chu 1972
Chu, Petra ten-Doesschate. "French Realism and the Dutch Masters: The Influence of Dutch Seventeenth-Century Painting on the Development of French Painting Between 1830 and 1870." Ph.D. diss. Columbia University, 1972.

Clairet, Montalant, and Rouart 1997
Clairet, Alain, Delphine Montalant, and Yves Rouart. *Berthe Morisot, 1841–1895: catalogue raisonné de l'oeuvre peint.* Paris, 1997.

Clark 1999
Clark, T. J. *The Painting of Modern Life: Paris in the Art of Manet and His Followers.* Rev. ed. Princeton, 1999.

Clay and Shepley 1983
Clay, Jean, and John Shepley. "Ointments, Makeup, Pollen." Translated by John Shepley. *October* 27 (Winter 1983): 3–44.

Collins 1978
Collins, Bradford R. "Manet's Luncheon in the Studio: An Homage to Baudelaire." *Art Journal* 38, no. 2 (1978): 107–113.

Coppens 2014
Coppens, Thera. *Suzanne en Édouard Manet: de liefde van een Hollandse pianist en een Parijse schilder.* Amsterdam, 2014.

Coppens 2022
Coppens, Thera. "Suzanne Manet and Léon Leenhoff: A Mystery Solved." *Burlington Magazine* 164, no. 1437 (2022) 1216–23.

Corradini 1983
Corradini, Juan. *Manet: La ninfa soprendida.* Buenos Aires, 1983.

Coue and Mödersheim 2002–3
Coue, Kris, and Sabine Mödersheim. "Homo Bulla: An Interview with Sabine Mödersheim." *Cabinet Magazine* 9 (Winter 2002–3); https://www.cabinetmagazine.org/issues/9/coue_modersheim.php.

Couture 1867
Couture, Thomas. *Méthode et entretiens d'atelier.* Paris, 1867.

Cuno and Kaak 2004
Cuno, James, and Joachim Kaak, eds. *Manet Face to Face.* London and Munich, 2004.

Curtiss 1981
Curtiss, Mina. "Letters of Édouard Manet to His Wife during the Siege of Paris: 1870–71." *Apollo* 113, no. 232 (June 1981): 379–89.

Daniel 1999
Daniel, Malcolm. *Edgar Degas, Photographer.* Exh. cat. Metropolitan Museum of Art; J. Paul Getty Museum; and Bibliothèque Nationale de France. New York. 1988.

De Clarac, 1832–34
De Clarac, Frédéric. *Musée de Sculpture Antique et Moderne.* Volume III. Paris, 1832–34. https://archive.org/details/b29325997_0010/mode/2up.

De Fels 1929
De Fels, Marthe. *La vie de Claude Monet.* Paris, 1929.

De Leiris 1969
De Leiris, Alain. *The Drawings of Édouard Manet.* Berkeley, 1969.

De Medeiros 2002
De Medeiros, Melissa. "The Document as Voice: The Manet Archive of the Pierpont Morgan Library." M.A. thesis. Hunter College, New York, 2002.

De Nittis 1895
De Nittis, Giuseppe. *Notes et souvenirs.* Paris, 1895.

Distel et al. 1994
Distel, Anne, et al. *Gustave Caillebotte: 1848–1894.* Exh. cat. Réunion des musées nationaux. Paris, 1994.

Dolan 2013
Dolan, Therese. *Manet, Wagner, and the Musical Culture of Their Time.* London, 2013.

Dombrowski 2013
Dombrowski, André. *Cézanne, Murder, and Modern Life.* Berkeley, 2013.

Dormoy 1932
Dormoy, Marie. "La Collection Ernest Rouart." *Formes* 24 (1932): 257–59.

Le Droit 1894
"Nécrologie." *Le Droit*, March 11, 1894.

Dumas et al. 1997
Dumas et al. *The Private Collection of Edgar Degas.* Exh. cat. Metropolitan Museum of Art and National Gallery. New York and London, 1997.

Duranty 1876
Duranty, Louis-Émile-Edmond. *La nouvelle peinture: à propos du groupe d'artistes qui expose dans les galeries Durand-Ruel.* Paris, 1876.

Duret 1902
Duret, Théodore. *Histoire d'Édouard Manet et de son oeuvre.* Paris, 1902.

Duret 1919
Duret, Théodore. *Histoire d'Édouard Manet et de son oeuvre, avec un catalogue des peintures et des pastels.* Paris, 1919.

École Nationale des Beaux-Arts 1884
Exposition des oeuvres de Édouard Manet. Exh. cat. École Nationale des Beaux-Arts. Paris, 1884.

Farwell 1975
Farwell, Beatrice. "Manet's 'Nymphe Surprise.'" *Burlington Magazine* 117, no. 865 (1975): 225–29.

Farwell 1981
Farwell, Beatrice. *Manet and the Nude: A Study of Iconography in the Second Empire.* New York, 1981.

Figaro 1909
"Figaro à Londres: la cour et la ville." *Le Figaro*, February 27, 1909.

Finckh 2017
Finckh, Gerhard, ed. *Édouard Manet.* Exh. cat. Von der Heydt-Museum. Wuppertal, 2017.

Fitzwilliam 2011
Work, Rest, and Play: Women and Children in Prints after Chardin. Exh. cat. Fitzwilliam

Museum, University of Cambridge. Cambridge, 2011.

Flament 1928
Flament, Albert. *La vie de Manet*. Paris, 1928.

Flescher 1978
Flescher, Sharon. "Manet's 'Portrait of Zacharie Astruc': A Study of a Friendship and New Light on a Problematic Painting." *Arts Magazine* 52 (June 1978): 98–105.

Fourreau 1925
Fourreau, Armand. *Berthe Morisot*. Translated by H. Wellington. New York, 1925.

Frey 2021
Frey, Angela. "The Soap Bubble Trope." *Art & Art History, JSTOR Daily,* June 16, 2021. https://daily.jstor.org/the-soap-bubble-trope/.

Fried 1969
Fried, Michael. "Manet's Sources: Aspects of His Art." *Artforum* 7 (March 1969): 28–82.

Fried 1996
Fried, Michael. *Manet's Modernism; or, the Face of Painting in the 1860s*. Chicago, 1996.

Friedrich 1928
Friedrich, Paul. "Édouard Manet: Retrospektive Ausstellung bei Matthiesen." *Berliner Börsen-Zeitung,* February 7, 1928.

Fry 1909
Fry, Roger E. "The Exhibition of Fair Women." *Burlington Magazine* 15, no. 73 (1909): 14, 17–18.

Fuchs 2008
Fuchs, Rachel. *Contested Paternity: Constructing Families in Modern France*. Baltimore, 2008.

Galerie Georges Petit 1924
Exposition Degas au profit de la Ligue franco-américaine contre le cancer. Exh. cat. Galerie Georges Petit. Paris, April 12–May 2, 1924.

Godet 1872
Godet, Anatole. *Reproductions de tableaux d'Édouard Manet: photographies*. Paris, 1872.

Groom and Westerby 2017
Groom, Gloria, and Genevieve Westerby, eds. *Manet Paintings and Works on Paper at the Art Institute of Chicago*. Chicago, 2017. https://publications.artic.edu/manet/reader/manetart/section/140020/140020_anchor.

Guillemet contre Préfet de la Seine 1865
Guillemet contre Préfet de la Seine, Cour de Paris, 1st chamber. *Bulletin de la Cour impériale de Paris* (February 18 and 21, 1865): 184–86.

Guillemet contre Ville de Paris 1868
Guillemet contre Ville de Paris, Cour d'Orléans. In J.-B. Sirey, *Recueil général des lois et des arrêts: en matière civile, criminelle, commerciale et de droit public* (January 25, 1868): 134–35.

Gunnarson and Brummer 2002
Gunnarson, Torsten, and Hans Henrik Brummer, eds. *Impressionism and the North: Late 19th-Century French Avant-garde Art and the Art in the Nordic Countries, 1870–1920*. Exh. cat. Nationalmuseum, Stockholm, and Statens Museum for Kunst, Copenhagen. Stockholm, 2002.

Gutton 1993
Gutton, Jean-Pierre. *Histoire de l'adoption en France*. Paris, 1993.

Hamilton 1954
Hamilton, George Heard. *Manet and His Critics*. New Haven, 1954.

Hanson 1966
Hanson, Anne Coffin, ed. *Édouard Manet*. Exh. cat. Philadelphia Museum of Art. Philadelphia, 1966.

Hansen 2021
Hansen, Dorothee, ed. *Manet and Astruc. Friendship and Inspiration*, Exh. cat. Kunsthalle Bremen. Bremen, 2021.

Harris 1970
Harris, Jean C. *Édouard Manet: The Graphic Work: A Definitive Catalogue Raisonné*. San Francisco, 1970.

Haskell 1951
Haskell, Daniel C. *The Nation: Volumes 1–105, New York, 1865–1917, Indexes of Titles and Contributors*. Vol. 1, New York, 1951.

Haskell 1971
Haskell, Francis. "Giorgione's Concert Champêtre and Its Admirers." *Journal of the Royal Society of Arts* 119, no. 5180 (1971): 543–55.

Heath 1874
Heath, James Dunbar. *The Complete Croquet-Player*. London, 1874.

Hendy 1974
Hendy, Philip. *European and American Paintings in the Isabella Stewart Gardner Museum*. Boston, 1974.

Higonnet 1990
Higonnet, Anne. *Berthe Morisot*. New York, 1990.

Holberton 1993
Holberton, Paul. "The Pastorale or Fête Champêtre in the Early Sixteenth Century." *Studies in the History of Art* 45 (1993): 244–62.

Hôtel Drouot 1927
Catalogue des tableaux, pastels, aquarelles, dessins, gravures, par Édouard Degas, dépendant de la succession de M. René de Gas. Hôtel Drouot, Paris, November 10, 1927. https://gallica.bnf.fr/ark:/12148/bpt6k321320z.

Huisman 1963
Huisman, Philippe. *Morisot Enchantment*. Translated by Diana Imber. New York, 1963.

Imperial International Exhibition 1909
Imperial International Exhibition. London 1909. Official Guide. London, 1909.

Ives, Stein, and Steiner 1997
Ives, Colta, Susan Alyson Stein, and Julie A. Steiner. *The Private Collection of Edgar Degas: A Summary Catalogue*. Exh. cat. Metropolitan Museum of Art. New York, 1997.

Ivey 2021
Ivey, Mary Frances. "Édouard Manet, The Croquet Party, 1871," documentation in *French Paintings, 1600–1945: The Collections of the Nelson-Atkins Museum of Art*. Edited by Aimee Marcereau DeGalan. Nelson-Atkins Museum of Art. Kansas City, 2021. https://doi.org/10.37764/78973.5.522.

Jamot 1927
Jamot, Paul. "Études sur Manet." *Gazette des beaux-arts* 15 (1927): 38–40, 42.

Jamot and Wildenstein 1932
Jamot, Paul, and Georges Wildenstein. *Manet*. 2 vols. Paris, 1932.

Jaskierny and Roberts 2016
Jaskierny, Diana M., and Samantha Roberts. "Madame Manet in the Conservatory: A Comparison Between Two Versions." Courtauld Institute of Art. London, 2016. https://courtauld.ac.uk/wp-content/uploads/2021/04/Final-Madame-Manet-in-the-Conservatory-Research-Forum-report-26062016.pdf.

Javel 1880
Javel, Firmin. "L'exposition de M. Manet." *L'Événement,* April 16, 1880.

Jean de Paris 1876
Jean de Paris [Adrian Marx]. "Nouvelles diverses." *Le Figaro,* April 19, 1876.

Jeanniot 1907
Jeanniot, Georges. "En souvenir de Manet." *La Grande revue* 44 (August 10, 1907): 844–60.

Jeanniot 1933
Jeanniot, Georges, "Souvenirs sur Degas," *La Revue Universelle*, November 1, 1933.

Jedlicka 1941
Jedlicka, Gotthard. *Édouard Manet*. Zurich, 1941.

Journal des débats 1909
P. V. "Au jour le jour: à l'Académie Royale de Londres." *Journal des débats*, March 14, 1909.

Jowell 2003
Jowell, Frances Suzman. "Thoré-Bürger's Art Collection: 'A Rather Unusual Gallery of Bric-à-Brac.'" *Simiolus: Netherlands Quarterly for the History of Art* 30, no. 1/2 (2003): 54–119. https://doi.org/10.2307/3780951.

Kern et al. 1996
Kern, Stevens, et al. *The Clark: Selections from the Sterling and Francine Clark Art Institute*. New York, 1996.

Krauss 1967
Krauss, Rosalind E. "Manet's Nymph Surprised." *Burlington Magazine* 109, no. 776 (1967): 622–27.

Kremnitzer 2020
Kremnitzer, Kathryn. "Manet's Watercolors: Transition and Translation in the 1860s."

Ph.D. diss. Columbia University, New York, 2020.

Kremnitzer 2023
Kremnitzer, Kathryn. "Manet and Photography: Looking at *Olympia*." *History of Photography* 46, no. 1 (2023): 20–30.

La Presse, 1875
Tribunaux," *La Presse*, September 26, 1875, np. URL: https://gallica.bnf.fr/ark:/12148/bpt6k541658v.

Leenhoff 1883
Leenhoff, Léon. "Registre manuscript: oeuvres d'Édouard Manet (peintures, pastels, dessins, et estampes) recensées dans son atelier en 1883 ou chez leur propriétaire." Bibliothèque Nationale de France. Paris, 1883. https://gallica.bnf.fr/ark:/12148/btv1b105469429.

Leenhoff 1900–1910
Leenhoff, Léon. "Ensemble de notes et de documents sur le peintre Manet recueillis et transcrits par Léon Leenhoff pour Étienne Moreau-Nélaton." Bibliothèque Nationale de France, Département des Estampes et de la Photographie. Paris, 1900–1910. https://gallica.bnf.fr/ark:/12148/btv1b10548955r.

Lees 2012
Lees, Sarah, ed. *Nineteenth-Century European Paintings at the Sterling and Francine Clark Art Institute.* Vol. 2, New Haven, 2012.

Lemoisne 1946–49
Lemoisne, Paul-André. *Degas et son oeuvre.* 4 vols. Paris: Arts et Métiers, 1946–49.

Lesage 1784
Lesage, Alain René. *The Adventures of Gil Blas of Santillane.* Translated by Tobias Smollet. London, 1784.

Lethbridge 2010
Lethbridge, Robert. "Zola, Manet et le premier jurisconsulte des Rougon-Macquart." *Les Cahiers naturalistes* (2010): 231–40.

Leymarie 1893
Leymarie, Léopold de. *Les Avocats d'aujourd'hui.* Paris, 1893.

Lobstein 2002
Lobstein, Dominique. *Manet.* Paris, 2002.

Lobstein 2012
Lobstein, Dominique. *Dans la maison de Manet.* Paris, 2012.

Lochard 1883a
Lochard, Fernand. *Three Albums of Photographs of the Work of Édouard Manet.* 3 vols. Morgan Library & Museum, New York MA 3950. https://www.themorgan.org/collection/lochard/album.

Lochard 1883b
Lochard, Fernand. *Reproduction des oeuvres d'Édouard Manet.* Bibliothèque Nationale de France, Département des Estampes et de la Photographie, 4-DC-300 (H). Paris, 1883.

https://gallica.bnf.fr/ark:/12148/btv1b84329137.

Locke 1991
Locke, Nancy. "New Documentary Information on Manet's 'Portrait of the Artist's Parents.'" *Burlington Magazine* 133, no. 1057 (1991): 249–52.

Locke 2001
Locke, Nancy. *Manet and the Family Romance.* Princeton, 2001.

Locke 2014
Locke, Nancy. "Visible Specters, Images from the Atmosphere." *nonsite* no. 14 (December 15, 2014). https://nonsite.org/article/visible-specters.

Loyrette 1991
Loyrette, Henri. *Degas.* Paris, 1991.

Lutz 2016
Lutz, Deborah. "Review of Harold Koda and Jessica Regan, *Death Becomes Her: A Century of Mourning Attire.*" Metropolitan Museum of Art, New York. *Victorian Literature and Culture* 44, no. 1 (2016): 217–22.

MacDonald 2003–10
Margaret F. MacDonald, Patricia de Montfort, and Nigel Thorp, eds. *The Correspondence of James McNeill Whistler, 1855–1903.* Online edition, University of Glasgow. http://www.whistler.arts.gla.ac.uk/correspondence.

Mairet 1907
Mairet, Jeanne (Mme Charles Bigot). "Des deux côtés de l'Atlantique—souvenirs." *Bibliothèque universelle et revue suisse* 48 (October–December 1907): 270–89.

Maisonneuve 1853
Maisonneuve, J.G.T. *Traite pratique des maladies vénériennes.* Paris, 1853.

Manchester Courier 1909
"International Society. Exhibition of Fair Women." *Manchester Courier,* February 22, 1909.

J. Manet 1979
Manet, Julie. *Journal 1893–1899: sa jeunesse parmi les peintres impressionnistes et les hommes de lettres.* Paris, 1979.

J. Manet 1987
Manet, Julie. *Journal 1893–1899: sa jeunesse parmi les peintres impressionnistes et les hommes de lettres.* Paris, 1987.

Manet 1928
Manet, Édouard. *Lettres de jeunesse, 1848–1849: voyage a Rio.* Paris, 1928.

Manet 1945
Manet, Édouard. "Lettres d'Édouard Manet sur son voyage en Espagne," *Arts* (March 16, 1945)

Manet 2010
Manet, Édouard. *Catalogue des tableaux de M. Édouard Manet exposés Avenue de l'Alma en 1867.* Paris, 2010.

Marcereau DeGalan 2021

Marcereau DeGalan, Aimee, ed. *French Paintings, 1600–1945: The Collections of the Nelson-Atkins Museum of Art.* Kansas City, MO, 2021.

Mathieu 2021
Mathieu, Marianne. *Julie Manet: La mémoire impressioniste.* Exh. cat. Musée Marmottan-Monet. Paris, 2021. French edition.

Mathieu 2022
Mathieu, Marianne. *Julie Manet: An Impressionist Heritage.* Exh. cat. Musée Marmottan-Monet. Paris, 2022. English edition.

Mathieu 2023
Mathieu, Marianne. *Berthe Morisot: Shaping Impressionism.* Exh. cat. Dulwich Picture Gallery. London, 2023.

Mauner 1975
Mauner, George. *Manet, Peintre-Philosophe: A Study of the Painter's Themes.* University Park, PA, 1975.

Mauner 2000
Mauner, George L. "Manet at le vie silencieuse de la nature morte." In Mauner and Loyrette 2000, 27–64.

Mauner 2001
Mauner, George. "Manet's 'Son.'" In *Horizons: Essays on Art and Art Research.* Edited by Juerg Albrecht and Kornelia Imesch. Ostfildern-Ruit, Germany, 2001, 123–33.

Mauner and Loyrette 2000
Mauner, George L., and Henri Loyrette, eds. *Manet: les natures mortes.* Exh. cat. Musée d'Orsay. Paris, 2000.

Meier-Graefe 1912
Meier-Graefe, Julius. *Édouard Manet.* Munich, 1912.

Meissner 2021
Meissner, Frank. *Edma Morisot (1839–1921): Souvenirs-Erinnerungen.* Exh. cat. Handwerkermuseum. Sittensen, Germany, 2021.

Meller 2002
Meller, Peter. "Manet in Italy: Some Newly Identified Sources for His Early Sketchbooks." *Burlington Magazine* 144, no. 1187 (2002): 68–110.

Mena 2003
Mena, Manuela, ed. *Manet en el Pardo.* Exh. cat. Museo del Prado. Madrid, 2003.

Mercure de France 1917
"Mort d'Edgar Degas." *Mercure de France* (October 16, 1917): 759.

Merridew 1874
Merridew, H. M. *Merridew's Visitor's Guide to Boulogne-sur-Mer and Its Environs; with Some Account of Its Early History, and a Notice of the Objects Most Worthy of Visiting in the City and District.* London, 1874.

Mew 1909
Mew, Egan. "Wagnerian Pictures at Brook Street: Fair Women at the New Gallery." *The Bystander* (March 3, 1909): 432–34.

Monneret 1979

Monneret, Sophie. *L'Impressionnisme et son époque*. Vol. 2 of 4, Paris, 1979.

Moore 1891

Moore, George. *Impressions and Opinions*. London, 1891.

Moreau-Nélaton 1925-26

Moreau-Nélaton, Étienne. *Catalogue général [manuscrit de l'œuvre d'Édouard Manet]: peintures et pastels, ca. 1925–26*. Bibliothèque Nationale de France, Paris, Département des Estampes et de la Photographie, 4-Z-89.

Moreau-Nélaton 1926

Moreau-Nélaton, Étienne. *Manet raconté par lui-même*. 2 vols. Paris, 1926.

Morris 2018

Morris, Richard E. "The Victorian 'Change of Air' as Medical and Social Construction." *Journal of Tourism History* 10 (2018): 49–65.

Musée de l'Orangerie 1932

Exposition Manet, 1832–1883. Exh. cat. Musée de l'Orangerie. Paris, 1932.

Nevitt 1997

Nevitt, Jr., H. Rodney. "Rembrandt's Hidden Lovers." *Nederlands Kunshistorisch Jaarboek (NKJ)/Netherlands Yearbook for History of Art* 48 (1997): 162–91.

News-Art 2014

"Agostino Carracci, Goltzius e Caravaggio: Singolari Convergenze." *News-Art* (November 2, 2014). https://news-art.it/news/agostino-carracci--goltzius-e-caravaggio--singolari-converg.htm.

Niehaus 1938

Niehaus, Kasper. "Een feest voor de oogen: de doeken der Impressionisten." *De Telegraaf*, August 20, 1938.

Nielsen 2017

Nielsen, Christina, Casey Riley, and Nathaniel Silver, *Isabella Stewart Gardner Museum: A Guide*. Boston, 2017.

Nizard 1977

Nizard, Alfred. "Droit et statistiques de filiation en France. Le droit de la filiation depuis 1804" *Population*, 32, no. 1, 1977.

Nord 1989

Nord, Philip. "Manet and Radical Politics." *The Journal of Interdisciplinary History* 19, no. 3 (1989): 447–80. https://doi.org/10.2307/204364.

Ollivier 1961

Ollivier, Emile. *Journal, 1846–1869*. Edited by Theodore Zeldin et Anne Troisier de Diaz. Paris, 1961.

Orienti 1967

Orienti, Sandra. *The Complete Paintings of Manet*. New York, 1967.

Orienti 1970

Orienti, Sandra. *The Complete Paintings of Manet*. New York, 1970.

Osenat 2018

"Lot 46," in "Collection Baudelaire et grands écrivains." Osenat, Fontainebleau, November 4, 2018. https://www.osenat.com/lot/94449/9451296-manet-Édouard-lettre-autograph.

Palais des Champs Élysées 1869

Explication des ouvrages de peinture et dessins, sculpture, architecture et gravure, des artistes vivants exposés au Palais des Champs-Élysées, le 1er mai 1869. Paris, 1869.

Patry 2018

Patry, Sylvie. *Berthe Morisot: Woman Impressionist*. New York, 2018.

Patry, Wilhelm, and Patin 2002

Patry, Sylvie, Hugues Wilhelm, and Sylvie Patin. *Berthe Morisot, 1841–1895*. Exh. cat. Palais des Beaux-Arts, Lille, and Fondation Pierre Gianadda, Martigny. Switzerland, 2002.

Péladan 1884

Péladan, Joséphin. "Le procédé de Manet: d'après l'exposition de l'École des beaux-arts." *L'Artiste* 1 (February 1884): 101–17.

Pennell 1909

N.N. [Elizabeth R. Pennell] "Art. A Show of Fair Women." *The Nation* 88 (March 25, 1909): 312–13.

Penny 2008

Penny, Nicholas. *The Sixteenth Century Italian Paintings. Volume 2. Venice 1540–1600*. London, 2008.

Pichois 1973

Pichois, Claude. *Lettres à Charles Baudelaire*. Neuchâtel, 1973.

Pickvance 1996

Pickvance, Ronald. *Manet*. Exh. cat. Fondation Pierre Gianadda. Martigny, Switzerland, 1996.

Pludermacher 2021

Pludermacher, Isolde. "From One Degas to the Other: Mademoiselle Malot, Dancer at the Opéra." *Degas: Dance, Politics, and Society*, 136–52. Exh. cat. Museu de Arte de São Paolo. São Paolo, 2021.

Proust 1897

Proust, Antonin. "Édouard Manet: souvenirs." *La Revue blanche* (February 15, 1897): 168–80. https://hdl.handle.net/2027/hvd.32044019999333.

Proust 1913

Proust, Antonin. *Édouard Manet: souvenirs*. Paris, 1913.

Pullins 2019

Pullins, David. *Manet: Three Paintings from the Norton Simon Museum*. Exh. cat. Frick Collection. New York, 2019.

Rabinow 2006

Rabinow, Rebecca A., ed. *Cézanne to Picasso: Ambroise Vollard, Patron of the Avant-Garde*. New Haven, 2006.

Reff 1962

Reff, Theodore. "The Symbolism of Manet's Frontispiece Etchings." *Burlington Magazine* 104, no. 710 (1962): 180, 182–87.

Reff 1964

Reff, Theodore. "Copyists in the Louvre, 1850–1870." *Art Bulletin* 46, no. 4 (1964): 552–59.

Reff 1970

Reff, Theodore. "Manet and Blanc's 'Histoire des peintres.'" *Burlington Magazine* 112, no. 808 (1970): 456–58.

Reff 2020

Reff, Theodore. *The Letters of Edgar Degas*. Vol. 1, New York, 2020.

Renard 1939

Renard, Marie. "In the Day of the 'Poseuse," *Verve* 4 (January–March 1939): 71.

Rinder 1909

Rinder, Frank. "'Fair Women' at the International." *Art Journal* (April 1909): 117–23.

Roberts 2017

Roberts, Jane. Editor and translator. *Growing Up with the Impressionists: The Diary of Julie Manet*. New York, 2017.

Rodary 2014

Rodary, Samuel, ed. *Correspondance du siège de Paris et de la Commune, 1870–1871*. Paris, 2014.

Rodary 2019

Rodary, Samuel. "Édouard Manet: A Selection of Letters, 1878–83." In Allan, Beeny, and Groom 2019, 161–82.

Rodary 2023

Rodary, Samuel, ed., *Berthe Morisot, Carnets*. Paris, 2023.

Rouart 1941

Rouart, Louis. *Berthe Morisot*. Paris, 1941.

Rouart 1950

Rouart, Denis, ed. *Correspondance de Berthe Morisot avec sa famille et ses amis*. Paris, 1950.

Rouart 1959

Rouart, Denis, ed. *The Correspondence of Berthe Morisot*. Translated by Betty W. Hubbard. New York, 1959.

Rouart 1987

Rouart, Denis. *Berthe Morisot: The Correspondence with Her Family and Friends*. London, 1987.

Rouart and Wildenstein 1975

Rouart, Denis, and Daniel Wildenstein. *Édouard Manet: catalogue raisonné*. 2 vols. Paris, 1975.

Rouart-Valéry 1960

Rouart-Valéry, Agathe. "Degas in the Circle of Paul Valéry." *Art News* 59, no. 7 (1960): 38, 60–64.

Roy 1849

Roy, Césaire. "Purge légale." *L'Éclaireur de l'arrondissement de Coulommiers, feuille d'annonces légales et avis divers* 59 (March 25, 1849): 3–4.

Rubin 2010

Rubin, James H. *Manet: Initial M, Hand and Eye.* Paris: Flammarion, 2010.

Rudd 1994

Rudd, Peter. "Reconstructing Manet's 'Velázquez in His Studio.'" *Burlington Magazine* 136, no. 1100 (1994): 747–51.

Salon Catalogue 1863

Catalogue des ouvrages de peinture, sculpture, gravure, lithographie et architecture: refusés par le Jury de 1863 et exposés, par décision de S.M. l'Empereur au salon annexe, palais des Champs-Elysées, le 15 mai 1863. Paris, 1863.

Salon d'Automne 1905

Oeuvres de Manet. Exh. cat. Salon d'Automne. Paris, 1905.

Sandberg 1964

Sandberg, John. "'Japonisme' and Whistler." *Burlington Magazine* 106, no. 740 (1964): 500–507.

Sandblad 1954

Sandblad, Nils Gösta. *Manet: Three Studies in Artistic Conception.* Lund, 1954.

Scheffler 1925

Scheffler, Karl. "Impressionisten bei Paul Cassirer." *Kunst und Künstler* (November 1925): 72–73.

Singletary 2017

Singletary, Suzanne. *James McNeill Whistler and France: A Dialogue in Paint, Poetry, and Music.* London, 2017.

Le Soir 1875

"Epilogue du drame de la Bourse (le procès Degas-Legrand)." *Le Soir,* September 25, 1875.

Soubiran 2004

Soubiran, Jean-Ronger. "Le bassin d'Arcachon: réinventé par les peintres du XIXe siècle." *Le festin revue des patrimoines, des paysages & de la création en aquitaine* 50 (June 2004): 37–45.

Spencer 1991

Spencer, Robin. "Manet, Rossetti, London and Derby Day." *Burlington Magazine* 133, no. 1057 (1991): 228–36.

Staffe 1891

Staffe, Baronne. *Usages du monde: règles du savoir-vivre dans la société moderne.* 24th ed. Paris, 1891.

Stedelijk Museum 1938

Honderd Jaar Fransche Kunst. Exh. cat. Stedelijk Museum. Amsterdam, 1938.

Steinberg 2023

Steinberg, Leo, ed. Sheila Schwartz. *Modern Art: Selected Essays.* University of Chicago Press, 2023.

Stéphane 1932

Stéphane. *L'art de la coiffure feminine: son histoire à travers les siècles.* Paris, 1932.

Sterling and Salinger 1967

Sterling, Charles, and Margaretta M. Salinger. *French Paintings: A Catalogue of the Collection of The Metropolitan Museum of Art.* Vol. 3. Nineteenth and Twentieth Centuries. New York, 1967.

Stevens et al. 2012

Stevens, Mary Anne, et al. *Manet: Portraying Life.* Exh. cat. Royal Academy of Arts. London, 2012.

Stuckey 1983

Stuckey, Charles F. "Manet Revised: Whodunit?" *Art in America* (November 1983): 159–77, 239–41.

Swicklick 1993

Swicklick, Michael. "French Painting and the Use of Varnish, 1750–1900." *Conservation Research* 41 (1993): 166.

Tabarant 1931

Tabarant, Adolphe. *Manet, histoire catalographique.* Paris, 1931.

Tabarant 1935

Tabarant, Adolphe, ed. *Une correspondance inédite d'Édouard Manet: les lettres du siège de Paris, 1870–1871.* Paris, 1935.

Tabarant 1947

Tabarant, Adolphe. *Manet et ses oeuvres.* 4th ed. Paris, 1947.

Tajan 2022

"An Exceptional Painting by Edouard Manet at Auction." Tajan, Paris, November 23, 2022; https://www.tajan.com/en/an-exceptional -painting-by-edouard-manet-at-auction/.

Tate 2023

"Art Term: Vanitas." *Tate*; https://www.tate.org .uk/art/art-terms/v/vanitas.

De Tijd 1938

"Impressionisme." *De Tijd,* September 23, 1938.

Thompson 1993

Thompson, Henry O. *The Book of Daniel: An Annotated Bibliography.* London, 1993.

Times 1909

"International Art. 'Fair Women' at the New Gallery." *Times* (February 23, 1909): 14.

Tinterow and Lacambre 2003

Tinterow, Gary, and Geneviève Lacambre. *Manet/Velázquez: The French Taste for Spanish Painting.* Exh. cat. Metropolitan Museum of Art. New Haven, 2003.

Tucker 1998

Tucker, Paul Hayes, ed. *Manet's Le Déjeuner sur l'herbe.* Cambridge, 1998.

Valéry 1941

Valéry, Paul, ed. *Berthe Morisot (1841–1895).* Exh. cat. Musée de l'Orangerie. Paris, 1941.

Van Anrooy 1941

Van Anrooy, Anton. *Impromptu.* The Hague, 1941.

Van Kempen and Van de Beek 2014

Van Kempen, Ton, and Nicoline Van de Beek. *Madame Manet: muziek en kunst in het Parijs van de Impressionisten.* Culemborg, 2014.

Verbeek 1958

Verbeek, J. "Bezoekers van het Rijksmuseum in het Trippenhuis 1844–1885." *Bulletin van het Rijksmuseum* 49, no. 3–4 (1958): 59–71.

Vollard 1924

Vollard, Ambroise. *Degas.* Paris, 1924.

Vollard 1937

Vollard, Ambroise. *Souvenirs d'un marchand de tableaux.* Paris, 1937.

Vollard 1938

Vollard, Ambroise. *En écoutant Cézanne, Degas, Renoir.* Paris, 1938.

Von Tschudi 1902

Von Tschudi, Hugo. *Édouard Manet.* Berlin, 1902.

Westheim 1928

Westheim, Paul. "Das Ende des Impressionismus." *Berliner Börsen-Zeitung,* February 16, 1928.

Willis 2014

Willis, Zoë. "The Melbourne Finding of Moses: Steps towards a New Attribution." *Art Bulletin of Victoria* 48 (January 29, 2014). https://www.ngv.vic.gov.au/essay/the -melbourne-finding-of-moses-steps -towards-a-new-attribution/.

Wilson 1977

Wilson, Juliet. *Edouard Manet: L' Oeuvre Gravé.* Exh. cat. Journées française. Ingelheim am Rhein, 1977.

Wilson 1978

Wilson, Juliet. *Manet: dessins, aquarelles, eaux-fortes, lithographies, correspondence.* Exh. cat. Galerie Huguette Berès. Paris, 1978.

Wilson-Bareau 1984

Wilson-Bareau, Juliet. "The Portrait of Ambroise Adam by Édouard Manet." *Burlington Magazine* 126, no. 981 (1984): 750–58.

Wilson-Bareau 1986

Wilson-Bareau, Juliet. "The Hidden Face of Manet: An Investigation of the Artist's Working Processes." *Burlington Magazine* 128, no. 997 (1986): i–v; vii–viii; 1–98.

Wilson-Bareau 1991

Wilson-Bareau, Juliet. *Manet by Himself.* London, 1991.

Wilson-Bareau 2003

Wilson-Bareau, Juliet. "Manet and Spain." In Tinterow and Lacambre 2003, 203–58.

Wilson-Bareau 2010

Wilson-Bareau, Juliet. "Édouard Manet dans ses ateliers." In *Manet et le Paris moderne.* Edited by Akiya Takahashi et al. Exh. cat. Mitsubishi Ichigokan Museum. Tokyo, 2010, 304–12.

Wilson-Bareau 2011

Wilson-Bareau, Juliet. "The Manet Exhibition in Paris, 2011," *Burlington Magazine* 153, no. 1305 (2011): 815–24.

Wilson-Bareau 2012

Wilson-Bareau, Juliet. "Édouard Manet dans ses ateliers." *Ironie* 161 (January–February 2012). http://interrogationcritiqueludique

.blogspot.com/2012/10/ironie-n161
-janvierfevrier-2012.html.

Wilson-Bareau 2017

Wilson-Bareau, Juliet, with the assistance of
Kathryn Kremnitzer and Genevieve West-
erby, "Manet, Cat. 12, The Races at Long-
champ: Curatorial Entry," para 26 in Gloria
Groom and Genevieve Westerby, eds.
*Manet Paintings and Works on Paper at the
Art Institute of Chicago*, Art Institute of
Chicago, 2017.

Wilson-Bareau and Degener 2003

Wilson-Bareau, Juliet, and David Degener, eds.
Manet and the Sea. Exh. cat. Art Institute of
Chicago, Philadelphia Museum of Art, and
Van Gogh Museum, Amsterdam. Philadel-
phia, 2003.

Wilson-Bareau et al. 2008

Wilson-Bareau, Juliet, et al. *Division and Revision: Manet's "Reichshoffen" Revealed*. London, 2008.

Witthaus 1930

Witthaus, Werner. "Malerei des 19. Jahrhun-
derts." *Kölnische Zeitung,* January 24, 1930.

Wivel, Finesen, and Wilson-Bareau 1989

Wivel, Mikel, Hanne Finesen, and Juliet Wilson-
Bareau. *Manet*. Exh. cat. Ordrupgaard
Museum. Copenhagen, 1989.

Wolohojian and Dunn 2023

Wolohojian, Stephan, and Ashley E. Dunn, eds.
Manet/Degas. Exh. cat. Metropolitan
Museum of Art. New York, 2023.

Zarobell 2015

Zarobell, John. "Paul Durand-Ruel and the
Market for Modern Art, 1870–1873." In
*Inventing Impressionism: Paul Durand-Ruel
and the Modern Art Market*. Edited by Sylvie
Patry. Exh. cat. National Gallery. London,
2015.

Zola 1867

Zola, Émile. *Éd. Manet: étude biographique et
critique*. Paris, 1867.

Zola 2003

Zola, Émile. *La fabrique des Rougon-Macquart:
edition des dossier préparatoires*. Edited by
Colette Becker with Véronique Lavielle.
Paris, 2003.

Index

Illustration Credits

First published to accompany the exhibition

Manet: A Model Family

Curated by Diana Seave Greenwald,
William and Lia Poorvu Curator of the Collection
at the Isabella Stewart Gardner Museum, Boston
October 10, 2024–January 20, 2025

Manet: A Model Family is supported in part by
the Ford Foundation, Amy and David Abrams,
Arthur F. and Alice E. Adams Charitable Foundation,
and by an endowment grant from the Mellon
Foundation and the National Endowment for
the Humanities.

The conservation of *Madame Auguste Manet* was
generously sponsored by the Richard C. von Hess
Foundation.

The Museum receives operating support from the
Massachusetts Cultural Council, which is supported
by the state of Massachusetts and the National
Endowment for the Arts.

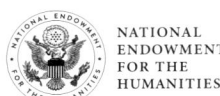
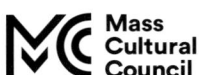
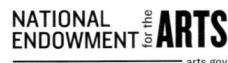

Published by Princeton University Press
41 William Street
Princeton, New Jersey 08540
USA
99 Banbury Road
Oxford OX2 6JX
United Kingdom
press.princeton.edu

Isabella Stewart Gardner Museum
25 Evans Way
Boston, MA 02115
www.gardnermuseum.org

Cover: *The Croquet Party (La partie de croquet)*, 1871
(detail of cat. no. 12)
Page 2: *Madame Auguste Manet*, about 1866 (detail of
cat. no. 1)
Page 6: *Reading (La Lecture)*, about 1868–73 (detail of
cat. no. 11)
Pages 10–11: *Interior at Arcachon (Intérieur à Arcachon)*,
1871 (detail of cat. no. 10)
Pages 98–99: *Monsieur and Madame Auguste Manet*, 1860
(detail of cat. no. 3)
Pages 118–19: *Fishing (La Pêche)*, about 1862–63 (detail
of cat. no. 6)
Pages 130–31: *The Croquet Party (La partie de croquet)*,
1871 (detail of cat. no. 12)

ISBN 9780691260662
ISBN (ebook) 9780691260655

Library of Congress Control Number: 2024000757
British Library Cataloging-in-Publication Data is available

Isabella Stewart Gardner Museum Publications
Elizabeth Reluga
Designed by Julia Ma and Tina Henderson,
Miko McGinty Inc.
Princeton University Press: Michelle Komie, Annie Miller,
Terri O'Prey, Jodi Price, Steven Sears, Kathryn Stevens
Printing by Conti Tipocolor, Florence
This book has been composed in Louize and Quire Sans

10 9 8 7 6 5 4 3 2 1

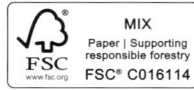

MIX
Paper | Supporting
responsible forestry
FSC® C016114